A HISTORY OF THE PUBLIC LIBRARY MOVEMENT
IN SCOTLAND TO 1955

A HISTORY OF THE
PUBLIC LIBRARY MOVEMENT
IN SCOTLAND TO 1955

BY

W. R. AITKEN

Senior Lecturer in Bibliographical Studies
University of Strathclyde

With an introduction by

W. B. PATON

County Librarian of Lanarkshire

SCOTTISH LIBRARY ASSOCIATION
GLASGOW
1971

Published by the Scottish Library Association, 1971
(Department of Librarianship, University of Strathclyde, Glasgow, C.1)

SBN: 900649 50 x

Z
791
S 35
A7
1971

Printed in Scotland by Macdonald Printers (Edinburgh) Ltd.
Edgefield Road, Loanhead, Midlothian

TO
BETSY MARY MURISON
MY WIFE

ACKNOWLEDGEMENTS

THIS STUDY was written in 1955, when it was submitted to the University of Edinburgh for the degree of Doctor of Philosophy, which was awarded in July 1956, and I am greatly honoured that the Scottish Library Association has chosen to publish it as the first of its series of Scottish Library Studies. It should be mentioned, however, that in 1964, through the good offices of Lawrence L. Ardern and the enterprise of the Council for Micro-photography and Document Reproduction (now the Microfilm Association of Great Britain), it was made available on microfilm and in "Copyflo" prints of the original typescript, and in these forms it may be found in a number of libraries. The thesis is now published as a book very largely as it was written in 1955; it has not been brought up to date, except by the addition of an occasional brief footnote and a supplementary bibliography, and by the inclusion of Appendix 5, the Scottish Library Association's survey of new library building in Scotland, 1960-69; but it has been revised here and there, an index has been provided, and it has been rewritten where necessary to remove such words and phrases as "recently" or "within the last ten years," which might have been misleading to the reader of a text newly published fifteen years after its original writing.

One of the sad results of the delay in publication is that so many of those to whom I acknowledged my indebtedness in 1955 are no longer living, among them Professor W. Croft Dickinson and Dr L. W. Sharp, the joint supervisors of this work. Nevertheless I print the acknowledgements in their original form:

In the preparation of this study the writer has been greatly assisted by the ready help of his colleagues in the public libraries, burgh and county, throughout Scotland. It would be invidious to single out any for special mention here: to all he extends his grateful thanks.

He owes a particular debt, however, to the librarians and staffs of the following libraries in which he has pursued his researches: to the National Library of Scotland and to the House of Commons Library; to Mr Minto and his staff in the Edinburgh Public Libraries; to the Rev. Dr John Campbell of the Church of Scotland Library; to Mr Tait, the city librarian of Perth; to Mr Small of Dundee Public Library; to Mr Paterson and the staff of the Mitchell Library, Glasgow;

to Mr Milne of Aberdeen Public Library; and to Mr D. C. Henrik Jones, librarian and information officer of the Library Association. To the present and to the past honorary secretaries of the Scottish Library Association, Mr Dow and Mr Stewart, he is indebted for the opportunity of access to the Association's records.

Professor Dickinson and Dr Sharp, under whose supervision this study has been prepared, have been unstinting in their encouragement and advice.

In the intervening years, as a result of this study, I have had an interesting and rewarding correspondence with a number of library historians, among them Dr Paul Kaufman of the University of Washington, Professor Thomas Kelly of Liverpool University, and Lionel Durbidge and James G. Ollé of the Loughborough School of Librarianship. Any new assessment of public libraries in Scotland would need to take account of their contributions to the subject.

For help with the book as now published I would thank my colleagues in the Scottish Library Association: W. A. G. Alison, chairman of the Publications Committee; R. S. Walker, the present honorary secretary; and James A. Tait, the Association's very active publications officer. The book is enhanced by W. B. Paton's foreword.

For permission to quote from the many reports, proceedings, minutes and papers referred to in this study I am grateful to the secretaries and other officials of the various authorities concerned, including the Director of Publications, H.M. Stationery Office.

My debt to my wife, in 1971 as in 1955, is most inadequately acknowledged by the dedication.

W. R. A.

CONTENTS

MAPS

FIGURE

INTRODUCTION

by W. B. Paton

I WELCOME THE OPPORTUNITY to contribute an introduction to this book for a number of reasons.

The first and most important must be to congratulate my friend and colleague, Dr W. R. Aitken, on an important literary achievement well performed. His twin enthusiasms for his native country and his chosen profession are happily and effectively wedded together in this history of the public library movement in Scotland. It was prepared in the first instance as a thesis for the Ph.D. degree of Edinburgh University, which is a guarantee of adequate research under supervision of experts in the field. The range of research has obviously exceeded minimum requirements, and well deserves the commendation of one assessor as "a good solid piece of work." Augustine Birrell speaks disparagingly of "that great dust heap called history," but Dr Aitken has succeeded in breaking through the arid formalism of a mere thesis and has produced a lively and interesting narrative which deserves to be read for both profit and pleasure.

It is unfortunately true that the university thesis seldom sees the light of day outside the dusty archives of the seat of learning which accepted it; and my second ground for congratulation arises from the wise decision of the Scottish Library Association to sponsor Dr Aitken's work for publication. Although the Association has published a journal and other pamphlet material from time to time, it breaks new ground with a real BOOK, and I hope that the commercial success of this publication (of which I have not the slightest doubt) will encourage similar ventures in the future.

I have read this book with a mixture of personal interest (having intimate knowledge of many of the events it describes), enlightenment (for it expands and illuminates familiar fields) and nostalgia for exciting occasions and hard fought battles with doughty colleagues and bonnie fechters of bygone days which its pages bring vividly to mind. "I hold it a noble task to rescue from oblivion those who deserve to be eternally remembered," wrote Pliny, and Dr Aitken's book fulfils this task in its own field.

Another writer has said: "Faithfulness to the truth of history involves far more than a research, however patient and scrupulous, into special facts. The historian must study events in

xi

their bearings near and remote; in the characters, habits and manners of those who took part in them. He must himself be, as it were, a sharer or a spectator of the action he describes." No more fitting compliment could be paid to Dr Aitken as author of this book than that of "sharer and spectator of the action he describes." He has lived with his subject; he knows it, through long personal experience, through study, by insight and inner conviction. He has accordingly assembled the facts in the most logical and effective order, has embellished them to produce an interesting narrative, and has correlated them to illustrate the sequence of historical development which forms such a striking feature of his book. It is a chastening thought to read (of the Rev. James Kirkwood's proposals for the establishment of public libraries throughout Scotland in 1699) that "this remarkable scheme anticipated by almost 250 years some of the most recent developments in the library world—library co-operation and the compilation of union catalogues, the operation of the British National Book Centre, and the standardization of cataloguing and classification made possible by the British National Bibliography —and it touched on topics still under discussion today—the self-sufficiency of the libraries in a given region, and the vital importance of abstracting services."

I fervently hope (and I see no reason to doubt) that this book will be widely read and studied by librarians and others throughout the country and beyond. It will be essential reading for students, because our distinguished countryman, Tom Johnston, was right when he wrote, "It is an abiding and indisputable truth that a people which does not understand the past will never comprehend the present nor mould the future." In the shaping of the future our successors will gain inspiration from Dr Aitken's fruitful excursion into the past.

> The course of life is like the sea
> Men come and go; tides rise and fall;
> And that is all of history.

Chapter 1

LIBRARIES IN SCOTLAND IN 1853

WHEN THE PUBLIC LIBRARIES BILL of 1850 was being read for the second time the member for Ayrshire, Alexander Oswald of Auchencruive, announced his intention to vote against the Bill, for he believed "that it was going to do by Act of Parliament what would be more efficiently done by private enterprise."

> In the boroughs of Ayr and Kilmarnock, and in almost every borough in Scotland, there were excellent libraries established without any help whatever from that House.[1]

At the Committee stage the same member insisted on the introduction of a clause to make it perfectly clear that the Act would not apply to Scotland.

That there were at the time libraries—often more than one—and frequently reading-rooms in almost every burgh in Scotland is corroborated by the New Statistical Account. There were similar libraries in many villages, and innumerable smaller collections—Sunday school libraries and the like. Most of these libraries had been established in the middle and late eighteenth and the early nineteenth centuries; in the early eighteenth century the General Assembly had organized a system of parochial libraries in the Highlands and Islands; and there were a few libraries that had been founded in the seventeenth century, or even earlier.

EARLY COLLECTIONS

The earliest public library in Scotland of which the books still exist is the Clement Little Collection that became the nucleus of Edinburgh University Library. In August 1580, the Town Council put on record that Clement Little, an advocate and one of the Commissaries of the burgh, had left "ane sufficient nummer of guid and godlie buikis to the ministrie of this burgh."[2] That "his zelous deid" might instigate other like-minded persons to give

---

[1] House of Commons, *Parliamentary debates (Hansard)*, vol. cix (1850), col. 849.

[2] J. Small, "Historical sketch of the Library of the University of Edinburgh," Library Association, *Transactions* 1880 (1881), p. 95-104.

their books for a similar purpose, "quhairby it may follow that ane commoun Librarie sall be erectit within this burgh," the Council thought it expedient and ordained that "ane Hous or Librarie be maid at the end of Mr James Lowsouns ministers studie."

In October of the same year the books were in place. Persons of honest conversation and good life (and no others) who were willing "to trauell and be exercised in the estait and vocatioun of ministerie, or vtherwayis of dewitie desyrous" were to have free access at all convenient times at the minister's pleasure "for reading and collecting the fruitfull knawledge be the saidis buikis, as it sall pleis God to distribute his graces to the reidaris." On each book was printed "the armes of the said vmquhile Maister Clement with thir wordis—

"I AM GEVIN TO EDINBVRGH AND KIRK OF GOD BE MAISTER CLEMENT LITIL THAR TO REMAN. 1580."

Four years later, on Mr Lawson's death, the books were transferred to the Town's College and they are still a treasured possession of Edinburgh University Library.

* * *

About a hundred years later Gilbert Burnet was minister at Saltoun for four years before his appointment in 1669 as Professor of Divinity at Glasgow. In 1666 he reported to the Presbytery that Mr Norman Leslie, late minister at Gordoun, had "mortified his Librarie to the Kirk of Saltoun for the use of the Minister thereof," and when Burnet himself died in 1715 he left a bequest for various philanthropic purposes in the East Lothian parish, including among them "the increase of a library which had already begun to be formed 'for the minister's house and use'."[3] But this library and the Leightonian Library at Dunblane—Robert Leighton (1611-84) was bishop of Dunblane from 1662 to 1669 —are scarcely public libraries.[4]

* * *

The Bibliotheck of Kirkwall is of historic importance. Not only can it claim to be one of the first public libraries in Scot-

---

[3] Extracts from the Acts and Proceedings of the Presbytery of Haddington relating to Dr Gilbert Burnet, and the Library of the Kirk of Salton, 1664-1669, *Bannatyne Miscellany,* vol. 3 (1855), p. 389-402; *New Statistical Account* (1845), vol. 2, Haddington, p. 112, 126.

[4] An Account of the foundation of the Leightonian Library, by Robert Douglas, Bishop of Dunblane, *Bannatyne Miscellany,* vol. 3 (1855) p. 227-64. Letters relating to the Leightonian Library, Dunblane, 1703-1710: ibid. p. 265-72.

2

land: it has a lineal connexion with the Orkney County Library that now administers the public library service in Kirkwall.[5]

Shortly before his death William Baikie of Holland in Stronsay, a man of property and a graduate of Edinburgh University, "being very tender in bodie, and having some few books, and not having any neire friends, in capacitie to make use of them, especially those of them which are not practicall," appointed his friend the Rev. James Wallace, minister of Kirkwall, to examine his books at his decease. After he had chosen from among them suitable gifts for Baikie's relatives, he was to take the rest, "which are more pollemick, large, and not practicall," to his own house "and reserve them there, and if any ministers within the country will add to them, Let them be reserved to your successors."

William Baikie died in October 1683, and in November of the following year Wallace laid before the Presbytery at Kirkwall "ane Catalogue of umqll Mr William Bakie's Bookes, . . . destined, mortified, and left be him to the Publicke Librarie of Kirkwall":

> Forasmeikle as Mr William Bakie of Holland, be his gift and and donatione, did leave and mortifie the above written Bookes to the ministers of Kirkwall successivlie, for a Publick Liberarie to be keept within the towne of Kirkwall, as they are named and ticketed, and of the volumes, numbers above specified, extending the number thereof to eight score, of the qlks number of bookes, according to the titles, volumes, and designations above written, I, Mr James Wallace, minister at Kirkwall, first in order thare, grant the receipt.

It seems clear that it was Wallace's idea to designate the collection a Public Library. He marked all Baikie's volumes:

> This Book belongs to the Bibliotheck of Kirkwall.
> Gifted be Mr William Bakie, 1684.

He also added considerably to the collection.

The Rev. James Wallace died in 1688, and in 1689 the Session of Kirkwall ordered "that a Press should be builded at the expenses of the Session for ye books mortified be Mr William Baikie and oyrs."

That the library was increased by later gifts, the inscriptions in the books show:

[5] J. B. Craven, *Descriptive catalogue of the Bibliotheck of Kirkwall (1683) with a notice of the founder, William Baikie, M.A., of Holland* (1897).

3

Given by the author, Dr Dillingham, July 1, 1689.
Giften to the librarie of Kirkwall be Wm Muidie of Melsiter,
June 6, 1691.
Gifted be Captain James Mackenzie to the librarie of Kirkwall,
June 30, 1691.
Given be Mr John Wilson to the Bibliotheck of Kirkwall, 1694.
This book belongs to the librarie of Kirkwall, gifted be Mr
Hugh Todde, schoolmaster of Kirkwall, Apr. 23, 1697.
July 11, 1699. Gifted by the Author to the Library of Kirk-
wall. (Thomas Forrester, Minister, and Principal of New Col-
ledge, in St Andrews. The hierarchical Bishop's Claim to a
Divine Right . . . Edinburgh, 1699).
To the librarie of Kirkwall, John Wilson, 1702.
John Edward of Solsgirth, 1752.
Will Anderson, his book, 1760.

One volume in the collection is noted as having at the end the
signature of the Knight of Cromartie, "Sr. Tho. Urquart"; the
volume later belonged to Pat. Clunes, parson of Wick, 1682-91.[6]
Eventually the old Bibliotheck was incorporated in the Orkney
Library, instituted in 1815, and in 1890, when the Public Libraries
Acts were adopted for the burgh, the Orkney Library was transferred by deed to the Library established under the Acts. The
Public Library Committee, however, found the older books
unsuitable for the new library and sold them by public roup in
February 1891, when the entire collection, with the exception of
about eight or ten, was bought by Archdeacon Craven, who published a Descriptive Catalogue of the Bibliotheck in 1897. On his
death the collection passed to Aberdeen University Library,
where it is still preserved.
The Kirkwall Public Library is now, in its turn, amalgamated
with the Orkney County Library that was founded in 1923;
indeed in the spring of 1955 the Kirkwall Library building,
replanned and redecorated, became the Headquarters of the
County system.[7]
The Orkney County Library is mindful of its heritage. Its
books carry a fine bookplate, with a quotation from a letter
written by Wm. Baikie, Founder of the Bibliotheck of Kirkwall,
1683:

> Faill not to keep your sone diligent reading
> . . . yt he losse not what he hes attained.

[6] See also J. Willcock, Sir Thomas Urquhart of Cromartie (1899), p. 57.
[7] Orkney Herald, 8 November 1955.

Innerpeffray Library, near Crieff, is mentioned in the will, dated 1680, of David Drummond, third Lord Madertie, who died about 1694.[8] Therein he states that he had "erected a library . . . to be augmented yearly in time coming for the benefit and encouragement of young students, and to be provided from time to time with a keeper," and this unique library, containing among its 3000 volumes "many rare and valuable works," still exists.[9] It is now accommodated in the building erected for it in 1750-1 by Robert Hay Drummond, Archbishop of York from 1761 to 1776, who inherited his grandfather's Perthshire estates, including Innerpeffray, in 1739. A catalogue of all books in the library printed or published before the year 1801 was compiled in 1927 by Dr W. M. Dickie, later librarian of Queen's College, Dundee.

> The books printed or published before 1801 number about 2000. They are not lent out and are very seldom consulted. The remaining 1000 volumes are borrowable by residents in the neighbourhood of the library, but of these there is no catalogue and the demand for them is small.[10]

The library is an interesting relic. There is virtually no borrowing now, but despite its inaccessibility, during the summer it receives a constant flow of visitors, attracted by its antiquity.

*　　*　　*

An eighteenth-century foundation of note is the Gray Library at Haddington.[11] John Gray was born in Haddington in 1646 and was inducted to the parish of Tulliallan in 1667. Thereafter he was in Glasgow from 1672 to 1684, when he was in close relationship with Gilbert Burnet whom he may have known when Burnet was minister of Saltoun. In 1684 he returned to East Lothian, and although he was removed from his charge in 1689, he continued to describe himself as "Minister of Aberlady" to the end. He died in 1717 and by a will dated 23 April 1711 he bequeathed his library "all and haill" to the town of Haddington. The bequest became operative in 1729 on the death of Gray's wife.

---

[8] It will be noticed that Madertie's will antedates William Baikie's, but as Baikie died first, it is evident that Kirkwall can claim to have the older public library.

[9] W. Stewart, *Innerpeffray Library and Chapel* (1916).

[10] W. M. Dickie, "Innerpeffray Library," *Library Association Record*, vol. 6. (n.s.), no. 22, June 1928, p. 100-5.

[11] W. J. Couper, *The Gray Library, Haddington* (1916); W. Forbes Gray, *Catalogue of the library of John Gray, Haddington* (1929).

The number of volumes left by Gray to the community must have exceeded 1300. When the library was catalogued by W. Forbes Gray he found it contained "fully 900 [items] on most of which . . . Gray has written the following inscription: Ex Libris Jo. Gray, Aberladie. Summa religionis imitari quem colis."

Although in the course of years many valuable books had disappeared, and some of those that remained were hopelessly dilapidated, the Gray Library was claimed (in 1929) to be "probably the finest thing of its kind in Scotland, a noble collection of early-printed books." In 1955 it was still preserved in Haddington in a small annexe to the Public Library in Newtonport.[12]

KIRKWOOD'S SCHEME: THE WORK OF THE GENERAL ASSEMBLY

The first—and a most ambitious—plan for the establishment of public libraries throughout Scotland was the work of the Rev. James Kirkwood.[13] In 1699 he published anonymously *An overture for founding and maintaining of bibliothecks in every paroch throughout this Kingdom* that outlined his ambitious scheme.[14]

Kirkwood had the unbounded optimism of the complete enthusiast. He did not foresee "any material objections" that could be made against his "easie and effectual" method for establishing and providing parish libraries. His plan, in brief, was:

1. In every parish there was to be a convenient place properly fitted for the keeping of books.

2. Every minister was to hand over all his books to the Bibliotheck of his own parish. The books were to be catalogued and four copies of the catalogue were to be made: one to be kept by the minister, and one by the heritors, the third for general use, and the fourth to be sent to the principal library in Edinburgh.

---

[12] Couper suggested that "such valuable and interesting collections as the Gray Library, and the equally important one at Innerpeffray, near Crieff . . . should be housed within [the National Library of Scotland, when it is set up], and so made easily accessible to students both of books and of history, even if special Acts of Parliament were needed to achieve the transfer." The transfer was in fact made in 1961.

[13] Born in Dunbar about 1650, for some time minister of Minto in Roxburghshire and later Rector of Astwick in Bedfordshire. When he died in 1706 he bequeathed his books to the Presbytery of Dunbar.

[14] Reprinted from the rare copy in the Free Public Library, Wigan, with introductory remarks by William Blades (1889).

3. From the catalogues sent to Edinburgh a "general cata-logue of all the Books in the Kingdom" was to be com-piled, and each book catalogued was to be valued.

4. This value was to be paid in full to the minister who gave the books, or to his heirs or assignees.

5. During a vacancy the presbytery and the heritors were to have powers to bestow the stipend of the vacant kirk on buying "such Books as they shall think most fit and necessary" for the library.

6. Every presbytery was to aim to be a "compleat Library within it self"; they should endeavour to have one copy at least of every valuable book extant in one library or other within their bounds. The ministers in a presbytery should compare their catalogues and should note both gaps and duplicates, and should exchange the books they had for those they wanted.

7. The librarian, who might be the reader or schoolmaster of the parish, was to find caution for the books and he was to lend books out only to heritors of the parish, to ministers of the presbytery, and to such residents in the parish as should find sufficient caution. The books were to be returned within such a set time as might be suffi-cient for reading them, but within one month at farthest. Each book was to be marked as belonging to the library "upon the reverse of the Title page and on the last leaf . . . so that wherever any Book shall be found want-ing the Title page and last leaf, it may be suspected to be stollen from the Libraries, and so may be confiscat to their use."

8. There was to be a bookbinder in every presbytery, to be provided with a house and "all the Instruments fit for his Trade." Alternatively, the librarian, or the minister's servants, might be taught to bind books.

9. All the libraries were to observe the same method of ranking and placing their books, and each book was to carry its shelf mark "written upon a piece of paper, and battered to the back of the Book."

These were the particulars Kirkwood thought necessary for the immediate founding of libraries in every parish, but for their maintenance he proposed further:

7

10. One month's cess was to be paid yearly, half by the heritors, to establish a fund "for buying and Printing all such books New or Old as shall be judged valuable and usefull to be distributed through the Kingdom," and every library was to get a copy of every book so printed.

11. For this end a "Printing-House and Paper Manufactory" was to be erected, and contact was to be maintained with all printing presses abroad throughout Europe, with the object of importing as soon as possible copies of all foreign books and of reprinting those judged fitting or worthy to be distributed.

12. A Commission of the General Assembly was to be appointed to revise all the new books brought home from time to time and to give some short account of them in print, to revise all the old books, and to determine what books should be printed every month.

This remarkable scheme anticipated by almost 250 years some of the most recent developments in the library world—library co-operation and the compilation of union catalogues, the operation of the British National Book Centre, and the standardization of cataloguing and classification made possible by the British National Bibliography—and it touched on topics still under discussion today—the self-sufficiency of the libraries in a given region, and the vital importance of abstracting services.

Two years later Kirkwood was writing to Bishop Burnet to acquaint him with "a little design which is set on foot about erecting some Libraries in the Highlands of Scotland for the use chiefly of ministers and probationers," but this scheme was much less ambitious.[15]

The whole number of Libraries which I design is but six; nor do we think to exceed forty or fifty pound for each Library at first.

A month later he was discussing the project again, expressing the hope that

as the design of printing the Irish Bibles was begun in time of Episcopacy and finished after Presbyterie was established, so who knows but that this design wch is begun in time of

---

[15] Letter to Bp. Burnet, 28 July 1701, in the Kirkwood Collection of MSS Prints and Books, 1687-1708, now in New College Library, Edinburgh.

Presbyterie may receive its consummation in time of Episcopacy.[16]

A modified scheme was outlined in Kirkwood's next pamphlet *A copy of a letter anent a project for erecting a library in every Presbytery or at least County in the Highlands,* published in 1702. This scheme can be read in conjunction with the broadsheet *An account of a design to erect libraries in the Highlands of Scotland: as also, in Orkney and Schetland for the use of ministers, probationers and schoolmasters.*[17] This account enumerates seven reasons for the scheme: the great scarcity of books in the Highland parishes, some of the ministers "hardly having so many as are worth twenty shillings"; and that the livings are so poor that the ministers cannot spare anything to purchase the books they need; the industry of, and the importance of counteracting, the "Romish missionaries"; the gross ignorance of the people, the "excellent parts and capacities of the ministers" and the extraordinary advantages of libraries to ministers, probationers, and "such young men as intend for the Sacred Office"; and finally, "their great distance from all such places where they might either buy or borrow such Books as are useful for them."

It was intended to have one library in every presbytery or rural deanery in the Highlands and in Orkney and Shetland, "besides three Parochial Libraries in each Presbytery for such Parishes therein as shall be found to have the greatest need of them." The number of presbyteries or rural deaneries in those parts was estimated at "about twenty-five."

In March 1703 the Society for Promoting Christian Knowledge appointed Kirkwood "a Corresponding Member . . . for the Kingdom of Scotland," and in November he submitted "Letters and Papers . . . concerning the Erecting of Lending Libraries in the Highlands" and later the same month attended a meeting and gave the Society "satisfaction about the Librarys for the Highlands in Scotland."[18]

The next year, at a meeting of the Society on 25 May 1704, "some objections being made against the Design of Erecting

[16] Letter to Bp. Burnet dated 22 August 1701. For Kirkwood's part in the distribution of Irish Bibles in the Highlands see G. P. Johnston, *Notices of a Collection of MSS relating to the circulation of the Irish Bibles in 1685 and 1690 in the Highlands and the association of the Rev. James Kirkwood therewith* (1904).

[17] There is a copy in the Kirkwood Collection of MSS.

[18] *A chapter in English church history*: being the minutes of the S.P.C.K. for the years 1698-1704; ed. by Rev. E. McClure (1888), p. 217, 243, 247.

9

Libraries in the Highlands of Scotland; Mr Kirkwood produced Answers to them in writing, which gave satisfaction to the Society." Kirkwood's reply, "An Answer to the objections of those who say, The books will be sould or burnt, etc.," considered first the problems arising from the different religious establishments in the two countries:[19]

> They who make the objections may say . . . there is more than a possibility, even a certainty or at least a great probability that they who are in the Government will sell or burn or change the books, the ruling party there being presbyterians, enemies to the Church of England.

But, he pointed out, the rules proposed for "ordering and securing the libraries" ordered

> that the library keepers shall give good security to leave the books in as good case as they were in when they were first put into their hands.

Elsewhere he had written:

> It is very evident that they [the Presbyterians] look upon it as absolutely necessary for ministers to have Books of all parties, even of such as they esteem to be hereticall.[20]

Another objection is considered and answered in this way:

> Some object that nobody will borrow nor make use of these libraries when they are sent to those parts. The reason of their saying this is, they have observed in several parts where there are such libraries no body comes near them.
>
> As to this I answer that tho a great many publick libraries are not so much frequented as might be expected yet there want not those who visit them and reap great benefit by this means. Besides that they are not more frequented it proceeds at times either from their not being put into a right method or from their being erected in such places where the Clergey are sufficiently provided with books and where they can borrow of one another such treatises as they have occasion for.

His "Answer" ends with the text:

> He that observeth the wind shall not sow; and he that regardeth the clouds shall not reap. Eccl. 11.4.

[19] MS in the Kirkwood Collection.
[20] MS: "An Answer to the objections against our list of books," Kirkwood Collection.

In 1704 the General Assembly in the Act anent libraries in the Highlands declared "their Approbation of that Design," and agreed upon the distribution of 31 libraries.[21]

The General Assembly does agree, that one of the saids Libraries be fixed at Dumbartoun, Two in the Presbytry of Dumblain, Three in the Province of Rose, One in the Presbytry of Southerland, Two in the Presbytry of Caithness, One in Orknay, One in Zetland, Four in the Province of Murray, Four in the Presbytry of Dunkeld, and Twelve in the Synod of Argyle, Including the Westren Isles, in such places, as the Respective Synods and Presbytries of these Bounds shall agree upon.

The same Assembly also passed an Act "agreeing to Rules for preserving the publick Libraries designed for the Highlands and Islands" and ordered the writing of "a letter of Thanks to the Society (in England) for Promoting Christian Knowledge and another to Mr James Kirkwood, Minister, for their kind offer and service to this Church with respect to Libraries in the Highlands."

The next year, upon the Report of the Committee to manage the affairs of the Highland libraries, a new scheme of distribution was adopted in place of the distribution agreed in 1704. This concerned nineteen Presbyterial libraries and 58 parochial libraries. A Committee, with Rev. William Carstares as moderator, was nominated to receive the libraries and arrange for their transmission to their destinations. The Committee was to print several copies of the rules for the libraries and "to digest in order some presses of books not methodized and sorted, and to distribute them to such places as have most need."[22]

In the next year, 1706, another Act concerning the Libraries contained some additional instructions and asked for a full account from the Committee.[23] Letters of thanks were sent to "Mr Strachan and others for their care and liberality in procuring some libraries for the use of this Church," and in 1708 to "some in and about Inverness who are benefactors to the Library there."[24]

---

[21] Church of Scotland, *The principal Acts of the General Assembly of the Church of Scotland* (1704), p. 18: Act XVII, 29 March 1704.

[22] ibid. (1705), p. 15: Act XII, 10 April 1705.

[23] ibid (1706), p. 18: Act XVIII, 16 April 1706.

[24] The very interesting story of the Inverness "Session" Library, which still exists, is fully told in Alexander Mitchell's *Inverness Kirk Session Records* (1902), p. 187-206.

An Act for Erecting publick Libraries in Presbyteries was adopted in 1709:[25]

> The General Assembly considering how much it might tend to the Advancement of Learning, that publick Libraries were settled, at least one in every Presbytery, and many Pious and Charitably inclined Persons having contributed toward that good design: and the Assembly, being desirous to encourage and promote the same, Does hereby earnestly recommend it to such of the Presbyteries of this Church, as have not received any of the Books sent for that end from England, to contribute amongst themselves in order to lay a Foundation for a Library at each Presbytery seat; and also endeavour to procure Collections in their several Parishes of more or less, according as their Parishioners are able and willing to give and bestow for that end.

The same Assembly noted the receipt of "a letter from Mr James Kirkwood concerning the libraries sent from London," and a letter of thanks was sent "to the said Mr Kirkwood."[26]

Presbyterial libraries usually contained around 100 volumes, and the parochial libraries about 40 volumes.[27] They were, in those days, subject to other dangers than fair wear and tear. On Monday, 10 October 1715, a party of armed Highlanders under the command of Lord Seaforth came to Alness where they resided till Saturday the 15th. Their visit had a sequel in May 1718 when Mr Daniel Mackilligin and Mr John Mackilligin, "Ministers of the Gospel at Allness," brought an action of Spuilzie before the Court of Session against "certain persons who were present with the rebels . . . when a spuilzie was committed," in which they averred that

> Kenneth Mackenzie, brother of George Mackenzie of Balmuchie, Roderick Mackenzie younger of Reidcastle, Lewis Mackenzie his brother, Donald Mackenzie of Kilcowie, John Chisholm of Knockfin, and Archibald Chisholm, his brother, . . . took possession of the houses, carried off a great part of

[25] Church of Scotland, *The principal Acts* . . . (1709), p. 19: Act XI, 26 April 1709.

[26] It is very probable that the copy of Richard Field's *Of the Church: Five Books* (2nd ed. Oxford, 1628) in the Bibliotheck of Kirkwall was sent there under Kirkwood's scheme: it is inscribed "Given to the Highland Library By the Poor Vicar of Shitlington in Bedfordshire."

[27] The catalogues of several presbyterial and parochial libraries are given in the Records of the Synod of Ross, 1707.

the household furniture, and cut and destroyed the rest, carried off, or tore and destroyed all the respondent Daniel's books, and likewise two parochial libraries, of all which the respondent Daniel was the keeper.[28]

In 1723 the Presbytery of Dunkeld decided that their library should be "safely lodged in the Schoolmaster's or Minister's house." Four years later:

Anent ye presbyterial library ye Clerk is appointed to give Mr Scobie in whose custody the said library now is a list of the books wanting and of the persons who borrowed them that the said Mr Scobie, Schoolmaster of Dunkeld may enquire for them between [now] and the next presbytery.[29]

Parochial libraries of this kind perished more easily than they were created. In the Statistical Account, three generations later, only three are mentioned. Few were in existence in 1807.[30] The Dumfries Presbytery Library, which dated from 1706, and was increased by later bequests, remained at Dumfries until 1885, when it was sent to the General Assembly's Library in Edinburgh.[31]

THE UNIVERSITY LIBRARIES AND THE ADVOCATES' LIBRARY

Although the university libraries do not fall within the scope of this study, it must be mentioned that in mid-nineteenth-century Scotland they claimed to be, and in a sense they still are, public libraries, and the library of the Faculty of Advocates in Edinburgh was declared to be "for all practical purposes a public library, and . . . the most accessible of all the great libraries in the United Kingdom."[32]

The Advocates' Library received books under the copyright Act—a privilege it still retains as the National Library of Scot-

[28] The ministers won their case; the Mackenzies and Chisholms appealed to the House of Lords, but failed to appear on the day appointed for the hearing, 6 February 1723. Judgement for the respondents was affirmed, with £100 costs. (D. Robertson, *Reports of cases on appeal from Scotland decided in the House of Peers*, vol. 1, 1707-27 (1807), Case 96, p. 431-5).

[29] Dunkeld Presbytery Records, 24 September 1723, 31 January 1727.

[30] John Anderson, *Prize essay on the state of Society and Knowledge in the Highlands of Scotland* (1807), p. 107.

[31] George W. Shirley, *Dumfriesshire libraries* (1933), p. 3.

[32] Parliamentary Return, Public Libraries, 9 March 1849 (18-II), p. 3.

land—and the libraries in the four Scottish universities had enjoyed the same right from 1709 until the privilege was withdrawn in 1836, when they were compensated for the loss by annual payments calculated on the annual average value of the books they had received. These privileges, it was maintained, gave the libraries concerned a public character. In 1849, the Solicitor-General, with the Advocates' Library in mind, could not imagine "that the privilege was intended to be given simply for use of a body of private barristers" and hastened to add that there was in fact "no library in Great Britain where the access given to the public generally is more liberal."[33] Edward Edwards of the British Museum was equally emphatic:

> The mere receipt of public money ought to involve, I think, a clear right of public accessibility.[34]

He did not mean that the general public should be allowed to use the libraries as freely as the members of the University: he thought it "a perfectly reasonable restriction to put upon the general public that they shall not come into the library and help themselves to books; they ought to be sent to a place apart to read them when brought."

From this point of view Edwards found the library at St Andrews "very liberally accessible to all persons who bring an introduction satisfactory to the librarian" and "by far the most liberally managed of the Scottish University libraries." He reported that access to the libraries of the Universities in Edinburgh and Glasgow was "very difficult, and very restricted," and that in Aberdeen "the library of King's College . . . is very much restricted, but not so much so as that of Glasgow."[35]

His statements on this point conflict with the replies from these libraries in the Parliamentary Return of 1849. There it was stated that at Edinburgh,

> Literary gentlemen or others, who have occasion to consult or to borrow books, on application to the Curators or to individual Professors willing to be responsible for them, are allowed every practicable facility;

[33] House of Commons, Select Committee on Public Libraries, *Report . . . together with the proceedings of the Committee, minutes of evidence, and appendix* (1849), 1443. (Afterwards referred to as: S.C. Report (1849). Precise references are given by quoting the question numbers.)
[34] S.C. Report (1849), 277.
[35] ibid. 378, 275.

14

that Glasgow University was open "to all respectable persons, properly introduced"; and that at Aberdeen "persons who are neither Graduates nor Students of the University, are allowed to take out books, if recommended by a Professor."[36]

When Edwards's attention was drawn to this discrepancy, he made the points that these privileges were, according to his information, by favour and not of right, and that in any event their availability was not widely known.

I find upon inquiry of persons living at Aberdeen, that practically that privilege cannot be obtained without the persons seeking it putting themselves under the same obligation that they would to the owner of a private library; it is just the same sort of favour. It is not known publicly in Aberdeen that under certain regulations such a privilege can be obtained.[37]

Edwards's opinion of the position in Aberdeen was corroborated by John Webster, an Advocate in that city, who maintained that the inhabitants of Aberdeen had no access at all to the University Library, or at least not a suitable access and "we feel it a disagreeable situation to be placed in"; and John Imray, a civil engineer who knew Aberdeen well, confirmed that although he imagined "no respectable person would find any great difficulty in getting access to a book," it was only possible indirectly through friends, members of the University, who had the privilege of borrowing books.[38]

Edwards also challenged the claim made for the Advocates' Library; that "any person of a decent appearance is allowed to consult the books."[39]

I believe the fact would be a great novelty to any person in Edinburgh. I have heard several persons express their astonishment that such a return should have been made.[40]

However, Edwards did know that the library had been "by special favour, in certain cases, a lending library, but not of right." In the Solicitor-General's opinion, this conversion of the Advocates' Library into "a common circulating library" was the

[36] Parliamentary Return, Public Libraries, 9 March 1849 (18-II), p. 3-5.
[37] S.C. Report (1849), 285.
[38] ibid. 722, 3129-34.
[39] Parliamentary Return, Public Libraries, 9 March 1849 (18-II), p. 3.
[40] S.C. Report (1849), 284.

"great defect" of its administration. The injury to the library had been "quite incredible."[41]

The position seems to have been that the general reading public was not properly aware of the library facilities the authorities were prepared to extend to them. In the Advocates' Library and the library of Glasgow University no records were kept of the number of persons, other than students, frequenting the library: but at Aberdeen, despite the opinions of Webster and Imray, the number increased steadily from 82 in 1836 to 246 in 1848; at St Andrews the number remained constant at 65 from 1838 to 1844 and then rose to 95 in 1847; at Edinburgh it was constant at 81.[42]

Today the Advocates' Library is the National Library of Scotland and all the university libraries readily lend their books at the request of the Scottish Central Library or the National Central Library to readers in any part of the country or beyond it.

CIRCULATING LIBRARIES

In 1725 Allan Ramsay, poet and bookseller, made history by opening in Edinburgh the first circulating library in Britain,[43] and in Glasgow a circulating library was established in 1753 by Mr John Smith, "who lent out books at one half-penny per volume."[44]

Although the circulating library survived as an institution for more than two centuries, from the very beginning it has been criticized and looked down upon. The Rev. Robert Wodrow lamented that

> all the villanous profane and obscene books and playes printed at London by Curle and others, are gote doun from London by Allan Ramsey, and lent out, for an easy price, to young boyes, servant weemen of the better sort, and gentlemen, and vice and obscenity dreadfully propagated. Ramsay has a book in his shope wherein all the names of those that borrou his playes and books for two pence a night, or some such rate, are sett doun; and by these, wickednes of

---

[41] ibid. 1444.
[42] Parliamentary Return, Public Libraries, 9 March 1849 (18-II), p. 2. The Signet Library, which Edwards cites as one of the "three public libraries in Edinburgh" (S.C. Report, 205), is not mentioned in this Parliamentary Return.
[43] B. Martin, *Allan Ramsay: a study of his life and works* (1931), p. 33.
[44] J. W. Hudson, *A history of adult education* (1851), p. 197.

all kinds are dreadfully propagat among the youth of all sorts. . . . A villanous obscene thing, is no sooner printed at London, than it's spread and communicat at Edinburgh;[45]

and in Sheridan's *Rivals* (1775) Sir Anthony Absolute maintained: "A circulating library in a town is as an ever-green tree of diabolical knowledge!—it blossoms through the year!"[46]

In 1849 it was noted that these small "shop libraries" dealt mainly in "the common popular cheap novel."[47] The circulating libraries of Aberdeen, which were much frequented by both "the middling and lower classes," provided "very much novels and other ephemera."

They do not at all supply the place of those public libraries which we wish for.[48]

READING SOCIETIES

The library of the Leadhills Reading Society was founded in 1741 by the men employed by the Scottish Mining Company. They worked in the mines only six hours in the twenty-four.

Having therefore a great deal of spare time, they employ themselves in reading, and for this purpose have been at the expence of fitting up a library, out of which every one who contributes to the expence receives books.[49]

That the library was instituted by the miners themselves is also stated in the New Statistical Account, but a local history published in 1876 claims that "the library was originally established by an overseer named Mr Stirling, who was a famous mathematician."[50] Certainly James Stirling of Garden in Stirlingshire, a distinguished mathematician, was appointed manager at

[45] R. Wodrow, *Analecta or Materials for a History of Remarkable Providences* (1842-3), vol. 3, p. 515-6.

[46] R. B. Sheridan, *The plays and poems,* ed. R. Crompton Rhodes (1928), p. 38.

[47] S.C. Report (1849), 2692.

[48] ibid. 751.

[49] Sir John Sinclair, *Statistical Account of Scotland* (1791-9) (*O.S.A.*), vol. 4, p. 512.

[50] *New Statistical Account of Scotland* (1845) (*N.S.A.*), vol. 6, p. 334; J. M. Porteous, *God's treasure-house in Scotland: a history of times, mines, and lands in the Southern Highlands* (1876).

Leadhills in 1735 "and prove extremely successful as a practical administrator."[51]

This is the "large library of long standing" that Dorothy and William Wordsworth heard of, but did not see, on their visit to Leadhills during their tour in Scotland in 1803;[52] and Dr John Brown in *The Enterkin* refers to it as "one of the oldest and best village libraries in the kingdom." He quotes, "as an indication of the wild region and the distances travelled," one of the Society's rules: "that every member not residing in Leadhills shall be provided with a bag sufficient to keep out the rain."[53]

As if in emulation the neighbouring village of Wanlockhead in Dumfriesshire established its Miners' Library in 1756.[54] This library still existed in 1932, "a testimony to the intelligence and tenacity of the villagers," although by that time it was "in a somewhat lugubrious condition."[55] Now "the County Library has taken on the role of book provider."[56]

Particular interest attaches to the Monkland Friendly Society, founded in the winter of 1788-9, for the purpose of buying books and circulating them among its members, for Robert Burns was "so good as take the whole charge of this small concern. He was treasurer, librarian, and censor to this little society."[57] This library survived until 1931 when it was formally disbanded, the older books being given to the Ellisland Trustees.

Later, in Dumfries, Burns was elected an honorary member of the Dumfries Public Library which he had helped to found in 1792 and to which he presented four books, two of them fiction.[58] Eventually the Dumfries Public Library was amalgamated with

---

[51] *Dictionary of National Biography*; Sir William Fraser, *The Stirlings of Keir* (1858), p. 98-102.

[52] Dorothy Wordsworth, *Recollections of a tour made in Scotland A.D. 1803,* ed. J. C. Shairp (1894), p. 19-22.

[53] Dr John Brown, "The Enterkin," *John Leech and other papers* (1882), p. 357.

[54] *N.S.A.* (1845), vol. 4, Dumfriesshire, p. 312.

[55] Shirley, *Dumfriesshire libraries* (1933), p. 3.

[56] "Upland Parish Pump: Plea for 200-Years-Old Library at Wanlockhead," *The Scotsman,* 22 July 1955.

[57] *O.S.A.* (1791-9), vol. 3, p. 597-8: see Burns's letter on the subject, signed "A Peasant," *Letters,* ed. J. Delancey Ferguson (1931), letter 469.

[58] R. Chambers, *Life and works of Robert Burns,* rev. W. Wallace (1896), vol. 4, p. 54-5. The novels were Smollett's *Humphry Clinker* and Mackenzie's *Julia de Roubigné*: the other books were Knox's *History of the Reformation* and De Lolme on *The constitution of England.* Burns had already presented to the Library, before it was a week old, a copy of his Poems.

18

the library of the Dumfries Mechanics' Institute, which later again was handed over to the Ewart Public Library on its establishment in 1903. Although many of the transferred volumes had to be discarded, in 1932 "a considerable number" of "The Dumfries Public Library" books were still in use.[59]

PUBLIC SUBSCRIPTION LIBRARIES

It was about the middle of the eighteenth century, at the time when the commercial circulating library was becoming established, that the idea of the public subscription library took root. A number of people in a community, interested in books, would join together voluntarily to launch a scheme whereby a collection of books could be bought and accommodated for the use of members who paid the required subscription.

An early Scottish example of this kind of library was opened at Kelso in 1751.[60] It is frequently mentioned in the diary of the Rev. George Ridpath, which begins in April 1755. Ridpath, who was minister of Stitchel from 1742 to his death in 1772, was an enthusiastic and active member of the Kelso Subscription Library. In 1759 he records the transfer of the Library to "a room in the town house which Ramsay has procured us the use of and at the expense of the Duke of Roxburgh made a very decent, convenient place," and how he arranged and catalogued the books:

Wednesday, December 19th—Employed forenoon and a great part of afternoon in putting up the books. I wrote also a catalogue of them, as they stand in the shelves, in order to make an alphabetical one from it . . .

Saturday, December 29th—Prepared for tomorrow and wrought more on the Library catalogue. Finished the aphabetical catalogue and also the contents of one of the presses in the order in which the books stand in the several shelves.

A year later Ridpath brought his catalogue up to date and prepared it for the press.[61]

The Diary's editor notes in his introduction:

It is wonderful in how short a time the newest publications came into his hands . . . It is astonishing to note the number

[59] Shirley, *Dumfriesshire libraries* (1933), p. 3-4.
[60] Library Association, *Transactions* 1880 (1881), p. 161.
[61] Rev. George Ridpath, *Diary 1755-1761*; ed. Sir J. B. Paul (1922), p. 283, 292-3, 355.

of solid books which this enterprising institution bought for the use of its members.

At the time of the removal of the books to the new Library Room its finances were in a "tolerably good condition": although only two years earlier the subscribers had found themselves so much in arrear, they could "commission no books. It will take all that we can raise for a twelvemonth to discharge what is already owing."

Forty years later the library could "boast of a collection of the best modern authors, being regularly supplied with every publication of merit."[62]

Proposals for a publick library at Aberdeen, issued in 1764, are worth quoting:

> As men of all Ranks and Professions in the present Age have frequent Recourse to Books for their Instruction or Amusement, and most Men can purchase but a very inconsiderable Part of the Books which they desire to peruse: Publick Libraries have been established by subscription in most considerable Towns where there is any Desire of Knowledge and Improvement. . . . In a publick Library properly furnished, not only the Architect, the Ship-Builder and the Farmer; but even the Tallow-Chandler and Pin-Maker may find the latest Improvements that have been made in his Profession.

> Several Gentlemen in and about Aberdeen, moved by these Considerations . . . have for some Months bygone, resolved to form a Society at *Aberdeen,* for establishing a publick library.[63]

At Duns in Berwickshire a public library was established in 1768, "consisting of about 60 shares, at £2 a share, and 6s a-year." From the original £2 for each share, and the subscriptions advanced for the year's reading, it was possible to buy at once "near £150 worth of books," and from £12 to £15 had been expended annually upon books over the next twenty years.[64] The *Catalogue of Books in the Public Library at Dunse,* published in 1780, is the "earliest catalogue noted of a private or non-commercial book society."[65]

[62] *O.S.A.* (1791-9), vol. 10, p. 597.
[63] Aberdeen, *Proposals for a publick library at Aberdeen* (1764; repr. 1893).
[64] *O.S.A.* (1791-9), vol. 4, p. 391.
[65] *Cambridge bibliography of English literature* (1940), vol. 2, p. 99.

The "elegant inn, with a library of books adjoining to it, chiefly for the amusement of travellers who may stop there," built and fitted up by Lord Gardenstone at Laurencekirk was visited by Johnson and Boswell in 1773.[66] Johnson "praised the design, but wished there had been more books, and those better chosen."[67]

In 1783, a number of gentlemen in Greenock, "to save themselves the expence of purchasing many books, and to avert the fatal effects which are sometimes occasioned by circulating libraries" founded a subscription library, which still maintains an independent existence.[68] It is now known as the Watt Library: in 1816 the famous engineer gave this library £100 "to form the beginning of a scientific library, for the instruction of the youth of Greenock."[69]

A public library established at Montrose in 1785 was to be available *gratis* to "the public teachers of youth and students at the universities."[70]

Such institutions, evidently tend to increase knowledge, and to diffuse a taste for learning, and therefore ought, as much as possible, to be encouraged.

Is there a touch of irony in the added footnote?—

Convinced of its great utility, several gentlemen have already presented to the library valuable books, and some have presented works of their own composition.

In the same year Mr Walter Stirling, a merchant and a magistrate, "considering that as a Public Library kept in a proper place in the City of Glasgow will be attended with considerable advantage to the Inhabitants," bequeathed to "the present Lord Provost of the City of Glasgow, and to his successors in office" the sum of £1000, and other assets, his tenement in Miller Street, and the books in his present library "for the sole and only purpose of purchasing a Library, and supporting a Librarian."[71] The Library was to be managed by a board of thirteen directors: the Lord Provost of Glasgow, as Preses *ex officio,* and three repre-

---

[66] *O.S.A.* (1791-9), vol. 5, p. 178.
[67] James Boswell, *Journal of a tour to the Hebrides,* ed. Frederick A. Pottle and Charles H. Bennett (1936), p. 52.
[68] *O.S.A.* (1791-9), vol. 5, p. 583.
[69] R. Orr "Presidential Address," S.L.A., *Annual Report 1925-6* (1926), p. 16-21.
[70] *O.S.A.* (1791-9), vol. 5, p. 34.
[71] Thomas Mason, *Public and private libraries of Glasgow* (1885), p. 36-69.

sentatives each from the Town Council, the Merchants' House, the Presbytery of Glasgow, and the Faculty of Physicians and Surgeons. In appointing a librarian the Directors were to prefer "one of the name of Stirling to any other of the candidates (providing he be equally qualified for the office)." All proper persons were to be allowed "to consult and read the books three hours each lawful day," but no book was to be lent out to any person, without an order signed by two of the Directors, and only if the borrower deposited a sum equal to the value of the book "to be forfeited, in case of his damaging or losing it." The Directors are recommended to purchase "rather rare and curious books, than of the common and ordinary kinds." The "primary view" of his bequest was "the constant and perpetual existence of a Public Library for the citizens or inhabitants of Glasgow."

Walter Stirling died in January 1791, and the Directors on assuming their responsibilities were immediately embarrassed by the inadequacy of the bequest. They resolved to amend the constitution to authorize the lending out of books to life subscribers of three guineas. Between 1791 and 1832, 607 persons were enrolled as members—377 during the first two years and only 270 in the ensuing 39 years. In the next 15 years the library declined rapidly. In 1833 the subscribers had numbered just over 300; by 1848 there were only 105.

In 1849 the Select Committee of Public Libraries noted:

In Glasgow there exists a free Public Library, "Stirling's Library" . . . to which it appears that the public, for some not very easily discoverable reason, do not resort.[72]

But a new Committee had already taken office and it had been agreed to admit annual members—118 applied for admission within the first month of the new arrangements. The Library had at last got under way.

The Perth Public Library was founded in 1786; the constitution that was then adopted embodied several clauses marked "Unalterable," including one that declared:

The said Library, with all its increase, being the property of the Subscribers, is by them consigned over to the Public; and conveyed in trust, for the purpose of the institution, to the

[72] S.C. Report (1849), p. vi.

22

persons holding and enjoying the following offices and characters—

whereon follows a list of *ex officio* Trustees.[73]

An excellent classified and annotated catalogue, compiled by David Morison, one of the notable Perth family of printers and publishers, was issued in 1824, in the introduction to which it was pointed out that the Perth Library was probably unique:

> Perth has the honour of having set the example of a Library— the property not of any Society or individuals, not even of the body of Subscribers, but unalterably secured to the Public, by a deed of settlement, and articles of agreement, which must for ever prevent it being turned aside from its original purpose, object and destination—that of being at all times patent to every member of the community, who subscribes to the Regulations by which it is conducted.[74]

It is sad to record that the Library got into debt, and was eventually taken over by the Literary and Antiquarian Society to become "the property of a private society."[75]

In Arbroath a library was opened on Christmas Day 1797, and in the same year libraries had been established in Cupar and Milnathort.[76] Forty years later the Milnathort library belonged to about 40 individuals who contributed 6s 6d annually; anyone might read the books by paying 1s a month, or 8s a year. Over the previous ten years funds had averaged £13 a year, and the library contained 1270 volumes.

By the middle of the nineteenth century, indeed, subscription libraries were ubiquitous. In Aberdeen there were several "extensive" subscription libraries, one containing 10,000 to 15,000 volumes. The Glasgow Public Library, founded in 1804, contained 16,000 volumes; the public library in Dundee about 6500.[77] The Edinburgh Supbscription Library in George Street had been instituted in 1794.[78] Kirkcaldy had five public libraries, the largest being a subscription library of 4000 volumes.[79] Ayr had a town

[73] Perth Public Library, *Abstract of Articles* (1786), p. 5-6.
[74] D. Morison, *Catalogue of the Perth Library* (1824), p. iii-iv.
[75] J. Minto, "A notable publishing house: The Morisons of Perth," *Perth Library and Museum Record,* vol. 1, no. 2, January 1900, p. 30-6.
[76] J. M. McBain, *History of the Arbroath Public Library 1797-1894* (1894), p. 9; *N.S.A.* (1845), vol. 9, Fife, p. 16, Kinross, p. 66.
[77] S.C. Report (1849), 3148, p. 303.
[78] Library Association, *Transactions* 1880 (1881), p. 154.
[79] *N.S.A.* (1845), vol. 9, Fife, p. 768.

library dating from 1762 with about 4500 volumes.[80] The public subscription library in Hamilton contained upwards of 3000 volumes; that in Stirling upwards of 2000.[81]

Even in the smaller towns there were considerable libraries supported by voluntary contributions. In Peterhead, for example, there was "a very handsome library, entirely supported by voluntary subscription, containing from time to time 2000 or 3000 volumes." It was open only to subscribers, and was managed on the principle that books were purchased and read, and thereafter sold, new books being bought partly with the proceeds of the sale of the books already read, and partly from the members' subscriptions.[82]

The "very good library in the small town of Kirkcudbright" was "kept up by private subscription, and . . . most extensively used by the inhabitants of the town, and by the inhabitants of the neighbourhood of the town."[83]

A Library and Reading Room was established in Earlston in Berwickshire in 1852. Major the Hon. Robert Baillie of Dryburgh, after consulting several of the inhabitants of the town, announced that he would present "Fifty Volumes of Books," if a Society were constituted on certain firm principles he laid down. The first of his five conditions stipulated that Earlston people should be invited to become members, "without distinction as to religious denomination or political opinion, and whether they do or do not belong to any Abstinence or Temperance Society." The second, however, insisted that one, at least, of the Committee of Management should be "a person who does *not* belong to any such Society." Somewhat surprisingly, in view of the tenor of the first two conditions, the fifth states emphatically: "That no intoxicating liquors be consumed on the premises on any pretence whatever." The third condition referred to the provision of "Newspapers and other Publications" that would be "generally useful and acceptable . . . and free from sectarian or political bias"; while the fourth prohibited the disposal of the books without the donor's consent.[84]

At a public meeting on 16 June 1852 it was unanimously resolved "that Major Baillie's munificent offer be gratefully

[80] S.C. Report (1849), p. 303.
[81] *N.S.A.* (1845), vol. 6, p. 291; vol. 8, Stirlingshire, p. 443.
[82] S.C. Report (1849), 3099, 3101.
[83] ibid. 1481.
[84] Earlston Library and Reading Room, *Catalogue and rules* (1909), p. 2

accepted, and that the formation of the Society be immediately proceeded with."

The Library and Reading Room that was first established in a two-roomed thatched cottage now occupies "impressive premises" in the Square, and the building provides accommodation for a branch of the Berwickshire County Library.[85] There was an interesting centenary celebration in June 1952 when the Earl of Haddington, a great-grand-nephew of the original founder, presented to the Library as a memento of the occasion the original National Covenant signed in Earlston Kirk in 1638:

> Its rightful place was in Earlston itself. It had, after all, been signed by the town's citizens, and it was a landmark in Earlston's history.[86]

*   *   *

Many of these libraries were remarkably long-lived and survived well into the era of the rate-supported libraries, burgh and county, with which they were frequently eventually amalgamated. Some instances have been mentioned: Sanquhar is another. The library founded there in 1800 was eventually merged with the Dumfriesshire Libraries when a new branch of the county service was opened in the burgh in 1935.[87]

The Cumbernauld Public Library was established in 1816: when its books were transferred to Dunbarton County Library in the year 1933-4, they were found to include first editions of several of the Waverley novels, Fielding's *Amelia,* Cobbett's *Rural rides,* a *Journal of a tour to the Hebrides,* the *Edinburgh Review,* 1809-27, early editions of the eighteenth-century poets, twelve volumes of British drama, 1817, the 1758 edition of Smollett's *History of England,* and twelve sermons by the Rev. James Boucher, minister of Cumbernauld in 1822.[88]

*   *   *

The subscription libraries, embodying as they did the principle of voluntary association, almost anticipated the public library idea. They had a resilience rarely found in libraries established by gift or bequest, unless these were generously endowed. The

[85] *Southern Reporter,* 15 May 1952; *Weekly Scotsman,* 5 June 1952.
[86] *The Scotsman,* 14 June 1952.
[87] *Dumfries Courier & Herald,* 9 January 1935.
[88] Dunbarton County Library, *Annual Report 1933-34* (1934).

number of persons directly interested in the library's welfare and
its continued existence was not only greater: their succession was
more certain. An almost inevitable failing of the subscription
library is underlined by a contemporary writer: [89]

> Their chief defect has been an exclusive and aristocratic
> spirit in their conditions of membership and in the choice of
> works supplied. In many instances they have been rendered
> subservient to the wishes of one or two individuals who have
> desired rare, expensive, and learned works, which were
> unsuited to the taste of the general reader. In this respect they
> have become, for the most part, intellectual catacombs of
> learning instead of repositories of useful knowledge.

He emphasizes his point in a footnote:

> The influence of a popular historian in Scotland, was sufficient
> to procure the Wellington Dispatches for his own reference.
> The cost of this work absorbed nearly the whole of the annual
> sum allowed to be expended in one book society to which he
> subscribed.

As the subscription library derives its income from its voluntary subscribers, their desires are a first consideration in its
purpose and policy. The public library is established for the community, and all pay their share of its expense whether or not they
use its service, or indeed even if they are unaware of its existence;
in this way library committee and librarian are responsible to the
community as a whole and should resist the influence of "pressure
groups."

*   *   *

In mid-nineteenth-century Scotland libraries, or at least small
collections of books, were found in almost every parish, established either by donation—the clergyman or perhaps a landed
proprietor giving 50 to 100 books—or by a subscription raised
in the parish. Some parishioner or other volunteered to be unpaid
librarian, and there were usually no funds for the maintenance of
the library, unless it enjoyed an endowment. [90]

Thomas Telford, the engineer, for example, was "so much . . .
impressed with the advantages arising from select libraries" that
he gave £1000 each to Westerkirk, his birthplace, and to Lang-

[89] Hudson, *Adult education* (1851), p. 195-6.
[90] S.C. Report (1849), 3086, 3090.

26

holm, the interest on which was to be "annually laid out in the purchase of books."[91] At Westerkirk the library had been instituted in 1792 by the miners employed in an antimony mine. After Telford's bequest a new building was erected for the library, where the books were exchanged "once a month, on the day of the full moon."

Readers of all ages and conditions—farmers, shepherds, ploughmen, labourers and their children—resort to it from far and near, taking away with them as many volumes as they desire for the month's reading.

Thus there is scarcely a cottage in the valley in which good books are not to be found under perusal; and we are told that it is a common thing for the Eskdale shepherd to take a book in his plaid to the hillside—a volume of Shakespeare, Prescott, or Macaulay—and read it there, under the blue sky, with his sheep and the green hills before him. And thus, as long as the bequest lasts, the good, great engineer will not cease to be remembered with gratitude in his beloved Eskdale.[92]

Within thirty-five years the Langholm Library contained "most of the standard works in English literature, and the popular periodicals of the present day."[93]

At the beginning of the twentieth century the Langholm library was accommodated in the post office buildings. Downstairs lived a rural postman called Grieve, whose son, whom we know as "Hugh MacDiarmid," had constant access to the library:

I used to fill a big washing-basket with books and bring it downstairs as often as I wanted to. . . . There were upwards of twelve thousand books in the library (though it was strangely deficient in Scottish books), and a fair number of new books, chiefly novels, was constantly bought. Before I left home (when I was fourteen) . . . I certainly read almost every one of them.[94]

[91] *N.S.A.*, (1845), vol. 4, Dumfriesshire, p. 435-6.
[92] S. Smiles, *Lives of the engineers* (1861), vol. 2, p. 492-3.
[93] *N.S.A.* (1845), vol. 4, Dumfriesshire, p. 427.
[94] Hugh MacDiarmid (C. M. Grieve), *Lucky Poet* (1943), p. 8-9. MacDiarmid was either a phenomenally voracious reader or his estimate of the number of books in the library is excessive; in 1932, G. W. Shirley, the Dumfriesshire librarian, described the Langholm Library as "an excellent collection of some 5000 volumes" (*Dumfriesshire libraries* (1933), p. 4).

Few of the libraries, however, were endowed. With no means of giving the libraries proper care, and in the absence of new books, enthusiasm generally—and naturally—fell off in the course of a few years. "The great part of the books is soon read."[95]

The parochial libraries were usually connected with the churches—the management of the Langholm Library, for example, was vested in the minister and kirk session—and consequently they were chiefly concerned "either with religious works, or with the literature of the particular church which they may be attached to."[96] Nevertheless, many included "history, travels and voyages" along with "books on moral and religious subjects," or "various useful and entertaining reading calculated to promote mental and moral improvement."[97]

From these libraries the books were usually lent out freely to everyone. When a charge was made it might be 1s yearly or 1d a month.[98] The libraries were well used:

> The books are thoroughly read; they are worn out, almost, they are read so much.[99]

In evidence given before the Select Committee on Public Libraries, John Imray, a civil engineer from Scotland who had resided during all his youth in the north of Aberdeenshire, and had had opportunities of seeing several parochial and village libraries there, agreed that landed proprietors might well encourage the formation of such libraries "for the sake of improving the habits of the population," but he pointed out that he had seen this happen very seldom.[100]

[95] S.C. Report (1849), 3091.

[96] ibid. 748.

[97] N.S.A. (1845), vol. 9, Fife, p. 259, 229.

[98] N.S.A. (1845), vol. 9, Fife, p. 144.

[99] S.C. Report (1849), 3096.

[100] ibid. 3084-5, 3104, 3110. Imray might well have heard of the "itinerating preacher," William Brown (1776-1829), who ministered for fourteen summers in Aberdeenshire and Banffshire, before accepting a call to settle at Inverurie. Brown was a strong advocate of libraries: "Endeavour to get libraries, consisting chiefly of history, travels, voyages, established for the benefit of the young, to keep them, if possible, from the perusal of plays, novels and romances"; "It might tend not a little to the diffusion of spiritual knowledge, were select Religious Libraries established pretty generally throughout the kingdom"; "The number of select Religious Libraries is yearly on the increase"; "It is evident that the libraries are doing good." (R. Penman, *Memoir of Mr William Brown* (1830), particularly p. 37.)

I think that the feeling has rather been that they were raising the lower classes too high by giving them information, and that it is better to keep them without it.

When pressed on this point, he replied that he did not mean there was any formal objection on the part of landed proprietors to the spread of information among the lower class, rather "they showed a want of inclination to assist."

His evidence in this respect can be compared with the information supplied to the Committee by the Rev. William Robert Fremantle, a clergyman of the Church of England at Claydon in Buckinghamshire, who was very sorry to say that the farmers in his district objected to "the extension of any but religious knowledge among the labourers."

I should be sorry to say anything unfavourable to farmers; I have a great respect for them, but I am afraid if they do not read themselves, they do not like to see the labouring class becoming really and truly wiser than themselves; if the farmers do not move forward, the labouring classes will be the wiser of the two. I have many young men in my parish better instructed than the farmers, and who could give a better answer to a question than many of the farmers themselves.[101]

On the other hand Thomas Maitland, the Solicitor-General for Scotland, thought that landowers, heritors, clergy, kirk sessions and farmers, all took an interest in education. Asked if there was no jealousy on the part of the farmers to the improvement of the peasantry, he replied:

Not the slightest, I think eminently the very reverse; the intelligent farmers of Scotland, if they came to select a workman, would rather have a man who spends his time in reading than anything else.[102]

Imray again was asked what suggestions he could offer for the improvement of "the system of parochial or village libraries, which has prevailed in Scotland." He thought assistance might be given from some "central fund," "because the localities themselves are generally very poor."

I should imagine that if in such towns as the county towns, if, for example, in Aberdeenshire, in the town of Aberdeen,

[101] S.C. Report (1849), 1397, 1402.
[102] ibid. 1484, 1486.

29

there were a large library formed, and portions of it were transmitted throughout the parishes in regular order, so that they might be read, by some such means many books might be brought within the reach of the rural population, at a very small expense.[103]

He thought, indeed, that "some system of itinerating libraries would be productive of great benefit."

ITINERATING LIBRARIES

The "itinerating libraries" referred to had been established in East Lothian some thirty years earlier by Samuel Brown, eighth son of the author of the *Self-Interpreting Bible*. The Select Committee had heard of them from Edward Edwards, and later the Committee examined the Rev. John Croumbie Brown, a son of the founder.[104]

Brown's plan was to provide a library, or a division, of 50 volumes in every town and village of the county, and he hoped to place the libraries at such distances that no individual might be more remote from one than a mile and a half. A division would be stationed in a place for two years; thereafter it would be passed on to another town or village and a new division would be sent in its place, and this in turn, would be exchanged after another two years.

The scheme was based on Haddington and began in 1817 with five divisions of 250 volumes.[105] In the first year the villages of Aberlady, Saltoun, Tynninghame and Garvald received libraries and the total issues of books at those stations was 1461, "every book being issued upon the average seven times in the course of the year." In the second year, however, the issues fell to 733. After the first exchange in 1819 the issues rose once more, to 1313; in the fourth year there were 928 issues—again a reduction.

The Rev. Mr Brown emphasized the alternation:

On every second year a similar reduction took place from that time on to the present. When the books were first sent to

[103] ibid. 3111-12.

[104] ibid. 307-12, 1769-1837.

[105] *N.S.A.* (1845), vol. 2, Haddington, p. 17, where there is a letter, dated 5 May 1835, from the founder, who was at that time Provost of Haddington. In Samuel Brown, jr., *Some account of Itinerating Libraries and their founder* (1856), p. 58, the original stock is given as "two hundred select volumes."

30

those villages, the number of issues was 1461. The second year the novelty had gone off, and the numbers fell; in the third year new books came, and again there was an increased demand for them, but a demand not so great as during the first year, only those who were really desirous of information reading; in the fourth year there was a falling off, but the number was greater than during the second year, a habit of reading having been acquired by a much greater number of individuals.[106]

Each division was placed in charge of a librarian, an individual who would accept the responsibility gratuitously and in whom the promoter of the scheme could trust. Teachers, shopkeepers and labourers were found as librarians:

The teacher, when he took an interest in it, made a good librarian. From the children being daily at school, they applied for books themselves and carried them home. But a shop is decidedly the best place for a library, rather than a private house. A stranger can go more freely to a shop than to a private house.[107]

The founder was emphatic that "the principal object of the East Lothian Itinerating Libraries is to promote the interests of religion," and a large proportion of the books (in general half or two-thirds of every division) were accordingly of "moral and religious tendency"; nevertheless there was "a number of volumes on all branches of knowledge which we could procure, of a plain and popular nature"—"history, biography, travels, and popular works on the arts and sciences":

This I am persuaded has made the institution much more popular, and also increased the number of religious books which have been read.

The libraries were used and the books read by "all ranks and all classes"

from families of the first respectability in the county down to the poorest and most distressed of its inhabitants—not excepting the prisoners in jail.[108]

---

[106] S.C. Report (1849), 1778-80.
[107] ibid. 1782-3, 1804, 1809. In 1828 the "gratuitous librarians" included a shoemaker, a draper, a labourer, a coalier, a baker, a tailor, a weaver, two saddlers, two smiths, three wrights and six teachers.
[108] W. Brown *Memoir relative to Itinerating Libraries* (1830), p. 4.

The scheme increased steadily until in 1830 there were altogether forty divisions (2000 volumes) in general circulation in Haddington and in thirty-one of the principal towns and villages of the county, and issues totalled 10,000. In 1835 there were "forty-three divisions of 50 volumes, besides about 450 volumes of new and agricultural books . . . in all 2600 volumes"; in 1836 there were "forty-seven libraries in circulatory motion through the county, containing 2380 volumes, exclusive of about 500 new books, which had not then been thrown into the general circulation"; and at Samuel Brown's death in 1839 "there were 3850 volumes; and if there had been sixty divisions or book-cases, instead of only forty-seven, no inhabitant would have been one mile and a half from one."[109]

The success of the scheme is underlined by citing the case of North Berwick:

In 1816 there was at North Berwick a library of 155 volumes, from which there were only 20 issues in the course of the year; an arrangement was then made by my father, and the 155 volumes were given to the East Lothian Itinerating Libraries, on condition that he would station two divisions in North Berwick and two others in neighbouring villages. Of the 100 volumes stationed at North Berwick, there were issued during the first year 769; every volume upon the average was issued more than seven and half times. During the second year there were 529 issues, while there had been only 50 before, so that a taste for reading was thus introduced into the district. Upon the average of six years there were 863 issues annually, every volume being read upwards of eight and a half times, upon the average.[110]

Nevertheless, the Rev. J. C. Brown had to report that in 1849 there were divisions only in the Western district of the county—about 20, all told—and although the books were still well read, the scheme on the whole was on the decline. For this he offered several explanations. Initially the books were issued gratuitously, although voluntary subscriptions were accepted, but in 1831 it was proposed to charge a penny per volume during the first year, while continuing to issue the books gratuitously the second year:

as a subscription, however small, might essentially impede the success of the scheme, and as it is of immense consequence to

[109] *N.S.A.* (1845), vol. 2, Haddington, p. 17; S. Brown, *Itinerating Libraries* (1856), p. 63.
[110] S.C. Report (1849), 1794.

bring the books within the reach of the whole population, particularly of the young, whom it is of peculiar importance to form to habits of reading and reflection.[111]

As a result of this charge the number of readers for the first year fell off. Then Samuel Brown had died in 1839, and there was no one to take the general charge of the divisions but his daughter. Others who had co-operated with him from the first were feeling the infirmities of age, and it was sometimes difficult to find new librarians who would take a deep interest in the scheme.[112]

Hudson suggests two other causes for the scheme's decline: that the proportion of theological and religious works generally increased, and that there was general dissatisfaction with the "irregularity" of the exchanges. The twenty divisions, he declared, were "almost entirely inoperative from the want of a sufficient amount of light literature and fiction."[113]

Writing in 1856, Brown's biographer also asserted, surely from experience:

Every centre of local circulation must have its manager as industrious, and imbued with the same spirit of devotion and love, as the unwearied founder; else the whole movements of egress, return, and exchange will be confused, retarded and inefficient.[114]

Originally Brown himself met a great deal of the expense of the scheme, "by engaging in the sale of religious periodicals, and devoting to this purpose the whole of the profits on these," but some friends aided him with contributions. Then, as new books were bought, they were kept in the first instance for the use of subscribers, and as a result the number of subscribers (at 3s a year) increased from 8 in 1821 to 162 in 1829, when the subscription was raised to 5s. Subscribers' collections were available at Dunbar and North Berwick as well as at Haddington.[115]

While the Select Committee was in session in 1849, William Ewart, its chairman, received from Samuel Smiles a letter, in which this writer referred perceptively to the "Itinerating Library system" with which he was, of course, familiar.[116] Smiles was

[111] W. Brown, *Itinerating Libraries* (1830), p. 7.
[112] S.C. Report (1849), 1798, 1816, 1817.
[113] Hudson, *Adult education* (1851), p. 198.
[114] S. Brown, *Itinerating Libraries* (1856), p. 72.
[115] S.C. Report (1849), 1786, 1787, 1792.
[116] ibid. p. 130.

born in Haddington in 1812, and after study in medicine at Edinburgh, he had settled in practice in his native town. He was convinced of the importance of the scheme: he noted the eagerness with which the books were read; he emphasized how readers were constantly attracted by "drafting off the books which had been read and become old in one district, to another where they had not been read and were still new"; and he appreciated the economy of a unified stock:

> Instead of having the same books, often expensive ones, in each library of a district, it would be necessary to have only a few sets, and keep them in regular circulation;

but he was not blind to the central fault of the scheme—that its success depended chiefly on its founder, and that since his death the system had lost in efficiency, and the divisions of books in attraction.

> The system is one that requires constant supervision, and the exercise of considerable judgement. But it might be matter for consideration, whether it would not be judicious economy to pay for such service, and to make it worth the while of a man of energy and judgement to devote his time and labour to the superintendence of the Itinerating Libraries of a district.

It is, of course, this "judicious economy" that the Education Authorities in 1918 were permitted to exercise; and the basic principles of the county library system we know today, as outlined in the Adams Report, are largely a variation and "future development" of Brown's pioneer scheme.[117]

Several other schemes of Itinerating Libraries were started in imitation of Brown's. About 1822 libraries of this kind were introduced into Berwickshire by George Buchan of Kelloe. Brougham, in his celebrated pamphlet *Practical observations upon the education of the people,* which went through twenty editions within a year of its publication in 1825, commended both Brown's "excellent plan" and Buchan's adoption of it in Berwickshire, "with this very great improvement, that the current expenses are defrayed by the readers who pay twopence a month, and I hope choose the books."[118] Samuel Brown's son told the Select Committee on Libraries in 1849 that Lord Brougham had urged his

---

[117] W. G. S. Adams, *A report on library provision and policy* (1915), p. 17; S.C. Report (1849), p. xii.
[118] H. Brougham, *Practical observations upon the education of the people* (1825), p. 7.

father "to abandon his other avocations, and give himself entirely to this enterprize."[119]

James Douglas of Cavers in Roxburghshire, after some correspondence with Brown, started a scheme in that county in 1829. In ten years there were twenty-six of these libraries there.[120] Douglas published in 1831 a pamphlet, *The prospects of Britain,* in which he spoke highly of Brown's work:

> Could Mr Brown's assistance be secured, and his whole valuable time be devoted to this object, which has indeed already absorbed a considerable portion of it, the plan might even now succeed over the whole country. It has already succeeded in the county where Mr Brown resides; at all events, it must sooner or later be generally adopted.

> Among all the various openings for liberality, none appears more satisfactory than this plan of itinerating libraries. . . .

> He who bequeaths a book to a moveable library leaves to posterity, like the Grecian author, "a possession for ever."[121]

The system of Itinerating Libraries was also introduced into the Highlands. In 1826 the General Assembly's Committee on Religious Instruction in Scotland reported that it had been considering the provision of "small and select libraries . . . for the use of the scholars."

> The practice of making these libraries, in some instances, itinerating (as has been done in East Lothian, and other districts, with the best effects), might be benefiicially adopted.[122]

A year later they were contemplating a plan for supplying schools with "a small and well-selected library—such as may afford at once instruction and amusement to the scholars."

> The plan of circulating these Libraries among different stations, as described in the last Report, will be observed wherever the localities of the district will admit of its being practised with convenience.[123]

[119] S.C. Report (1849), 1828.
[120] S. Brown, *Itinerating Libraries* (1856), p. 71.
[121] J. Douglas, *The prospects of Britain* (1831), p. 48.
[122] Church of Scotland, *Report of the General Assembly's Committee on . . . Education and Religious Instruction* (1826), p. 15.
[123] ibid. (1827), p. 13

In 1828 the arrangements were "now very far advanced."

The books have been selected, and are in the hands of the binder. They contain as many suitable volumes of translations in the Gaelic language as could be procured; and the rest are in the English language—there being in whole 150 different volumes. . . . Every three schools shall have a whole set of these books equally divided among them, by appropriating 50, in the first instance, to each station, which they shall, after an interval of two years, interchange with each other; so that in six years, each station shall have enjoyed the whole 150 volumes. It will be seen from the description of these books, that they are intended, not merely for the use of young people attending school, but to be accessible, through the scholars, to the whole grown-up population, who, it is believed, have seldom in the Highlands enjoyed any benefit of this kind.[124]

The libraries consisted "partly of books of a religious description and partly of such as contain useful and entertaining knowledge—interesting histories—voyages and travels—biographies—sketches in civil and natural history."[125]

In their Report submitted to the General Assembly in 1829 the Committee had the satisfaction of reporting that in December 1828 their arrangements had been completed.

Early in the month of January, they issued books from the Depository for the formation of Libraries at no less than fifty-five different stations, each Library consisting of fifty-six volumes English and Gaelic.[126]

The Committee recalled that it was "considerably more than a century since 19 Presbyterial and 58 Parochial Libraries were planted in the Highlands by the General Assembly . . .: hardly a vestige of these Libraries now remains."

---

124 ibid. (1828), p. 11-12.
125 ibid. (1829), p. 13. A full list of the "Books selected for School Libraries" is given on p. 48-50 of the 1828 Report: it includes such books as *The Cottagers of Glenburnie, Robinson Crusoe, Sandford and Merton,* Ossian, Goldsmith's *Deserted Village,* Thomson's *Seasons,* Boston's *Fourfold state, The Vicar of Wakefield,* Falconer's *Shipwreck,* and various travels; the Gaelic books are mostly religious, and include Dugald Buchanan's *Songs on sacred subjects, The Pilgrim's Progress,* and Boston again.
126 "Regulations for managing the Assembly's School Libraries" are printed on p. 33 of the 1829 Report.

In February 1831 a further 25 libraries were established, and the first "exchange" of the original libraries was ordered to take place at Whitsunday of that year. Hitherto the issue of books had been gratuitous, it was now proposed "to exact one-halfpenny per month from each scholar." Although "almost an elusory payment," this would supply "a fund sufficient to maintain the libraries, and to reproduce them as they decay." As there had been 2130 scholar-borrowers in the previous year, we can calculate the estimated revenue as less than £55.

Some of the schoolmasters' comments on the libraries are worth quoting:

"The Library induces them to read good books, and they read to their parents in the long winter nights."

"On return of the books, I examine every one on what he has read."

"When examined on the ordinary school lessons, they show an acquaintance with the subject, which, but for the use of the Library, they must have been quite unacquainted with."

"They are acquiring some little information, for I sometimes hear them talk together of the subjects contained in books which two or more of them have read."

"Many an hour is profitably employed in reading these books, that would otherwise be spent in idleness and folly."

"The good effects of the Library are seen in the civil deportment and peaceable disposition the scholars evince . . . and the almost total abolition of falsehood."

"The desire for information prevents them visiting their neighbours' houses, so as to misspend their time."[127]

Eleven years later, in 1843, the Assembly's Committee was remarking how little indication there was in the Presbyterial and Parochial Reports "of the existence of school libraries," and in 1851 Hudson noted:

The Itinerating Libraries established in the Highlands of Scotland have been for a long time inoperative, and the stock is much dilapidated or destroyed.[128]

---

[127] Church of Scotland, *Report of the Committee on Education and Religious Instruction* (1832), p. 32-4.
[128] ibid. (1843), p. 33; Hudson, *Adult education* (1851), p. 198.

In his evidence to the Select Committee (1849) Brown's son mentioned that the system had been introduced into Peeblesshire by the Free Church in 1849, and Brown himself had been invited in 1834 to supervise a similar scheme with twenty-one centres in Edinburgh and Leith.[129] An earlier Edinburgh attempt had proved "a complete failure."[130]

In 1837 a subscription library at Crossgates in Fife that had been founded in 1809 and had continued for twenty-five years "with varied success" was re-formed as an Itinerating Library:

> Novelty gave a slight stimulus and brought a few donations. Dr S. Brown delivered two lectures, and by renewed exertions four hundred and fifty volumes were collected and annually divided between Crossgates and seven surrounding villages.

None of the divisions ever did well, however, except those immediately under the minister's superintendence, and when he left the parish, "the whole rapidly declined."[131]

Hudson recorded also the "almost unanimous" opinion of those connected with the work in Scotland that it was only "as a missionary task" that the system could be revived and carried on, "even if fiction entered largely into the new libraries." Nevertheless, the committee of the Northern Union of Mechanics' Institutions (of which Hudson was founder) had established an itinerating library to provide each associated Institute with a certain number of volumes, and in six months the experiment had proved so successful that the Committee were unable to meet the demand.

Samuel Brown's brother, the Rev. William Brown, M.D., in his *Memoir relative to Itinerating Libraries*, argued enthusiastically for the expansion of the system.[132] He drew attention to "an important characteristic of these libraries" that he called "a principle of Self-production." A "British and Foreign Itinerating Library Society," able to raise £5000 a year might, "within a moderate period of time, cover the whole of Europe with such Institutions," by issuing divisions of fifty volumes each on loan for 25s a year, "which many individuals would willingly pay, as they

[129] S.C. Report (1849), 1818, 1835; *N.S.A.* (1845), vol. 2, Haddington, p. 17.
[130] S. Brown, *Itinerating Libraries* (1856), p. 71.
[131] Hudson, *Adult education* (1851), p. 198-9. The Dr S. Brown may have been the founder's son: he was a chemist of note and in 1843 a candidate for the chair of chemistry in Edinburgh University.
[132] Published in 1830; reprinted in *East-Lothian Literary and Statistical Journal*, vol. 1,, no. 10, April 1831, p. 298-308.

might more than reimburse themselves by lending out the books."
After some years, he suggested the Society would be able to print
books for itself: he compiled an elaborate table to show that in
fifty years libraries of this kind could be provided "for nearly
every 600 of the inhabitants of our globe!" After this astro-
nomical calculation, it is not surprising to read "that the Society
could not be carried on without expense," and that "it would be
vain to expect that it could be conducted by gratuitous agency."

On a smaller scale, the author estimated that a Society of this
kind for Great Britain and Ireland could in twenty years provide
a library for every 524 persons (taking the population at
20,000,000), and in twenty-five years for every 294 persons. In a
footnote he particularized even further:

> If a Society were established in Edinburgh with an income of
> £250 a-year, it would, in twenty-five years, furnish nearly
> four libraries for every parish in Scotland.

It is perhaps too easy to laugh at this elaborate computation.
The founder is not to be blamed for the excesses of his followers.
In the memoir of Samuel Brown published in 1856, at a time when
the future fortunes of the scheme were "now left with a Christian
public," his plan for sending books "in the state of perpetual
motion over the face of the earth" is justly described as "a devout
and a noble thought."

MECHANICS' INSTITUTES

There is another movement that developed rapidly in the first
half of the nineteenth century which claims consideration with the
types of library we have been discussing—the endowed, the subscription, the parish and the itinerating—as a forerunner of the
public rate-supported library. In Scotland in 1850 there were,
according to Hudson, 55 Literary and Mechanics' Institutions, with
a total of almost 60,000 volumes in their libraries and an issue of
154,747 books.[133]

That a library was essential to the success of a Mechanics'
Institute was repeatedly emphasized in the evidence heard by the
Select Committee in 1849. Samuel Smiles, for example, reported
that all the institutions in the Yorkshire Union had libraries
attached to them:

[133] Hudson, *Adult education* (1851), p. vi, vii.

They find in the libraries a bond of union, as it were, for the institution; that it is necessary to have a library to keep the institution together;

and John Baxter Langley affirmed that if it were not for their libraries, the Mechanics' and Scientific institutions he was familiar with would cease to exist: they held a continued existence in consequence of the attraction which the library afforded. In a later reply he underlined his point of view:

The permanent success of the institutions depends completely upon the libraries. Where the institutions have either not the advantage of a large gift of books from some benevolent party, or where they have not succeeded in making a large collection of books, they are upon the most insecure footing.

The name Mechanics' Institute is known to be inaccurate. In 1849 Smiles took care to point this out:

The mechanics' institutes in the large towns, generally speaking, are not Institutes of mechanics; they are for the most part Institutes of the middle and respectable classes, and a small proportion, in some cases not so much as a half, of working men; a class superior to working men, and a small proportion of working men receiving comparatively high wages, support those institutions; generally speaking, they are not Mechanics' institutes, and it is a misnomer to designate them as such.

Mechanics' Institutes were so named, for they trace their origin to the "gratuitous course of elementary philosophical lectures" that Dr George Birkbeck first offered in 1800 to the mechanics and artisans he had met in Glasgow.[134] The year before, Birkbeck, a Yorkshire man and Quaker born in 1776, had been appointed professor of natural philosophy at Anderson's University. He was so impressed by the eagerness for knowledge he found among the men in the workshops he went to for the apparatus he required that he began his "mechanics' class" for their benefit. His first lecture in the autumn of 1800 was attended by seventy-five workmen; the second by two hundred;

[134] Hudson claims for Birmingham "the earliest Mechanics' Institution or Society in Great Britain"; but the Society founded there in 1789 was called the Sunday Society, its later title being the Birmingham Brotherly Society, while its associated library was called the Birmingham Artisans' Library (*Adult education* (1851), p. 29-31).

40

the third by three hundred; and "exactly one month after he commenced his course, Dr Birkbeck was listened to with rapt attention by five hundred working mechanics."[135]

Birkbeck left for London in 1804, but his successor, Dr Andrew Ure, continued the class and "by his exertions a library was added in 1808, to the original design." In 1823, after arguments with the Directors about the ownership of the library, the mechanics seceded, and on 5 July 1823 they formed the "Glasgow Mechanics' Institution," with Birkbeck as Patron.

In Edinburgh a School of Arts (which has evolved over the years into the present Heriot-Watt University) had been founded in April 1821.[136] The prospectus announced courses of lectures on Mechanics and Chemistry, to begin in the following October, and the opening of "a Library of Books upon the same subjects, for perusal at home as well as in the room."

A "Mechanics School of Arts" that was commenced in Haddington in 1823 grew "out of the Haddington itinerant libraries."[137] The movement spread rapidly throughout Great Britain. Institutions were established in many Scottish towns in the early 1820s: in Aberdeen, Dundee, Dunbar, Hawick and Perth, for example; and all included libraries.

In Aberdeen, where the Institute was founded in 1824, a "well-selected scientific library of 800 volumes" had been collected as early as 1825.[138] The Mechanics' Institute in Dundee was called the Watt Institution, and its chief features were its museum and library.[139] In 1850 a news and reading room had been recently added, and there were 3250 volumes in the library. At Dunbar, as at Haddington, according to the Rev. J. C. Brown, the Mechanics' Institute originated out of the interest excited there by his father's Itinerating Libraries.

In Greenock, when an Arts and Sciences Lectures Association came to an end in 1829, a deputation of workmen appealed to the custodian of the Association's library of 201 volumes for the continued use of the books.[140] The custodian "freely complied, but

[135] J. G. Godard, *George Birkbeck* (1884), p. 26.

[136] Brougham, *Practical observations* (1825), p. 19.

[137] *N.S.A.* (1845), vol. 2, Haddington, p. 15; S.C. Report (1849), 1827.

[138] G. M. Fraser, *Aberdeen Mechanics' Institute* (1912), p. 3, 7; Hudson, *Adult education* (1851), p. 59.

[139] Dr Sharp has drawn attention to "the influence of James Watt on this movement for general education with its bias towards science and technology" (S.L.A., *Proceedings* . . . *Dumfries* (1950), p. 15).

[140] R. M. Smith, *A page of local history: being a record of the origin and progress of Greenock Mechanics' Library and Institution* (1904), p. 10-12.

stipulated that the guarantee for their preservation should be undertaken by a small joint body of men from the shipyards in the east and in the west ends of the town." The books were being circulated by July 1830 and early in August it was resolved by a majority to name the organization Greenock Mechanics' Library.

The Tradesmen's and Mechanics' Library in Dunfermline resulted from an amalgamation of the Tradesmen's Library established in 1808 and a Mechanics' Library dating from 1832. By 1844 it contained 200 volumes, well selected, covering science and art, moral and political philosophy, history and theology.[141]

Not all the libraries were well selected, however. Many of the books were donated, "turned out of people's shelves," and were never used. The selection of books was "very imperfect, and frequently injudicious." Several of the witnesses before the Select Committee (1849) were worried by the "large proportion of works of fiction" in these libraries, though they were confident that "a taste for a better description of literature" was evidently increasing, and that the circulation of works of fiction was diminishing.

> Where the institution is new the first demand is chiefly for works of fiction; and if you trace out the readers, you find their names attached first usually to narratives and tales, then to novels, then to biographies and histories, and then to philosophy.

Another witness reports:

> We find that in regard to novels, which form the majority of books taken out, the proportion is diminishing, and the proportion of historical and philosophical works is increasing. The novels, in some libraries, are in the minority.

To this reply the Kenyon Committee in 1927 added the laconic comment: "This claim has been made many times since!"

The historian of the Greenock Mechanics' Library had a different tale to tell:

> From being the seat of a severe erudition, as its founders aimed it to be, it came by the hand of inflexible circumstance to the level and estate of an undistinguished circulating library, the bulk of whose readers moved and had their being in a routine that may excite but does not always instruct or elevate.

[141] *N.S.A.* (1845), vol. 9, Fife, p. 903.

According to Hudson in 1850 the library with the "largest circulation in the kingdom" was the Edinburgh Mechanics' Subscription Library, founded in the year 1825. In its early days this library was handsomely assisted by "munificent donations" from the leading booksellers and publishers—Black, Blackwood, Constable and others—and some of these granted, in addition, "credit to any amount required—an accommodation of vital service to an infant institution."[142] In 1850 the library contained nearly 18,000 volumes; thirty years later, nearly 22,500.

A parallel development to the mechanics' libraries is referred to in a letter printed in the Select Committee's minutes of evidence. A Farmers' library and club had been formed in Wigtownshire in 1843, and similar libraries "of great utility" had been established in the counties of Argyll, Lanark and Berwick. More recently a Farmers' club had been formed in Langholm (it met there once a month), and another in Lockerbie, and the "Dumfries and Galloway Farmers' Club and Library" had been instituted.

> Much good has resulted from these, and I think the upper classes ought systematically to patronize and promote such means of spreading sound rural statistical and economical knowledge throughout Great Britain and Ireland.[143]

THE MOVE TO PUBLIC LIBRARIES

It was William Ewart, the Member for Dumfries, who moved in the Commons on Thursday, 15 March 1849, "That a Select Committee be appointed on the best means of extending the establishment of Libraries freely open to the Public, especially in large Towns in Great Britain and Ireland."[144] At the Committee's first meeting, he was appointed Chairman, and he conducted the proceedings throughout. The Committee met on sixteen occasions over the next two and a half months and its report is dated 23 July 1849.

The Report fills eleven and a half foolscap pages, and the minutes of evidence, with maps and appendices, extend to over three hundred pages. It has been described as "a document of the first importance. Its excellence lies both in its comprehensive

[142] Library Association, *Transactions* 1880 (1881), p.154-5.

[143] S.C. Report (1849), p. 253-4; *N.S.A.* (1845), vol. 4, Dumfriesshire, p. 428.

[144] There is an admirable brief biographical sketch of Ewart and an estimate of his work by Mrs M. D. McLean, Librarian of the Ewart Library, Dumfries, in S.L.A., *Proceedings . . . Dumfries* (1950), p. 2-4.

character and in the liberal spirit which inspires its recommendations."[145] Seventy-five years later the Departmental Committee of the Board of Education was to make this significant statement:

> We find that the general lines of our report correspond with those of the report of 1849, and that in many instances we have only to reaffirm the recommendations which were made in that report but have never been implemented, or have been implemented only on a small scale. Notwithstanding the great changes in social feeling during the same period we find in the report hardly one expression of opinion on contemporary society which we would hesitate to endorse today. To this report must be attributed the legislation which authorized the provision of libraries by Town Councils and all subsequent developments.

The first and most important witness examined by the Select Committee was Edward Edwards, then an assistant in the British Museum. His valuable evidence is summarized in the long reply he gave on his third appearance before the committee in answering the Chairman's question: "Have you any suggestion to offer to the Committee with respect to the formation of new public libraries?"

> I think, first of all, there are the libraries that we need in the capital cities; next to these are the libraries that are needed in provincial towns; and then there are the village libraries, the formation of which ought to be encouraged in rural parishes: those seem to me to be three classes of libraries which ought to be separately looked at. With respect to London, I think it is of the highest importance that there should be at least two new libraries founded, strictly of a public kind, and such as should keep pace with the progress of literature, in addition to the library of the British Museum, and that they might with great advantage be adapted to a different class of readers, so as in some degree to draw away from the reading-room at the British Museum certain of what I may venture to term, in a literary sense, the less important class of readers: such a change would enable that establishment better to meet the wants and requirements of the higher class of students. I think those libraries might be rather what one would term educational libraries, the British Museum Library continuing to be a

[145] Board of Education, Public Libraries Committee, *Report on Public Libraries in England and Wales* (1927) (The Kenyon Report), p. 10.

library which should be encyclopedical, having all sorts of books, bestowing its funds not only on the purchase of books of intrinsic value, but also on those of curiosity and rarity. If new libraries were formed in London they ought not to go beyond the books that are instrinsically valuable, not seeking to purchase curiosities or rarities; and it would deserve consideration whether advantage might not result from giving to every such new library a special and distinctive character, in respect to the classes of books of which it shall mainly consist, one being chiefly legal, another chiefly medical, and so on. In Edinburgh there is also great need of a new public library; Edinburgh has several libraries, but to none of them is access unrestricted. Dublin also is in great need of a library that shall be at once accessible to the public and contain a good supply of modern and foreign books; there is no such library at present, but there is an excellent groundwork for one in Archbishop Marsh's library. With regard to provincial towns, I think, as I have said before, that particular attention ought to be paid to the literature of the locality, a sort of topographical character ought to be given to them. Most of our great towns have no libraries at all that can in any proper sense be termed public, so that what has to be done there is entirely from the beginning. I think it would also be important that the claims of country parishes should not be overlooked; an entirely different class of libraries is needed there from those which are required in the great towns, and I think the plan which has been already suggested of itinerating libraries eminently deserves the consideration of the Committee; the adoption of that plan has certainly done great good in Scotland, and I think it would be worth trying whether it could not be brought into operation in England.

Edwards pointed out, incidentally, that three Edinburgh Libraries (the University Library, and the libraries of the Faculty of Advocates and of the Writers of the Signet) contained a total of 288,854 printed books, or about 219 volumes to every 100 inhabitants—a proportion that compared very favourably with the $24\frac{1}{2}$ volumes to every 100 inhabitants in London.

Other witnesses included several eminent foreigners, and a large number of persons connected with the existing libraries in Great Britain and Ireland. George Dawson, Samuel Smiles and J. B. Langley spoke knowledgeably of the libraries in the mechanics' institutes; and the Rev. J. C. Brown discussed his father's system.

45

The witnesses were unanimous in the importance, social, moral and educational, they attached to the establishment of free public libraries:

I have always found that when the people read most they are the least open to be played upon by mere appeals to feelings.

I think that . . . by establishing public libraries which should be open at all times, especially in the evenings, a taste for reading would be greatly promoted. Give a man an interesting book to take home with him to his family, and it is probable that the man will stay at home and read his book in preference to going out and spending his time in dissipation or in idleness; and, therefore, the formation of those libraries would be favourable to the improvement of the moral and intellectual condition of the working population.

I have known men of from 20 to 30 who, when they came, smoked their pipes in the school-room, overturned the forms and did all kinds of mischief, and now they are perfectly quiet and orderly, and they dress better; instead of rags, they come with whole clothes (though of the poorest kind still), and they sit down in the library with the greatest quietness and decorum, and read the books.

We give the people in this country an appetite to read, and supply them with nothing. For the last many years in England everybody has been educating the people, but they have forgotten to find them any books. In plain language, you have made them hungry, but you have given them nothing to eat; it is almost a misfortune to a man to have a great taste for reading, and not to have the power of satisfying it.

It appears to me that the second-best gift which the Government could bestow on the working classes of this country, next to a good system of secular instruction, would be a library in every town and village of the empire. The only public libraries to which the poor have any access are those of the mechanics' institutions, and of course the fee, though very small, limits the circulation materially. . . . I think that the best method of doing it would be by empowering every corporation to levy a rate on the inhabitants for the purpose, with a Minister of Instruction and Progress in the Government, to watch over these and similar objects, to take care that the powers so lodged did not remain a dead letter, and to check abuses. We want the interest in these matters which local management alone permits, and we want the efficiency which a central and controlling power alone confers.[146]

In its Report the Committee argued for an "improvement" that "yet remains to be accomplished, hitherto almost untried in this country—the establishment of Public Libraries, freely accessible to all the people." Such libraries had long existed on the continent, and the United States had already anticipated us in the formation of public libraries. The principal British libraries—those "entitled to receive a copy of every new work on its publication" —are then referred to, and the Committee gives its opinion that "libraries thus privileged" should, "in the absence of any valid reason to the contrary," throw open "their literary treasures (so far as they reasonably can do so)." Certain "local libraries" are mentioned by name—including Stirling's Library in Glasgow—and cathedral and parochial libraries are discussed.

After this survey the report continues:

Whatever may be our disappointment at the rarity of Public Libraries in the United Kingdom, we feel satisfaction in stating that the uniform current of the evidence tends to prove the increased qualifications of the people to appreciate and enjoy such institutions. . . .

There can be no greater proof of the fitness of the people of these institutions than their own independent efforts to create them. Evidence will be found in the subjoined Minutes of the extent of the Libraries connected with Mechanics' Institutes. . . .

The recent successful literary efforts of several of our working men is another reason for encouraging them by the formation of Public Libraries. . . .

It would seem, from the Evidence, that few countries are better calculated to profit by Public Libraries than Scotland. A respect for education and reading, long fostered by the ancient and excellent system of instruction by means of parochial schools, is hereditary in the people of Scotland. Even in distant rural districts Libraries have been formed. Your Committee observe with satisfaction the tendency in Scotland to form Farmers' Libraries; this is a wise proceeding, by which the theory of books is brought down to the test of practice. "Itinerating Libraries" (hereafter to be described) had their

[146] S.C. Report (1849), 1266, 2001, 3213, 1308, 2014.

origin, and still remain, in Scotland. The successful formation of a Library at Peebles, and its results in promoting literary taste and temperate and moral habits among the inhabitants, are shown in a letter to the Chairman of this Committee from the celebrated publisher, Mr Wm. Chambers. But these tendencies to the acquisition of knowledge deserves further development, both by the formation of Libraries in towns, and the dissemination of Village Libraries throughout the rural population of Scotland. . . .

A reference to "the demand for 'Lectures' " follows, with the comment:

It is almost a necessary consequence, that lectures should lead to reading. The lecturer himself frequently needs the assistance of books. His hearers naturally wish to pursue, by means of books, the subject on which his lectures have interested or instructed them. The power of access to standard works in a Public Library would tend to render the lecturer less superficial, and to promote investigations among his hearers. It would even be serviceable to our provincial press.

The Committee then consider how such institutions as public libraries could be established and maintained. The Committee suggest that if buildings can be provided, for library or museum, "The materials to fill these buildings would easily, and in many cases, voluntarily, be supplied."

Your Committee are convinced that the first great step in the formation of Libraries (and of similar institutions) is to establish a place of deposit, a local habitation for the books. That once formed, measures should be taken . . . for securing the property—the buildings as well as the books—in the town council of the place, or in some fixed and perpetually-renewable body. . . . There can be no doubt that these two conditions once fulfilled—a fixed and proper place of deposit, and a due investment of the property—Donation will abundantly supply the books. Donation has been the source of the principal libraries which have ever or anywhere, been formed. . . . It is not easy to conceive that a benevolent and enlightened citizen can leave a more pleasing or lasting monument behind him than a donation of books to a Public Library; constituting a department, on which his name might be inscribed as a benefactor, not only to his own times but to future ages.

They accepted, in fact the general principle, so emphatically underlined by later observers, that voluntary effort must be backed by some statutory organization. Edwards in his *Memoirs* ten years later, after the first Act had been amended to permit the purchase of books, restated the position:

> Without some assured provision of the means of continuing increase—as well as of simple preservation—no man ever secured to posterity the true advantage of a public library. To those persons, therefore, who took thought of such matters, two principles to start with seemed plain. The one that the new libraries should be formed in a catholic spirit. The other, that they should be freed from all dependence, either in gifts or in current "subscriptions" for their permanent support. The first principle involved the corollary that the new institutions and their management should stand entirely aloof from party influences in Politics or in Religion. . . . The second principle involved the corollary that the maintenance must be by rate, levied on the whole tax-paying community, and administered by its elective and responsible functionaries.[147]

This same point was still to be emphasized about eighty years later.

> Without the stability and continuity which good administration alone can give—without assured ways and means—without adequate equipment—how short-lived and ineffectual, for all their enthusiasm, such voluntary movements are apt to be! Not that organization and efficient administration can ever supersede voluntary effort. . . . No great work is ever done unless it can go on inspiring an ever-renewing voluntary effort. But neither can any real lasting work be done unless the enthusiasm of voluntary effort gets embodied in institutions, and is helped by a structure of administration and equipment which will preserve the gains of the past—which will prevent enthusiasm having to waste itself in beginning again each time from the beginning—which will by co-ordination and organization make the achievements of all the heritage of each.[148]

The Committee underlined the need of two sorts of libraries— "libraries of deposit and research; and libraries devoted to the

[147] E. Edwards, *Memoirs of libraries* (1859), vol. 1, p. 775.
[148] A. D. Lindsay (afterwards Lord Lindsay), "Presidential Address," *Library Association Record*, vol. 6, new series, December 1928, p. 235.

general reading and circulation of books." Existing libraries might be made more available to the public if they were "thrown open in the evening."

Government grants-in-aid are suggested:

It would be a far less objectionable appropriation of the public money than many other unopposed modes of expending it.

The Committee further recommended that Town Councils should be given the power "to levy a small rate for the creation and support of Town Libraries." "Topographical Libraries . . . where history may find a faithful portraiture of local events, local literature and local manners" should be found in "all our chief provincial towns."

Special Libraries would, no doubt, form themselves in appropriate localities. . . . In our large commercial and manufacturing towns, as well as in our agricultural districts, such libraries would naturally spring up, illustrative of the peculiar trade, manufactures, and agriculture of the place, and greatly favourable to the practical development of the science of political economy.

Village libraries are also important:

It is the opinion of this Committee, that much of the future character of our agricultural population, social, moral and religious, may depend on the extension and due formation of Village Libraries.

Interesting evidence has been given by the Rev. John Crombie Brown on the formation of "Itinerating Libraries in Scotland." By the location of 50 volumes in each village or hamlet, and its replacement by a new set of books at the end of two years, a constant supply of fresh works was afforded to an extensive district in the Lothians. This system, though not now in vigour, appears to have been, while it was in active operation, successful. It still exists; and a record of it (as capable of future development) appears to be a duty imposed on Your Committee.

The Committee then summarizes its recommendations so far:

Your Committee revert to the more general question. They have recognized in the establishment of Libraries, the general principles that they should be based on a firm and durable

50

foundation; that they should be freely accessible to all the public; that they should be open during the evening; and that they should, as far as possible, be Lending Libraries. The last consideration is one of great importance. Many men, in order to derive the fullest advantage from books, must have them not only in their hands, but in their homes.

An opinion on catalogues is given, with more than a hint of our present-day idea of Union catalogues:

There is no doubt that every Library should have a printed Catalogue, and that all Catalogues should (as far as possible) be published for general consultation. A man may find great use in a printed Catalogue, without going into a Library. It shows him what he can procure, and where he can procure it. . . . Until a nation possesses a good system of Catalogues, it cannot know the extent of the literary wealth which it possesses. In all the great Libraries of Deposit, there should not only be a collection of all the Catalogues of Libraries existing in the country, but so far as possible, a collection of the Catalogues of all the Libraries in the world. A great Library should in fact contain within it a Library of Catalogues.

The report concludes with references to the internationael interchange of books between France and the United States, and "less extensively," between the United States and Britain; and to fiscal regulations "of various kinds" and in particular their effect on the importation of foreign books.

Acknowledgements to the foreign witnesses and to Edward Edwards follow and the report ends:

Your Committee feel convinced that the people of a country like our own—abounding in capital, in energy, and in an honest desire not only to initiate, but to imitate, whatsoever is good and useful—will not long linger behind the people of other countries in the acquisition of such valuable institutions as freely accessible Public Libraries. Our present inferior position is unworthy of the power, the liberality, and the literature of the country. Your Committee believe that, on such a subject as this, Inquiry alone will stimulate Improvement. . . . It will be a source of sincere satisfaction to Your Committee if the result of their labours shall be, still further to call out, to foster, and to encourage among their countrymen, that love for literature and reverence for knowledge, of which during the course of their inquiries, they have had the gratification to trace the spontaneous development.

The Bill that Ewart introduced in February 1850 had a stormy passage through the house—the second reading was carried by only seventeen votes, 118 votes to 101—but it nevertheless received the Royal Assent on 14 August 1850.[149]

It was a permissive Act and applied only to towns in England and Wales with a population of 10,000 or over, and then not until the ratepayers had signified their assent by a two-thirds majority at a public meeting called for the purpose, of which at least ten days' notice had been given. If this majority was not obtained, two years had to elapse before a similar poll could be held. If adoption was authorized, the town council might then provide buildings and furnishings, heat and light, and appoint a librarian. Money could be borrowed subject to Treasury consent. There was no provision to permit the purchase of books. Admission to libraries and museums under the Act was to be free, and the rate that could be levied was limited to $\frac{1}{2}$d in the £.

Three years later a Bill to extend the Act to Ireland and Scotland was introduced to the Commons on 21 June 1853. Throughout its passage it provoked no debate in either House. The Bill received the Royal Assent on 20 August 1853.[150]

[149] House of Commons, *Parliamentary debates* (*Hansard*), (1850) vol. cviii-cxiii.
[150] ibid. (1853) vol. cxxviii-cxxix.

CHAPTER 2

THE FIRST RATE-SUPPORTED LIBRARIES

THE PUBLIC LIBRARIES ACT, 1850, was extended "to the Municipal Boroughs in Ireland and the Royal and Parliamentary Burghs in Scotland" by an Act of 1853 (16 & 17 Vict. c. 101) which became law on 20th August. Airdrie Town Council was the first to avail itself of the new powers. On 6 October in that same year the council considered the Act and "instructed the Provost to give the necessary statutory notice (at least ten days) required by said Act."[1] At a public meeting of electors on 1 November the Act was adopted by 211 votes to 20, and three days later the Town Council appointed a committee "to form rules and regulations for carrying out the provisions of the Acts." In July of the following year the first rate was levied and two months later the library of the Mechanics' Institute was purchased for £40. There follows a gap of almost eighteen months, until January 1856 when the Directors of the Mechanics' Institute requested the Town Council that the Library be opened to the public as soon as possible. In November of that year the council resolved "to open Public Library and allow parties inclined to read in Town Hall, till a more convenient place can be provided," and in due course the first rate-supported library in Scotland was opened.

There was an interval of thirteen years before another Scottish town took action to establish a rate-supported library. In the meantime the original Act of 1853 had been superseded, in so far as it concerned Scotland, by the Public Libraries (Scotland) Act, 1854, which allowed a maximum rate of 1d in the £ and permitted the erection, furnishing and maintenance of suitable buildings on land the town council might purchase or feu, the purchase of books, maps and specimens of art and science, and the appointment of salaried staff. Admission to all libraries and museums established under the Act was to be free.

An Act of 1866, applicable to England and Wales as well as to Scotland, provided for the adoption of the Acts whatever the population of the parish or burgh, and reduced the majority

[1] Airdrie Town Council Minutes; Airdrie Public Library, *A century of reading: 1853-1953* (1954).

required from the two-thirds of the earlier Acts to a simple majority.

Dundee was the second town in Scotland to adopt the Acts. Subscriptions had been collected for an Albert Memorial, following the death of the Prince Consort, and it was decided to establish the Albert Institute of Literature, Science and Art. The Acts were adopted unanimously in 1866, the rate was first collected in 1867-8, and the libraries and reading-room were opened in 1869 with a stock of 17,051 books in the lending department and 3671 in the reference department.[2] The library board acquired all the books and exhibits of the Watt Institution Library and Museum.[3] The great western hall, designed as a reference library was opened in 1874, in the same year as the museum and art gallery. The Albert Memorial fund went towards providing the building, but an outstanding debt of £10,000 incurred in building the art gallery and museum was paid off in 1887 by a Jubilee gift from Mr J. M. Keiller.

In Paisley the Acts were adopted by a considerable majority. The library owes its origin to the initiative of the Paisley Philosophical Society, founded in 1808.[4] One of this Society's aims was the collection of books and objects of antiquarian and scientific interest. Soon after the middle of the century its collections had so increased that the Society had to face the problem of a permanent abode. It was suggested that a fund of £3000 should be raised, when Mr (later Sir) Peter Coats offered a site and building at his own expense, if the Libraries Act was adopted by the burgh. At a public meeting in the Gaelic Church on 19 March 1867, the Act was adopted by a vote of 483 to 21. The rate was first levied in 1871 and on 11 April the same year a building was formally opened that included a large museum, library, reading-room and lecture hall. The Paisley Library Society, founded in 1802, transferred its library to the new buildings, and the Philosophical Society handed over its various collections, including 5000 books. Eleven years later Sir Peter Coats added another museum, a picture-gallery and a reference library.

In 1867 the Public Libraries Act (Scotland) 1867 was passed to amend and consolidate the Libraries Acts relating to Scotland. It was to remain the principal Act for twenty years. It continued

[2] Dundee Public Library, *Annual Report* 1898, which contains a review of thirty years' work.

[3] House of Commons, Parliamentary Return, Libraries (168) 11 April 1870.

[4] Paisley, The Free Public Library and Museum of Paisley: Paisley Public Library, *First Annual Report* (1907).

the existing provisions for adopting the Acts, conferred the power to borrow for capital expenditure and repay the loan by instalments, and left the rate limit untouched at 1d. It enacted that the general management of the library should be entrusted to a committee of not more than twenty, drawn equally from the town council and the ratepayers.

The Public Libraries Act (Scotland, 1867) Amendment Act of 1871 added certain powers —to make by-laws, and to recover by a small debt action, if necessary, penalties laid down therein, to lend books not only to ratepayers and residents but to the inmates of certain kinds of institution, and to print and issue catalogues. The power to borrow was now limited to a capital sum not exceeding twenty years' purchase of a farthing rate.

Before a further Scottish adoption of the Public Library Acts can be recorded the first of the rejections must be reported. In Edinburgh, on 19 November 1867, at a meeting in the Free Church Assembly Hall, with the Lord Justice General Inglis in the chair, Lord Neaves moved, and the meeting adopted, this resolution:

> That this meeting heartily approve of the Free Library Amendment Act, 1867, and desire that the same may be adopted by the citizens of Edinburgh as a means of promoting the enlightenment, recreation and general benefit of the community.[5]

It was resolved further to request the Lord Provost to call the necessary meeting of citizens at which it might be decided whether the Act should be adopted or not.

Shortly afterwards a meeting of those who opposed the movement was convened and a committee was appointed that set about obtaining signatures to a declaration opposing the establishment of a rate-supported library. This committee also issued a statement pointing out that free libraries were unnecessary in Edinburgh as there were already over fifty institutions where books could be obtained at nominal rates. Petitions were also presented to the Town Council from various bodies of workmen, asking the council to refrain from imposing any additional assessment for the purpose of a free library.

The Lord Provost's Committee, asked to report on the matter, expressed the opinion "that in the circumstances no necessity existed for such a proposal," and their decision was accepted by the council. Nevertheless, the promoters presented the usual

---

[5] T. Mason, *The free libraries of Scotland* (1880), p. 16.

request for a public meeting which was duly held in the Music Hall on 18 May 1868. The meeting was very noisy, refusing to hear the speakers on either side. On a show of hands the amendment, that the Act be not adopted, was carried by an overwhelming majority—1025 to 68.[6]

There is no doubt there was no lack of libraries or books in Edinburgh. When the university librarian, as chairman, welcomed delegates to the third annual meeting of the Library Association, held at Edinburgh in October 1880, he listed the libraries that would be thrown open for their inspection, and mentioned others "worthy of attention," libraries that in the aggregate represented "a total of upwards of 75,000 volumes available to the literary public of Edinburgh." Yet at the same conference it was pointed out that for the most part these libraries either were "of a professional character, where the books are mostly of a technical nature" or charged subscriptions that "put them practically beyond the reach of working men," and that "much yet remains to be done before it [Edinburgh] has secured for its poorer citizens the same facilities for intellectual advancement which other large towns (where the Libraries Acts are in operation) have provided for their humblest dwellers."[7]

Undoubtedly there was a widespread dislike of the additional rate, and there was the opposition of the proprietors of circulating libraries who feared that their businesses would suffer. Even in Paisley, where, as we have seen, the Acts were adopted with comparatively little opposition, this point of view found expression.

Local taxes were already burdensome and oppressive . . . Any respectable man could have books free from the libraries of our churches, and, for a very small sum, from our circulating libraries . . . Our local taxes already amounted to 5s 4d on a £5 rental . . . The good from the proposed library would be of a trifling character and confined to a few who could easily supply their wants otherwise.[8]

In Aberdeen also the move to adopt the Acts met strong opposition, although even in 1854 the Town Council had discussed repeatedly the advisability of a public library for the city.[9] In July 1871 at a public meeting the proposal was unanimously

[6] Parliamentary Return, Libraries (168) 11 April 1870.
[7] Library Association, *Transactions* 1880 (1881), p. 19-20, 54.
[8] *Paisley Gazette*, 23 March 1867.
[9] Aberdeen Public Library, *On re-opening of the Lending Department on open access* (1925).

rejected. The next year the matter was considered again at a meeting in the Music Hall when upwards of 1500 persons were present.[10] In support of the motion that the Act be adopted it was mentioned that a suitable building had been offered rent free, that subscriptions to the amount of nearly £4000 were expected to be given, and that the library of the Mechanics' Institute would probably be handed over. The opposition argued that a rate-supported library was unnecessary as the Mechanics' Institute library was not supported to the extent it might be, which seemed to indicate there was no real desire for an extension of reading facilities. Fewer than half of those present voted: the motion was rejected by 488 votes to 134. The source of some of the opposition is perhaps recalled in a paper read to the Aberdeen Philosophical Society by John Duguid Milne eleven years later, in March 1883, when the supporters of the library movement were active again: *The success of Free Public Libraries in Industrial Towns and the Necessity for a Free Public Library in Aberdeen.*

> Booksellers who feared they [public libraries] would injure their trade find that they create a taste for reading and multiply their customers. Subscription libraries find that the Free Libraries, so far from injuring them, serve as pioneers for them.[11]

Glasgow also refused to adopt the Acts. As early as February 1863 Bailie Blackie, who later that year became Lord Provost, had pressed for an inquiry into the matter and a very able and elaborate report was submitted.[12] It reviewed library provision on the continent and in the United States, and then turned to Great Britain and Ireland, coming to the conclusion that "it cannot but appear, from the most cursory perusal of the foregoing statements, that Great Britain is far behind other nations in the possession of public libraries, open to all ranks of the people."

> Public libraries, commensurate with the wealth, and adequate to the requirements, of the nation . . . had no existence in this country till twelve years ago, when the first movement was made for establishing them in the large provincial towns, the chief seats of our teeming population and varied industries.

[10] T. Mason, *The free libraries of Scotland* (1880), p. 21.

[11] J. D. Milne, *The success of free public libraries* (1883), p. 9.

[12] Glasgow Town Council, *Report on free town libraries and museums* (1864).

The public libraries in Manchester and Liverpool were then described in some detail, and a note on museums was appended. Surprisingly, since Airdrie is no distance from Glasgow, the report stated: "The Act has not yet been adopted by any town in Scotland." The report concluded:

> Although it is essentially a question for the citizens, inasmuch as they must determine it by their individual votes, your committee feel justified in assuming that it is highly desirable that Glasgow should have a free public library, and also a museum.

When the report came before the Town Council on 18 February 1864 the Lord Provost spoke at length in its favour and formally moved its adoption. The council approved, but no further action followed.

Ten years later, in April 1874, Mr Stephen Mitchell died suddenly leaving a bequest of £67,000 to be put out to interest until it reached £70,000 and then to be used for the establishment of a public library for the city of Glasgow to be managed by a committee of the town council.[13] The Philosophical Society took an active interest in the matter and appointed a strong committee to push the question. As a result of its activities the question of a public library again arose. A public meeting took place in the City Hall on 17 April 1876, where the adoption of the Act was proposed with the usual amendment, the direct negative. A show of hands was taken, but the numbers were apparently equal and a poll was demanded, which showed a majority of 786 against the adoption of the Act (for the amendment, 1779; for the motion 993).[14]

The fourth Scottish town to adopt the Library Acts was Forfar.[15] At the statutory public meeting convened by the Provost on 14 March 1870 the voting was 507 to 150 in favour. The library was opened the following year with 2423 volumes and there was an issue of 12,860 volumes in the first year.

In 1872 the Acts were adopted both in Galashiels and in Thurso. In Galashiels the idea of a public library for the town was first brought forward in November 1871 when it was suggested that the initial expense of the buildings might be met by opening a voluntary subscription list. £1000 was raised by the committee on a first canvass, in a very short time more than £2000 had been subscribed, and the Acts were adopted at a meet-

[13] T. Mason, *Public and private libraries of Glasgow* (1885), p. 101, 102.
[14] T. Mason, *The free libraries of Scotland* (1880), p. 26.
[15] Library Association, *Transactions* 1880 (1881), p. 52.

ing of ratepayers in February 1872. In 1874 the library was opened to the public temporarily in May, when the lower part of the unfinished building was opened as a reading-room, and formally in October, when the building was completed, by G. O. Trevelyan, M.P. for the Border burghs. The initial stock was 2104 volumes.[16]

In Thurso a proposal to adopt the Acts had been rejected in 1870, but the library, when it was opened in February 1875, was an immediate success. Indeed five years later it was claimed:

In regard to both the quantity and quality of the reading this little place in the far north exceeds all the Scotch and most of the English Free Libraries, the issues last year being at the rate of nearly two volumes to each inhabitant. . . . Altogether, the citizens of this far northern town seem to make an intelligent use of their institution.[17]

And in 1890 Greenwood could write:

The Thurso Library, after a considerable number of years' work, seems as fresh and vigorous as ever. . . . To outsiders it is a continual marvel how a Public Library in any form or with any success can be carried on with an income of £40; but seeing that the Thurso one manages to exist with all the freshness of its early years on this slender income, the wonder is increased.[18]

The library began with about 800 volumes, but the stock was increased within a few months to over the thousand by a donation from the Thurso Young Men's Mutual Improvement Society. At that time the penny rate yielded only £38 a year. To supplement this income an Industrial and Fine Art Exhibition was organized in 1876. The exhibition was opened by the Prince of Wales and yielded a surplus of £100.

Another Scottish town rejected the Acts in 1873. At Arbroath there had been for a considerable time letters in the local newspapers complaining of the lack of a good public library. There was, of course, the Mechanics' Institute library, founded in 1832, containing about 3000 volumes, and the Arbroath Subscription Library, which dated from 1797. But, it was pointed out, many of the books in the former, "though valuable, were scarcely of a

[16] ibid. p. 52, 159.
[17] T. Mason, *The free libraries of Scotland* (1880), p. 18; Library Association, *Transactions* 1880 (1881), p. 53.
[18] Thomas Greenwood, *Public libraries* (1890), p. 246-7.

kind suitable to the popular taste," while the latter was "practically closed against the bulk of the community—the annual subscription being half-a-guinea." Several attempts to popularize this library by reducing the subscription were unsuccessful, and it was decided to call a public meeting to consider the adoption of the Acts. At this meeting, on 25 March 1873, "the promoters were ignominiously defeated." Subsequently, however, in January 1875 the Arbroath Subscription Library, "augmented to the extent of several thousand volumes of the freshest and most varied literature," was opened to the general public "at the extremely modest annual charge of half-a-crown."[19]

In 1878, then, twenty-five years after the first Public Library Act had been extended to Scotland, the position was that there were six rate-supported libraries—in Airdrie, Dundee, Paisley, Forfar, Galashiels and Thurso. Two towns, Inverness and Hawick, had adopted the Acts (in 1877 and 1878 respectively), but the Hawick Library did not open until March 1879 and it was June 1883 before the library in Inverness was opened. On the other hand four towns—Edinburgh, Aberdeen, Glasgow and Arbroath had emphatically rejected the Acts.

*　　*　　*

The next adoption of the Public Libraries Acts in Scotland is of particular importance. Andrew Carnegie promised to his native town, Dunfermline, the gift of £8000 for a public library on condition that the Public Libraries Acts were adopted; the Acts were adopted in Dunfermline on 11 February 1880 and the Carnegie Library was opened in August three years later.[20] This was the first of many grants that Andrew Carnegie was to give—in Great Britain more than half of the towns with rate-supported libraries have been assisted by his generosity, in Scotland fifty out of the seventy-seven.[21] As we shall see later, these benefactions continued after his death through the interest and encouragement of the Trusts he founded, in particular the Carnegie United Kingdom Trust.

[19] J. M. McBain, *History of the Arbroath Public Library* (1894); T. Mason, *The free libraries of Scotland* (1880), p. 22-3.
[20] Dunfermline Public Libraries, *Report for the Jubilee Year of the first Carnegie Library* (1934); B. J. Hendrick, *The life of Andrew Carnegie* (1932), vol. 1, p. 236.
[21] A. L. Hetherington, "The late Dr Andrew Carnegie," *Library Association Record,* vol. 21 (1919), p. 284.

As we have mentioned, the Library Association of the United Kingdom held its third annual meeting in Edinburgh in October 1880, and a month later is was noted that a fresh impetus had been given to the public library movement in the city.[22] The Trades Council secured the signatures of a thousand working-men ratepayers to a petition requesting the Lord Provost and Magistrates to test the question by a plebiscite and early in the next year a public meeting endorsed the request.

This alternative method of ascertaining the opinion of the ratepayers was permitted under the Public Libraries Amendment Act of 1877, which had been framed and introduced by Mr George Anderson, a Glasgow M.P., following the rejection of the Acts at Glasgow in 1876.[23] The Act applied to the United Kingdom as a whole, and in addition to the simple vote "Yes" or "No," gave ratepayers an opportunity of demanding a lower library rate than the maximum penny. In Edinburgh the opponents of the movement were well organized. A committee sat daily and canvassed the city vigorously. Files of sandwich-men marched through the leading streets, bearing huge bills:

RATEPAYERS :

Resist this Free Library dodge,

And Save Yourselves from the Burden of £6000

of Additional Taxation.

Return your cards marked "NO."

Be sure and sign your Names.

The university, however, supported the idea of a public library:

Its Chancellor (Lord President Inglis), its Lord Rector (the Earl of Rosebery), and its Principal (Sir Alexander Grant, Bart.), were all in favour of the Free Library movement. So also were the Librarians of the great Libraries of Edinburgh, viz., Mr Clark of the Advocates' Library, and Mr Law, of the Signet Library. Evidently the great Libraries of Edinburgh felt no jealousy of the proposed Free Library. If any such jealousy was shown it was by the owners of small Circulating libraries throughout the city, and by libraries formed for workmen, but which, being far inferior to such as the Library

[22] Library Association, *Monthly Notes* (1880), p. 87.
[23] Public Libraries Amendment Act 1877, sect. 1; Minto, *History* (1932), p. 107.

61

Acts afford, had failed to enlist the support of the working classes.[24]

Of 41,853 cards distributed only 23,327 were returned. Of these 15,708 were against adopting the Acts, and only 7619 for their adoption.

Following this defeat the implementation of a scheme for establishing "district subscription libraries" was begun with the opening early in 1882 of the Morningside Athenaeum in the old United Presbyterian Church there: a similar library was proposed for Stockbridge.[25]

Further rejections followed in Ayr (1882), Cambuslang (1883) and Elgin (1884).[26] At the "exceedingly stormy" meeting in Ayr the adoption of the Acts was moved by Rev. Mr McCrie and seconded by a carpet manufacturer supported by another clergyman. The opposition was moved by a clerk and seconded by a grocer, and supported by a bookseller. Those who spoke in favour of the Act were received with "strong expressions of disapprobation." On a show of hands the amendment was carried by an overwhelming majority, "about three-fourths of the entire audience supporting it."[27]

In 1884 and 1885 the question was again under discussion in Glasgow.[28] An influential committee published "statements, tracts and leaflets" explaining the objects and operation of the Acts, and organized meetings addressed by leading citizens. After an enthusiastic public meeting a requisition was presented to the Lord Provost for a plebiscite under the Act of 1877. The promoters were confident of success, there had been little sign of opposition, but when the votes were counted the rejection was carried by 29,946 to 22,755.

The committee thereupon reconstituted itself as the Glasgow Public Libraries Association "to secure the adoption by the city of Glasgow of the Public Libraries Acts, and, if necessary or expedient for this end, to originate or support any amendment of these Acts which may render them more equitable in their operation."[29] Three years later, however, in another plebiscite the majority against adoption was even greater, when there were 22,987 noes and only 13,550 ayes.

[24] Library Association, *Monthly Notes* (1881), p. 38-41.
[25] ibid. (1882), p. 36.
[26] ibid. (1883), p. 163; J. J. Ogle, *The free library* (1897), p. 54.
[27] Library Association, *Monthly Notes* (1882), p. 15.
[28] Greenwood, *Public libraries* (1890), p. 250-2.
[29] Minto, *History* (1932), p. 109-10.

In no town or city in the entire United Kingdom and Ireland has the organization been stronger and more comprehensive, and the fight better marshalled than in Glasgow, and yet in no place has the result been more crushing and disheartening. . . . The figures appeared to make it clear that the movement is making the reverse of headway.[30]

In the meantime the movement had won a success in Aberdeen. In their report for 1881-2 and in a special memorandum issued with it, the directors of the Mechanics' Institution proposed to offer their "property and funds applicable for library purposes to be made over to the Town Council, contingently on the adoption of the Free Library and Museum Acts."[31] The books in the library, the shelving and fittings, and the proportion of the Institution's general estate "to be dealt with as held for library purposes" were valued at almost £4000. In March 1883 John Duguid Milne had read to the Philosophical Society the paper from which we have already quoted.[32] Therein he emphasized "that as a whole, the great manufacturing and industrial towns of England have eagerly adopted the Free Library Acts, and that the Free Library has already become a national institution for all, and especially for the working classes." He pointed to Aberdeen as "one of the great towns that have stood by their Mechanics' Institutions," but argued that the time had come when a Free Library was a necessity for the town and reminded the inhabitants of the offer the directors of the Institution had made.

That same year an anonymous pamphlet was published, *The Free Public Library Question discussed—with Special Reference to Aberdeen,* in which the author "Sigma," actually James Sinclair, the librarian of the Mechanics' Institution, pointed out how far this country lagged behind the United States and the Empire:

Sydney has a large Free Public Library. . . . The finest building in Melbourne is the Free Public Library. . . . In Toronto the resolution to establish a Free Public Library was carried on the first of January of the present year [1883] by the large majority of 2500. There are also Free Libraries in Cape Town, Graham's Town, Petermaritzburg, Hobart Town (Tasmania), and in New Zealand.[33]

[30] Greenwood, *Public libraries* (1890), p. 249-50.
[31] Library Association, *Monthly Notes* (1883), p. 14, 16.
[32] Milne, *The success of free public libraries* (1883).
[33] [James Sinclair], *The free public library question discussed* (1883), p. 4.

Following this the Provost convened and presided at a meeting on 25 March 1884, when the adoption of the Acts was decided by 891 votes to 264.[34]

The Aberdeen Public Library Committee held its first meeting within a month's time, and at once began negotiations with the directors of the Mechanics' Institute. As a result it was agreed that the Institute building with its library and furnishings, should be transferred to the town. A reading room was opened in August and on 12 March 1886 the lending department was opened in the Institute Hall in Market Street. But a new building was required; after prolonged discussion a site was found; and a new public library, towards the cost of which Mr and Mrs Andrew Carnegie had each contributed £1000, was opened in July 1892.[35]

In Edinburgh a third attempt to secure the adoption of the Acts was successful. In 1886 Carnegie offered a gift of £25,000, subsequently increased to £50,000, to build the library, if the Acts were adopted.[36]

The Scotsman was strong in its support of the movement.[37] Later Greenwood was to say:

> Never since the Ewart Act of 1850 was passed has there been in any paper articles so pungent and so ably written, urging upon the citizens the advisability of adopting the Acts as were printed in this well-known Scotch paper.[38]

At a public meeting in October only twenty of the 2500 estimated to have been present voted against adoption of the Acts, and most of them "quickly resumed their seats in some confusion, caused by the outburst of laughter with which they were greeted." Carnegie laid the foundation stone of the library in July 1887 and the building was opened by Lord Rosebery in 1890. Edinburgh, he remarked, without a free library of this kind was like men starving in the midst of a granary.

*   *   *

[34] G. M. Fraser, *Aberdeen Mechanics' Institute* (1912), p. 62.

[35] Aberdeen Public Library, *On re-opening of the Lending Department on open access* (1925).

[36] Greenwood, *Free public libraries* (1887), p. 89.

[37] In April 1955, when the Public Libraries (Scotland) Bill was in jeopardy, Dr Savage recalled how "in the early days of public libraries, *The Scotsman* was the greatest advocate the service had in the United Kingdom." (Letter in *The Scotsman*, 28 April 1955.)

[38] Greenwood, *Free public libraries* (1887), p. 90.

At this time Scottish library legislation was embodied in four separate Acts—the Public Libraries Act (Scotland) 1867, the Public Libraries Act (Scotland, 1867) Amendment Act 1871, and the Public Libraries Amendment Act 1877, which have been mentioned in their chronological order in this chapter, and a further amending Act, the Public Libraries Act 1884, which enlarged on the question of buildings for public libraries, public museums, schools for science and schools for art, and attempted to clarify certain "doubts that have arisen." These were the Acts operative at the time of their second rejection in Glasgow in the plebiscite of 1885.

One of the purposes of the Glasgow Public Libraries Association that was formed thereafter was, as we have seen, "to originate or support any amendment of these Acts," and the Association's honorary secretary, Richard Brown, was asked to draft a consolidating measure. The Bill was ready in 1886, and was introduced to Parliament in January 1887. It was immediately withdrawn, but was re-introduced by A. Cameron Corbett and R. B. Cunninghame Graham. It passed through Parliament without discussion and became law on 16 September.[39] The Public Libraries Consolidation (Scotland) Act, 1887 (50 & 51 Vict. c. 42) remains the principal Act for Scotland. As a consolidating measure it contained little new matter, although for the first time library committees were given specific powers to provide "suitable rooms" in which books, periodicals and newspapers might be read.

Seven years later another bill drafted by Richard Brown was introduced to amend this Act, and made its passage through Parliament without opposition.[40] It allowed the town council in a burgh to adopt the Acts by resolution at a special meeting of which one month's notice had to be given to each member of the council: if such a resolution were passed, it had to be promulgated in the local newspapers and had to come into force on an appointed day not less than one month later.

In 1899 the principal Act was further amended to restore the provision originally contained in the Act of 1866, but not continued in the consolidating Act of 1867, to permit any two or more neighbouring burghs or parishes to combine in implementing

[39] Minto, *History* (1932), p. 110. The withdrawn bill is not printed in the sessional volumes of Parliamentary Papers: there it appears as a title-page only, as the Free Libraries Acts Consolidation Bill (1887 (115) vol. II, p. 339).
[40] The Public Libraries (Scotland) Act, 1894 (57 and 58 Vict. c. 20).

the Libraries Acts, the expenses to be shared by agreement.[41] In only a few cases was this Act ever taken advantage of, but it was on this power of neighbouring parishes to combine for the purposes of providing a joint library service that the Carnegie United Kingdom Trust was prepared to rely in transferring their pioneer rural library schemes to the local authorities, when, however, the Education (Scotland) Act of 1918 introduced a much simpler expedient.

*   *   *

It is not proposed to continue a detailed account of adoptions of the Acts year by year—chronological lists are to be found in Tables 1a and 1b—but a few of the later adoptions call for particular comment.

"The year 1887," Ogle reminds us, was "the jubilee year of our beloved Queen's happy and glorious reign."[42] The year before, the first edition of Thomas Greenwood's *Free public libraries: their organization, uses and management* had been published. Ogle continues:

His enthusiastic advocacy of free libraries found a response in many hearts, and the erection or establishment of free libraries became for the first time a popular form of celebration of the Queen's jubilee. No year has witnessed so many adoptions of the Acts as the year 1887.

In Scotland, however, there were only two adoptions of the Acts in 1887, and that number had been equalled in the two adoptions of 1872.

The Victoria Public Library in Grangemouth had its origin as part of the town's jubilee commemorations. The library was opened temporarily in two rooms above the Town Hall on 11 July, and when Mr and Mrs Carnegie came to the town to launch a ship in September of that year they were asked to open formally the temporary premises. Just over a year later the foundation stone of the permanent building was laid, and the finished building, towards which Carnegie had given a grant of £900, was handed over to the Library Committee on 30 January 1889.

In December 1883 the parish of Tarves in Aberdeenshire had made history by adopting the Libraries Acts—the first adoption

[41] The Public Libraries (Scotland) Act, 1899 (62 and 63 Vict. c. 5).
[42] Ogle, *The free library* (1897), p. 56.

66

in a purely rural district.[43] The population of the parish in 1881 was 2558. A former subscription library founded in 1878 was taken over, and its librarian became parish librarian.[44]

Carnegie's offer of £10,000 for a library building in Ayr carried the adoption of the Acts in that town "by a majority of votes sufficient to constitute all but absolute unanimity."[45]

In the Jubilee year of 1887 Falkirk had failed to follow the example of Grangemouth. A proposal to adopt the Acts was rejected, even though a gift of £1000 was offered conditionally upon their adoption. The gift, however, was entrusted to the local Y.M.C.A. to be administered in line with the donor's intentions, and nine years later the Acts were at length adopted.[46]

It was in 1896 that Arbroath at last adopted the Acts. The evolution of the Arbroath Public Library from the subscription library founded in 1797 is worth recalling.[47] After the defeat of the proposal to adopt the Acts in 1873 the directors and share holders revived and slightly amended a scheme that had been put forward by one of their number, a Mr Alexander Gordon, a few years earlier. Briefly, the original proposal was that the directors should endeavour to raise a sufficient sum to pay the expenses of the management for two years and to purchase a selection of new books for the library; that the library should be thrown open free for two years, and that it should be open for an hour or more every evening; at the end of two years, if the number of readers should amount to 600, the books should be handed over to the community to form the nucleus of a Free Public Library, if the Acts should be adopted. As modified, free membership was abandoned in favour of a nominal subscription, the number of years the scheme was to operate was increased to five, and the minimum number of readers was fixed at 400. A joint committee representing the subscribers and the community was appointed, over a thousand subscribers were enrolled, and the guarantee fund of £1000 was oversubscribed by £200.

But interest waned, the number of subscribers dropped steadily till it fell below 600, and when towards the end of the lustrum the proposal for the adoption of the Acts was again considered, it

[43] Greenwood, *Public libraries* (1890), p. 245-6.
[44] Greenwood's *Library Year Book* (1897), p. 199.
[45] Greenwood, *Public Libraries* (1891), p. 240.
[46] ibid. (1890), p. 249; *British Library Year Book 1900-01* (1900), p. 127.
[47] I am indebted to Mr Norman Crawford, burgh librarian of Arbroath, for the opportunity to examine the minute book of the Arbroath Subscription Library; see also McBain, *History of Arbroath Public Library* (1894).

was again defeated—by 1632 votes to 966. For another sixteen years the library struggled on. In 1881 the half-crown subscription was raised to 5s but with the increased rate the number of subscribers was so reduced that no greater income was realized and the subscription was reduced once more.

In 1896 it was rumoured that a local manufacturer had acquired the Old High School and intended to fit it out as a library and art gallery for the town, if the Acts were adopted. The Town Council rose to the bait, and the Acts were adopted. Carnegie provided a grant of £1000, and on 14 June 1898 the library was formally opened by Mr Alexander Gordon of Ashludie who had pressed so ardently for the adoption of the Acts almost thirty years before.

It was only in 1899, eleven years after the third rejection of the proposal to adopt the Libraries Acts, that Glasgow was empowered to levy a library rate. Even then the Libraries Acts were not adopted, but clause 29 (1) of the Glasgow Corporation (Tramways, Libraries &c.) Act 1899, which became law on 1 August that year, provided:

The Corporation may establish and maintain free public libraries;

and Clause 39 added:

The Corporation may assess and levy (equally on owners and occupiers) an annual assessment not exceeding one penny per £.

The Mitchell Library, managed by a committee of the Town Council, had been opened in November 1877 in temporary premises in Ingram Street, where it remained for more than thirteen years.[48] Francis Thornton Barrett, sub-librarian in the reference library in Birmingham, had been appointed librarian in the previous January, and under his care the library developed rapidly. By the time of the removal to more commodious premises in Miller Street in 1891 the initial stock of 14,432 volumes had increased to more than six times that number.

More than eleven years before Glasgow had the power to rate for libraries Barrett had outlined a scheme of district libraries for the city. Later proposals were published in a preface to the second edition of his *Concise Guide to The Mitchell Library* (1894):

[48] Mason, *Public and private libraries in Glasgow* (1885), p. 112.

I. A large central library, including

(a) The principal reference or consulting library, to be developed and made as complete as possible.

(b) Central news-room, with a large collection of newspapers and periodicals, representing all localities, trades, opinions, and interests, with a selection of American and Continental serials.

(c) Central lending library, with large collection of books for home reading.

(It does not necessarily follow that the several departments of the central library must be in the same building, but they should be conveniently placed within the central area of the city.)

II. A series of branch or district libraries, not less than six or seven in number, and so distributed throughout the several quarters of the city as to secure that every inhabitant will have one within a convenient distance of his dwelling. Each of the branch libraries would have the same features, in a smaller scale, as the central library, namely, a collection of reference books for consultation at the library only, a lending or circulating department, from which books would be drawn for home reading; and a newsroom, with a selection of the papers of the day and of the week, and a number of magazines and other periodicals.

Subject to the necessary rules and regulations, all the inhabitants of the city would be entitled to the enjoyment of all the privileges furnished by such a series of public libraries without any payment beyond the rate of one penny in the pound of rental (one shilling a ycar on a £12 house), which is the largest sum leviable under the Act.

In order to extend the value of the libraries to the utmost, borrowers would have the liberty to draw books from any or from all of the lending departments. By means of a daily express service books could be brought from branches for the use of readers in other districts, thus placing the resources of all the libraries at the disposal of borrowers, in whatever part of the city resident.

In 1899, when it was at last possible to implement proposals of this kind, the city librarian was instructed to prepare a report which was submitted to the Libraries Committee in February and received the approval of the Corporation in May 1900. Under the scheme each district of the city was to be provided with either a branch library or a reading-room. The eight branch libraries were each to include a home-reading department, a small collection of reference books, and a general reading-room. The five reading-rooms in outlying districts would contain newspapers and magazines and a small collection of books for reading on the premises, but no lending departments. Possible sites for the branches were indicated, and it was estimated that when the scheme was complete about 90 per cent. of the population would be within three-quarters of a mile of one of the eight branches or of The Mitchell Library.

With the offer of £100,000 for branch libraries from Andrew Carnegie in 1901, this scheme was amended and expanded. Libraries were to be placed in localities which under the former scheme were provided with reading-rooms only. It was suggested that the district libraries should be of three grades, estimated to cost £8500, £7000 and £5000 respectively and that there should be four first-grade libraries, six second-grade and three third-grade.

The first district libraries, Kingston and Anderston, were opened in 1904. Three others were opened in 1905, five more in 1906, and two in 1907. At this stage Carnegie's gift of £100,000 was exhausted, but he generously gave a further £15,000 to continue the work.[49]

* * *

The fact that it was now possible for a burgh to establish a rate-supported library service did not, of course, mean an immediate end to the establishment of mechanics' institutes or endowed public libraries.

There were, we have seen, 55 mechanics' institutes, most of them with libraries, in Scotland in 1850.[50] By 1884, according to Godard, there were 160.[51] Many of these institutes were destined to form the nucleus of a public library. We have seen how this happened in Aberdeen in 1884; in the burgh of Blairgowrie and Rattray it took place as recently as 1937, when the Mechanics' Institute, which incorporated a Working Men's Library first founded in 1853, was taken over "as a going concern" by the

[49] Glasgow Corporation, *Public libraries 1874-1954* (1955), p. 27-30.
[50] J. W. Hudson, *Adult education* (1851), p. vi.
[51] J. G. Godard, *Life of George Birkbeck* (1884), p. 226.

Town Council (on their adoption of the Public Libraries Acts) with the collaboration of the County Education Authority. In 1954-5 the Blairgowrie and Rattray Public Library was the busiest branch of the Perth and Kinross County Library[52]

Greenwood in his advocacy of public libraries was quick to see the connexion. He pointed out that rate-supported public libraries were not antagonistic to mechanics' institutes and work-men's clubs:

> But they certainly are endeavouring to do on a larger and more practical scale the work which those institutions originally set themselves out to accomplish. . . .

> The one vital difference between mechanics' institutes, work-ing-men's clubs and rate-supported Public Libraries is that the management of the two former has no representative character attaching to it, whereas in the other case the continuity is assured by the corporate nature of the institution. A Public Library forms part of the corporate life of the town, and is administered by the elected representatives of the people, who have to give an account of their stewardship to those who elect them to the governing body in which they sit. This applies to the smallest parish which may adopt the Acts, up to the very largest city. . . .

> Mechanics' Institutes, being proprietary institutions, are not subject to this popular control and administration, and if the cause of failure to meet the educational and reading needs of the day is looked into, it will be found that the absence of this popular control largely accounts for it.[53]

These institutions, he argued, would form a good nucleus for a public library. In some places the committee of management had "well and wisely" offered to hand over their institution as a public library, if the town adopted the Acts.

> An excellent beginning has thus been made by a happy wedding of the old love with its creditable past and the new love with its enlarged prospects and solid chances of success. . . .

[52] Information supplied by the clerk to Blairgowrie Public Library Com-mittee; Perth and Kinross County Library, *Annual Report 1954-5* (1955), p. 3.

[53] Greenwood, *Public libraries* (1890), p. 473-4; *Free public libraries* (1887), p. 116.

71

In no better way can these buildings be preserved for the educational benefit of the public and also for rational amusement than by turning them into Public Libraries.[54]

Greenwood saw a similar future for the "very large number of institutions called 'Public Libraries' which are really subscription libraries."

> Many of these institutions and others scattered throughout Scotland would form an excellent nucleus for turning themselves into Public Libraries in the full sense of the term, and securing the adoption of the Acts. This is especially the case as regards the parochial libraries of which there are hundreds capable of being transformed into comparatively large and vigorous institutions, after the pattern of pioneer Tarves.[55]

Among private endowments a Free Public Library had been founded in Stirling in 1855 by a John Macfarlane whose name is still perpetuated in the Reference Library in Stirling Public Library.[56] In 1882 there were over 8500 volumes in the library, and the Trustees had also distributed, free of charge, "about 1000 volumes to twelve different villages and libraries around Stirling."[57]

A library in Corstorphine village was founded in 1856 by a Dr Fowler who presented 100 volumes. In twenty-five years the library had increased to 4000 volumes and had nearly 100 subscribers. The committee were always favourably disposed to admit free of charge readers who were unable to subscribe, but could only continue this free list to a very limited extent—unless they were supported by subscriptions from the public—"thus furnishing another proof of the necessity of a library being either supported from the rates or from public generosity, if poor people, who are unable to pay subscriptions, are to be benefited by it."[58]

The Chambers' Institution in Peebles was established in 1859 by the publisher, William Chambers, a native of the town, to continue the good work begun by the library he was associated with some ten years earlier. This earlier foundation is described in a statement from its secretary that Chambers sent to William Ewart while the Select Committee of 1849 was taking evidence:

[54] Greenwood, *Public libraries* (1890), p. 474.
[55] Greenwood, *Public Libraries* (1891), p. 268.
[56] Parliamentary Return, Libraries (168) 11 April 1870.
[57] Library Association, *Monthly Notes* (1882), p. 112.
[58] ibid. (1883), p. 62.

The library received a fair start, and the public interest in it is gradually increasing. The number of volumes has risen from 150 to 730; the number of readers is also progressively increasing. During the summer months the number of readers is smaller than during the winter, but at present there are 55 who have out books. The number of readers during winter will be at least 70.

It is impossible to estimate the benefit which will ultimately accrue to the population from the library.[59]

The Hon. William Ogilvy of Loyal, from the regard which he had "to the Town and Parish of Alyth and with a desire to increase the opportunities of reading and knowledge therein," by a deed of bequest dated 7 February 1870 bequeathed £500 sterling and the whole of his library

> including printed books of every description, and Illustrated Books or Folios, Maps, Atlases, and whole Books bound or unbound now belonging, or which shall belong to me at the time of my death, as the same may be in my Mansion House at Loyal or elsewhere, excepting only any devotional Books that may be in my seat in the Episcopal Church of Alyth,

to constitute a public library in the town of Alyth to be called The Loyal Alyth Public Library.[60] The library is now part of the Perth and Kinross County Library and its valuable books are highly treasured.

Baillie's Institution in Glasgow, a free reference library that still maintains its independent existence, was opened in September 1867, the bequest of George Baillie, a Glasgow lawyer.[61] In 1952 this library found a new home in Blythswood Square.[62]

In Kirkcaldy a public library was opened in 1899 under the will of Provost Michael Beveridge who had died in 1890. A "Branch Beveridge Library" had been opened in Pathhead three years earlier when there was as yet no main or central library. It

[59] Select Committee, Report (1849), p. 252.
[60] Deed of Bequest by Capt. the Hon. William Ogilvy of Loyal, dated 7th February 1870. Recorded in the Books of Council and Session 15th April 1871.
[61] Greenwood, *Public libraries* (1890), p. 445.
[62] Since 1966 Baillie's Library has been accommodated in premises provided by the University of Glasgow at 69 Oakfield Avenue, W.2. See the article by Hugh Mackay, the present librarian of Baillie's Library, *SLA News* 93 (1969), p. 376-9.

is interesting to note that the branch was maintained from the Beveridge Bequest and it was a clause in the Kirkcaldy Corporation and Tramways Act of 1899 that authorized the levy of a library rate of one penny in the £. Kirkcaldy did not adopt the Public Libraries Acts until 1925, and then only in respect of the Museum and Art Gallery. It was not until 1928 that the Acts were applied to the library.[63]

There is an attractive and widely-held belief that public libraries were established as a result of the public demand for them, but it has been shown on the contrary that the public library was largely the work of philanthropists and reformers who saw it as an ameliorating moral and educational force they were devotedly willing to further.

> There is very little evidence proving a popular demand for libraries before the enactment of legislation authorizing their establishment; and even after the passing of an Act by the British Parliament and a Bill by the General Court of Massachusetts, it was in both cases a group of scholarly and influential citizens who planned, established, and directed the first public library. The chief motivating forces appear to have been reformative, philanthropic, and educational, all three being strengthened by the liberal policy so characteristic of the late nineteenth century.[64]

To the efforts of those progressive and public-spirited citizens was added the "powerful stimulus of private munificence."

[63] P. K. Livingstone, *Kirkcaldy and its libraries* (1950).
[64] J. H. Wellard, *Book selection* (1937), p. 60.

74

CHAPTER 3

THE CARNEGIE LIBRARIES AND THE ACT OF 1920

THE NAME OF ANDREW CARNEGIE is inseparably connected with the development of public libraries. When he laid the foundation stone of the Edinburgh Public Library he said it was the fifth public library he had been permitted to found and he wished for himself no happier lot than that he might be allowed to add infinitely to the number. At his death 380 separate library buildings in the United Kingdom were associated with his name, and his influence continued long after his death through the Trusts he founded.[1]

The first Carnegie library was opened in Dunfermline in 1883, and his early benefactions included £50,000 to Edinburgh, £10,000 to Ayr, and smaller grants to Aberdeen, Grangemouth, Inverness, Kirkwall and Peterhead. In 1897 Carnegie appointed an executive officer for library gifts and "the 'business' was reorganized on new lines."

The earlier gifts belonged to what Carnegie sometimes called the "retail system"; now he projected his benefactions on the more congenial "wholesale" plan.[2]

The immediate effect of the Carnegie grants was a great increase in the number of places adopting the Acts. Even in 1894 Greenwood had observed this trend:

Poll a northern town on the Public Library question on the simple merits of the case, and it is not usually successful. But let some generous citizen present a library to the town, or offer to do so on condition that the Acts be adopted, and it is surprising how speedily and unanimously the movement becomes an accomplished fact. . . . The history of the Public Library movement in Scotland is a history of Mr Andrew Carnegie's generous gifts to these institutions.

[1] A. L. Hetherington, "The late Dr Andrew Carnegie," *Library Association Record,* vol. 21 (1919), p. 284.
[2] B. J. Hendrick, *The life of Andrew Carnegie* (1932), vol. 2, p. 205.

Through Carnegie's influence there were in Scotland seven more adoptions of the Acts in the decade 1899-1908 than there had been in the forty-five years from 1853 to 1898, and only six of the thirty-five libraries established between 1900 and 1909 did not receive grants from his ever-open purse. In addition to his grants for new libraries Carnegie helped several of the earlier foundations, including Airdrie, to develop and improve their services in various ways.

The policy followed in giving these grants was later summarized by Professor Adams in this way:

(1) All grants have been made in aid of local effort. With minor exceptions, these grants have been to a public library authority, the condition being laid down that this authority shall adopt the Library Acts and shall impose the 1d rate. In certain cases where boroughs had obtained special powers of rating, it has been a stipulation that a higher rate shall be imposed.

(2) Grants have been almost exclusively for library buildings, including, in many but not all cases, furnishing. It has been a practice to require that the local authority will provide a site free of cost. Plans of the building had to be submitted, with estimates of cost. It has not been the practice, where the actual building exceeded the estimates in the original grants, to provide supplementary grants.

(3) Grants have been definite in amount, and the liability or obligation of Mr Carnegie ceased with the individual grant. Except in two isolated instances, continuing obligations have not been incurred, nor have grants been made by way of endowment, for maintenance, librarianship, or the purchase of books.[3]

In Carnegie's own words:

No millionaire will go wrong in his search for one of the best forms for the use of his surplus who chooses to establish a free library in any community that is willing to maintain and develop it.[4]

There is no doubt that the Carnegie grants greatly advanced the library movement as a whole. When the Kenyon Committee were asked in 1924 to inquire into "the adequacy of the library

[3] W. G. S. Adams, *A report on library provision and policy* (1915), p. 11-12.
[4] A. Carnegie, *The gospel of wealth* (1901), p. 30-1.

provision already made under the Public Libraries Acts and the means of extending and completing such provision," they pointed out in their Report that but for Andrew Carnegie's efforts "there could at the present time be no possibility of completing library provision throughout England and Wales."

> The Carnegie benefactions . . . made possible at many centres a development which would not otherwise have come into existence.[5]

The chief criticism of the Carnegie grants is summed up by Professor Adams in the word "overbuilding."

In the American benefactions the general requirements had been "that the community provide a site and bind itself to an annual maintenance charge of 10 per cent of the cost of the building," but in this country with the library rate limited, as it was at the time, to 1d in the £, the annual incomes of many of the grant-aided libraries fell far below this ratio of 10 per cent, particularly in the smaller places. According to the Adams Report Carnegie grants were given to forty Scottish libraries where the rate-income did not exceed £750, and of these forty libraries only three had a rate-income of or exceeding 10 per cent of the grant received; of the thirty-one places with a yield of rate not exceeding £200 per annum, the rate-income exceeded 10 per cent in only one case; among the twenty-three places where the rate-income did not exceed £100 there was no instance in which the rate yielded as much as 10 per cent of the grant. In many cases the grants—and the buildings erected with them—were out of all proportion to the library's income. Libraries had been provided that involved an expenditure on upkeep that left "no sufficient means for the main purpose and object of the library."

A large part of the Adams Report is devoted to this problem. In the "Extracts from letters relating to Carnegie Library Benefactions" in Appendix III of the Report it is frequently mentioned.

> The grand building needs in the first place to be cleaned and kept in order, and for this a caretaker and cleaners have to be employed. Then there is the lighting and heating and other building charges. Then you have the actual staff—the librarian and his assistants. Only last of all, under these conditions of foundation, can you consider the books. . . .

> It is extremely desirable that buildings only of such a size and character should be erected as can be adequately maintained. The rate of a penny in the pound is said to be swallowed up

---

[5] Adams, *Report* (1915), p. 13.

in administrative charges, allowing little or nothing for the purchase of books, or for the payment of librarian's salary. Over-ornate buildings are being locally taxed to the full, leaving the book fund "wiped out," or sadly too small to be of any service in keeping the library in an efficient state. *The whole success of the library depends upon its book-purchasing capacity.* . . .

Appendix IV gives nine examples of "overbuilding." Three at least of the examples can be identified as Scottish libraries. One of these is Hawick:

EXAMPLE B.—In 1902 Mr Carnegie gave £10,000 for a library building—the penny in the pound produces £300. The gift was too great in proportion both to the size of the town (16,887 pop.) and to the yield of rate. Salary of librarian is £100; and in 1914, £11 17s 5d was spent on books. Local effort has started a book-club, which transfers the books, bought by subscription, to the public library after one year.

The former librarian writes, that previously the library had "accommodation in the Municipal Buildings, and out of a revenue of £300 spent £80 on books. Grant of £10,000 obtained, and the cost of maintenance swallowed up the whole income, and nothing was left for the purchase of books. In this case a Carnegie grant seriously crippled a prosperous library."

Another case given "sad prominence" is Dumfries:

EXAMPLE D.—In 1898 Mr Carnegie gave £10,000 for library building, finally erected and opened in 1904. Meantime no rate had been levied, so that on opening £1000 was borrowed for purchase of books. Added to the strain of repayment of loan, the yield of rate was taxed by the unsuitability of the site and of the planning of the building. The librarian gets £140 without a house. Only £1 spent on books last year; on building loans and rates, £67 17s.

The librarian writes: "Since 1908 I have devoted myself not to the library but to the finances. I have kept down every expenditure and ignored our requirements. Every member of the staff is underpaid."

The case of Dumfries was further discussed twenty years later when the Dumfriesshire librarian was president of the Scottish Library Association. During the years from 1904 to 1920 the expenditure on books and binding averaged £28 per annum.

During 1910-19 it was respectively £5, £4 13s, £1 15s, £5, £33 (this sudden rise was due to my enlistment without an allowance, my wife taking on my job at a reduced salary), £1 10s, 13s 9d, 14s 11d, 2s 11d.[6]

While it is obvious that in these cases of "overbuilding" there was an unfortunate disproportion between the size and maintenance costs of the building and the authority's income from the library rate, it might be argued that it was not so much that the buildings were larger than necessary but that the income was restricted by the rate limit. Certainly, in his presidential address already quoted, Mr Shirley emphasized the unfortunate effects of a restricted rate and a "mean and narrow" concept of what a public library should do.

On the other side Stanley Jast comments on the "fallacy [that bricks and mortar are the prime necessity of a library] which reached its culmination in the buildings which Mr Carnegie, infinitely well-meaning but infinitely ill-advised, showered on library authorities whose funds were exhausted in the effort to keep them up."[7]

It is perhaps worth pointing out that by 1955 no fewer than sixteen of the twenty-nine Scottish libraries established with Carnegie grants between 1900 and 1909 had been incorporated in joint schemes or had amalgamated with their respective county libraries, and a further four ought to have considered a move of the kind.[8]

Towards the end of 1913, when Carnegie was almost 78 years old, he founded the Carnegie United Kingdom Trust "to put into the hands of a permanent body the future oversight and extension of certain experiments to which he had already set his own hand and, notably among these, the provision of public libraries." The Trust Deed was signed in October and registered in December of the same year.[9] The first meeting of the Trustees was held later in that month and the first meeting of the executive committee in February of the following year.

It is interesting to note that just as Carnegie's first gift of a public library was to his native town of Dunfermline in 1883,

[6] Scottish Library Association, *Report, May-December* 1934 (1935), p. 25.
[7] L. S. Jast, *The library and the community* (1939), p. 43.
[8] The trend has continued. Now (1970) twenty are included in joint schemes of one kind or another, and probably no more than five justify their independence by present standards.
[9] The Trust Deed is reprinted in full in the Trust's *Annual report* for 1914 (1915), p. 20-3.

there is recorded in the first annual report (1914) of the Trust he created, the payment of £2000 of the promised grant of £5000 towards the building of Dunfermline Public Library's extension.

The executive committee of the new Trust, as a preliminary to its work for libraries, decided to inquire into the general results of the grants, and invited Professor W. G. S. Adams, Gladstone Professor of Political Theory and Institutions in the University of Oxford, to report on "the existing public library provision in the United Kingdom, with special reference to the extent to which Mr Carnegie's benefactions had been instrumental in furthering the library movement." Professor Adams was also asked to suggest "any further directions in which the library movement might wisely be assisted in future."

The Adams Report, *A Report on Library Provision and Policy,* was ready in October 1914 and was referred to in some detail in the first annual report which the executive committee submitted to the Trustees early in 1915. The Trustees decided to publish "those parts of the report which are not of a confidential character," and this was done the same year. The central recommendation of the Adams Report, that the Trustees should take the initiative in developing rural library services, is discussed in the next chapter.

The report, as we have seen, also drew the Trustees' attention to the "error of overbuilding" in connexion with burgh libraries. The executive committee in a summary of "collated statistics" based on the report drew attention to an allied problem—the effect on a library's budget of the presence, or absence, of loan charges.

The effect of the non-existence of loan charges is to increase the relative expenditure upon purely library items. This is shown in the following table: [10]

PERCENTAGE OF EXPENDITURE ON SALARIES, BOOKS AND PERIODICALS
(i.e. on purely library items)

	All libraries	Loan charge Libraries	Non-Loan charge Libraries
England	65.12%	63.76%	71.6%
Scotland	64.04%	62.53%	71.7%
Ireland	64.12%	60.5%	76.6%
Wales	63.37%	59.51%	78.37%
United Kingdom	64.9%	63.35%	72.17%

[10] CUKT, *Annual report* 1915 (1916), p. 38-9.

The Trustees found that most of the libraries in respect of which these charges occurred were established before the Carnegie grants were begun. The more progressive towns had acted first in the matter of adopting the Libraries Acts and had consequently erected their buildings by loan. If they had waited, they might have benefited from his generosity, and in these circumstances the Trust was prepared to make "capital grants for the partial extinction of the loan, so as to release additional income for the purchase of books." These grants were given on the condition that the library rate was not reduced, and that the increased income made available was used for purely library expenditure.

These loan charge grants, "which were really in the nature of retrospective building grants," continued to be a minor part of the Trust's library policy for several years. Scottish libraries which benefited included Bonnyrigg (£25), Ayr (£350) and Rutherglen (£120). In their report for 1921 the Trustees pointed out that the removal of rate limitation in England and Wales, and its increase to 3d in Scotland, had done away with the main reason which underlay their borough library policy, "that the raising of a loan for building purposes left too small a margin of the 1d rate for maintenance purposes."

At the end of 1925 two important lines of the Trust's library policy came to an end. No further applications were to be considered for grants for new buildings (these had been continued during the last ten years, but on a small scale only) and the offer of grants for the establishment of county libraries was withdrawn. The Trustees' new policy was to stimulate and strengthen the libraries that already existed:

It is unfortunately clear that many of the Carnegie Public Libraries are insufficiently supported by the rates. Purchase of books is in these cases manifestly inadequate; salaries are too low to attract competent librarians; circulation shows that from these two causes public interest is at a low ebb.

The Trustees' new book-purchase grants were given on a "definite undertaking on the Authority's part to bring the service up to a prescribed level of efficiency on accepted modern lines."[11] Later they were rigidly confined to libraries serving populations between 10,000 and 50,000. In difficult cases the Trustees first obtained a report from a leading librarian. In the case of "very small towns"

[11] CUKT, *Annual report* 1926 (1927), p. 16.

It is further made a condition that every effort will be made to effect . . . co-operation on the Middlesex-Hanwell basis with the County Library, either at once or as soon as the county service has developed sufficiently to make such co-operation feasible. In one instance, co-operation with a larger contiguous Town Library has been recommended.

The underlying idea of the policy was an attempt to ensure better use of existing buildings and to make the libraries more efficient at a minimum of extra cost. Its success led the Library Association to appoint a strong committee

to review the whole question of Small Libraries, with the object of preparing a practical Memorandum for the guidance of Local Authorities desirous of bringing their libraries into line with the best modern practice.

Small municipal libraries: a manual of modern method was published in 1931, with a second edition three years later.

An interim indication of the effect of the Trust's book-purchase grants is to be found in the figures given in the report for 1929:

	Pop.	First effective year of Grant	Stock prior to Grant	Stock at end of 1929	Issues for year prior to Grant	Issues for last year
Clydebank	50,000	1929	18,231	25,000	179,193	262,258
Kirkcaldy	42,000	1929	22,694	25,078	117,555	184,694
Hamilton	39,420	1929	16,358	12,292	124,477	130,795
Falkirk	38,000	1927	22,839	29,488	103,624	114,212
Dumfries	21,873	1928	15,466	19,384	75,509	97,948
Bo'ness	13,446	1928	7,544	9,488	28,695	42,410
Larbert	12,389	1928	4,100	5.900	25,419	43,210
Peterhead	13,000	1927	6,449	8,826	32,863	43,827
Fraserburgh	10,514	1929	5,434	7,283	33,106	31,148
Elgin	7,776	1928	8,753	10,000	23,511	32,580

It is clear that the grants, both directly and indirectly, have either initiated or assisted in a very striking forward movement in the libraries which have received them.

This policy continued until 1935 by which time £135,000 had been expended.

The Trust's policies of loan charge grants and book-purchase grants were both aimed at mitigating the crippling effects of rate-limitation, which persisted for a considerable time after the limitation was removed or increased. Libraries that had got into a bad condition were difficult to improve, and committees that had been forced to spend little often lacked the vision and the inspired (and inspiring) staff to spend more. Carnegie himself had been aware of the inhibiting effect of the rate limit, and in at least one instance, in offering a grant for branch libraries to the city of Dundee, he made it clear that the gift was conditional on the Authority's seeking and obtaining permission to levy a 2d rate.[12]

Nevertheless, sixty-five years after the raising of the library rate limit from ½d to 1d, by the Act of 1854, the rate limit of 1d in the £1 was still effective, although several towns had freed themselves from the limitation by means of local Acts, a step first taken, as early as 1865, by Oldham.[13] In Scotland in 1914 the penny rate no longer affected Dundee, Glasgow, Kilmarnock and Dunfermline, and Aberdeen Town Council resolved in December 1918 to apply for powers to increase the limit to 2d.

In 1905, indeed, the Convention of Royal Burghs had made representations to the Scottish Office urging the increase of the maximum rate to 2d in the £1, but it was the marked rise in prices during the years of World War I that brought matters to a head and made the abolition of the penny rate a matter of real necessity.[14] A special general conference of the Scottish Library Association was held in Glasgow on 27 March 1919 when the then city librarian, S. A. Pitt, read a paper on *The library rate in relation to the financial position of public libraries,* subsequently printed and circulated.

The speaker dealt exhaustively with the hampering effect of the statutory rate limit, and the subsequent discussion was wholly sympathetic. A resolution submitted by Mr Pitt on behalf of the council was unanimously adopted:

That in view of the extreme urgency of the present financial position of public libraries, and the necessity for remodelling and reorganizing this branch of the public service for the better education and information of the people, it is essential that the present limit of the penny library rate, which hampers the efforts and work of public libraries on every side—whether in the larger centres or in the smaller communities—be extended or abolished. This restriction, imposed as far back as 1854, on

[12] Information from the Dundee City Librarian; the power to levy a 2d rate was obtained by the Dundee Corporation Libraries Order of 1902.
[13] Minto, *History* (1932), p. 125.
[14] Convention of Royal Burghs, *Minutes* 1905-6 (1906), p. 20, 5 April 1905.

the provision of books for the people, is a fetter upon public authorities and their constituents. The abolition of this restriction would leave to each locality, power to decide for itself as to its library requirements in like manner as power is vested for other branches of public service.

This meeting, representative of library authorities and others interested in education throughout Scotland, hereby expresses the view that the removal of the limitation on the library rate is absolutely necessary if public libraries are to take their proper place in the movement for reconstruction.

In May a strong deputation was received by the Secretary for Scotland (the Rt. Hon. Robert Munro, P.C., K.C., M.P.). Some twenty library authorities were represented, and the Scottish Library Association sent its president, its vice-president, its honorary secretary, and three members of council. The Secretary for Scotland admitted "that the case for relief as it had been laid before him was very strong, and promised to give consideration, without undue delay—but after having assured himself that there is no real opposition to the demand—as to means by which the necessary extension of public library incomes may be brought about."[15]

The question before him, he said, was not a purely Scottish concern: it affected England and Wales also, and it was "unthinkable" that there should be different laws on this matter on the two sides of the Border.[16]

In May also the Carnegie United Kingdom Trust addressed a circular letter to all library authorities and Members of Parliament:

For more than sixty years Public Libraries have had to be conducted with the financial means derived from the produce of a 1d rate, except in towns where steps have been taken by private Act to exceed the statutory limitation.

Serious though the financial strain has been in the past, the position of Public Libraries today is precarious. Unless early and effective steps are taken to allow each town to decide for itself what annual sum is necessary to conduct efficiently one of its most popular institutions, it appears highly probable that many Public Libraries will have to close their doors or be administered unsatisfactorily.

[15] SLA, *Report* 1915-19 (1919), p. 6.
[16] *Library Association Record,* vol. 21 (1919), p. 244.

It is probable that these apprehensions are shared by your Council, for no doubt it has had cause from time to time to consider the difficulties under which its Library has been conducted. The Trustees venture to address you on the subject as they feel that, as an impartial body, they are in a position to express an opinion which might influence your Council to press the Government to give Local Authorities the right of self-determination in the matter.

In June the Third Interim Report of the Adult Education Committee of the Ministry of Reconstruction recommended the removal of the limit; in July, at the Scottish Library Association's eighth annual general meeting in Aberdeen, the city librarian, G. M. Fraser, raised the matter again; and the conference of the Library Association at Southport in September adopted a resolution on the subject.

As a result of these representations a Bill to amend the law of England and Wales in this respect was introduced on 28 November and the Public Libraries Act, 1919, received the royal assent on 23 December. The Act did not apply to Scotland, but on the same day the honorary secretary of the Scottish Library Association wrote to the Secretary for Scotland, urging a similar measure of freedom for Scottish libraries. At the same time a letter explaining the situation was sent to all Members of Parliament representing Scottish constituencies.

Early the next year questions were being asked in the House.[17] A further letter to the Secretary for Scotland was sent on 24 February and there were more questions in the House.

A special conference of public library authorities in Scotland met in Perth on 18 March under the chairmanship of Lord Provost Wotherspoon. Resolutions urging the removal of the rate limit were adopted and it was agreed "to request the Convention of Burghs to support by resolution the claim of Local Authorities in Scotland to permissive powers corresponding to those conceded to Local Authorities in England and Wales by the Public Libraries Act, 1919." Copies of the resolution were sent to the 203 town councils represented in the Convention.

The question was duly considered by the Convention on 6 April, when it was decided "by a large majority" that the Convention was of the opinion that the limit should be extended to 3d, after an amendment urging upon the Government the "absolute

[17] House of Commons, Parliamentary debates, vol. 130 (5 s.), 16 February 1920.

necessity for the removal of any limitation of the Library Rate" had been withdrawn.[18]

The long-awaited Bill was introduced on 22 June: it embodied the suggestion of the Convention. A Scottish Library Association deputation waited on the Secretary on 8 July to protest against the proposed restriction of the library rate to 3d in the £. The inequality between the library laws of England and the proposals for Scotland was brought to his notice and it was pointed out that in Ireland the Local Government Board had been given power to extend the rate to 6d in the case of county boroughs. The Secretary entrenched himself behind the April decision of the Convention and gave no hope of the removal or extension of the limit in the Bill.

Again the honorary secretary wrote to all Members of Parliament representing Scottish constituencies urging them to try to obtain for Scotland powers in this matter at least equal to those proposed for Ireland.

When the Bill was read for the second time the Lord Advocate maintained that the maximum now suggested was quite "suitable."[19] Mr Wm. Graham, M.P. for Central Edinburgh, protested against the limit: he had been advised by the Scottish Library Association that the case of Scotland "might be met by including in the Bill the second clause of the Irish Bill." Arguments were advanced both for and against the new limit. One M.P. who claimed to share Mr Graham's point of view said he had been reassured by the Lord Advocate's statement. Another stated that the Bill met "all the requirements of the case." Sir George Younger maintained it was "not at all a novel thing to have a maximum rate." Dr Murray on the other hand declared that "one of the most necessary elements in our social life in these times" was "an efficient library." The House, he asserted, was seeking to protect Scotsmen from levying a rate on themselves.

In the event Graham's amendment was incorporated in the form of a proviso to the clause increasing the limit to 3d:

Provided that the Secretary for Scotland, or, where the rating authority is a parish council, the Scottish Board of Health, may, as regards any burgh or parish, as the case may be, sanction a further increase in the amount of the library rate to an amount not exceeding threepence in the pound.[20]

---

[18] Convention of Royal Burghs *Minutes* 1920-1 (1921), p. 4, 6 April 1920.
[19] House of Commons, Parliamentary debates, vol. 132 (5 s.), 22 July 1920, col. 803.
[20] House of Lords, Parliamentary debates, vol. 41 (5 s.) 9 August 1920.

In the House of Lords, Lord Stanmore presented the Bill. The Duke of Buccleuch declared he was against the Bill on economy grounds. The Earl of Crawford, as one would expect from a bookman, stressed the Bill's urgency: it was possible that free libraries in Scotland would be forced to close.

At the committee stage the Duke of Buccleuch moved to omit the proviso: if economies had to be made, he said, it certainly would not be quite as convenient on cold days, for a certain number of young men would not get their betting news so early. Lord Stanmore explained the proviso, and gave an assurance that its authority would be sparingly used, but when a vote was taken the proviso was deleted by 28 votes to 19.

On the Bill's return to the Commons the Secretary of State pointed out that the amendment had not been in the original Bill: it had been accepted on two counts—that there was no restriction in the corresponding English measures and that the Irish Act permitted elasticity of this kind.

A great deal was said in another place about economy. No doubt that is a desirable thing, but whether it is desirable to economise in the matter of public libraries may be a matter for discussion and even dispute.

However, he was prepared to accept the Lords' judgement. Dr Murray said he was sorry the proviso had been altered.

With these brief comments the Bill was passed, and ten days later, on 20 August 1920, received the Royal Assent.[21] The threepenny rate was to be effective in Scotland for thirty-five years.

On commenting on this sad progression the annual report of the Scottish Library Association's council deplored the "particularly ill-informed criticism" that the Bill and its new clause received in the House of Lords.

There is a touch of irony in the fact that the Act of 1920 introduced between England and Scotland this invidious distinction in the matter of rating, when only fifteen months earlier the Secretary for Scotland had made it an excuse for postponing purely Scottish legislation on the question that it was unthinkable there should be different laws on the matter on the two sides of the Border. An explanation of the retention of a limit in Scotland when the limit was abolished in England and Wales will be found in chapter 9.

In this connexion it is perhaps worth pointing out that at least one prominent Scottish librarian is convinced that, provided the

[21] House of Commons, Parliamentary debates, vol. 133 (5 s.), col. 368, 678.

limit represents a reasonable level of expenditure to cover the needs of the service, it is no bad thing to have a rate limit: in his experience he has found that when there is a legal maximum, although the library committee certainly cannot exceed it, the finance committee of the town council rarely cut the library committee's estimates; the finance committee feel that library expenditure is safely limited. Without the degree of security—and immunity—that a legal maximum provided he fears that the detailed scrutiny of the finance committee may sometimes result in a reduction of the library estimates.

It is not easy to estimate the effect of the Act of 1920. In Dumfriesshire the county librarian was asked "to prove there was a demand which would justify an increased rate."

There was no direct evidence available. No one had written to the papers complaining, one-time readers had drifted away, the books available were dirty, obnoxious and out of date. By general consent the Library was regarded as a white elephant and myself as the occupant of a superfluous post. And on the lines the library was forced to run in these days these conclusions were just. I resorted in my difficulty to a graph showing the relationship of expenditure on books and issues and to my surprise there was demonstrated a much closer interaction than I had thought possible. I cannot bore you with details but it showed that starting in 1904 with a stock three-quarters fresh, an issue of 83,000 was secured to a population of 23,000, 3.6 per head of population; with two exceptions it fell steadily over a period of 16 years to 17,600, 0.76 per head. . . .

Most illuminative were the years immediately following 1922 when for the first time in our existence we began to spend money on books. The issues responded very closely with the amounts spent.

Putting it broadly, when once the stock was in good condition and the fact had reached the public every £100 spent brought 25,000 issues, over one per head of population. So in 1931-2 we touched 150,000 issues, 6.5 per head with an expenditure of £550. . . . That issue should have been achieved by 1910, in seven instead of thirty years.[22]

*   *   *

[22] G. W. Shirley, Presidential Address, SLA, *Report, May-December* 1934 (1935), p. 24-5.

Few burgh libraries have been established in Scotland in the last fifty years. The last of the large burghs to adopt the Acts was Clydebank (1911), and the largest of the small burghs, Buckhaven, adopted the Acts in 1919, and opened its library in 1925. The rapidly developing county library services, although they began as rural libraries, soon provided for the towns and small burghs that had not yet adopted the Acts. Where the Acts have been adopted in these last fifty years it has usually been to provide certain local facilities supplementary to the county library service —a reading room, for example—or to continue, or as in Helensburgh to accept and develop, an endowment.

The only new central burgh libraries to be built in Scotland between 1918 and 1955 are those of Airdrie (1925), with the help of the Carnegie Trust, Kirkcaldy (1928), the gift of Mr John Nairn of Forth Park, and Buckhaven (1935), although there have been conversions, adaptations and modernizations, notably and most recently at Airdrie again (in 1951 and 1953), at Stirling (in 1953) and in Glasgow, when the Royal Exchange Building, purchased in 1949 for £105,000, and extensively altered to accommodate Stirling's Library, the Commercial Library and the Library of Patents, was formally opened in 1954.[23]

> Glasgow Corporation Public Libraries Committee merits the warmest praise for the quite superb job it has done in converting the Royal Exchange Building into Stirling's Library, and the tearoom underneath the Exchange into the Commercial Library and Library of Patents.
>
> Members of the Chamber are urged to pause one day while passing Wellington's statue and to look into the main hall of what used to be the Royal Exchange. We have long envied Edinburgh some of its late Georgian and early Victorian libraries such as the Signet and the University Libraries, but Stirling's Library, as it has been repaired, painted and furnished, bears comparison with the best.
>
> Less spectacular but perhaps even more astonishing is the changing of the musty and most undistinguished old tearoom into a bright and most attractive commercial library.[24]

---

[23] There have been a number of developments since that date. For a survey of new premises for the period 1960-9 see Table in Appendix 5.
[24] Glasgow Chamber of Commerce, *Monthly Journal*, vol. 37 (1954), p. 163.

CHAPTER 4

COUNTY LIBRARIES

IN THE DEVELOPMENT of county library services the Carnegie Trustees are again the main driving force. The *Report on Library Provision and Policy* which Professor Adams submitted to the Trustees in 1914, on their invitation, drew attention to the fact that despite the remarkable advance of the public library movement—only 19 out of 222 towns with a population of 30,000 and over had not adopted the Acts—not more than 57 per cent of the population of the United Kingdom, and in Scotland only 50 per cent, resided within library areas. The smaller towns and country districts remained to a great extent unprovided for.

This problem of village and rural libraries had exercised the Select Committee of 1849. Edwards considered village libraries "highly desirable," and another witness agreed that "a library in a rural district containing standard works and books of a more expensive character . . . would be exceedingly useful." The Committee themselves could not doubt that the village library would "in the course of time, be an object of encouragement and support to our landed proprietors and clergy, and an object of natural interest and reasonable pride to our rural population."[1]

A Bill to extend "the free library system to counties" which had been introduced in the Commons in 1876 did not reach a second reading.[2]

Four years later, John Maclauchlan, the chief librarian and curator of the Dundee Library and Museum, read before the Library Association a paper entitled "How the Free Library System may be extended to Counties," in which he outlined a scheme that reads in part surprisingly like a blueprint for later practice—for each county there would be a chief librarian and a

---

[1] Select Committee Report (1849), 341, (Rev. F. R. Fremantle) 1434-5, p. xii.

[2] Library Association, *Transactions* 1880 (1881), p. 59. There is no record of this Bill in the appropriate sessional volume: it may have been the *Not printed* Bill presented by A. J. Mundella, Sir John Lubbock, and others on 9 February 1876 and withdrawn on 4 July (1876 (35) vol. II, p. 383).

staff, large or small, according to the size of the county; in the county town there would be a building, "better described as a central office or depot for books, than as a library," where all work connected with the selection, the cataloguing and so on would be done; there would be branch libraries in every parish, in the larger parishes more than one, and the school is suggested as a suitable centre; there would be little or no difficulty in getting some "intelligent workman" to undertake the duties of branch-assistant for £10 or £20 per annum. But the book-stock apparently was to be static and the libraries, apart from donations, identical: all books purchased were to be in duplicate, as many copies being bought as there were branches. Maclauchlan rounded off his paper by showing how the scheme could be applied to two Scottish counties: Perthshire, "one of the most unfavourable counties in Great Britain for the successful working of my scheme," and Stirlingshire. With the product of the 2d rate that he claimed to be "essential," he demonstrated that in Perthshire about £26 a year could be spent on the purchase of new books for each of eighty branches, and in Stirlingshire about £40 a year for each of twenty-five branches.[3]

In the successive editions of his manual, Thomas Greenwood had pressed "the case for Rural Public Libraries."[4] In the 1887 edition he quoted the draft of a Bill "for the institution of National School Libraries for Scotland," which proposed the establishment of parochial libraries in every School Board district, except in towns where the Public Libraries Acts were in operation, and it was clearly the intention of this Bill that these Parochial Libraries should be made available "not only to the children and young persons attending schools . . . but also to the adult population."[5]

The Library Association had considered the matter seriously. It had published in 1895 a pamphlet, *Books for Village Libraries,* which included "Notes upon the organisation and management of Village Libraries" by James Duff Brown, who had already contributed to *The Library* an article on "The Village Library Problem," taking Dumfriesshire as his example. There were three

[3] Library Association, *Transactions* 1880, p. 58-66.
[4] T. Greenwood, *Free public libraries* (1886), p. 260-76; (1887), p. 190-7; *Public libraries* (1890), p. 328-36; (1891), p. 438-47.
[5] Greenwood, *Free public libraries* (1887), p. 202-3. There is no trace that the draft Bill Greenwood quotes was ever introduced into Parliament: it is, indeed, amateurishly drafted, and even Greenwood doubted if it would pass "in this form."

articles on county libraries in the *Library Association Record* in 1906 and 1907.[6]

Nevertheless, when Professor Adams made his inquiry for the Carnegie Trust in 1914, there was still no legislation permitting the establishment of libraries for areas larger than the burgh or parish, apart from the power conveyed by the Public Libraries (Scotland) Act of 1899, whereby neighbouring burghs or parishes might combine. This power had been exercised in eight instances only, and in each case it was a burgh and its surrounding parish that had combined.[7] In 1913 it was estimated that while 79 per cent of the urban population of Great Britain had access to public library facilities, less than 25 per cent of the rural population had the same advantage.

In the rural districts of Scotland, however, there were a number of libraries—of a kind; others had been established and had died. Tarves in Aberdeenshire was acclaimed by Greenwood in 1890 as "the only rural parish [in Scotland] that has a library under the Acts," and at the best there were just over a dozen parishes that chose to adopt them.

The rural libraries that immediately preceded the rate-supported county libraries were almost invariably the gift of some benefactor. Greenwood praises the "little village library at Long-forgan, near Dundee . . . designed principally for the use of the older school children and of the younger adults."

> The schoolmaster of the village undertook the management of the library and the care of a microscope given for use both in the school and by any capable of using it. The cost of the books, bookcase, stamp, microscope, etc., was about £50. The issues for one year were 1012 volumes, exclusive of those issued for use during school hours. It is evident that this library has been a success. The success points to the moral that the wealthy in any district have assuredly an easy way of giving great pleasure and conferring a great boon, or that a small community itself might with moderate effort and little outlay open a lasting spring of joy and good.[8]

[6] H. Farr, "The libraries and the counties," *Library Association Record*, vol. 8 (1906), p. 169-77; H. W. Fovargue, "Suggested library legislation for counties," vol. 9 (1907), p. 15-18; J. Daykin, "Village libraries," p. 169-77.

[7] The eight instances can be identified in the list given as Table 1 (*a*).

[8] Greenwood, *Public libraries* (1890), p. 334-5.

There was also the library presented in 1885 to Iona by Thomas Cook, the tourist, that could still be seen in the school there seventy years later.

*   *   *

The name of James Coats of Ferguslie, Paisley, is as closely connected with the provision of libraries in rural Scotland as Andrew Carnegie's name is identified with the establishment of libraries in all parts of the world. In the early years of this century, Coats presented to towns and villages throughout the country, not only collections of books but the bookcases to hold them. To at least one place Mr Coats gave in addition "Bibles for the old . . . and a fountain pen for the librarian," while to the same place at the same time another Paisley philanthropist presented "sixty pairs of spectacles to those in need of such physical aid to reading."[9]

The origin of these benefactions is told in the *Rambling Recollections* of another member of the Coats family:

> I had several trips in the "Gleniffer" to the West Highlands. In July 1901, we started from Gourock, and Mr James told us he would order the Captain to go wherever we wished on condition that, before returning, we put into Stornoway. . . . Mr James had a suite of rooms for his own use, consisting of bedroom, bathroom and sitting-room. In the latter there was a bookcase, and the last time I had been on board it was fairly well filled. So, on leaving, I went down to get a book of some sort, but, to my surprise, found none but a Bible, and Hymn-book and the yacht register. I asked him what had become of the books, and he told me that, a few days before, he had landed at Ailsa Craig, and had sent them all ashore to the solitary lighthouse-keepers. This was the beginning of an extensive distribution. His fine sense of fairness led him to say to himself, "Why should I do this for the Ailsa men only?" and so he added to the work which he began that day by supplying a large number of books to every lighthouse on the Scottish coast, accompanied by two pounds of tobacco and two pipes, and this he continued to send every New Year's Day for ten years until he died. This was followed by his providing libraries with book-cases to about 4000 towns, villages and schools throughout Scotland.[10]

[9] *Library Association Record,* vol. 8 (1906), p. 328.
[10] G. S. Coats, *Rambling recollections* (1920), p. 182-3.

The figure quoted for the Coats benefactions (4000), although far in excess of Professor Adams's estimate, is probably no exaggeration. As far as Adams had been able to ascertain, there were 336 of these libraries, 150 in the islands and 186 on the mainland; but there were in Perthshire at least ten times the eight libraries Adams records, and in Fife where Adam reported only "scattered libraries," there appear to have been about forty.[11]

These libraries were usually housed in the school, and in the first instances were extremely popular: "a great want had been supplied." But the collections at their largest were still small—"most places received about 300 or 400 volumes, but in some areas altogether 600 or 700 volumes were given"—and no provision was made for the exchange or renewal of books or for the purchase of new books, although this was sometimes done by local effort.

In course of time the Coats libraries have become part of our present-day county library service: what remained of value among the books has been incorporated in the county stocks, and in many a rural centre the Coats book-cases are still used to house the village collections of county library books. In 1920 when the Perthshire Education Authority sought formal permission from the Executors of the late James Coats to incorporate the Coats libraries in Perthshire in the recently formed Rural Library, they were informed: "While they [the Executors] will not raise any objections to the course you indicate, they cannot accept any responsibility in the matter, and have no suggestions to offer."[12] This cautious reply the education authority construed as approval.

At the annual meeting of the Scottish Library Association at Montrose in 1914 the burgh librarian, Mr James Christison, referred to an attempt that had been made in Angus some years before to extend the burgh library services to the surrounding districts. He had found that this extension was widely desired by readers in the neighbourhood of Montrose, and he wrote to the other burgh library authorities in Angus—Arbroath, Brechin and Forfar—to suggest concerted action in this direction. The proposal had been heartily taken up, and embodied in petitions, largely signed, which were presented to the county council. That council had agreed to make in return grants of £20 per annum to each library, and this was acceptable to the library committees.

[11] A. Anderson, *The old libraries of Fife* (1953), p. 20.
[12] Letter from Neil Buchanan, on behalf of the Executors of the late James Coats, jr., dated 5 January 1920.

The Secretary for Scotland, however, could not see his way to give his sanction to the County Council's application, and consequently the scheme had to be abandoned, greatly to the disappointment of the petitioners.[13]

In view of Christison's obvious interest in the problem of extending library services to the county, it is not surprising to find that one of the Carnegie Trust's pioneer schemes was based on Montrose and that it was signally successful.

*　　*　　*

The most important aspect of the Adams Report was its advocacy of rural libraries. Professor Adams declared that "the question of small towns and country districts and of the large population which is scattered through them deserves first consideration." Urging the Trustees to adopt a policy of "taking the initiative" in rural library provision, Professor Adams suggested that experiments should be carried out in perhaps five areas in different parts of the United Kingdom to demonstrate what an effective rural library could achieve.

In these experimental areas there would be: (1) a central library, from which the books are distributed at regular intervals, and from which also there should be supervision of the whole area. (2) Village libraries, usually placed in the school, with the schoolmaster as librarian. This local library should consist of (a) a permanent collection of certain important reference books and standard works; (b) a circulating library which would be exchanged each three months, or at such times as may be arranged.

This "outstanding recommendation" of the report was warmly welcomed by the library profession and immediately accepted by the Trust.[14] The first annual report of the executive committee included a map indicating the distribution of the Carnegie library grants and underlining the fact that Carnegie benefactions had been directed "almost entirely to providing facilities in urban districts. Rural areas have had no similar advantages." It also announced the decision "to act upon Professor Adams' recommendation that a limited number of experiments in rural book

[13] Scottish Library Association, *Annual report of Council* 1914-15 (1915), p. 22-9.
[14] B. Wood, "The Report and Rural Libraries," *Library Association Record,* vol. 17 (1915), p. 533-9.

supply should be instituted." A year later, in the executive committee's second annual report (for 1915), it was possible to state that "a number of experimental schemes have been set on foot."

All have the same underlying principle, viz. to circulate, from one or more centres, collections of books to the villages, over a fairly wide area, using the village schools as a rule as the final distributing units from which the books may pass to their readers.

A scheme for the supply of books to the Orkneys, the Shetlands and the Island of Lewis was the first to be established. A "fairly detailed description of the arrangements devised for the administration of the scheme" appeared as an appendix to the Trust's annual report for 1915 and the "development and progress of the Scheme" was explained "in considerable detail" in an appendix to the report for 1916.

The North of Scotland Scheme, as it was called, was conducted from Dunfermline so that it might be kept under "immediate supervision and control." The Trust's other rural library schemes were organized on one or other of two alternative patterns which were described in the report for 1915.

The first pattern, of which Staffordshire was the type case, was a county scheme placed under the direct control of the education committee of the county. Nottinghamshire, with the public library of Worksop as centre, was the initial experiment in the second pattern, which consisted of linking up the various parishes within a given area, so that they might collaborate to provide library facilities they could not hope to provide on their individual rate resources. The parishes were offered a supply of books free for a trial period of one year, at the end of which each parish would adopt the Libraries Acts and, by levying a rate, pay its share in the scheme or lose the book supply.

"This form of scheme," the 1916 report noted, "may prove of greater applicability in Scotland than in England and Wales," for at that time control of primary education in Scotland was not vested in a county authority (as was the case south of the Border) but in parochial school boards, and it was the Worksop pattern that was followed when the next Scottish rural library schemes were organized—from Montrose in 1916 and from Perth in 1917.

In the Montrose scheme the Montrose public library committee commenced the work of organization on 25 July 1916, and a large and representative general committee was formed after several conferences with "H.M. Inspectors of Schools, teachers,

96

chairmen and members of public boards, clergymen and others interested in the movement." Eight parishes with thirteen centres were selected to start the experiment, and on 8 December the first consignment of books, "selected partly from lists and requests made by the teachers, and partly by the librarian," were dispatched to all the centres. "In no case was the number of volumes sent to any of the centres less than 150. In the larger centres, such as Bervie, Johnshaven and Hillside, it has been found necessary to send 250 to 300 volumes." The "commodious Hall" of the Montrose Public Library formed an "ideal" central repository.

The Perth scheme was established in 1917, and by April 1918 arrangements were completed for the distribution of books from the Sandeman Public Library in Perth to twenty-four centres in neighbouring parishes.[15] Following the Worksop pattern, the parishes concerned were to be asked after the trial period (in this case two years) to adopt the Libraries Acts, and then amalgamate their resources to finance the scheme, but a simpler procedure was found when in 1919 the education authority of the county, taking advantage of the powers granted by the Education (Scotland) Act of 1918, assumed responsibility for the Trust Scheme.[16] Perthshire can claim to have had the first rate-supported county library in the country.

The Education (Scotland) Act of 1908 had allowed a school board to provide the pupils within its area with school books.[17] Section 5 of the 1918 Act now permitted the education authority of a county to provide books for general reading:

It shall be lawful for the education authority of a county, as an ancillary means of promoting education, to make such provision of books by purchase or otherwise as they may think desirable, and to make the same available not only to the children and young persons attending schools or continuation classes in the county, but also to the adult population resident therein.

For the purposes of this section an education authority may enter into arrangements with public libraries, and all expenses incurred by an education authority shall be chargeable to the county education fund.

[15] Perth Rural Library Committee Minutes.
[16] As from 1 August 1919: Perthshire Education Authority Minutes, 11 August 1919.
[17] Education (Scotland) Act, 1908, sect. 3 (6).

A lengthy proviso exempted any burgh or parish that levied a library rate under the Public Libraries Acts from payment of the part of the county education rate that related to the cost of the county library service, unless the "county library rate" exceeded the local rate, when the excess only would be collected by the education authority.

The county library service in Scotland as we know it today was authorized by the last eight words of the first paragraph quoted just above. The slow development and painful elaboration of burgh library legislation has been traced in some detail in chapters 2 and 3; here, by contrast, an important and entirely new extension of the library service is based on a phrase in an Education Act, which, as it happens, does not contain the word "library" at all. There is no administrative detail and no financial limitation. The Act has been generally interpreted by the Scottish county education authorities "as a mandate for setting up a county library system designed to give dwellers in rural and other areas outwith the burghs that had adopted the Libraries Acts similar facilities to those already enjoyed in these burghs," although it has been pointed out that the Act permitted the provision of books only, and that the acquisition or erection of buildings and the appointment of the necessary staff must be justified under the phrase "to make the same available."[18]

The Education (Scotland) Bill was introduced by Robert Munro (the late Lord Alness) on 18 June 1918. In its passage through Parliament the proposal now embodied in section 5 of the Act was welcomed:

The provision of books for young persons and adults in places where the Public Libraries Act does not operate has no detractors.

There is another proposal in this Bill that so far has not been referred to, but which is a very important one, and shows an advance upon the English Bill. The Right Hon. Gentleman has recognized that libraries are an educational institution and should properly be, if not under the direct management of the educational authority, at any rate regarded as a serious part of

[18] Scottish Education Department, Advisory Council on Education in Scotland, *Libraries, museums & art galleries: a report* (Advisory Council Report) (1951), p. 21; see, for example, G. M. Fraser, "Burghal and rural libraries in Scotland," SLA, *Annual Report* 1928-29 (1929), p. 28-30, who discusses "the disadvantages of having library service introduced as, in a sense, a side issue."

our educational system to be worked in close co-operation with our schools and in that clause I think he will be able to point the way to England to show a great development in the use of what has been in many cases a much neglected possibility in education, namely, the use of the public library.[19]

The Scottish Library Association council, on the other hand, in considering the Bill, while "in complete sympathy with the proposal for the supply of books to children attending school . . . felt that the needs of adults would be more effectually and conveniently met if such work were placed in the hands of a library authority co-ordinate with the education authority." Their representations to the Scottish Secretary, however, had no effect; the Bill became law on 21 November 1918.

At the Association's annual meeting in 1919 "the possibilities opened up by Section 5 of the Act" were discussed "in optimistic terms," and thereafter the council of the Association sent to each county education authority a letter

> drawing attention to the powers given under Section 5 of the Education (Scotland) Act, 1918, to the clamant need for exercise of these powers and to the fact that in most areas Public Libraries with which arrangements might be made for the working of schemes under Section 5 were in actual operation.

The reaction of the education authorities may be gauged from two sample cases. In Perthshire, at the second meeting of the newly constituted education authority on 19 May 1919, Miss Haldane of Cloan, one of the original Carnegie Trustees and an enthusiastic supporter of the county library movement, proposed "the appointment of a Special Committee—to be known as The Library Committee— . . . which would deal with matters connected with rural Libraries," and, as we have seen, this committee of the authority assumed responsibility for the Carnegie Trust's pioneer scheme as from 1 August of that year.

Ayrshire, by contrast, was "rather a laggard" in putting into operation the permissive powers given to education authorities under the 1918 Act.[20] It was not until 1924 that the authority began to discuss with any seriousness the organization of a library service. The initial impetus, as usual, was a letter from the secre-

[19] House of Commons, Parliamentary debates, vol. 107 (5 s.), col. 1144, 1186.
[20] W. A. F. Hepburn, "Five Years have past," SLA, *Annual Report 1935* (1936), p. 49.

tary of the Carnegie United Kingdom Trust, Lt.-Col. J. M. Mitchell, drawing attention to the grant-in-aid offered by his Trustees and suggesting that he might meet a committee of the authority. This letter was received by the authority in November 1923 and the suggested meeting took place the following January. In February a motion, "that steps be taken to operate the provisions of the 1918 Act with regard to Libraries," was remitted to Ayrshire's central committee on school management for consideration, and in March this committee appointed a sub-committee "to go into this question and report." Later that month it was agreed to recommend that the authority should exercise their powers under the Act, and in May formal application was made to the Carnegie Trust "for the usual grants." In June the authority decided to proceed with the appointment of a librarian, who eventually took up his duties in October. That same month, the authority had learned that the Carnegie Trustees had sanctioned a grant of £1800 "of which not less than £1500 is to be spent on books."[21]

*   *   *

The Carnegie Trustees had been enthusiastic in welcoming the Act: indeed the library clause in the Education (Scotland) Act of 1918 and the Public Libraries Act, 1919, which empowered county councils in England and Wales to adopt the Libraries Acts and to establish libraries within their areas, were largely the outcome of the representations the Trust had made to the government departments concerned.

The Trustees' enthusiasm was infectious—and powerfully supported by the practical encouragement of generous grants and the personality and persistence of Col. Mitchell. In their executive committee's sixth report (1919) it is noted:

The outstanding event of the year as regards Rural Libraries in Scotland has been the coming into operation in May of Section 5 of the Education (Scotland) Act, 1918. . . . To stimulate the Authorities in the establishment of schemes, the Committee made to each County Authority an offer to consider the making of a grant to meet the necessary capital outlays.

Definite proposals already formulated by the county education authority of Caithness, to whom the Trust had promised a grant

[21] Ayrshire Education Authority Minutes, November 1923-October 1924.

100

to cover their capital outlays and maintenance for a period of five years, are then outlined:

> It has been decided to use the Public Libraries at Wick and Thurso as distributing centres, the former for the Eastern part of the County, the latter for the Western. A room in each of these buildings is being provided by the respective Library Committees for use as a repository, not only rent free, but free also of heating, lighting and cleaning charges. The librarians of the Public Libraries will act as librarians also for the Rural Scheme, and will receive salaries from the Education Authority for the work done.

Later in the same report it is recorded that

> The scheme worked from the Montrose Public Library has been continued and extended. The soundness of the experiment is abundantly proved by the fact that the Educational Authorities of both Forfarshire and Kincardineshire (districts of which areas are supplied by the Montrose centre) are investigating its operation with a view to the adoption of schemes under Section 5 in their respective Counties.

The story is continued in the subsequent reports of the Trust. In the seventh report (1920) is recorded a decision of policy regarding grants in respect of county library schemes: maintenance grants and grants for the erection of special buildings were to cease since, in the first case, "County Authorities could now provide the amount required from public funds," and, in the second, "it had become clear that the work at the central repository could be carried on efficiently from a room of adequate size in an existing building." Grants instead would cover the capital costs of books, boxes and shelving and other accessories.

> In order to fix a scale which would be applicable to all counties alike, it was decided that the grant in respect of (a) books should be, in general, at the rate of one book per five of school population, and that the sum allowed for (b) boxes should be in proportion to the number of centres which each Authority ultimately proposed to serve. Experience showed that grants based on these principles would normally cover all capital expenditure for the first four or five years, after which it would be for each Authority to consider in the light of its own experience the scale upon which expenditure should be incurred.

The Trustees admitted that this scale of book supply would not enable authorities to provide all the expensive books individual students might need, but the justification for the allocations, they pointed out, "was two-fold."

(1) It would enable Trustees within the reasonable period of six years to meet the immediate needs of every county in Great Britain, and (2) the provision of literature for students was at the same time guaranteed by a special grant of £1000 a year, for the years 1920 to 1925 inclusive, to the Central Library for Students, on the explicit agreement that this Library would supply such works (costing 6s and upwards) to all County Library Systems founded on Trust Grants, on demand and on payment of carriage only.[22]

In this way, it was argued, "Authorities could devote practically the whole of the book-grants to the purchase of cheaper works (averaging 3s 6d) in general demand, relying for technical and specialist literature upon the Central Library for Students."

Two years later the Trustees noted that "the initial stock thus scheduled was not an ideal, but a compulsory average maximum on the basis of the funds available." They then reported:

It has now become obvious that the stock thus provided does not meet the needs of counties in which the Authority and the Librarian give the scheme a fair chance. The figures show that the demand outruns the supply, and the Trustees have decided to reconsider the matter in March with a view to finding out whether they can . . . make supplementary grants in those counties where the keenness of the readers and the devotion of the librarians appear to have earned special treatment.

As a result, during 1923 supplementary grants were offered to nineteen counties, five of them Scottish.

Elsewhere in the 1920 report three lists were given showing: (1) counties or areas where pioneer rural schemes had been financed or assisted by the Trust prior to 1920, (2) counties to which grants had been sanctioned in 1920, and (3) counties where

[22] The establishment and development of the Central Library for Students (now the National Central Library) in London and the Scottish Central Library to supplement the resources of public, academic, and other libraries by their book-stocks and by the organization of inter-library loans is discussed in chapter 6.

102

authorities were negotiating for a grant. Scottish names in the lists are:

(1)	(2)	(3)
Perthshire	Sutherland	Kirkcudbright
Caithness	Clackmannan	Nairn
Montrose district	Renfrewshire	Fife
	Forfar and Kincardine	West Lothian
	Midlothian	
	Berwickshire	
	Peeblesshire	
	Dunbartonshire	
	(*not yet accepted*)	
	Inverness	

By March 1924, when the Trust's tenth report (for 1923) was published, with a comprehensive survey of the rural libraries of Great Britain, it was claimed that twenty-five of the thirty-three Scottish counties were operating libraries, and six—Argyll, Ayr, Banff, Dumfries, Inverness and Sirling—were known to be considering the question. The attitude of the remaining two counties, Aberdeen and Bute, was not known.[23]

The Rural Library Report, 1923, which forms appendix I to the Trust's tenth report extends to thirty pages, with in addition two folding sheets tabulating comparative statistical information. The twenty-five Scottish county libraries are all mentioned. Statistics are given for seventeen of them, one of these being the joint library for Angus and Kincardine. Four others "had not made sufficient progress in the start of their schemes to be able to report to the Trustees in the year 1923," while three "had not made a start."

Two years later the Trust's report for 1925 summarized the results and the lessons of the period 1921-5, "the second quinquennium of systematic policy," and announced:

The Trustees have had the satisfaction of sanctioning initial grants [for county libraries] to all except seven (England 5, Wales 1, Scotland 1) of the counties of Great Britain.

The only Scottish county which had not accepted the offer was Argyllshire.

[23] As a matter of fact, both Aberdeen and Bute (to a degree) began their library service within the next two years: it was Argyllshire that was to remain without a county library for more than twenty years.

This means that the County Library policy, to which the Trustees committed themselves in 1915 on the recommendation contained in Professor Adams' Report, and which so rapidly commended itself to general approval as to be embodied in the law of the land by the Scottish Education Act of 1918, and the Public Libraries Act of 1919, has extended, within the prescribed period, to 46 English, 11 Welsh and 32 Scottish counties, or, roughly, 99 per cent. of the total population not served in 1914 under the older Acts.

The spread of the county library movement throughout Scotland from 1919 to 1926 is demonstrated in the accompanying series of four maps which show the counties whose education authorities had taken steps to make some provision under the Act of 1918 at the end of 1920, 1922, 1924 and 1926 respectively.

One slightly unfortunate result of the county library movement's connexions with the education authority and the schools was that the impression got abroad—it persists in some places even yet—that the libraries were intended for pupils only. The county librarian of Caithness made this point in his report for 1924:

Owing to the Library Scheme having been placed under the charge of the Education Authority, it is sometimes assumed that young people of school age are alone catered for. This is, of course, by no means the intention of the scheme, and it is now time to aim at a further development of interest among the general population of our rural districts.

*   *   *

About this time it was increasingly realized that the county library movement, which was at its outset almost entirely a rural library movement, had a responsibility for these populous places in its area, whether burghs or not, that were not independent library authorities. One of the first county library branches in Great Britain was opened by Midlothian County Library in Musselburgh in September 1925: "a bold attempt to provide a library service to a populous area out of a very limited county stock, but . . . a practical one based on commonsense and experience."[24] A house was being built for the janitor of one of the burgh's principal schools and a composite building was planned to

[24] CUKT, *County Library Conference* 1926 (1927), p. 72-3.

COUNTIES WHOSE EDUCATION AUTHORITIES
HAD BEGUN TO PROVIDE LIBRARY
SERVICES UNDER THE EDUCATION
(SCOTLAND) ACT, 1918, BY THE END
OF **1920**

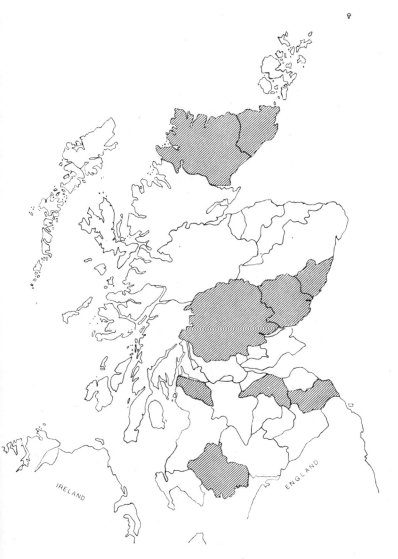

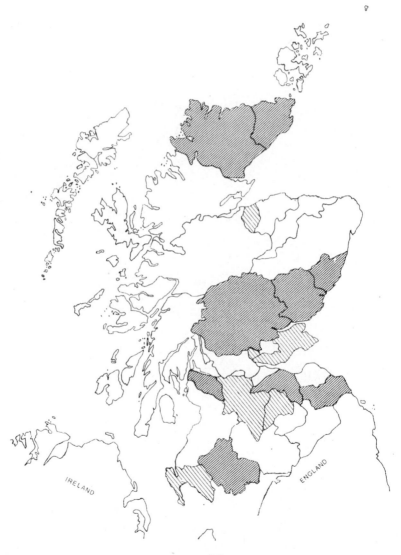

COUNTIES WHOSE EDUCATION AUTHORITIES
HAD BEGUN TO PROVIDE LIBRARY
SERVICES UNDER THE EDUCATION
(SCOTLAND) ACT, 1918, BY THE END
OF **1924**

COUNTIES WHOSE EDUCATION AUTHORITIES
HAD BEGUN TO PROVIDE LIBRARY
SERVICES UNDER THE EDUCATION
(SCOTLAND) ACT, 1918, BY THE END
OF **1926**

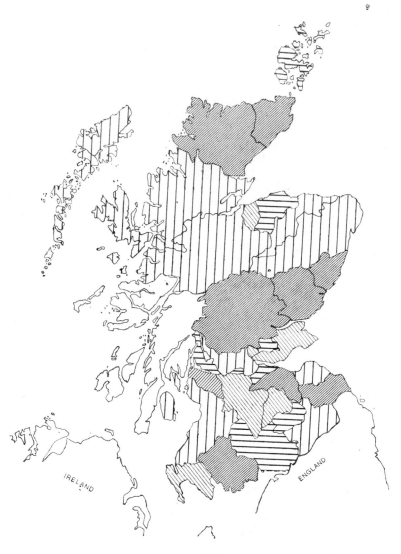

accommodate the library on the ground floor with the house above. Shelving for 4000 volumes was provided and the first collection of books amounted to 3000 volumes of which roughly 2000 were fiction. At first the branch was open for four hours on three evenings of the week and staffed from the library's headquarters in Edinburgh.

> The public came in hundreds. . . . The available floor space was crowded to the utmost during the whole of the four hours, and for most of the time the queue at the barrier and far into the street suggested a popular theatre rather than a very small branch library.

After a few weeks the service was extended to six and a half hours of opening instead of four as formerly, but early in 1926 a daily service (Saturdays excepted) with a permanent staff was begun.

About the same time also, responsible opinion abandoned the idea that a county library service was or could be provided cheaply. It is undoubtedly true that the county library movement in Great Britain would not have developed as rapidly as it did without the enthusiastic support and encouragement and the financial assistance of the Carnegie Trust, but it can be maintained that the Trust did the movement one grave disservice by pointing out so frequently in the early days how little a county library service would cost.

In the important *Memorandum on the Rural Library Policy of the Trustees,* which was prepared for the Adult Education Committee of the Board of Education in 1922, it is emphasized that "a rural library system can be provided at a very low annual cost."

> No case is yet recorded of the cost exceeding the equivalent of a $\frac{1}{2}$d rate. On the other hand, it is also clear that the scheme offers opportunities of development which, when further expenditure is thought desirable, would be productive of excellent results. It may, therefore, be well to base estimates for the future on $\frac{1}{2}$d as the average rate required.

The example of Gloucestershire is quoted. There the expenditure in 1920-1, even making allowance for an increase in the librarian's salary, represented a rate of "almost 3-10d in the £, or about 1-7th to 1-10th of the rate which was to be levied for the maintenance of an efficient borough library."

Again, a year later:

It is still true that a ½d rate is the highest levied, and this rate is reached only in a few of the smaller and poorer counties.

Large additions to stock and heavy repairing bills are not yet imminent; but it is quite clear that, unless and until the demand grows to such an extent that the ratepayers themselves are content to pay more, a rate of from one to three farthings in the £ will provide a good working scheme.

But in 1926 it was noted:

There is in some quarters a disposition to point out that in early days the Trustees indicated a rate of ¼d as the probable average expenditure, and that most counties will have to levy at least an average of ½d rate to carry out the new conditions. The contention is literally true, but the justification for the new conditions is obvious. Even so recently as 1921, no one could foresee how large the demand would become, nor was it contemplated that large urban centres would be required. It has become clear, however, that urban communities with a population of less than 30,000 can be served far better and more economically as part of a county system than as independent Library units, and also that it is a source of strength to the county service to incorporate these industrial areas.

As a result, it is pointed out, the small staff and modest headquarters which would have sufficed for a rural programme were inadequate. Library committees and librarians were acquiring a new status and larger responsibilities. More books and more expensive books would have to be provided.

If, as the outcome of this extended policy, the County Library enables the Authority to obtain fuller value for the money expended in formal education, it will be readily agreed that the increased scale of expenditure is justified.

The Kenyon Report (1927) scotched the idea of a cheap service:

It would be idle to suppose that the cost of the county library service can be permanently kept within the limits already existing. . . . County Library Committees must cease to think in terms of a rate of one-tenth of a penny. The older the library, the more the expenditure per caput must approximate to that obtaining in urban libraries.

The challenge has been repeated at intervals: by George W. Shirley in 1934, for example:

110

It requires little consideration to realise that an adequate service throughout a county will cost more than a similar service to the concentrated population of a town, yet no County in Scotland is spending per head what towns of comparable size are;

and by L. R. McColvin in 1949:

It is a universal axiom that it must cost more to give adequate library services the more sparse the population.[25]

Yet the average expenditure per head in county library services in Scotland in 1953 was still less than three-quarters the average expenditure per head in urban library services, although it must be pointed out that the average expenditure per head on books was higher in counties than in burghs by about one-third.[26]

* * *

At the end of 1935 the Carnegie Trustees announced that no further grants would be made to municipal or county libraries, apart from grants to a limited number of authorities in respect of amalgamated small urban libraries and provision for new housing estates. The Trustees felt they had helped

to set up a standard of achievement which should enable those who are responsible locally to carry on the work and develop it adequately, and that to give further help would stultify the pioneer principle which is at the root of the policy which their Founder laid down.

The Trust's report for 1935 also referred to the "valedictory conference" held in November of that year that "marked the end of the longest and most intimate of all the Trustees' experiences." The total of the Trust's county library grants in the United Kingdom from 1915 to 1935 was approximately £500,000.

The Trustees, in completing their main programme, confidently hope that Authorities, with all the facts before them as set forth in this and other Reports, will feel it incumbent upon them to develop the service on sound and generous lines. . . .

[25] G. W. Shirley, "Presidential Address," SLA, *Report, May-December 1934* (1935), p. 30; L. R. McColvin, "The North Scotland Survey," *Library Association Record*, vol. 51 (1949), p. 109.

[26] The figures for 1952-3 were: average expenditure per head: burghs 4s 7.2d, counties 3s 0.9d; average expenditure per head on books: burghs 10.6d, counties 1s 1.9d.

It is agreed by all concerned that the grant money has been well spent, and it would be exceedingly unfortunate if, with the cessation of the grants, a service which is doing such excellent work were allowed in any way to deteriorate.

One of the minor legacies of the Carnegie Trust to the county library movement, perhaps, but a legacy none the less arresting, was the county library sign—"a torch of learning . . . with a red cartouche bearing in white lettering the words COUNTY LIBRARY."[27] The selected design was submitted by a 15-year-old boy at Bradford College of Arts and Crafts, and the Trustees presented to each County Library, at a total cost of approximately £4000, as many of these signs as were required—about 15,000 in all. In response to special requests from Wales and Ireland signs were also provided with the words, "LLYFRGELL Y SIR" and "LEABHARLANN NA CONNTAE," but no similar request was received from the Gaelic-speaking areas of Scotland. The first sign was displayed in 1928 at the school-centre at Brownhall, some two miles from Dumfries.

* * *

The Local Government (Scotland) Act of 1929 had in the meantime become law. This Act affected the library movement in Scotland in several ways: it abolished, as at 15 May 1930, two authorities concerned with the provision of libraries—the parish council and the education authority. The powers and duties of the education authority in each county were transferred to the county council, as were the powers of a parish council as library authority, and detailed provision was made for the administration of any parish library so transferred.

The Act also repealed the proviso to section 5 of the Education (Scotland) Act, 1918, and in future the expenditure of the county council as education authority met from local rates, including any expenditure on the county library service, was to be levied as a flat rate throughout the county area, including any burghs that might be levying their own library rates. The effect of the repeal of the proviso and the reaction of burgh library authorities to it is discussed in the following chapter, and again, from the point of view of the legislative problems it created, in chapter 9.

* * *

In the twenty years from 1935 to 1955 the county library services in Scotland continued to develop. New headquarters

[27] CUKT, *Annual report* 1928 (1929), p. 33.

112

buildings were opened in Hamilton (for Lanarkshire) in 1936 and in Kirkcaldy (for Fife) in 1938. Argyllshire appointed its first county librarian in 1946 and began operations the next year with a grant of £1500 from the Carnegie Trust. The service in Bute was re-organized in 1950 with the Norman Stewart Institute Library at Rothesay as headquarters, after a four-year experiment during which a library service for the islands had been provided by Kilmarnock Public Library.

The book-stocks of Scottish county libraries increased from a total of 440,822 in 1928-9 to 1,290,928 in 1938-9 and to 2,089,913 in 1950-1.[28]

Between 1946 and 1951 the number of full-time branches increased from 33 to 47; part-time branches increased from 44 to 73; three libraries on wheels took the road, and the number of exhibition or delivery vans—an experiment initiated by the Perthshire Education Authority in 1920—increased from four to six.[29]

But despite the vastly increased stocks of books that are available the central problem of any county library continues to be the provision for its readers of reasonable access to the books they co-operatively possess. This problem scarcely exists in a burgh library service where the majority of the books the community owns and the facilities the library offers are often concentrated in one central building. In contrast, the county library's resources are continually dispersed and there is frequently no single point where they are all displayed to their best advantage. Often the largest collection of county library books that can be examined under one roof is the stock at the headquarters, but this rarely contains more than a third of the books the library possesses, while the remaining two-thirds or more, are distributed over the library area—over hundreds if not thousands of square miles.

Even with travelling libraries it is physically impracticable to offer the readers in remote places direct access to all the books they own in their county library. They are, unfortunately, denied the pleasure of browsing around the well-stocked shelves of a large public library, and they may miss the peculiar satisfaction of an unexpected find. Nevertheless, with request systems and

[28] Library Association: County Libraries Section, *Statistical reports,* 1934-35, 1938-39; *Statistical and policy survey,* 1951 (1952).
[29] CUKT, *Proceedings of Carnegie Rural Library Conference* . . . 1920 (1921), p. 51. There is an illustration of a suggested travelling library —horse-drawn—in James Duff Brown's *The village library problem* (1894), p. 4. (*Library,* vol. 6 (1894), p. 102).

postal services neither the general reader nor the student, however isolated his house, is entirely cut off from the opportunities for recreation, study or research that the public library service affords. The day is long past when a prominent city librarian could deplore "the lamentable state of rural Scotland in respect of facilities for studious reading."[30]

[30] G. M. Fraser of Aberdeen Public Library at the 8th annual meeting of the Scottish Library Association, Aberdeen, 4 July 1919; SLA, *Annual Report* 1919-20 (1920), p. 3.

CHAPTER 5

BURGH AND COUNTY

BY 1928 THE OLDEST COUNTY LIBRARIES in Scotland had been in existence for ten years. That the new kind of library service was authorized by an Education and not a Libraries Act did not hinder its rapid development. Here and there throughout the country, indeed, schemes of co-operation were discussed and adopted. In some cases there may have been jealousies and petty differences, but by and large it was recognized that in effect the Education (Scotland) Act of 1918 had extended the Public Libraries Acts to cover the country.

There was no overlapping of the two types of library. Section 5 of the Education Act explicitly stated that that part of the county education rate from which the expenses of the county library service were met should be levied on a burgh or parish that raised its own library rate only if it exceeded, and only to the extent that it did exceed, the burgh or parish library rate. As no education authority in the early days of county libraries was spending more, as a rate, than any independent library authority within its area, the proviso was invariably operative, and no burgh or parish that levied its own library rate was required to contribute at all towards the cost of the county scheme. It should be noted, however, that although there was in fact no "double rating," the principle was there.

The Act, however, had explicitly permitted county education authorities to "enter into arrangements with public libraries" and it was soon appreciated, particularly in the rural counties and if small burgh libraries were involved, that co-operation could be mutually advantageous, although there was a certain anxiety among burgh librarians that co-ordination might mean the absorption of the burgh library by the county education authority.[1]

The Carnegie Trustees had frequently urged the importance of co-ordination between burgh and county libraries.

[1] CUKT, *Scottish Central Library for Students: Transactions of a Conference . . . Stirling . . . 1923* (1923), p. 28-30, 39-42; J. M. Mitchell, *A report on the public library system of Great Britain and Ireland 1921-1923* (1924), p. 7-8

The Trustees, however, are not in a position to take the initiative beyond pointing out the importance of the principle. The experiment involves a mutual arrangement between two distinct statutory authorities serving distinct bodies of rate-payers under separate Acts of Parliament. Moreover, the problem is not the same in all counties. In a few counties big burgh libraries exist which could derive little or no benefit from co-ordination but could confer a great deal. In other counties the relationship is reversed, so that it is the burgh libraries—starved and short of books—which could benefit by participation in the constantly-fresh county stock.[2]

As early as 1921 the education authority of Midlothian had arranged that the lending department of Bonnyrigg Public Library should be incorporated in the county scheme. Even earlier the education authority of Caithness and the library committees of the burghs of Wick and Thurso had arrived at a complete unification of the library services in that county.

At the Stirling Conference in 1923 the education officer of the Stewartry of Kirkcudbright described how the county library scheme in his area had taken over the stock of several stationary village libraries which were in a state of decay. His authority, he stated, were negotiating with the public library committee in Castle Douglas with a view to a similar arrangement.

This the Trustees considered "a most important case, since the Library in Castle Douglas is a rate-aided library of the usual type."

> At first sight it would appear that, pending some modification of the Public Libraries Acts, the only way is a mutual arrangement on a voluntary basis by which the Public Library would receive periodical collections of current literature in return for an agreed contribution to the Rural Library Funds, and for certain concessions in respect of its stationary stock. There can presumably be no pooling of the two stocks, since each exists under a separate enactment and is owned by a different group of ratepayers.

By 1926, however, the town council and the education authority had come to an arrangement under which the burgh library building became the county library repository, the education authority providing the library service for the burgh, while the town council remained responsible for the upkeep of the building.

[2] Stirling Conference Transactions (1923), p. 19.

116

In Aberdeenshire the education authority offered the burgh libraries loan collections of books, on the same scale as given to the rest of the county, if the burgh paid annually to the education authority a sum equal to the amount payable if there had been no burgh library, or alternatively collections of county library books were lent to the burgh library at an agreed payment per 100 volumes. It is worth noting that by the first of these methods the proviso to section 5 of the 1918 Act already ceased to have effect.

For the large burgh libraries, on the other hand, with their greater resources, co-operation with the county library service was at that stage unnecessary; there was perhaps only a general air of condescension in their attitude to the junior service.

The Local Government (Scotland) Act of 1929 completely altered this relationship. The two types of library could no longer work side by side without overlapping. Subsection 5 of section 18 repealed the proviso in the Education Act, and every independent library authority found that it had to pay in addition to its own library rate its due proportion of the expenditure on the library service of its county.[3]

When the Act had been introduced as a Bill, the Scottish Library Association council had foreseen the situation that would arise and had called a special general meeting of the Association, where a resolution approving clause 18 (5) was adopted "with the proviso that where a burgh is operating a library under the Public Libraries Acts, it shall be given, for the portion of the County Assessment for libraries raised for it, an equivalent service"; and although a second motion expressing the meeting's disapproval of the council's recommendation of the Bill was defeated, there was a general feeling of dissatisfaction. Nevertheless the Bill became law, with this clause intact.

Almost immediately the burgh library authorities began to clamour for some return for this contribution towards the cost of a county library service from which they did not benefit. The county councils, on the other hand, resented the immediacy and the insistence of the burghs' demands. An authority that levies a rate as a flat rate over a large area, as the county education rate is levied, is rarely able—or finds it rarely advisable—to spend the rate over the area in direct proportion to its incidence. Again, many of the county library services were still developing and there

[3] The sub-section reads: "The proviso to section five of the Education (Scotland) Act, 1918 (which relates to burghs or parishes in which a library rate is levied) shall cease to have effect."

117

were sometimes considerable groups of county ratepayers who had been patiently paying for years their contribution towards a service they hoped to enjoy some day. In the face of these considerations the almost immediate demand from the burghs for a *quid pro quo* seemed ill timed and ungenerous.

In March 1931 the Carnegie United Kingdom Trust and the Scottish Library Association jointly convened a conference at Dunblane, the main purpose of which was "to discuss the new relation between County and Burgh Library Authorities created by the relevant clauses of the Local Government (Scotland) Act, 1929."[4]

Upwards of 180 delegates attended the conference, representing forty-four burghs and twenty-nine counties (only six or seven library authorities had been unable to send representatives), along with Mr Thomas Johnston, Parliamentary Under-Secretary for Scotland, Mr W. W. MacKechnie of the Scottish Education Department, and representatives of the Association of County Councils, the Convention of Royal Burghs, the Educational Institute of Scotland, the Workers' Educational Association, and the British Institute of Adult Education.

Principal R. S. Rait of Glasgow University, in an opening address, made a general statement on the issue at stake. He explained the purpose of the cancellation of the proviso.

> The object of the Section which removed the exemption was simply to enforce what has been adopted as a cardinal principle in educational administration in Scotland, a flat rate for the County. The consequent inequality of rating as between Burgh and County residents was recognised to be an evil, but it was regarded as a lesser evil than the introduction, or retention, of an exception to the principle that differential rating is to be regarded as inadmissible. On the other hand, it remains true that the Burgh resident who pays an additional Library rate receives a double Library service.

The ways and means of providing this "double library service" were discussed in two papers that followed. The speakers were Mr Andrew Shearer, town clerk of Dunfermline and later honorary legal adviser to the Scottish Library Association, and Mr W. A. F. Hepburn, who was at the time director of education for Ayrshire.

[4] This Dunblane conference is discussed again in chapter 9. The Conference proceedings were published later in 1931.

Mr Shearer very fairly presented not only his own but the other sides of the problem, as he saw it:

There is no necessity for the whole of the Library activities within a Burgh being taken over as an educational matter by the Education Authorities. . . . It is for experienced Committee members and expert Librarians to determine by what methods mutual arrangements can best be carried out to achieve economy, to avoid overlapping, and to identify the Public Libraries with the County scheme with the object of providing the best possible service, including a return to the Burgh rate-payers for the levy made upon them.

Short of restoration of the status quo, it has been suggested that the County Council should simply hand over to the Town Council the whole product of the County Library rate collected from the Burgh citizens in their Education rate and allow the Burgh Public Library Committee to apply that money towards the Burgh Library expenditure, with the effect of reducing the Burgh Library rate. The County Council, however, through their Education Committee, are the people vested with the statutory duty of administering the money collected for County Library purposes in the Education rate, and simply to hand that over to the Town Council might be a desertion of responsibility.

The County Council's library work will be planned and financed as a whole without admission of any rule that each different area of the County must receive in services exactly what it has contributed in rates.

He went on to elaborate the questions discussed in Dunfermline burgh:

(a) What additional library services can profitably be given in the Burgh? (b) How far can these be adequately rendered by the County Education Library, or how far can they be most suitably given by the existing Burgh Library at the cost of Education rate?

queries directed, as he frankly admitted:

to obtaining for the Burgh a return from the County in respect of the additional rating; but any scheme of arrangements must also take into account something more, namely, assistance by the Burgh Librarians to the County Education Library System.

He then detailed six possible methods of co-operation that were being considered in Dunfermline:

(1) Co-operation, to enable County readers to borrow through their own Library scheme such books as the Burghs might possess and vice versa, with the formation of a joint card catalogue of non-fiction books. . . . With the established stocks in the Burgh Library the preponderance of advantage in this co-operation would at first probably accrue to the County, but in course of time as the County Library stocks increase the balance of advantage might pass to the other side.

(2) Supply or loan of books for adult education classes within the Burgh—as an appropriate charge against the Burgh's rate contribution.

(3) (a) Provision of school libraries, or (b) development of juvenile section in Burgh Library (with Children's Room and Supervisor) . . . subject to general approval by the County Education Committee.

(4) Aid in purchase of expensive books for the Burgh Library as an appropriate charge against the Burgh's rate contribution to the County Scheme, together with co-operation in book selection and buying.

(5) Facilities of Burgh Library to extra-burghal readers:

(6) Contribution from County Education Committee towards book purchases, etc.

In conclusion he emphasized a point that some county authorities would have heartily endorsed even twenty-five years later:

The provision under the Public Libraries Act in any populous neighbourhood of a comfortable and attractive place of resort in the nature of a library with accommodation and equipment proportionate to the population should be made out of local resources rather than out of a widespread Education rate mostly paid by ratepayers from elsewhere, and should be managed by or under Local Councils.

Mr Hepburn then spoke as a county representative. He too suggested methods of co-operation between burgh and county, with the qualification that as hardly two library areas in Scotland are "identical in needs and conditions it would be wide of the mark to dogmatise regarding the type of co-operation which will be found most practicable." His suggestions may be summarized as follows:

(1) The interloan of books should be developed systematically. The final aim should be to give every reader in an area his choice of the area's total book supply.

(2) Adjacent authorities might each choose a field in which to specialize. "A case in point is that of the County town, in whose library one naturally expects to find a full range of works dealing with local records, history, and topography. . . . Similarly, the County Library, organized by the Education Committee, might specialize in books dealing with education and allied topics."

(3) Residents on the fringe of the Burgh "are often, on a payment, allowed to use the Burgh Library. The new situation should bring these readers definitely within the ambit of the Burgh service."

(4) The possibility of the Burgh Library acting as "distributing centre" for a district should be kept in view.

(5) School and class libraries are provided by some Education Committees. "Such facilities are excellent and should be developed. The Public Library Committee (1927) advocated 'the universal formation of juvenile departments (lending as well as reading) in public libraries with personal access to the shelves.' Here is a field common to Burgh and County." Financial assistance to develop juvenile departments within the Burgh Library might be given by the County Authority.

(6) Finally Mr Hepburn referred to the Departmental Committee's conclusion "after a careful sifting of the evidence, that the County Authority was able to undertake the service to urban areas with a population of less than 20,000, that is to say in Burghs defined as small by the recent Act. . . . As the County schemes mature, small Burghs will tend to turn for guidance and support to the County Authority. . . . The degree of autonomy preserved by the small Burghs will be a matter of arrangement, but much can be done through Joint Committees, which are a well-tried device of local government."

It is interesting to note, after the acrimonious bickering of the ensuing quarter of a century, that Mr Shearer's suggestions (1), (3) and (5) are identical with Mr Hepburn's (1), (5) and (3), that the latter's second suggestion might be considered a special case of the "co-operation in book-selection and buying" of Mr

121

Shearer's fourth suggestion, and that the remaining suggestions put forward from the two camps are not inconsistent.

An invaluable appendix to Mr Hepburn's paper details the arrangements made (up to February 1931) between certain county education authorities and the independent library authorities within their areas.

In the subsequent discussion the town clerk of Stirling asked for "the maximum consideration from the County Authorities" and deplored "the absence of the spirit of true co-operation" revealed, according to Mr Hepburn's appendix, in the arrangements made by one education committee.

The county clerk of Dumfriesshire, Mr Robson, also spoke. He could not see the County Councils' Association agreeing to the suggestion that a burgh's contribution to the county library service "should be ascertained down to shillings and pence and paid over automatically to be administered by the Town Council of the Burgh that may have happened to adopt the Free Libraries Acts and to have made a certain amount of provision under these Acts."

> The assessment will be levied by the County Council. They are responsible for the administration of the assessments they collect, and it is their duty, whatever one may say, to see that the service is properly administered and that the rates they have collected are efficiently expended.

He then passed from the general to the practical:

> We have in our own County our own problem . . . we have one large Burgh which has had a Public Library for a long time. I cannot say that I can speak from personal knowledge, but I have every reason to believe that it is efficient. They have a certain amount of assessment, but it is doubtful whether that assessment is sufficient for all their needs. They must maintain a staff, and when they maintain a staff and pay them reasonably they have not as much left for providing books as they ought to have. Then we have six small Burghs and two of these have adopted the Libraries Act. Now, I am not wanting to criticise them, but they have not the means to provide an efficient Library service. They have some ancient buildings and some ancient books and some ancient shelves. Now, these are cases in which I am perfectly certain the County Authority could co-operate and provide the books, which are the essentials. . . . We have other burghs that have not yet adopted the Act, and in these at present the County

122

Library service is supplying the needs fairly efficiently. I have no doubt we will manage our own problem at home, and from the general point of view, as I said before, any proposals will be reasonably received.

The problem in Dumfriesshire was certainly "managed," and a most satisfactory and statesmanlike solution found, within little more than a year. In October 1931 at a conference of town council and county council representatives a joint committee was appointed "to consider and report whether the library services . . . in the burgh of Dumfries . . . and in the education area of the county of Dumfries . . . should be unified and, if so, under what arrangements."

Six months later, after several meetings, the joint committee issued its report and recommendations.[5] It reviewed the existing situation in burgh and county in the light of the legislation under which the two kinds of library service operated, and then announced the joint committee's unanimous conclusion—

that, pending further legislation, library provision should be made under the Education Acts and at the cost of the education fund throughout the whole education area.

Certain specific provisions and arrangements were then suggested, of which the most important were:

that the Ewart Library buildings in Dumfries should be leased to the County Council to be used as part of their library accommodation for the whole county, the Council Council undertaking to maintain the buildings and to continue the services which were at that time provided by the Town Council as burgh library authority;

that the books in all the libraries in the county should be pooled;

that branch or district sub-libraries should be established at Annan and Lockerbie, if satisfactory arrangements were reached with the Town Councils of these burghs;

that other branch or district sub-libraries should be established elsewhere, if necessary, and that the existing county service should be continued;

that there should be one library staff under one librarian;

[5] Report by Joint Committee of the County Council of the County of Dumfries and the Town Council of the Burgh of Dumfries . . . April 1932. The report is an important document and is reproduced in full in appendix 3.

that the service should be administered by a committee of the County Council, to be known as the "Library Committee," consisting of thirteen County Councillors, seven representing the landward area of the County, four to represent the burgh of Dumfries, and two to represent the small burghs in the county, and that this committee's annual estimate of expenditure should be transmitted to the Education Committee who should include it in the education estimates, with "such observations on the details or amount . . . as they may consider called for," and transmit both the library estimates and any observations on them to the Finance Committee of the County Council.

It was recommended that if the county council and the town council of Dumfries approved, the new arrangements should become operative "as from and after 15 May 1932."

No time was lost. The report was adopted by the town council on 26 April, and by the county council on 11 May, and a formal minute of agreement was sealed and signed by the burgh representatives on 12 May and by the county representatives on 18 May.[6]

By the time that the librarian of the Dumfriesshire Libraries (G. W. Shirley, previously the librarian for Dumfries burgh) presented his annual report for the libraries' first year, 1932-3, he was able to record that a similar minute of agreement between the county council of Dumfries and the town council of Lockerbie had been signed in October 1932. It was not until May 1943 that the third of the Dumfriesshire agreements, between the county council and the town council of Annan was signed.

The importance of the Dumfriesshire amalgamation is that it voluntarily and successfully achieved what it may have been hoped subsection (5) of section 18 of the Act of 1929 would accomplish—a unification of library services on a county basis. It served as a model for the amalgamation that followed four years later in Clackmannanshire, and it may have encouraged the agreements reached in Inverness-shire and Orkney; it anticipated by almost twenty years the solution of the problems of rate-limitation and double-rating contained in the Report of the Advisory Council in Education. It does not, of course, necessarily follow from the success of the voluntary amalgamation in Dum-

[6] County Council of Dumfries, Minute of Agreement with the Town Council of Dumfries as to unification of library service, May 1932; *The Scotsman,* 12 May 1932.

124

friesshire that other amalgamations of the kind would have been equally successful, particularly if the amalgamations were enforced by law. The Dumfries experiment owed its success to the true spirit of co-operation that existed between the parties to the agreement and to the enthusiasm, energy and foresight of a distinguished librarian.[7]

A similar readiness to co-operate was found in Clackmannanshire when a director of education with vision suggested an amalgamation of the library services of Alloa burgh and Clackmannan county.[8] There the situation was slightly more complicated, in that the Alloa Library accommodation in the town hall was not suitable for use as the headquarters of an amalgamated county system. However, the former museum buildings became available opportunely, and proved admirably suited for the purposes in view. The combined Clackmannan County Library came into being at 16 May 1936 (when Alloa burgh ceased to levy a rate for library purposes) under the librarianship of Mr Egarr who had been appointed chief assistant in the Dumfriesshire Libraries on the amalgamation there four years earlier. So the example and the influence of Dumfriesshire spread.

That the Dumfriesshire amalgamation was an immediate success is revealed by the librarian's report for the first year (1932-3): that the success persisted was pointed out by his successor twenty years later:[9]

The way out of the difficulty [of double rating] chosen by Dumfriesshire has proved with the passage of time an amicable and beneficial one for all concerned. In 1932 the burgh of Dumfries (and later Lockerbie and Annan) pioneered a scheme of amalgamation under which the education authority became responsible for all library service within the county area. . . .

That both services benefited under the new regime was quickly apparent. The county service, which in 1932 was in the early stages of its development, was strengthened by the incorporation of the old-established bookstock of the Ewart Library while the burgh service drew fresh life from the increased flow of books of current interest which percolated from the younger service and from the proceeds of the education rate.

[7] George W. Shirley, 1879-1939.

[8] A. C. Marshall, CBE, MA, LLB, FRSE, 1890-1959.

[9] Mrs M. D. McLean, *Fifty years a-growing: the Ewart Library attains its jubilee* (Reprinted from the *Dumfries and Galloway Standard*, 1954).

In Clackmannanshire, the amalgamation that was carried through despite the protests of some members of the former Alloa burgh library committee was similarly beneficial.[10] If the burgh library, although much of its stock was moribund, possessed many books of genuine value, the county service had certainly more books "of current interest" and a greater flexibility in its approach to the problems of librarianship, and their combination under a young librarian of promise (Mr Egarr was only 25 when he was given the appointment) was destined to succeed. In issues alone the improvement was startling. For several years before the amalgamation the issues from Alloa Burgh Library had been decreasing steadily: 1932, 76,239; 1933, 73,560; 1934, 68,675; 1935, 61,509. From Alloa Public Library as a branch of Clackmannan County Library the issues in 1936-7 were 116,479; in 1937-8 they were 165,170.

The agreement between the two libraries in Inverness-shire was of a very different kind.[11] In Dumfriesshire and Clackmannanshire the burgh library committees surrendered their powers to the education committee, the town council ceased to levy a rate for library purposes under the Public Libraries Acts (although Dumfries continued to levy a rate under these Acts for the maintenance of its town museum), and the library service for the entire education area was administered under the Education (Scotland) Act of 1918. In the agreement in Inverness-shire that came into operation on 16 May 1933, the library services were to be under the control of a joint committee, to be known as the Inverness Burgh and County Public Library Committee, with the powers of a library committee as provided in the Public Libraries Act of 1887, or as provided for by the Education Acts, and of the committee's twenty members ten were to be appointed by the town council, in accordance with the Act of 1887, and ten by the county council. The chairman would be appointed from among the burgh representatives. The expenses of the libraries were to be borne by the town

[10] One member of the burgh library committee had asked that his protest should be minuted: "The Draft Scheme is an unblushing proposal to 'dish' or swallow the Burgh side of the proposed amalgamation of the two Libraries and digest them into a 'Sub-Committee of the Education Committee'—a sort of minor School Management Committee affair. I cannot conceive of any Scheme that could be further removed, so utterly repellent to the wish of the venerated Donor of Alloa Public Library" (Alloa, Joint Committee on Library Facilities, Minute, 13 January 1936).

[11] The agreement is printed as an appendix to C. S. Minto's report, *Public library services in the North of Scotland* (1948).

council and the county council equally, and were to be requisitioned from the two councils as required by the joint committee, except that the committee was not to requisition more than £2500 in all without the sanction of both councils. The existing book stocks were to be made available for the joint use of the burgh and the county, and were to be interchangeable, but in the event of the scheme's being discontinued

> all books at the commencement of this scheme belonging to each of the combining Authorities shall remain the property of the Authority to which they belonged at the commencement of the Joint arrangement, and shall as far as possible be returned to such Authority.

Books purchased during the subsistence of the scheme were also to be "inter-changeable," and were to be divided as far as possible equally between the two combining authorities, if the agreement were ended. The public library buildings in Inverness were to be placed at the disposal of the joint committee free of rent; the reading room, reference department, and museum conducted by the burgh library committee were to be continued, and their cost was to form a legitimate charge on the joint fund. The distribution of books to centres throughout the county was to be maintained.

In the other agreements we have discussed the burgh had surrendered its powers as a library authority for the greater good of both. In this agreement it appeared that two authorities of different kinds, burgh and county, recorded their will to combine; but the independent status of the two contracting parties was fictitious. However proud and independent a Scottish burgh may be, it is only a part, though frequently a most important part, of the administrative area of the county council as education authority. The Inverness agreement, it should be noted, neither solved the problem of double rating nor circumvented the rate limit, while the Dumfriesshire agreement did both.

Nevertheless, the agreement might have worked better than it did, if the joint committee had been in a position to appoint one chief librarian to have charge and control of the combined service; but at the date of the agreement there were two librarians, a burgh librarian and a county librarian, and the agreement saved the joint committee the invidious task of appointing the one or the other (or any third person) as chief librarian, by allowing it power to appoint "librarians."

Fifteen years later Mr Minto noted the effect of this provision:

> In practice this has led to virtually separate systems neither of which gains any advantage from the existence of the other. No correlation of book stocks exists.[12]

In Selkirkshire a joint agreement of a third type has been working "satisfactorily" and with "no complications" since November 1948. Galashiels Public Library administers the library service for the county "as agents of the County Council as Education Authority." The former county library's books and equipment were transferred to the public library committee and the book stocks were completely merged:

> The rural centres will get their fair share of new books. All the facilities of the Galashiels Public Library will so far as available be open to dwellers in the County Area, including the opportunity to select books from the shelves when visiting Galashiels.

The "whole library" is governed by the Galashiels Library Committee, and the sum that the County Council pays annually "in respect of expenditure incurred and services rendered" is determined by joint consultation.[13]

*　　*　　*

The agreements in force between burgh and county authorities in Scotland cover a wide range from the minimal interconnexion represented by the county's handing over unconditionally to an otherwise independent burgh library authority a "reasonable return" in respect of double rating to the complete amalgamation of the two types of service—by the absorption of the burgh authority into the county scheme, by the administration of the county service by the burgh library committee, or by the appointment of a joint committee, that "well-tried device of local government." In many small burghs the burgh library committee, if it still survives, now provides from its own resources only premises and staff, and perhaps a reading room with newspapers and magazines, while the entire book stock is maintained by the county authority.

[12] Minto Report (1948), p. 12

[13] Galashiels Public Library Draft Proposals, 23 September 1948. The proposals have not been embodied in a formal agreement.

But whether the co-operation between burgh and county is complete or almost non-existent, there is at least no case of the "absurdity" of direct competition between the services, although it is theoretically possible that there might be in a Scottish burgh "two independent library services—one operated by the education committee of the county council under the Education Act and another operated by the library committee of the burgh under the Public Libraries Acts."[14] The county authority invariably serves a burgh library area through the burgh library service by supplementing the burgh's service, more or less, either directly by a "reasonable return" in cash or kind, or indirectly by offering additional specialized services—perhaps to schools in the burgh, to adult education classes, to prisons or to hospitals—or by both direct and indirect means. Inevitably there must be some sort of arrangement or other between the two types of authority in any county education area for the authorities cannot escape the interconnexion imposed by the Act of 1929.

*　　*　　*

Another and older library agreement must be examined in detail, for it combines for library purposes two independent authorities of the same kind. The Angus and Kincardineshire Joint County Library, to give it its official name, came into being in 1920 as a continuation and development of the Montrose experiment which the Carnegie United Kingdom Trust initiated in 1916. As we have seen, this scheme began as a service to certain parishes in Forfarshire (as it was then called) and Kincardineshire and it was based upon the public library at Montrose. The original organization of the scheme was soundly built, and when the Education Act of 1918 enabled county education authorities to establish or assume responsibility for library services, it was natural that the neighbouring authorities of Forfarshire and Kincardineshire should combine to take over the scheme. The formal minute of agreement is dated 5 June 1929, but its preamble refers to the authorities' agreement "to take over the existing Montrose Rural Library Scheme" as from 15 November 1920.[15]

Thirty-five years later the agreement was still functioning smoothly. The management is vested in an executive committee consisting of four members from each of the Angus and the Kin-

---

[14] L. R. McColvin, *The public library system of Great Britain* (1942), p. 53.
[15] The agreement is given in full in appendix 4.

cardineshire education committees, and three from Montrose burgh library committee, for the headquarters of the joint county library is still housed at Montrose Public Library, and, as it happens, the librarian of the Joint County Library is also, as her predecessor was, burgh librarian of Montrose. The Montrose representatives sit on the committee "for their interest" but they have no vote on purely executive matters. The county representatives are constituted as sub-committees of the education committees to which they report. The representation of the two authorities on the committee is equal, but the cost of the service is borne by the Angus and by the Kincardine education committees in the ratio of two to one.

> The allocation of costs between Angus and Kincardine was made on a rather arbitrary basis but although the question has been reviewed from time to time neither side has seen fit to suggest any variation in the two to one formula.[16]

This earliest instance of the combination of authorities for library purposes, appropriately originating in a pioneer Carnegie Trust rural library service, could well have provided the pattern for similar arrangements in other parts of Scotland, to the general advantage of the library service.[17] There is this precedent and there is good legal authority for such joint schemes. The Local Government (Scotland) Act, 1947, repeated the provisions of the Act of 1929, that "any two or more local authorities may combine for any purpose in which they are jointly interested," and the Education (Scotland) Act 1946 continued the provisions of the second schedule of the Act of 1918 for co-operation between education authorities "in the exercise of any power under this Act."

> Any education authorities, or education authorities and town councils or county councils or other local authorities, may from time to time join in making such arrangements with regard to the conduct and management of their business, and the distribution of such business among their officers, and the joint use of offices or buildings, or otherwise, as shall seem to them, in the whole circumstances of the case, to be most effective and economical.[18]

[16] The director of education for Angus in a letter to the author dated 19 March 1955.
[17] For further discussion of this point see chapter 10.
[18] Education (Scotland) Act, 1946, sect. 23 (3).

130

Such questions as representation of the combining authorities on a joint committee and the allocation of its expenses would be specified in the agreement covering the combination.

A curious anomaly in this story of amalgamation, combination and co-operation is the instance of Moray and Nairn. By the Local Government Act of 1929 the county of Nairn was combined with the county of Moray, and the joint county council became the education authority for the combined counties.[19] However, the two education authorities then superseded had each established a county library service, Nairn in 1922 and Moray in 1924, and the two libraries were to retain some appearance of an independent existence, each with its own librarian, until the appointment of a qualified librarian for Moray and Nairn in 1960. Throughout these thirty years of apparent independence there was in fact one library committee, a sub-committee of the education committee of the joint county council, for the two libraries. In 1955 it consisted of nine members of the education committee, two of whom represented Nairnshire, and three headmasters, one of whom was the rector of Nairn Academy. For each library there was a small sub-sub-committee of three or four persons. There was one budget for the two libraries, levied in the normal way on the education rate. The amount estimated for the purchase of books was then allocated between the two libraries, and each librarian was responsible for the purchases for her own library. Books were exchanged between the two libraries "from time to time," and there was a union catalogue of the non-fiction books.[20]

It is difficult to understand why this show of independence was maintained. As Mr Minto pointed out in 1948:

> Neither county has a population sufficiently large for economic administration. There is no doubt in my mind that a better service would result from the amalgamation of the present separate services.

*   *   *

It will be noted that in this survey of the different kinds of combination of library authorities that are to be found in Scotland, there is no mention of one of the five instances that

---

[19] Local Government (Scotland) Act, 1929, sect. 10 (7) (a).
[20] The director of education for Moray and Nairn in a letter dated 17 March 1955.

McColvin cites in his report.[21] The counties of Perth and Kinross were combined for a variety of local government functions, including education, by the Act of 1929, as were the counties of Moray and Nairn, and from that time library provision throughout the combined county has been the responsibility of the education committee of the joint county council. This is not an example of the voluntary combination for library purposes only of two otherwise independent authorities, and it should not be grouped with the other four.

[21] McColvin Report (1942), p. 102.

CHAPTER 6

THE SCOTTISH CENTRAL LIBRARY AND THE REGIONAL LIBRARY BUREAU OF SCOTLAND

THE COUNTY LIBRARY ORGANIZATION that emerged from the Adams' Report and the Trust schemes—"the idea of assembling, on a county basis, books which could be lent to individual readers in their homes"—almost inevitably led on to the idea of central lending libraries that would supplement the resources of existing library systems. The first institution of this kind was the Central Library for Students in London, now known as the National Central Library. It was established in 1916, largely through the generosity of the Carnegie United Kingdom Trustees, and "its immediate aim was to improve the supply of books to students in organized classes of adult education." Indeed, it developed from a library established by the Workers' Educational Association in conjunction with Toynbee Hall as a direct result of the Adams' Report of 1915:

> A central lending library, common to the Workers' Educational Association, the Adult School movement, and all other organizations of working men and women which are carrying on systematic study work, would be an institution of great public utility.[1]

As the library was designed mainly to assist the adult education organizations, only a few public libraries shared in the scheme at the start. In 1919 the Adult Education Committee of the Ministry of Reconstruction recommended that "the Central Library for Students should be regarded as a nucleus of a much larger central circulating library." This recommendation was welcomed by the Library Association at its Annual Meeting at Southport in September 1919. There it was resolved:

> That this Annual Conference of Librarians and Members of Library Committees records its agreement with the view expressed in the Third Interim Report of the Adult Education

[1] W. G. S. Adams, *Report on library provision* (1915), p. 21.

Committee as to the value of the Central Library for Students; suggests to public libraries the desirability of making an annual subscription to the Central Library; and strongly recommends a Government grant to the Library in order that it may fulfil the objects for which it is formed.

THE SCOTTISH CENTRAL LIBRARY FOR STUDENTS

A Scottish Central Library for Students was established, again by the Carnegie United Kingdom Trust, in Dunfermline in the autumn of 1921, "primarily as a repository to supplement the resources of the fifteen Scottish county library systems which were then in operation and to supply books to individual readers in counties not yet provided with library services."

In an address delivered on 7 June 1922 before the Scottish Library Association at its annual meeting, held that year in Dunfermline, the secretary of the Trust, Lieut.-Col. J. M. Mitchell, outlined the policy and purpose of the library. He pointed out that the circulating system adopted in the Carnegie rural library scheme "in itself makes little or no provision for the more serious readers in rural areas who want particular works of a learned kind."

> Moreover, it is quite likely that in the whole county, to say nothing of the villages, the readers of any one of these books would not number more than two or three in a year. Therefore it is not only improper to send them as part of the three months' supply for one village; it is actually improper—speaking generally—to buy them for the county stock at all. Just as they would occupy an unfair share of the village box, so they are too costly to be charged to the county book bill, having regard to the comparative fewness of their probable readers. . . .

> What is the answer ? . . . That what the village and even the county cannot afford to stock, they must be able to borrow from a national or a district stock, the clientele of which is big enough to bear and to justify the necessary expenditure.

> The National or Central Library is, in the view of the Trustees, the keystone of the arch. . . . The aim of the Central Libraries in London and Dunfermline is . . . to supplement the meagre resources of the village and the county area.

Further on in his address Col. Mitchell discussed certain principles "gradually emerging as experience grows":

134

Applicants will not normally be supplied with books costing less than 6s or more than £2. . . . In general terms the system is intended to supply standard modern works on serious subjects of study. We do not as a rule supply books, which, having been superseded by subsequent works, have ceased to be of first-rate authority. . . . As a rule the best English book on a subject would be preferred to a book in a foreign language, and if no good English works exist a translation would be sent rather than the original. . . . Lives of living men would generally be excluded, since they are rarely if ever genuinely historical. . . . For similar reasons one would not supply the works of a contemporary poet who is not yet a classic.

Col. Mitchell added: "It is rare that an applicant waits a week from the time his post card is sent."

Then he referred to the possible development of the system "in relation to municipal libraries" and concluded:

Every book that is bought by public money should, during its period of activity in the intellectual sense and so long as its material strength allows, serve the maximum number of readers and spend the minimum number of days in the expensive harbourage of the library. A County or a Borough Library rate should be used primarily to subserve the general educational needs of the community and its reasonable demands for relaxation. The connoisseur, the antiquarian, the bibliophile, the literary dilettante must be content to get his books from a national store, the nation or the big district being the only unit rich enough to afford them. The isolated local institution has soared too high and burned its wings.

The Trustees decided in the first instance to limit the operation of the scheme to county areas in which rural library schemes were already established under section 5 of the Education (Scotland) Act of 1918. This meant that in June 1922 the Scottish Central Library for Students was serving some seventeen or eighteen county areas.

In July 1922 the Trustees decided to extend the scheme, after a year's working, to the remaining county areas. When Col. Mitchell's address was published by the Trustees in September 1922 he could write in the prefatory note:

It is enough to say that any reader is eligible who resides in Scotland outside those cities, burghs, or parishes in which a public library rate is levied.

It is then pointed out that readers in municipal library areas might still apply through the burgh librarian to the Central Library for Students in London.

Ultimately these areas also may be included in the Trustees' Scottish scheme.

The pamphlet containing Col. Mitchell's address, with an appendix indicating the type of book supplied, was distributed in November 1922, along with a leaflet of instructions to individual borrowers and a covering letter, to rural ministers throughout Scotland. "The Trustees," the letter said, "would be glad of your co-operation in making known the facilities provided by the Library to any who may be eligible."

A second edition of the pamphlet in January 1923 contained revised instructions for individual borrowers, a partly re-written prefatory note, and an enlarged appendix. The chief alteration in the procedure for individual borrowers is in the paragraph headed "Period of loan." Under the original instruction, "readers are permitted to retain books for a maximum period of three months"; under the revised procedure, "the normal loan period is one month, but extensions may be granted."

The appendix is "not a catalogue in the ordinary sense."

It is simply a record of books acquired up to December 31st 1922, in response to actual requests. The great majority have been specifically asked for; of the remainder, the bulk have been selected in response to requests for advice as to the best book or the most suitable set of books for an individual student or a reading-circle. . . . In the nature of the case, a catalogue is an impossibility, since the Trustees' system is to obtain books (provided they are of the right calibre) *as they are required.*

The point is well and truly driven home:

It is important to realise that the list in no sense represents a comprehensive collection in any one group. It is a plain record of books actually applied for and supplied.

The total stock of the Scottish Central Library numbered "only about 300 books" when Col. Mitchell delivered his address in June 1922; by September it had "increased to 650," by January 1923 to a thousand.

In June 1923 a conference was assembled by the Carnegie United Kingdom Trustees in Stirling to consider the possibility

136

of extending to burgh and parish libraries the service provided by the Scottish Central Library for Students. The opening address of the conference was given by Miss Haldane of Cloan and the proposed extension was outlined by Lieut-Col. Mitchell. In Scotland, he pointed out, according to returns received that year from a total of sixty-seven public libraries, there were

25 libraries with an income of less than £250 a year.
13 libraries with an income of less than £100 a year.
34 libraries which spend less than £50 a year on books.
42 libraries which spend less than £100 a year on books.

In the course of his address Col. Mitchell restated the main issue—in his own words, "the creation of a National Reference Library by post"—and reviewed the existing machinery: the Central Library for Students in London, and the separate Central Library for Scotland set up by the Carnegie United Kingdom Trustees two years before. For the time being the Scottish burghs and parishes were still required to make application to the London Central Library.[2] No charge was made for the service other than the cost of postage, but of the 160 public libraries in the United Kingdom who made use of the London service in the year 1922-3 "128 made voluntary contributions varying in amount from 10s 6d to £5, and totalling about £190. The only Scottish contributions shown in the current subscription list are from Dundee, Falkirk and Perth (totalling £3 11s 6d)."

Col. Mitchell then discussed the principle of supplying public libraries on a voluntary basis. First, nothing must be done which might encourage local authorities "to shirk their just responsibilities." He anticipated the danger that "obscurantist members of library committees" might, in the knowledge that "books of the proper kind" could be obtained on application at the cost of postage only, neglect the reference library and the more serious sections of the lending library in favour of ephemeral literature. He suggested then that "some charge should be made and that a preferential rate should be offered to those libraries which levy a rate of (say) 2d or more"; while at the other end of the scale "those very small libraries which have no real reference stock at all . . . the Trustees would probably treat exactly as they treated Rural Schemes, charging postage only, on the principle that for different reasons Reference Libraries were impossible in both."

[2] In the discussion that followed Col. Mitchell's paper it was emphasized that "the Central Library for Students in London was too remote to become an integral factor in Scottish Library provision."

As to the charges and the basis of contribution, Col. Mitchell preferred a contribution based *ad valorem* upon the actual borrowings during each year to one based *pro rata* upon library income, as it would take some account of the service rendered:

> I suggest, as an experiment, that all libraries which levy a 2d rate or upwards and spend a fair proportion upon reference books, be entitled to borrow books from the Central Library at the rate of 5 per cent. of the published net price, and that those which levy less than a 2d rate be, in the discretion of the Trustees, charged 7½ or 10 per cent. . . . The proportion of the net price would have to be taken from rates; but the Trustees have no objection to the postage, one way or both, being debited to the borrower, which is a common practice in the case of County Library Schemes.

Very few libraries, he estimated, would borrow more than fifteen or twenty books in a year, "at all events in the first year. . . . Their expenditure would, therefore, not exceed £1 (plus postage) on the 5 per cent. scale, and £2 on the 10 per cent. scale—not, I venture to think, an exorbitant charge when it is realised that it brings to individual readers £20 worth of books which would otherwise be unattainable."

Col. Mitchell discussed also the provision of books for adult classes, the minimum and maximum price of books supplied, and the scope of the Central Library system.

Subsequent papers at the Stirling Conference were "Possible means of co-operation between burgh and rural libraries" by E. A. Savage, city librarian of Edinburgh, and "The Central Library for Students in rural areas" by James Christison, Montrose.

There was some lively discussion at the conference, in the light of which the whole question was considered by the Trustees at their meeting in July. The Trustees were satisfied that the extension of the Scottish Central Library to cover Scottish burgh and parish libraries was widely desired, and they decided it should come into operation on 1 October 1923. In the conditions laid down by the Trustees Col. Mitchell's suggested scale of charges was abandoned, and only two classes of library were recognized: small libraries which manifestly could not afford to maintain an adequate stock of serious literature were required to pay postage only; the larger libraries, which had stocks which were normally adequate, but which required help "in respect of the more expensive works which are too little in demand to justify their purchase," would in addition pay five per cent of the cost of the works actually supplied. "It is left to the discretion of the local Library Committee whether the above charges are paid out of public funds, or charged (wholly or in part) to borrowers."

This then was the pattern of library co-operation in Scotland that was to remain for some fifteen or sixteen years. The Carnegie United Kingdom Trustees, by their central library policy, enabled the burgh and county libraries to possess jointly a pool of first-class books which they could not all own severally. Certain of the Scottish university libraries were prepared to lend books at the request of the Scottish Central Library for Students, and the National Central Library in London with its chain of "outlier" libraries was always ready to help.[3] With the extension of the Scottish Central Library service to burghs and parish libraries in 1923, the National Central Library ceased to have direct contact with any library in Scotland, other than "outlier" or university libraries.

Throughout, the initial principle, that books are bought for stock only when they are asked for, has been generally maintained. The library is entirely postal and it does not aim to be an "ideal collection." "At any given moment the actual stock is simply an accumulation of books supplied on actual applications," but "with the passage of time and the improvement in the book stocks of the public libraries, applications have increasingly tended to be for the rarer, more expensive and specialized books."[4]

In 1923 it was urged that "the Trustees should publish and circulate a catalogue of the books they were prepared to lend." This the Trustees were reluctant to do, for "once a reader understood the principle upon which applications were granted, he was sure within wide limits, of getting any book he asked for." Nevertheless, catalogues were issued in 1923, 1924, 1927 and 1931, and

---

[3] "An outlier library is one which undertakes to lend its books to other libraries through the agency of the National Central Library." The outlier library system was established through the foresight of the Carnegie Trustees, who from 1922 onwards made their grants to a special library conditional on the library's undertaking to make its books "available to readers in all parts of the country through the Central Library for Students, as the National Central Library then was." Among the first outliers were the Scottish Marine Biological Association, Millport, the Rowett Research Institute, Bucksburn, Aberdeen, and the Royal Scottish Society of Arts. (L. Newcombe, *Library co-operation in the British Isles* (1937), p. 75; CUKT, *Annual report 1923* (1924), p. 23).

[4] Stirling Conference Transactions (1923), p. 37; CUKT, *Report by the Advisory Committee on the Scottish Central Library for Students* (1947), par. 8.

a supplement to the last of these, a list of books added to stock from September 1931 to December 1936, appeared in 1937. Repeatedly it is underlined that the list "simply contains the names of books which have been bought in response to applications received. . . . Borrowers need have no hesitation in applying (through their Burgh and County Librarian) for books not mentioned in the list."[5]

The rule that "No book is supplied if its price is below 6s or above £2 2s, except in special circumstances" was not meant to deter the serious student.

> Books of a lower value than 6s are never purchased, simply because it is felt that there is no local library that cannot afford to purchase standard works that are published below this price. . . . [The rule] was framed to guard against frivolous requests for expensive books. "Special circumstances" will always be taken into consideration. From the point of view of the Trustees, indeed, it may often be a better investment to spend four or five pounds on an important monograph than to buy for the same sum four or five books of a more general nature. The monograph is likely to have a long literary life, while books of general interest are often quickly superseded. Students of history, especially, frequently require to consult works that have been out of print for fifty years or more. Such works may be difficult to obtain, and that only at a price considerably in excess of two guineas. It would clearly be a mistake to miss the opportunity of obtaining them for a national collection simply because the price was high.[6]

CO-OPERATION AMONG SCOTTISH LIBRARIES

Co-operation, in the form of inter-lending among the Scottish libraries, was more difficult to establish. The Public Libraries (Scotland) Act of 1887 specified certain categories of persons to whom books could be lent, and it was maintained that this detailed specification implied that books could not be lent to others. The interchange of books between public libraries was held to be illegal and as a result Scotland was the last area in Great Britain

[5] Scottish Central Library for Students, *List of books in stock at 15th September 1931* (1932), p. viii.
[6] W. E. C. Cotton, "The Scottish Central Library for Students": CUKT, County Library Conference 1926, *Report of proceedings* (1927), p. 104.

to establish a regional library system. The Scottish Library Association's long campaign to clarify the position and to establish the legal right of a public library committee to lend books and other library material to other library authorities, from the Dunblane conference of 1931 to the enabling Act of 1955, is traced in chapter 9.

Nevertheless, some libraries were prepared to make arrangements for the interloan of books. As early as 1900 in Aberdeen anyone entitled to borrow books from the public library was allowed on a payment of 5s per annum to borrow books (two at a time) from the university library, an arrangement that was claimed to be "the first of its kind in the country";[7] and in Glasgow in 1917 fifteen learned and scientific societies, such as the Scottish Aeronautical Society, the Institutions of Engineers and of Shipbuilders, the Mining Institution of Scotland, the Royal Technical College, Glasgow University, the Institute of Electricians, and the Electrical Engineers, accepted a suggestion of the Public Libraries Committee that permits might be issued at the public libraries to enable readers to obtain from these special sources books that were not available in the municipal libraries.[8]

A certain amount of interlending was organized by the Scottish Central Library for Students. Applications for books with a particular local connexion in Scotland were frequently transferred to libraries likely to satisfy them. A record of locations was kept, and in certain subjects libraries were invited to report their holdings. In 1937 a card catalogue of Scottish family histories was compiled at the Central Library from lists of holdings supplied by thirty-six Scottish libraries—a catalogue that "repeatedly proved its value as a means of locating material required by readers both within Scotland and beyond Scotland."[9]

The introduction of the regional library systems may be classed, according to Col. Newcombe, "among the five epochmaking events in the history of library development in the British

[7] Aberdeen Public Library, *Annual report* 1900. The librarian further reported there were already 16 subscribers, classified as follows: "cabinet-maker (employer) 1, clergyman 1, civil engineer 1, commission agent 1, doctors 2, ladies 2, draper 1, photographers (employers) 3, press reader 1, solicitor 1, teacher 1, writer 1—Total 16."

[8] Baillie A. Campbell, Convener, Glasgow Public Libraries Committee, in Library Association, *Public libraries: their development and future organization* (1917), p. 76-7.

[9] Letter from Scottish Central Library to all Scottish libraries, 10 March 1953.

Isles."[10] The first fully-organized system, the Northern Regional Library Bureau, came into operation in January 1931; it covered the four northern counties of England. By the spring of 1937 all England and Wales was covered by a network of regional bureaux.

In Scotland the first move towards a bureau was made in 1925 when the Scottish Library Association, at its annual meeting in Greenock, adopted a resolution, introduced by S. A. Pitt of Glasgow and seconded by G. M. Fraser of Aberdeen, which was remitted to the council with powers:

> This meeting expresses the view that, in order to render the national library resources as effective as possible, and to facilitate interchange between local libraries, it is desirable that a system of co-operative cataloguing of the books added to the public libraries of the country should be devised.

The council after a full discussion, decided to forward a copy of the resolution adopted at the annual meeting to the Board of Education Public Libraries Committee.

The Dunblane conference of 1931 recommended, among other things:

> That Public Library Committees should be empowered to enter into arrangements with other Library Authorities for the interloan of books and other library material.

During the year 1932-3 the council of the Scottish Library Association appointed a special committee to draft a regional library scheme for Scotland, and to make application to the Carnegie United Kingdom Trust for a grant to defray the cost of the scheme during its initial stages. A series of draft proposals for the establishment of a Scottish Regional Library Bureau was submitted the next year to the Trust, and the Trustees announced that:

> On the assumption that the Scottish scheme will be similar to those existing in England and Wales, they are prepared to make a grant of not more than £2000 towards the cost of providing a union catalogue.

[10] L. Newcombe, *Library co-operation in the British Isles* (1937), p. 83. "The other four are the Public Libraries Act of 1850, the abolition of the rate limit in 1919, the institution of the County Library service in 1915, and the establishment of the Central Library for Students— now the National Central Library—in 1916."

Almost nine years after this matter was first raised in Scotland, at a conference in the Heriot-Watt College, Edinburgh, on 24 January 1934, three resolutions moved on behalf of the Scottish Library Association by its president, G. W. Shirley, and seconded by Dr Savage, were unanimously adopted:

1. That this meeting is in favour of establishing a Scottish Regional Library Bureau to operate throughout Scotland; that membership of the Bureau be voluntary; and that the function of the Bureau be to promote co-operation between Scottish libraries.

2. That for the present the Bureau be situated at the Scottish Central Library for Students, Dunfermline.

3. That a Committee of Inquiry be appointed forthwith to prepare a scheme for the Bureau and to report at a future meeting of the Conference.[11]

The committee of inquiry sought the opinion of the Secretary of State for Scotland as to the legality of the proposed regional scheme, and representatives of the committee and the council of the Association were invited to the Scottish Education Department office in October 1934 to meet representatives of the local authority associations together with officers of the Scottish Office and the Scottish Education Department.

Thereafter the Committee of Inquiry on Regional Library Co-operation reported to a further conference of Scottish library authorities in Edinburgh on 30 January 1935. The conference agreed "that the establishment of a Regional Library scheme for Scotland is of great importance in the development of the library service and is a matter of urgency" and approved a draft constitution for a Regional Library Bureau for Scotland. "It was recognized, however, that the establishment of the Bureau could not be achieved until the necessary amendment to Scottish Public Library legislation had been secured."

The Carnegie United Kingdom Trustees generously offered a sum of £2000 towards the capital cost of the Bureau and in view of the legal difficulty consented to hold open their offer until 31 December 1936, later extending their time limit, first to the end of 1937, and later to the end of 1938. During 1938, the Scottish Library Association's committee of inquiry, in the absence of the necessary permissive legislation, decided to ask the Trustees "either (a) to extend the time limit once more, or (b) to release

[11] SLA, *Annual report* 1933-4 (1934), p. 12-13.

143

their grant (or part of it) so that an immediate start might be made with the compilation of the Union Catalogue while the negotiations for new legislation were proceeding." The Trustees were willing to consider the second alternative and a third conference of library authorities was held in Edinburgh in April 1939 at which it was resolved:

> That, pending a solution of the legal difficulty which has hitherto prevented the establishment of a Regional Library Bureau for Scotland, a start shall be made as soon as possible with the compilation of a Union Catalogue of books in Scottish libraries;

and that the administration of the Catalogue should be entrusted to a sub-committee of the committee of inquiry, to be entitled the Scottish Union Catalogue committee.

Miss I. A. Carbis, B.A., F.L.A., was appointed as editor and began her duties on 1 September 1939 in accommodation provided in the Mitchell Library, Glasgow. The committee intended to use the catalogue of the Glasgow Public Libraries as the basis of the Scottish Union Catalogue and to circulate copies of the Glasgow catalogues to the other Scottish libraries co-operating in the scheme, which would report their holdings and any additions. The outbreak of the Second World War modified this programme slightly. Eighty-one library authorities had agreed to take part in the scheme, but in the first instance slips were circulated to only twenty-two libraries.

These were divided into two groups, around each of which one of two carbon copies of the catalogue was circulated.[12] The eleven libraries in the western circuit were Lanarkshire, Airdrie, Clydebank, Paisley, Renfrewshire, Kilmarnock, Ayrshire, Midlothian, Dumfriesshire, Galashiels and Hawick. The eastern circuit comprised Falkirk, Stirlingshire, Clackmannanshire, Dunfermline, Fife, Kirkcaldy, Perth, Dundee, Arbroath, Aberdeen and Caithness. Galashiels, Stirlingshire and Clackmannanshire had to withdraw temporarily during 1941.

A copy of the Union Catalogue as it proceeded was made available in the Scottish Central Library for Students and soon proved itself invaluable.

For the portion of the alphabet covered by the Scottish Union Catalogue more than half of the books for which a search is

[12] Scottish Union Catalogue Committee, *Report of progress to* 15 *May* 1943 (1943), p. 2.

made are located, although the resources of only 23 out of 80 libraries are recorded, and the proportion would be much higher if the S.C.L.S. (which supplies from its own stock fully 75% of the books for which it is asked) were not used as the first line of supply. . . .

Many of the books which have been borrowed with its help could have been obtained in other ways—by purchase for the S.C.L.S., by borrowing from the N.C.L. or an outlier, or even, after protracted inquiry, from a library in Scotland. The great value of the Catalogue, is that it enables the S.C.L.S. to locate instantly books in libraries where their presence would never have been suspected.[13]

A table in the Scottish Union Catalogue committee's first report showed that 377 books had been lent by the libraries co-operating in the compilation of the catalogue during the year 1942-3. In the next year the loans arranged through the catalogue numbered 610. In 1944-5 the total was 807.

These figures are quite satisfactory, considering that by the end of 1944-5 only one-third of the alphabet was available for consultation at the Scottish Central Library for Students. To judge from past experience there will have been a very big increase in the use made of the Catalogue by the time that the whole alphabet has been covered and the holdings of more libraries have been incorporated.[14]

By 1942 it was clear that the catalogue could not be continued beyond April 1943, when the grant of £2000 given by the Carnegie United Kingdom Trust would be exhausted, unless fresh funds were forthcoming. In view of this the Union Catalogue committee decided to ask the Scottish library authorities to express in writing, as they had already expressed verbally, their willingness to subscribe to the cost of a Regional Library Bureau in accordance with the scale of subscriptions agreed at the conference held in 1935. There was, of course, no precise legal sanction for such contributions from burgh authorities. The counties and the counties of cities, as education authorities, possessed the power to contribute under section 9 (4) of the Education (Scotland) Act of 1918.

[13] ibid. p. 3.
[14] Scottish Union Catalogue Committee, *Annual report* 1944-45 (1945), p. 2.

The response to the appeal was encouraging. By 15 May 1943 £290 had been received. In the first full year (1943-4) subscriptions from 55 authorities amounted to more than £475, and the following year the amount received from subscriptions (£520) almost covered the year's expenditure.

Early in 1945 it seemed opportune "to reconsider the whole question of regional library co-operation." It was apparent that:

> The scheme which had been inaugurated on a temporary basis in 1939—pending the enactment of new legislation—could in 1945 be regarded as having established itself as a permanent agency to promote co-operation between Scottish libraries.

The Regional Library Bureau of Scotland was formally established at a conference in Edinburgh on 26 September 1945 when a resolution in the following terms was adopted: "This Conference approves the immediate establishment of the Regional Library Bureau of Scotland in accordance with the Constitution adopted by previous Conferences in 1935 and 1939."[15] There still remained some doubt as to the Bureau's legality, but it was clear that the interlending that had followed on the inception of the Scottish Union Catalogue had been to the general advantage of the library service as a whole, and there had been no official prohibition either of interlending or of the payment of subscriptions by the burgh authorities. "Commonsense has triumphed over a technical legal difficulty." The executive committee elected at the conference took over the work of the Scottish Union Catalogue committee, with the librarian of the Scottish Central Library as its *ex officio* honorary secretary. It was empowered to apply to the Carnegie United Kingdom Trust for a supplementary grant of £2000. This application was endorsed by the Trustees in December, and a first payment of £500 was made in the year 1946-7.

The future of the Scottish Central Library itself was at the time under discussion. At the Scottish Library Association conference at Hawick in September 1946, the chairman of the Carnegie United Kingdom Trust, E. Salter Davies, c.b.e., had delivered an address on "The future of the Scottish Central Library for Students." The Trust, he said, had decided that the time had come for a radical change in the administration of the Scottish Central Library for Students. The first step would be to form a responsible and representative body to govern the new library.

[15] Regional Library Bureau of Scotland, *Annual report* 1945-46 (1946), p. 1.

The conference decided "that the matter be remitted to the Scottish Library Association Council for consideration and report."

As a result the Trustees appointed a committee of fourteen, representative of the various interests concerned, with Professor Sir Alexander Gray, Professor of Political Economy in the University of Edinburgh, as chairman, and the librarian of the Scottish Central Library as secretary. Its report was completed by September 1947 and adopted by the Carnegie United Kingdom Trust. The report examined the relationship between the Scottish Central Library and the Bureau and noted:

> The Scottish Central Library acted as a clearing-house for Scottish inter-library loans until September 1945, when the Scottish Union Catalogue Committee reconstituted itself as the Regional Library Bureau of Scotland, and became nominally responsible for arranging Scottish inter-library loans. We have noted, however, that in practice, the Scottish Central Library has continued to function exactly as it did previously, and the Executive Committee of the Regional Library Bureau of Scotland has largely confined its activities to the compilation of the Scottish Union Catalogue and the raising of funds for this purpose. We consider it anomalous and undesirable that there should be two bodies, separately administered, with virtually identical aims, and therefore recommend that close consideration be given to the practicability of a merger of the Scottish Central Library and the Regional Library Bureau.[16]

This recommendation was studied both by the Carnegie Trust and by the executive committee of the Bureau and there was complete agreement on its desirability. At the second annual meeting of the Regional Council held in September 1947 it was agreed that when the time was ripe the bureau should be merged with the Central Library. The only question that remained was the timing of this amalgamation, and it was felt on both sides that it was advisable to await the recommendations of the Advisory Council on Education in Scotland, to whom the whole question of library provision in Scotland had been remitted.

The other main recommendations of the Gray Report were:

> (ii) The Scottish Central Library has firmly established itself as the natural headquarters of library co-operation in Scotland and should be assured of continued existence. It should not be merged with the National Central Library but should con-

[16] CUKT, *Report on the S.C.L.S.* (1947), par. 32-3.

147

tinue, as hitherto, to work in the closest co-operation and consultation with that Library. . . .

(iv) The Carnegie United Kingdom Trustees cannot be expected to maintain the Scottish Central Library much longer and the time is now ripe for its establishment on an independent basis, with a body of Trustees to hold its property and a governing body to manage its affairs. The governing body should be largely representative of the co-operating libraries.

(v) The objects of the Library, thus constituted, should be defined as follows:

(a) To maintain a reservoir of books to supplement the resources of Scottish libraries and to lend, at their request, books for study which cannot conveniently be obtained from other sources.

(b) To facilitate, and to act as a clearing-house for Scottish inter-library loans.

(c) To provide bibliographical information to Scottish libraries.

(d) To take such other action as will facilitate access to books and the development of co-operation (a) between Scottish libraries and (b) between Scottish libraries and libraries outside Scotland, in association with the National Central Library.

(e) To maintain a Union Catalogue of books in Scottish libraries.

(vi) Although the co-operating libraries should be expected to make some continuing contribution to the costs of the Central Library, the latter may legitimately look to public funds for the main part of its revenue.[17]

To review library co-operation in Scotland had been included by the Secretary of State for Scotland in his remit to the Advisory Council on Education in Scotland on 9 January 1947. The Carnegie United Kingdom Trustees accordingly passed the Gray Report to the Advisory Council as a memorandum of evidence, and a delegation from the Bureau appeared before the appropriate committee of the Advisory Council in September 1948, and received "a sympathetic and encouraging hearing." The Advisory Committee's report published in 1951, recommended, so far as regional library co-operation was concerned, that the Central Library should be administered by a Library Council for Scot-

[17] CUKT, *Report on the S.C.L.S.* (1947), par. 55.

148

land, that the Library "should hold the key position for the whole lending library system," that "its functions should include the completion and maintenance of the Union Catalogue system," and that apart from an annual grant from Treasury sources, a share of the expenditure of the Central Library should be borne by compulsory contributions from local authorities in proportion to their population.[18]

Meanwhile the Carnegie United Kingdom Trust were advised that their plans for the independent establishment of the Scottish Central Library need not necessarily be delayed for the report of the Advisory Council. Accordingly, the Gray committee was continued to draft a constitution for the library. This was subsequently approved and is now the governing instrument of the library. The principals of the four Scottish universities then in being (Aberdeen, Edinburgh, Glasgow and St Andrews) agreed to act *ex officio* as joint trustees of its property and the management of the library was to be in the hands of an executive committee representative of the various interests concerned.[19]

In their report for 1949 the Carnegie Trustees were able to announce that new accommodation had been found for the library in Edinburgh.[20]

The destined home of the Library is a typical Edinburgh "land" or tenement, known as Fisher's Close, on the south side of the Lawnmarket. The building, which is about two hundred and fifty years old, is scheduled for preservation as one of the historic buildings of the Royal Mile of Edinburgh, and the necessary work of securing the external fabric has already been carried out by the Ministry of Works on behalf of the City Corporation, which now owns the property and is willing to make it available for the purposes of the Scottish Central Library. Internally, the building is in a ruinous state and complete reconstruction will be required before it can be used for any purpose whatever. This reconstruction, for which the Trustees have agreed to make themselves responsible, is to take the form of the erection, inside the existing shell, of a new structure in steel and concrete, to which the old walls can

[18] Scottish Education Department, Advisory Council on Education in Scotland, *Libraries, museums & art galleries: a report* (1951).

[19] CUKT, *Annual report* 1949 (1950), p. 3.

[20] More than twenty-five years earlier the opinion had been expressed that "Dunfermline . . . was the wrong place for the library: it should be in Edinburgh" (D. E. Edward, Burgh Librarian of Ayr: Stirling Conference Transactions (1923), p. 21).

149

be pinned. Apart from surface work and the removal of derelict shop fronts at street level, the old facade is to be left unaltered. Behind it, a new building comprising of ground floor and five upper storeys should be able to meet the needs of the Library for many years to come.

It was also reported that the Treasury had agreed to ask Parliament to approve from 1 April 1949 a maintenance grant which, under the Goschen formula, would be eleven-eightieths of the grant provided for the National Central Library. The grant for 1949-50 amounted to £3100.

By 1951 the principals, as Trustees, stood possessed of the building at Fisher's Close, and on 1 July 1952 the administration of the library formally passed from the Carnegie United Kingdom Trust to its independent governing body, along with the book stock and equipment.

In the meantime the Regional Library Bureau of Scotland continued its independent existence and its work on the Scottish Union Catalogue. In 1948 it was decided "to suspend the 'circuit' method" of compiling the catalogue "after the letter H had been completed, and that thereafter the Editorial Staff should proceed to incorporate the balance of the following non-fiction stocks concurrently—Glasgow Lending, Edinburgh Lending and Lanarkshire."[21] The Carnegie United Kingdom Trust supplementary grant of £2000 was exhausted with the payment of the fourth instalment of £500 in the year 1949-50, but a further approach to the Trust was sympathetically received and the Trustees agreed to set aside the sum of £1000 "to enable the Bureau to continue its work during the period which must elapse pending the merger of the Bureau with the re-constituted Scottish Central Library." This supplementary grant was paid in two instalments of £500 each in the financial years 1950-1 and 1951-2.

Following the publication of the Advisory Council Report the Regional Council of the Bureau at its annual meeting in Aberdeen in September 1951 agreed to address a formal communication to the Scottish Education Department expressing the Bureau's satisfaction with the Advisory Council's references to its work. This communication also referred to the financial problem which would confront the committee, with the expiry of the final Carnegie Trust grant, and a reference was made to the possibility of a grant-in-aid from public funds to enable the compilation of the catalogue to continue without interruption. The Scottish Educa-

[21] RLBS, *Annual report* 1947-8 (1948), p. 2.

tion Department eventually agreed to help the catalogue financially and promised a grant-in-aid of £500 for the financial year beginning 1 April 1953, without committing itself to future grants.

By the middle of 1952 it seemed very likely that the merger of the Bureau and the Central Library would "become practicable in 1953."

The Bureau may be said to be nearing a momentous phase in its history, constitutionally as well as financially.[22]

Later in the year, when responsibility for the Scottish Central Library was transferred from the Carnegie Trust to the independent board of library trustees and an executive committee, the time appeared to be ripe for the long-delayed amalgamation.

At the annual meeting held in Airdrie in September 1953 the committee brought positive recommendations before the Regional Council of the Bureau:

(1) That this Council approves the unanimous recommendation of the Executive Committee that, as from 1st October 1953, the Scottish Union Catalogue should cease to be the responsibility of the Regional Library Bureau of Scotland and should become the responsibility of the Scottish Central Library. . . .

(2) That the Regional Library Bureau of Scotland shall be deemed to be dissolved, as from 1st October 1953.

The resolutions, moved by A. B. Paterson, city librarian of Glasgow, as chairman of the executive committee, and seconded by R. Butchart, city librarian of Edinburgh, as honorary treasurer, were adopted unanimously.

In 1953, when the Bureau was merged with the Scottish Central Library,

the Scottish Union Catalogue . . . recorded the locations of close on a quarter of a million books contained in over twenty-five Scottish libraries. As many of these titles show four, five, six, or more locations, it is safe to say that locations are known for over a million copies. This is no mean achievement and has opened up rich and previously unknown resources for students and serious readers throughout Scotland, and furth of Scotland.[23]

[22] RLBS, *Annual report* 1951-52 (1952), p. 2.
[23] RLBS, *A historical note* (1953), p. 3.

It is only since its establishment on an independent basis that annual reports on the work of the Scottish Central Library have been published. For the library's history before 1952 there are only the brief references in the Carnegie Trust reports and the bare statistics in the reports from the National Central Library.

For the greater part of its first thirty years the Scottish Central Library was wholly financed by the Carnegie Trust. In 1949 the Treasury made a grant-in-aid, and since then annual grants have been made, at first on a scale of eleven-eightieths of the grant voted to the National Central Library. The library continued to receive grants from the Carnegie Trust, however, but in approving their grant for 1953-4 the Trustees intimated

> that they felt obliged to place a time-limit, provisionally fixed at two years, on their commitment in respect of the maintenance of the Library.

It is the policy of the Trust "to assist pioneer enterprises, not to maintain them permanently."

As the Central Library is "the servant, the supplement of all other [Scottish] libraries," it seemed desirable "that Scottish libraries themselves should take over that part of the financial responsibility hitherto borne by the Trust."[24] The Library's executive committee expressed the hope that

> the goodwill earned by the Library over the past thirty years will be reflected in a willingness on the part of every Scottish library authority to bear its share of responsibility,

but recognized that in face of the continued existence of a 3d rate limit for the burgh libraries "it would be unrealistic to expect hard-pressed authorities to find contributions to a Scottish Central Library."

In the absence of new library legislation for Scotland the executive committee decided to seek an interview with the Secretary of State for Scotland to present its urgent case for a new Act that would

> (a) place the legality of inter-library lending beyond question, and (b) ensure a stable and adequate revenue for the Library from co-operating libraries.

[24] Sir Alexander Gray, letter in *The Scotsman,* 23 April 1955; SCL, *Annual report* 1953 (1953), p. 6.

By the middle of 1954 it became generally known that new library legislation was "under active consideration," and after a discussion between representatives of the library and officials of the Scottish Education Department, the executive committee invited the three local authority associations to appoint delegates to join in considering the financial position of the library "in view of the announced withdrawal of Carnegie U.K. Trust support at the end of 1955."

After discussion the local authority association representatives intimated their unanimous agreement on the following conclusions, subsequently ratified by their parent bodies:

(1) That financial contributions to the Library from Local Authorities should be calculated in ratio to population as determined on a particular date (e.g. 30th June).

(2) That these contributions should be made obligatory in new library legislation.

(3) That Local Authority representation on the Library Executive Committee should be increased to twelve, i.e. three additional representatives from each of the three Local Authority Associations. If, after a period of trial, the enlarged Committee should prove unwieldy, this Committee could be altered to form a Council, from which a smaller Executive Committee could be appointed.

(4) That, in the first year in which these recommendations took effect, the Local Authorities' financial contribution to the Library should total £5500; in the second year £6000; and in the third, fourth and fifth years, £6500 p.a.

(5) That the Local Authority financial contributions should be determined quinquennially.

These proposals the Executive Committee found highly satisfactory and they were welcomed

as convincing evidence that the importance of the Library's work was fully recognised by Scottish Local Authorities.

Eventually a clause in the Public Libraries (Scotland) Bill, which passed into law on 6 May 1955 as the Public Libraries (Scotland) Act, 1955, gave full legal sanction to the decisions the local authorities had already agreed to implement. As the Joint

Under-Secretary of State for Scotland pointed out, the section made "an informal agreement into a formal agreement."[25]

Since its establishment as an independent "non-statutory library authority," with the principals of the four older Scottish universities as *ex officio* trustees, the day-to-day management of the library's affairs has been in the hands of an executive committee representative of "a wide range of library, educational and local government interests in Scotland." By the original constitution the executive committee was to consist of not more than twenty-two members, but in 1955 when the local authority associations agreed to levy compulsory subscriptions to aid the library their representation on the executive committee was increased, as we have seen, from three to twelve so that the committee could number 31. Very appropriately the first executive committee appointed Sir Alexander Gray as its chairman, and he continued in that office until 1957. Scottish librarians and librarianship owe Sir Alexander much: a minor debt, but one gladly acknowledged, is his happy inspiration for the motto of the library, RAX ME THAT BUIK, adapted from the words used by the Rev. Dr John Erskine at a meeting of the General Assembly of the Church of Scotland in 1796.[26]

The library's new premises have been briefly mentioned already. A detailed description of the building and of its official opening on 5 November 1953 by the Duke of Edinburgh will be found in the annual report of the executive committee for the year ended 31 March 1954. The conference room was soon proved to be an excellent venue for the meetings of various "bodies and groups concerned with the promotion of libraries and librarianship in Scotland."

The actual removal of the library from Dunfermline to Edinburgh took place in October 1953: one newspaper described it as "'Operation Rubicon': Moving a library across the Forth."[27] Within a few months of the move to Edinburgh the committee noted "the benefits of functioning in the immediate vicinity of other important libraries in Edinburgh," with their rich bibliographical resources.

It would be difficult to think of a finer site for the Library. It stands on the Royal Mile, a few hundred yards west of St

[25] Public Libraries (Scotland) Act, 1955, sect. 2; House of Commons, Parliamentary debates, Scottish Standing Committee: Official Report, Public Libraries (Scotland) Bill, 26 April 1955, col. 47.
[26] See the entry for John Erskine in the *Dictionary of national biography*.
[27] *Dunfermline Press,* 12 September 1953.

154

Giles' Cathedral, the National Library of Scotland, and the Signet Library. Round the corner, in George IV Bridge, is the Central Public Library, and within a few minutes' walk is the Library of the University of Edinburgh.[28]

An advantage held in mind as the new premises were designed was the housing of the Scottish Union Catalogue (which as we have seen became the responsibility of the library with the dissolution of the Regional Library Bureau of Scotland) and its staff "as an integral and important department" under the same roof as the library. The physical transfer of the Catalogue took place in December 1953. Unfortunately at the removal Miss I. A. Carbis, editor of the catalogue since its inception in 1939, found she had to resign for health reasons.[29] A new editor assumed office in March 1954 and the year that followed was a "busy and productive one." At the end of the year the stocks of thirty Scottish libraries were wholly or partly included in the Union Catalogue —a total of 262,780 separate titles. In the year to 31 March 1955 over 102,000 entries were checked by the staff. Previously unrecorded titles numbered 18,399, while 84,372 duplicate locations were noted.

> The percentage of new titles ranges from as low as 8 per cent in the case of general stocks to as high as 25 per cent in more specialised collections. The new entries produced by the completion of Lanarkshire's catalogue, for example, amounted to 17 per cent, i.e. one title in six was new to a Union Catalogue of a quarter of a million entries. Paisley's stock produced one new title in ten, and Arbroath one new title in seven, showing that every library, regardless of size, has a unique quota to bring to the common pool. The duplicate locations thrown up are welcomed as a means of reducing the number of calls made on a few libraries which have hitherto borne the brunt of lending, and of distributing requests more evenly among co-operating libraries.[30]

It is obvious that the Union Catalogue must be "of inestimable value in tracing the whereabouts of books which the Library is asked to supply" and, as one would expect, the executive com-

[28] With the opening of Edinburgh University's new library in George Square in 1968 the walk has become a few minutes longer.
[29] Miss Carbis died in August 1968.
[30] SCL, *Annual report* 1955 (1955), p. 3.

mittee of the Central Library has agreed that it is "highly desirable" that the Catalogue be completed and kept up to date.[31]

One characteristic of the Scottish Central Library cannot be over-emphasized. Its stock of approximately 34,500 volumes "has not been built up as a planned or balanced collection." Its purchases are confined to "books for which it is specifically requested and which cannot, for one reason or another, be borrowed from some other source."

Nevertheless the library's policy in regard to book purchase has changed over the years. When the library was founded it was to provide books "to supplement the meagre resources of the village and the county area," for it was openly suggested that it was actually "improper—speaking generally" to include books for the more serious readers in the county library book stock at all.[32] Later it was made clear that while the library imposed few restrictions, it should not be necessary "to purchase for the Central Library books which ought to be in every Public Library."[33]

The restriction that the 3d rate limitation imposed on Scottish burgh libraries naturally affected the situation. To the executive committee of the Regional Library Bureau it was clear that if Scottish libraries were in a position to purchase most of the books in print which they were obliged to borrow from others, the Scottish Central Library would be

correspondingly freed to concentrate on its principle function, i.e. the supply and purchase of highly expensive, recondite or out-of-print books.[34]

In 1955 the executive committee of the Library hoped

that one early effect of the rate abolition proposed in the Library Bill will be an increase in local book funds which will reduce the calls made on the Scottish Central Library for new books in wide demand. The more generous provision of this type of book locally will in turn enable the Scottish Central Library to develop further its apparatus and capacity for tracing and supplying, from resources in Britain and abroad, out-of-print and obscure books and journals, in any period or

[31] ibid. 1954 (1954), p. 9; SCL, *Report of the Executive Committee's conclusions on the document "Recommendations on library co-operation"* (1955), p. 2.
[32] J. M. Mitchell, *The Scottish Central Library for Students* (1922), p. 7-8.
[33] SCLS, *List of books in stock* (1931), p. vii.
[34] RLBS, *Annual report* 1948-9 (1949), p. 4.

language. It is this last function which gives the Library its unique place in Scotland.[35]

And in a similar context the executive committee affirmed "the basic principle . . . that the Scottish Central Library does not buy a book if it can borrow it."[36]

It would appear that over the years the emphasis has gradually moved from the library's original function and the first of its stated objects: "To maintain a stock of books to supplement the resources of Scottish libraries . . ." to the second: "To facilitate and to act as a clearing-house for Scottish inter-library loans."[37] Indeed, on more than one occasion Sir Alexander Gray has underlined the uniqueness of the Central Library by pointing out that paradoxically "it is a library which need not possess books on its shelves."[38]

In the executive committee's first annual report, the library's principal function is defined thus:

> To endeavour to supply on loan either from its own stock, or from co-operating libraries, books which are not available to readers from their local libraries.

In the year 1954-5, 16,568 volumes were lent to readers through its agency.

> Bearing in mind the fact that all these books, often urgently required, would be unprocurable in the absence of machinery of this kind, it is clear that the service is of the highest value and cannot be measured in terms of finance.[39]

The twenty-nine Scottish county libraries and the service for the Isle of Man, which uses the Scottish Central Library, borrowed 9020 volumes; the burgh libraries borrowed 4748. The university and special libraries lent 1,176 and borrowed 743 volumes.

The number of university and special libraries using or co-operating with the Scottish Central Library in the years 1952-5 exceeded 50. In half of these cases the traffic was two-way. The libraries of the four universities and of Queen's College, Dundee, and New College, Edinburgh, both borrowed and lent. Over these

---

[35] SCL, *Annual report* 1955 (1955), p. 9.
[36] SCL, *Report of Executive Committee . . . on . . . "Recommendations on library co-operation"* (1955), p. 4.
[37] The constitution of the Scottish Central Library is printed as an appendix to the Library's *Annual report* 1953 (p. 17-24).
[38] *The Scotsman*, 23 April 1955.
[39] CUKT, *Report on the SCLS* (1947), par. 10.

157

three years these six libraries had borrowed just over 600 volumes while they had lent almost 2000 volumes (1568 volumes to other Scottish libraries and 415 to libraries outwith Scotland). Of this total Edinburgh university library alone provided 846 volumes, 603 for other Scottish libraries and 243 for libraries furth of Scotland.

Among others on the list are the libraries of the Teachers' Training Colleges, of the Colleges of Art in Dundee, Edinburgh and Glasgow, and of the Technical and Agricultural Colleges in both Edinburgh and Glasgow; there are the specialist libraries of research institutes, research associations, learned societies, and government departments. Most of these libraries have come to borrow from the Scottish Central Library, or to lend books through its agency, in a free spirit of co-operation to the mutual advantage of all. The executive committee would seem to be justified in its opinion,

that the machinery of the Library is well adapted to meet the needs of special libraries and research organizations in Scotland.

An indication of the library's international range is given in the annual report for 1955:

The books lent have come from all corners of Great Britain, and many from overseas. From Paris, books were lent to St Andrews University, Airdrie, Ayrshire, Edinburgh, Lanarkshire and Paisley. Cologne University lent books to Edinburgh, Stirlingshire, Queen's College (Dundee) and the Brown Trout Research Laboratory. Books were also lent to various Scottish readers by libraries in Berlin, Berne, Brussels and Rome.
The Library of Congress in Washington has been particularly helpful in lending American publications, not located in Scottish libraries.

Scottish libraries also lent books, at the request of the Scottish Central Library, to libraries throughout Britain and overseas. Caithness lent Reid's *Earls of Ross and their Descendants* to Copenhagen, Aberdeen University lent Macdonald's *Fairy Tales* to Czechoslovakia, Midlothian lent Dalyell's *Fragments of Scottish History* to Stockholm, Perth lent Keir Hardie's *Speeches and Writings* to Cologne. Other Scottish libraries lent books to France, Germany and Hungary.

Despite the Scottish Union Catalogue and the "good deal of miscellaneous information about Scottish library resources" that had been accumulated over the years, there were known to be certain books of Scottish interest for which the library had no location. As an experiment, in October 1952 a "Locations wanted" list was circulated to co-operating libraries. Any library holding any of the books listed was asked to report the fact to the Scottish Central Library, and every location traced in this way was noted in the Scottish Union Catalogue for future reference. One hundred and eighteen locations were notified for 43 of the 71 scarce books on the eight lists between October 1952 and March 1953. For many of the books, however, only a single location was found. There inevitably remained "a residue of Scottish items for which no location has been found" and a selection of these was listed in the executive committee's third annual report.

The Scottish Central Library carries on a variety of miscellaneous activities. On various occasions it has helped to "place" "duplicates, gifts of books, and surpluses brought to its notice," although it does not set out to supersede the work of the British National Book Centre.[40]

In July 1953 a questionnaire was circulated to Scottish libraries "asking for information on their holdings of Scottish newspapers, old and new." From the replies it was hoped to edit a union list of Scottish newspapers in Scottish libraries, to be issued as a printed catalogue. A progress report on the list was released in April 1955: over 350 separate Scottish newspapers had been reported from 45 libraries:

> The gaps in the list may be as important as the titles included. . . . No complete set has yet been reported of the *Edinburgh Evening Courant,* founded in 1718. . . . No public library seems to have a complete set of the *Inverness Journal,* the first newspaper in the Highlands, and issues for 1832-48 are unrecorded.

> If some current newspapers are not being preserved in any library, it is hoped that the deficiency may be made good in the future. Already, we suppose as a result of the inquiry, some libraries have come to realise the importance of such local records.[41]

[40] SCL, *Annual report* 1953 (1953), p. 9; for the BNBC *see* R. F Vollans, *Library co-operation in Great Britain* (1952), p. 9.
[41] *The Scotsman,* 30 April 1955. The list, *Scottish newspapers held in Scottish libraries,* compiled by J. P. S. Ferguson, was published by the Scottish Central Library in 1956, with a "characteristically witty and perceptive" foreword by Sir Alexander Gray.

A function of the Scottish Central Library not included in its constitution is to act as gad-fly to the less lively public library authority.

The Scottish Central Library has earned many tributes: one testimonial appeared in the correspondence columns of *The Scotsman* when it seemed that the Public Libraries (Scotland) Bill, 1955, was in jeopardy. Sir Alexander Gray had pointed out that the Scottish Central Library existed

> to get for readers books otherwise inaccessible, so that the remote scholar in Caithness may, if he needs it, get the use of a book of which the only known copy is in Plymouth.

A few days later a "remote scholar in Caithness" replied:

> The library is, indeed, unique. More than that, to a student outside a university town, it is indispensable. . . . It has got for me, with the minimum of delay, rare book of reference after book of reference. Nothing has been inaccessible, nothing too much trouble. . . .

> It will get a rare book for you more easily than will any of the great reading libraries and (as few of them will do) to your own fireside. If ever a library deserved help and encouragement, it is the Scottish Central Library—today one of Scotland's richest and most enviable treasures.[42]

The Scottish Central Library is primarily concerned, as was the Regional Library Bureau also, with the organization of inter-library lending in Scotland; but library co-operation is international, and there is a two-way traffic not only across the border but over the seas. In England and Wales there are the National Central Library and the regional library bureaux; in Scotland the Scottish Central Library is both central library and regional bureau. It is important that in Great Britain there should be a considerable degree of uniformity in policy and practice in the central libraries and in the bureaux. The National Committee on Regional Library Co-operation was formed in 1931 to ensure this desirable uniformity.[43]

In 1949 a joint working party of this National Committee and the National Central Library was set up—the librarian of the Scottish Central Library was one of its members—to consider

---

[42] Letters in *The Scotsman*, 23 and 27 April 1955.
[43] L. Newcombe, *Library co-operation in the British Isles* (1937), p. 98; P. H. Sewell, *The regional library systems* (1950), p. 28.

160

means of improving the efficiency and the comprehensiveness of the system of library co-operation in Great Britain. An independent survey of the existing position was commissioned and undertaken by R. F. Vollans, depute city librarian of Westminster. His report appeared in 1952.[44]

The report is in two parts. Part one records "the facts as the Surveyor saw them; the second part attempts to evaluate these facts and produce suitable recommendations." The surveyor emphasized that his recommendations were confined to England and Wales, "since concrete proposals concerning library co-operation in Scotland are already contained in the recent Report of the Advisory Council on Education in Scotland"; but his survey contains several references to Scotland. The history of inter-library lending in Scotland is briefly summarized, there is a note on the Scottish Union Catalogue, and another on the finances of the Scottish Central Library and the Regional Library Bureau, and there is an extremely interesting analysis of the system at work—a survey of the inter-library loans on a selected day. The service of the Scottish Central Library emerges from the scrutiny in a way that goes far to justifying the claim that the library "in degree of coverage and effectiveness is unrivalled anywhere in the world."[45]

A series of recommendations, largely based upon the Vollans Report and again primarily for England and Wales, was drafted by the joint working party. Both documents, nevertheless, contained conclusions equally relevant to Scotland, and their recommendations were considered in detail at a special meeting of the executive committee of the Scottish Bureau. In the light of comments made by interested parties final recommendations were issued in June 1954 in the names of the National Central Library and the National Committee on Regional Library Co-operation. The recommendations, it should be said, involved no "major changes." "The general structure of library co-operation and inter-lending is sound."

The recommendations were carefully studied by the executive committee of the Scottish Central Library, and a report detailing the committee's conclusions was submitted in 1955 to the annual meeting of contributories to the library. The executive committee recorded its agreement with the recommendations in almost every case, although there were certain reservations. For example, the suggestion that entries for British books could be notified to

[44] R. F. Vollans, *Library co-operation in Great Britain* (1952).
[45] W. B. Paton, letter in *The Scotsman*, 23 April 1955.

regional library bureaux by means of British National Bibliography numbers was turned down "in view of . . . the fact that many Scottish libraries do not take the B.N.B."

One important recommendation suggested

> that each region should consider what co-operative arrangements can be made to ensure that all applications to the bureaux for current British material, except for material in excluded categories, are supplied from resources within the region,

and the executive committee, in agreeing, authorized the preparation of "an outline of a Subject Specialization Scheme for Scottish libraries."

Again, in accepting the recommendation that "as much material as possible should be made available for loan," the executive committee agreed that it was "desirable in principle that books in Public Library Reference Collections should not be rigidly excluded from the inter-library lending system," but held the Mitchell Library, Glasgow, "to be in a special category."

The Scottish Library Association's Scottish Fiction Reserve Scheme is mentioned and the "valuable *Union Catalogue of Periodicals in Edinburgh Libraries.*"

A recommendation with which the executive committee concurred suggested that

> no charge should be made to readers for any service rendered by the inter-loan service, except for notifying readers that books have been obtained.

This is perhaps a minor question, but it is one in which uniformity is desirable. The whole scheme of library co-operation seems a little ridiculous, if it is found that neighbouring libraries —sometimes a burgh library and a county library in the same town—observe different principles in this matter.

The recommendations finally "at the risk of re-stating the obvious" affirmed that

> the most effective contribution which the individual library can make to the success of library co-operation is to improve its own book-stock and its service to its own readers.

CHAPTER 7

SURVEYS AND REPORTS:
DEVELOPMENT OF SERVICES

(1) SURVEYS AND REPORTS

FOR SIXTY-FIVE YEARS, from 1850 to 1915, there was no
official survey of the library services in this country. In the
forty years following the Adams report of 1915 there were no
fewer than six surveys, undertaken or sponsored by the Carnegie
United Kingdom Trust (the Mitchell report, 1924), a Departmental Committee of the Board of Education (the Kenyon report,
1927), the Library Association (*A Survey of Libraries,* 1938, and
also the McColvin report, 1942), the Scottish Library Association
(the Minto report, 1948) and the Advisory Council on Education
in Scotland (the Advisory Council report, 1951). The reports vary
in importance and impact, but viewed in succession they indicate
in a general way how library services developed over these
forty years. The Adams report has been dealt with in chapters 3
and 4; the Advisory Council report will be considered in chapter 9.

THE MITCHELL REPORT

In 1924 the Carnegie United Kingdom Trustees published *The
Public Library System of Great Britain and Ireland, 1921-23,* a
report prepared for them by their secretary, J. M. Mitchell, as a
sequel to the Adams report of 1915. Its purpose was "to
summarise the present position and to indicate new lines of
development"; its occasion, "the rapid growth of the County
Library Policy and the consequent importance of a full and early
inquiry into the future co-ordination of the borough and the
county service." The report pointed out that the disappearance of
the penny-rate limitation—abolished in England and Wales and
raised to 3d in Scotland—"in itself would justify a new edition of
the Adams report."

The first part of the report discussed "Arguments for co-
ordination." The basic principle of the county library service was
re-iterated:

163

The aim of the Rural Library is to take books to villages whose inhabitants *cannot visit any central library*. . . . In so far as . . . a central county library is desirable—and, of course, it *is* desirable—it should be housed in, and be part of, an existing Borough Library.

This was the first argument which suggested co-ordination between the borough (stationary) and the county (circulating) scheme. There was also the case of the smaller stationary library:

Even the meagre box of fifty fresh books renewed four times a year, distributed by the local teacher (who is at least an educated man or woman), is vastly more efficient than a derelict stationary library in charge of a caretaker. . . . In the Trustees' view the only hope . . . in cases like these is co-ordination with a vigorous county scheme.

Several examples were then given to show how co-ordination could be mutually profitable. One was the case of Forfarshire.

In this county there is one library belonging to the relatively small class of those which are rich enough to stand upon their own feet—that of Dundee, which from a 2d rate enjoyed an income (to September 1922) of £10,468 (plus £315 from other sources), bought (or replaced) books to the value of £1996, and paid a bill for salaries and wages of £5531. Beside Dundee there are in Forfarshire four old-established Burgh Libraries—those of Arbroath, Brechin, Forfar, Montrose. . . . A total population of 47,509 spent a total of £2386, of which only £199 (8.3 per cent) went in purchase of books, and £801 in salaries to nine officials. £196 was spent on newspapers and periodicals.

Here . . . co-ordination is obviously required, but in Dundee there is a library which should serve as the pivot and centre for the whole county, including the admirable county scheme which for some time past has been with growing efficiency supplying the villages of Forfar and Kincardineshire (where there is no public—burgh or parish—library). The desiderata here are even more simple of achievement, thanks to the Dundee stock of nearly 200,000 volumes. A joint County Committee, representing Dundee, the four burghs, and the joint County Library Committee of Forfarshire and Kincardineshire, should be able to set up a system of co-operative service—with the Scottish Central Library for Students in

164

reserve—which could be a model of economy and efficiency, so far, i.e., as concerns the lending system solely which is all that, at present, the Rural scheme attempts to provide.

Here is a plan for regionalization almost on the McColvin scale. The point the report sought to drive home was that "the money spent in the smaller towns would be far more productive if there were a business-like system of co-ordination."

The report then glanced at the rates levied since the limit was abolished or raised, and indicated the extent to which authorities had taken advantage of their increased rating powers. Of the 64 Scottish libraries whose figures were analysed, 49 had exceeded the penny rate, but 15 (10 burghs and 5 parishes), or 23.4 per cent of the Scottish libraries still levied a rate of 1d or under. (In England and Wales the comparable percentage was 17.6.)

In considering staff salaries the report pointed out:

One fifth of these 445 libraries have a total salary-list of less than £100; 186 (more than two-fifths) of less than £300—the minimum imposed by the Trustees for the librarian only in all County schemes where more than 100 centres are served. Only 206 (less than a half) pay more than £500, and of these all but 28 are in England.

In Scotland the number of libraries with a total salary list of less than £100 was 25, or just over two-fifths of the number of Scottish libraries reporting. Thirty-seven (or 60.7 per cent) had a total salary bill of less than £300, and only 18 (or less than 30 per cent) paid more than £500 in salaries.

It would seem to be clear that ratepayers in very few towns are paying salaries such as are likely to attract men and women who are competent to guide the great mass of the reading public. In about half the public libraries of the country the chief posts are apparently less attractive, financially, than those which are offered by County Library schemes. The argument for co-operation in these cases is surely conclusive.

The fourth topic discussed was the provision of newspapers and periodicals. Attention was drawn to the surprising number of libraries where more was spent on newspapers and periodicals than on books. The report was emphatic that this was wrong:

The casual reader of the daily press who spends an hour or so studying the sporting and athletic columns costs a great deal more (and on the average contributes a great deal less)

165

than the steady reader who borrows three or four books a week. It would seem, therefore, that admitting to the full the value of the news-room, a Library Committee has a case for giving prior consideration to the other departments.

In this respect Scotland was shown to be neither better nor worse than the country as a whole. Approximately two-thirds of the libraries submitting returns had spent more than half as much on newspapers and periodicals as they had spent on books.

The final section of chapter 1 of the report summarized the data concerning rent, rates and taxes, "a special question . . . of much importance before the removal of the limit of the library rate." With the passage of time the problem largely resolved itself. By the 1950s libraries and similar public buildings were usually rated, although they were, however, exempt from the payment of Income Tax under Schedule A.

At the time of the Mitchell report, only 7 out of 59 Scottish libraries were paying rent, but on the other hand only 4 were free of rates. The report considered it "an anomaly" that so many libraries (in Scotland 93.3 per cent)

are called upon to pay back to the local authority a greater or smaller contribution out of the very rates which are levied for their upkeep.

The Kenyon report, on the other hand, justified the principle and pointed out that

the public libraries which at present escape that burden [of rates] probably owe their exemption to the circumstance that the rating authority does not enforce the liability. . . .

So far as rates on public libraries are concerned the cost of a remission of rates falls either on the ratepayers who support by their payments the public library or on some other body of ratepayers. In the former case payment of rates becomes mainly a matter of book-keeping. In the latter case the case against exemption is stronger since exemption means the payment of part of the cost of the library by ratepayers who are not liable for its support.[1]

The second chapter of the Mitchell report was concerned with the "External Relations of Public Libraries," and set out to show

to what extent Public Libraries are extending their usefulness

[1] Kenyon report (1927), p. 56.

166

by co-operation with one another, and with external institutions, especially educational bodies.

Out of 430 libraries, it was reported, 174 (or 40 per cent) still confined their service to residents—the percentage for Scotland alone was much higher, 37 out of 64, or 58 per cent—the remainder making provision for extra-urban readers, usually on the basis of an annual subscription "varying as a rule from 2s 6d to 5s (in a few cases, 10s 6d)."

The interesting point here is that although there is legal authority for lending libraries in England and Wales to be made available "to persons not being inhabitants of the district, either gratuitously or for payment," the Scottish library authority has no power to make such a charge.[2] On the other hand, it has no explicit powers to make its books available at all to persons who are not householders or inhabitants of the district, other than to persons carrying on business or employed within its area or to the inmates of certain kinds of institution therein.

The report later discussed a similar question, the extension of a library service to the

> person who neither resides nor is rated, but works daily within the rated area,

and pointed out that it seemed

> reasonable that the borough should make some charge in this type of case, particularly if borrowing facilities are granted . .; there could be no complaint against a charge of 1d to 3d per volume, or an annual subscription.

Here again the report's recommendation ran counter to Scottish library law, for the Public Libraries (Scotland) Act of 1887 specifically authorized the extension of library services at the Committee's discretion "to any person carrying on business within the limits of the Burgh or Parish, or to any employee engaged in employment therein, although such person or employee may not be a householder, and may not reside within such limits," without, however, suggesting any modification of the general principle that all libraries should be open to the public free of charge, and that no charge should be made for the use of books or magazines issued for home reading.[3]

[2] Public Libraries Act 1892, sect. 11 (3); Public Libraries Consolidation (Scotland) Act 1887, sect. 32.
[3] Public Libraries Consolidation (Scotland) Act 1887, sect. 21, 32.

The report continued with an examination of the use that public libraries made of the central libraries, a survey of the relationship between libraries and a variety of educational agencies, the provision of lectures and collections of books on local industries, and a note on library hours. In the course of this, reference is made to the *ad valorem* charge for service rendered that the Trustees had imposed on Scottish public libraries using the Scottish Central Library for Students and to the collections of books "bearing on local industries" in the libraries at Dunfermline ("a large collection useful for those engaged on damask art-designs") and Aberdeen ("all books relating to the granite and fishing industries").

A list of rural library schemes "existing or in immediate contemplation" immediately preceded the 80 pages of statistical tables. The costs of sixteen county schemes in Britain, all of which had been in operation for more than three years, were tabulated and analysed, with a naive pride in the fact that

> one only exceeds the product of a $\frac{1}{2}$d rate, and that by an inconsiderable fraction in a county which has an abnormally low rateable value (Cardiganshire). Two others have levied roughly a $\frac{1}{4}$d, and the other thirteen range from one-fifth of a penny down to one-tenth.

It is interesting to find in the tabulation no separate column for expenditure on books and binding. This is explained in footnote and commentary:

> The Trustees have in all cases made an initial grant for the purchase of books believed to be sufficient for the first five years. Some counties have, even before the end of that period, purchased further supplies of books out of the County rate. Eventually annual purchases of books will have to become a regular item of expenditure. . . .

> It is only now being discovered what additional expenditure will be necessary for book purchase, as the original stock is gradually worn out. It is noteworthy that quite substantial sums are included for this purpose in the (very modest) aggregate totals of six counties.

The statistical tables, "offered as a quarry for the student, and as a general guide to the position of the library service," have provided material for the statistical appendix to this study.

The reviewer of the Mitchell report in the *Library Association Record* called it "this all-important conspectus of the public libraries of the country, separately and collectively as they exist today." It formed a sequel to the Adams report of 1915:

The essential fact emerging from consideration of these two reports is that individualism, an admirable quality in youth, has had its day in the public library movement, and that all hope of future progress lies in co-operation. The success of the rural library and the comparative failure of the small urban library are indications that cannot be ignored.[4]

It is an indication of the contemporary relevance of the Mitchell report that today it is largely forgotten: its conclusions are, to a great extent, embodied in present-day practice.

THE KENYON REPORT

The *Report on Public Libraries in England and Wales* prepared by the Departmental Committee appointed by the President of the Board of Education was issued in 1927. The committee had been appointed in October 1924

to enquire into the adequacy of the library provision already made under the Public Libraries Acts, and the means of extending and completing such provision throughout England and Wales, regard being had to the relation of the libraries conducted under those Acts to other public libraries and to the general system of national education.

The committee's chairman was Sir Frederick Kenyon, principal librarian of the British Museum, its secretary C. O. G. Douie, and its members included Mr (afterwards Sir) John Ballinger, librarian of the National Library of Wales, E. Salter Davies, director of education for Kent and a Carnegie Trustee, Dr Albert Mansbridge, founder of the Workers' Educational Association, Lt.-Col. J. M. Mitchell, secretary of the Carnegie United Kingdom Trust, Frank Pacey, honorary secretary of the Library Association, and S. A. Pitt, librarian of Glasgow Public Libraries.

At the outset of the report the committee drew attention to the fact that "between the years 1850 and 1924 no Committee was appointed by the Government with terms of reference specifically relating to public libraries."

The appointment by Mr Charles Trevelyan, the President of the Board of Education, of this Committee in the autumn of

[4] *Library Association Record,* vol. 2 (N.S.) (1924), p. 19.

1924 marked an interest on the part of the Government in public libraries such as had not been manifested for three-quarters of a century.

The report is a document of the first importance, and although the committee's terms of reference limited its scope to England and Wales, and its recommendations are made with the conditions in these countries in view, the report is both relevant to Scottish libraries and has had a marked influence on Scottish conditions. More than twenty years later, for example, the Scottish Library Association was quoting this report in support of its opposition to the Advisory Council's recommendation of the transfer of public libraries to the control of education committees.[5]

The report begins with a brief historical introduction which pays tribute to the "liberal spirit" which inspired the report of the Select Committee of 1849.

The "present state of library provision" is then reviewed:

So far as the inclusion of the population within library areas is concerned, the position may be regarded as very satisfactory. But unfortunately a library area does not necessarily provide a library service. . . . Nor does the existence of a library service necessarily imply that the service is in any way adequate.

After careful consideration the opinion is expressed

that there comes a point where economic factors become so strong as to defeat the efforts of any community to provide itself with an efficient library. . . .

A very relevant factor is the remuneration which a small community can offer to a librarian. . . . Clearly the great majority of library authorities with a population under 20,000 are not in a position to offer a remuneration which a trained librarian can accept. . . . On the whole we consider that any town of over 20,000 inhabitants must be regarded as able to maintain a library in a reasonable state of efficiency. We have assumed this figure throughout our report.

It is interesting to note that this same figure of 20,000 was adopted by the Scottish Library Association at a later date.[6]

[5] SLA, *Statement . . . on the Report of the Advisory Council . . .* (1951), p. 4, 6.
[6] SLA, *Statement on essential requirements of new library legislation* (1947). clause 3.

170

The urban library service, the county library system, and special libraries are then discussed in lucid detail, and an outline of an organized national service follows. Its principal elements are:

(i) co-operation, on financial terms varying according to the circumstances, between neighbouring libraries, whether they be borough, urban district, or county libraries;

(ii) the grouping of public libraries round regional centres, which will generally be the great urban libraries;

(iii) a federation of special libraries pooling their resources in the service of research;

(iv) acting as centre of the whole system, a Central Library.

The "linking up of co-operating libraries into larger groups, each centred on some great library which may be conveniently described as a regional library" is a recommendation that has not been fulfilled quite in the manner the report suggests, but the regional library bureaux embody the principle here enunciated.

A specific recommendation that the Central Library for Students should be supported by Government grant was implemented without undue delay, although the committee's scheme that the library should become "a special department of our greatest national library, the British Museum," was not accepted. The Central Library for Students was reconstituted in 1931 as the National Central Library, and was granted a Royal Charter in the following year.

The report's remaining chapters deal with adult education, library law and a number of miscellaneous items. The establishment of a central cataloguing agency is suggested; it is noted as desirable that public libraries should adopt either the Dewey Classification or that of the Library of Congress; select lists and bibliographies are discussed; recommendations are made on the supply of government publications to public libraries; and the question of a discount for libraries on the purchase of new books is considered. This last recommendation was implemented when the Library Licence Agreement became effective in 1929. This was a joint agreement of the Publishers' Association, the Booksellers' Association and the Library Association to the effect that libraries which "grant access to the public free of charge" and spend more than £100 per annum on new books may receive a licence which entitles them to receive from the booksellers named in the licence a commission not exceeding 10 per cent.

171

The report is particularly sound in its statement of the aims and functions of the library service:

Even now we should not venture to say that the possibilities of the public library are always adequately recognised.

The public library should be the centre of the intellectual life of the area which it serves. That intellectual life covers all stages, from the incipient curiosity of those whose intelligence is only beginning to awaken to the advanced research of the highly-trained specialist. The library has to serve not only the earnest seekers after knowledge, but also those who are merely gratifying an elementary curiosity, and those who are seeking relaxation and recreation. . . .

The librarian aims, therefore, at supplying recreational literature of as good quality as his public can digest; at placing at their disposal the information necessary for the ordinary duties of a citizen; and at supplying all their needs for intellectual culture and for the knowledge that they require in their several professions and occupations. It is his duty to see that, so far as the means placed at his disposal permit, the books that they require, whether for recreation, for information, or for research, are on the shelves of his library. . . .

The function of the public library is to supply, or to assist to supply, books for the use of (a) the young, (b) the ordinary adult public, (c) the adult student in organised classes, (d) individual adult students, (e) the technical worker and those who need special information for commercial and business purposes. . . .

It may be convenient if we set out here the aims which, in our opinion, those responsible for a county library policy should have in view: —

(i) To relieve the tedium of idle hours quite irrespective of intellectual profit or educational gain. It is sufficient to satisfy this purpose that the rural inhabitant should be rendered a happier (and not necessarily a more learned) man by the provision which is made for him.

(ii) To secure that the taste for good English which should be acquired in the elementary school is kept alive and developed by a provision of good literature after school years have ended.

(iii) To enable the rural inhabitant to acquire, without diffi-

172

culty, that general knowledge which alone can enable him to appreciate to the full what he sees and hears.

(iv) To impart that knowledge of public affairs and of the history of his own neighbourhood which a citizen must possess if he is to perform with intelligence his duties as a member of the community ultimately responsible for the government of the parish, rural district, county and country.

(v) To provide facilities for the study of the arts, trades and professions which constitute the occupation of the inhabitants.

(vi) To remove as far as possible all obstacles from the path of the serious student of any subject.[7]

The characteristic freedom, independence and informality of the library movement is repeatedly referred to:

It is of the essence of the public library service in England and Wales that (apart from the limitations of finance) it has grown up in an atmosphere of freedom. . . .

We believe an atmosphere of freedom to be an essential condition of healthy library progress. Compulsion can only lead to resistance, to grudging compliance, to resentment, which will ensure unpopularity for the very idea of a library. Persuasion and example are the stimuli on which we should rely. . . .

Tempting as it may be to use compulsion in order to turn a bad service into a good service, the Committee are not convinced that compulsion would have that result. It is contrary to the whole spirit of the library movement, which has derived its main value from the fact that it is a spontaneous growth. . . .

The essence of intellectual culture is freedom, and the strength of the library movement as it exists today lies in the liberty which admits of experiment and of adaptation to local needs, and in the encouragement of initiative on the part of able and experienced librarians.[8]

Outstanding, too, is the report's insistence on the importance of the "able and experienced librarian":

For the large majority of the population the librarian and his staff are the guides who introduce them into the kingdom of

---

[7] Kenyon report (1927), p. 39, 40, 44, 95.
[8] ibid. p. 49, 38, 108, 148.

knowledge. For such a service no qualifications can be too high, while it is a disaster to the community if they are too low. It means that a potential mechanism of cultivation is running at less than its full power, and that the country is obtaining much less than full value for its library expenditure. . . .

For the welfare of the library service it is essential to recognise that librarianship is a learned profession.[9]

The report also includes tributes to the generous benefactions of Andrew Carnegie and the Trust he established, and to the foresight of Professor Adams, on whose report county library policy had been based.

The Kenyon report was not only "a most valuable and lucid survey;"[10] it was and it has remained an influence and an inspiration. The first object of the report, and its great achievement, was "to establish the public library service as a national service and to emphasize its national importance."[11] The service we know today derives much of its form and its strength from this report.

THE LIBRARY ASSOCIATION'S *Survey of Libraries*

During 1936 and 1937 the Library Association, with financial assistance from the Rockefeller Foundation, organized a survey of the library service at home and abroad, in which Scotland was covered in three reports—Northern Scotland by Duncan Gray, South-West Scotland (along with North-West England and Northern Ireland) by A. S. Cooke, and South-East Scotland (with North-East England) by R. W. Lynn. Gray found in the area he surveyed, Scotland north of and including Edinburgh, "libraries and librarianship in every stage of development from the completely ineffective to the well-nigh perfect." The buildings were on the whole good. He specially mentions the two new libraries at Kirkcaldy, the Sandeman Library, Perth (then undergoing alteration and extension), Dunfermline, with a recently-opened children's room, Buckhaven (opened in 1935) and Fraserburgh, "a modern building made very attractive by a small but tastefully-planted garden." He commented pointedly on the "numerous

[9] Kenyon report (1927), p. 78, 79.

[10] W. A. Munford, *Penny rate* (1951), p. 51.

[11] Sir Frederic Kenyon in Proceedings of the Fiftieth Anniversary Conference of the Library Association . . . Edinburgh . . . 1927, *Library Association Record*, vol. 6 (N.S.) (1928), p. xvi*.

evidences" of over-building and deplored "the indiscriminating acquisitiveness of certain of the local authorities in accepting gifted buildings without counting the cost in upkeep and administration charges."

The surveyor referred with surprise to the continued existence in one of the larger city libraries of a " 'book club' with an annual subscription of one guinea," and recorded that in the "Reference Corner" of one of the very small libraries "two of the more important books were the ninth edition of the *Encyclopaedia Britannica* and an eight years old *Who's Who.*" The reference library at Falkirk and the music collection of Aberdeen County Library were particularly commended. In discussing the rebinding of books, mainly undertaken by book-binding contractors, he mentioned that "the cost of transport from the Shetland Islands is so heavy that books are not rebound but discarded when rebinding becomes necessary."

In two cases Gray found the county librarian was also burgh librarian: "an obvious wisdom in areas where there are small scattered populations and low rateable values." On the other hand, he recorded his disapproval of three cases where "the county librarian was a part-time officer, his main occupation being his other office."

> It was hardly surprising to find that in one such library the views of a firm of booksellers as to suitability of novels was sought and accepted unquestionably on the grounds that the experience of this firm was such that no unsuitable book was offered for purchase—in effect a guarantee of suitability.

The one-man library was fairly common, and Gray expressed his surprise that "at least two of these one-man libraries were extremely efficient within their limits,"

> but the presence of a card catalogue at one of them was made possible only by the supply of catalogue cards with the books by a library bookseller.

He was worried by the problem of getting "information on technical matters to small libraries with inexperienced staffs" and suggested "establishing recognised correspondents to whom the librarians of smaller libraries might be induced to write more fully and freely," the correspondence to be reinforced by personal visits "in cases of special difficulty."

Gray pointed to the "pressing need for guidance in book selection" and urged the Library Association "to help librarians, particularly of small isolated libraries, in the selection of suitable books by compiling and distributing carefully constructed and well-annotated book lists."

In south-east Scotland the surveyor, R. W. Lynn, found that the "small burgh and county libraries between Edinburgh and the Border," in a large proportion of which "several factors in combination militate against efficiency," approached "in very few instances . . . the recognised minimum standards for a modern library service." Over-building, "for the district is one in which Andrew Carnegie made numerous grants," was one but not the chief cause of the low standard of library provision.

> In many of the small burghs the proportion of the income required to maintain the fabric is so large that any development of other essential parts of the service is impossible. Thus book funds are generally inadequate to a pitiable degree, and there are far too few trained and qualified librarians and assistants among staffs which are very small numerically.

The rate limitation must be removed before real progress could be made and there must also be "much closer co-operation among, or perhaps amalgamation of, small authorities in neighbouring districts."

Lynn considered that no library in south-east Scotland was adequately staffed.

> That the librarian-caretaker-cleaner is still found in many libraries indicates that the status of librarianship is very low. There are instances in which the entire administration of the library, including book-selection, is carried out by the committee, without reference to any professional guidance. Salaries of officers employed in the small towns vary from £30 to £100 per annum with house, ignoring one where the librarian has accommodation on the premises but no salary, and the highest salary paid in this area is £300 per annum. There are county libraries of considerable size and income in which the entire staff consists of the librarian and in more than one instance this officer is expected to perform other duties in the education department. In one county where the expenditure on books amounted to £2000 per year, the librarian worked alone for the majority of the time because no assistant would stay for long at the low wage offered.

Several authorities, however, provided services "which are remarkable when all the difficulties are understood." The surveyor praised Hawick, "an example of economic efficiency" with "a fine special Border collection," and Galashiels, "while ratepayers in Kelso, Bo'ness and a few other places cannot complain that they do not receive full value for their expenditure on the public library."

While the surveys of northern and of south-east Scotland are not exactly flattering, their measured criticism is near enough the mark to be both just and acceptable. On the other hand, the survey of south-west Scotland by Miss A. S. Cooke raised an immediate outcry. So many of its statements were so wild and sweeping.

There was a dreary sameness about all the buildings. A stuffy staleness and an odious smell of scented disinfectant pervaded nearly all of them. One had the feeling that air and sunlight were never admitted. . . .

No new books have been added to the libraries for years. What books are on the shelves are filthy dirty and worn to shreds. The so-called reference libraries are worse than useless as they contain no up-to-date books at all. . . .

The librarians are as a rule part-time caretakers. . . .

I am convinced that had I been a resident within the area of my survey I should not have registered as a borrower at any of the libraries, with the exception of the Mitchell Library, Glasgow, or the new County Library of Lanarkshire. . . .

In Scotland, particularly, little effort seems to be made to recruit to the service assistants holding the qualifying examinations. Therefore they take little interest in the work of the Library Association and enter the library service only because it is something to do in their own home town. The majority appear to be without ambition and as they look round at the library service in the area it is easy to understand that to them the Library Association examinations seem "highfalutin" and useless. There is certainly little incentive to make them want to study. . . .

The book stocks throughout the area were in a woeful condition—dirty, out-of-date, laden with germs, dog-eared, and without any attraction whatsoever. That people borrow the books at all shows what a real desire for reading there must be.

Perhaps the most distressing factor was that so many librarians were quite complacent about it, had presumably never seen anything different, and took it for granted that it must be so. . . .

Only a small proportion of the libraries have separate children's rooms. . . . As a general rule the children's books were shelved in a corner of the lending library, and were shabby and very tattered.

The cumulative effect of these criticisms was so damaging and so unfair to the reputations of many reasonably good libraries, that it is not surprising that at the Scottish Library Association annual meeting in September 1938 the following resolution was moved by W. B. Paton, then burgh librarian of Airdrie, seconded by the Rev. R. P. Fairlie, Dumfriesshire, and after some discussion carried unanimously:

That this Annual General Meeting of the Scottish Library Association deplores the publication of Report 2 on libraries in South-west Scotland in the *Survey of Libraries* published by The Library Association, on the grounds that the Report is untrue and misleading, and requests (1) that the *Survey of Libraries* be immediately withdrawn from circulation, *or alternatively,* that an official repudiation of Report 2 on libraries in South-west Scotland be published in *The Library Association Record,* and (2) that a re-survey of the libraries in South-west Scotland be made and published, and that a copy of the new Report be issued to all subscribers to the *Survey of Libraries* for replacement or correction of the original Report 2.[12]

In considering this resolution the council of the Library Association asked for "a statement of the facts which are alleged to be misrepresented in the Report," and this was duly prepared and submitted.[13] The Library Association, in reply, refused to withdraw *A Survey of Libraries* but invited the Scottish Association to produce a survey of the area which the Library Association would undertake to publish. The Scottish Council felt this did not meet the requests made in the original resolution. They argued that the onus of preparing any report or survey arising from the published report rested with the publishers, but the Library Association refused to undertake any further survey.

[12] SLA, *Annual report* 1938 (1939), p. 9. See also the letters of protest from the librarians of Motherwell & Wishaw and Coatbridge, *Library Association Record,* vol. 40 (1938), p. 519-23.
[13] *Library Association Record,* vol. 41 (1939), p. 12-19.

As a result a motion went forward to the 1939 annual general meeting of the Library Association:

That this Annual Meeting of The Library Association repudiates Report 2 (Part 1) in *A Survey of Libraries* published by The Library Association, on the grounds that it is untrue and misleading, and instructs the Council to publish and issue to all subscribers without delay a new Report embodying the facts contained in the report sheets on which the original Survey was based, supplemented by re-inspection of the area.

The motion was carried by a large majority, and later a joint committee of six, three nominated by the council of the Library Association and three by the council of the Scottish Library Association, was formed "to make a preliminary survey of the whole question and offer suggestions on procedure." The joint committee's first meeting was called for 7 September 1939, but with the outbreak of war it was cancelled, and the committee never met.

At the end of 1941 the Scottish Library Association asked the emergency committee of the Library Association when it was proposed to take action in the matter and was met with a new suggestion—that an article should be written by Mr McColvin based upon a recent visit to south-west Scotland in connexion with another survey. The Scottish Library Association council agreed to this suggestion provided that the article be submitted for the scrutiny of their officers prior to publication, and that off-prints of the article, along with copies of the 1939 resolution, be circulated to all purchasers of *A Survey of Libraries*. As the Library Association considered these proposals "impracticable," the Scottish council resolved to let the matter drop, and so this international dispute ended.

THE McCOLVIN REPORT

The origins and occasion of the McColvin report of 1942 are explained in its introduction, and its scope is indicated by its title and sub-title: *The Public Library System of Great Britain: a report on its present condition with proposals for post-war re-organization.* Lionel R. McColvin, city librarian of Westminster, and at the time honorary secretary of the Library Association, was asked by the emergency committee of the Library Association "to devote six months to a study of war-time conditions and post-war possibilities." It is emphasized that the report as published "unless and until it receives approval . . . has no 'official' status."

This is a personal report, incorporating the impressions and views of one man.

But as one would expect from "the outstanding librarian of his generation," the impressions are vivid and accurate and the views are radical and provocative.[14] The McColvin report must be studied with care and attention: its importance cannot be exaggerated.

Certain impressions of Scottish libraries emerge from the report. In the course of his journeys and visits the surveyor "had the privilege of attending a meeting of the Council of the Scottish Library Association," and among other acknowledgements he thanks in particular the honorary secretary of the Scottish Library Association, W. B. Paton, "who arranged every detail regarding my most interesting visit to Scotland."

Chapter V of the report is entitled "Scotland" but it deals solely with the legal position and problems—difficulties that are, as the surveyor points out, "not so easy to explain—or even, for a Sassenach, to understand." Nevertheless, "so far as one can judge by visits to several and a study of the data concerning many more, Scottish libraries as a whole can be compared not unfavourably with those of England."

There are some interesting references to Scottish libraries throughout the report. In the survey of urban library systems Perth and Dunfermline are cited in the group serving populations between 30,000 and 40,000, along with Pontypridd in Wales and Kidderminster in England:

All four enjoy the services of keen and capable librarians, this resulting in clean, well-arranged premises, sound, well-chosen stock and a general air of efficiency and purpose. It is such active libraries as these which have in the past provided the arguments in favour of maintaining the independence of these medium-small authorities. No doubt there are several other examples—and no system of re-organization would be desirable that did not recognize their value and achievement and seek to increase their sphere of influence rather than to limit it.

Nevertheless there are certain features which make present achievement possible but which also may militate against

14 The phrase is Dr Munford's (*Penny rate* (1951), p. 54).

further development. Only one of the four has any branch service (though in two it is certainly needed); the librarians have wisely concentrated on doing well the first and most important part of their task—but this does not mean that the rest has not to be attempted in due course. Only one has any loan charges to bear (and here they are small). None pay good salaries to their assistants. Two enjoy substantial funds from endowments or trusts (in one case equivalent to nearly 12 per cent of the total expenditure). Two expend over 2s per head of population. One raises a rate of nearly 4d, another of 3d, a third of over 2d, plus a substantial contribution from the county.

In McColvin's next group, serving populations between 40,000 and 50,000, "three good Scottish libraries . . . illustrate the effect of the 3d rate limitation. . . . One of them reaches the limit but 1d goes on art galleries and museums, so that the library gets a maximum of a 2d rate; one—tell it not in Gath—considerably exceeds it; the third is only $\frac{1}{4}$d short."

In the next group, the burgh of Motherwell and Wishaw, McColvin found, spent up to the legal limit;

but what is done is well done in two most attractive libraries —one, an old building recently modernized, the other a striking new building admirably situated. About 9d per head is spent on books.

In the next group again, Paisley and Greenock are commended.

It is interesting to note that McColvin found in Scotland the only instances of the combination of authorities for library purposes, although all library authorities enjoy the right to combine. That these examples of combination should have been found in Scotland is of particular interest in view of the fact that at the time Scottish libraries were not empowered to co-operate fully with one another.[15]

The third and most striking part of McColvin's report is his "Proposals for the future," in which he suggests and describes a new organization for the public library service in the United Kingdom with 93 library units to take the place of the 604 existing library services.[16] In this scheme Scotland is divided into nine

[15] Legal sanction was only given by the Public Libraries (Scotland) Act 1955.
[16] McColvin's proposals are considered at length in V. D. Lipman, *Local government areas, 1934-1945* (1949), p. 347-50, 420-8.

THE LIBRARY UNITS PROPOSED FOR
SCOTLAND IN THE McCOLVIN REPORT
(1942)

1.

2.

3.

4.

6.

7.

8.

9.

Aberdeen

Dundee

Dunfermline

Dumbarton

Paisley

Glasgow

Edinburgh

Hamilton

Ayr

IRELAND

ENGLAND

182

units. Before giving details of the proposed units the report emphasizes:

We do not suggest that this is an ideal and final scheme. On the contrary, we hope it can be improved as a result of discussion and suggestions from those with a more intimate knowledge of the circumstances of each area. . . .

The primary objects of this list are to demonstrate, in concrete terms, exactly what we mean by the unit system and to show that it is a practical, workable, complete project.

The Name of the Unit is in each case merely a suggestion. As a rule we have avoided using the name of an existing library authority so as to remove any impression there may still be that the unit system means the taking over of one authority by another; it does not mean this—it means the creation of new areas.

Certain parts of Great Britain, it is pointed out, offer special difficulties. In Scotland "four of the units—two in the North and two in the South, cover exceptionally wide areas. This cannot be avoided owing to the absence of large towns suitable as main libraries. The two Highland units in particular will need to develop a sound transport system in which sea, and even air, communications will be utilized to supplement road and rail."

Here, then, is McColvin's plan for Scotland:

Name of Unit & Headquarters	Composition of Unit	Total Pop. in thousands	Grade of Unit
1. NORTH SCOTLAND Aberdeen	The Counties of Aberdeen, Banff, Caithness, Inverness, Kincardine, Moray, Nairn, Orkney, Ross and Cromarty, Sutherland, Zetland	682	2
2. WEST SCOTLAND Dumbarton	The Counties of Argyll, Bute, Dunbarton (less Clydebank), Stirling	359	4
3. ANGUS and PERTH Dundee	The Counties of Angus and Perth	393	3
4. FIFE and DISTRICT Dunfermline	The Counties of Clackmannan, Fife, Kinross ...	324	4
5. GLASGOW and DISTRICT Glasgow	Glasgow, Glasgow Parish, Clydebank, Rutherglen, Cadder Parish	1221	1*
6. CLYDESIDE Paisley	The County of Renfrew ...	317	4

183

Name of Unit & Headquarters	Composition of Unit	Total Pop. in thousands	Grade of Unit
7. SOUTH-WEST SCOTLAND Ayr	The Counties of Ayr, Dumfries, Wigtown, The Stewartry of Kirkcudbright	436	4
8. UPPER CLYDE Hamilton	The County of Lanark *except* those areas allotted to Glasgow and District	463	3
9. EDINBURGH-TWEED Edinburgh	The Counties of Berwick, East Lothian, Midlothian, Peebles, Roxburgh, Selkirk, West Lothian	799	2*

* denotes a Regional Library.

McColvin elaborated his plan in considerable detail, to show how these library units would be organized and financed, how they would function, and how they would be staffed.

A plan on this scale cannot be criticized in a sentence. With its general principles there is considerable agreement: the greater efficiency of a larger unit is conceded, although there may be some misgivings over the dangers of remote control, if an area is too large. It is its detailed application—particularly to the sparsely populated areas of Scotland—that is contentious. The Scottish Library Association council after careful deliberation, "while expressing appreciation of the vision, thought and diligence brought by Mr McColvin to the formulation of comprehensive proposals . . . agreed that the project as a whole was on too ambitious a scale and too revolutionary in principle to gain for it the approval of the authorities by whom the necessary decisions would be made."[17] The council felt that McColvin's proposals were "impracticable in Scotland." The Advisory Council on Education went farther and maintained they did not even deserve "serious consideration."[18] But the idea of "regionalisation," as it has been called, is still alive.

The "North Scotland" area of the McColvin report (with the omission of Kincardine) was the subject of a special survey carried out during April 1948 for the council of the Scottish Library Association by C. S. Minto, then deputy librarian, Edinburgh Public Libraries, and the first paragraph of his report, *Public Library Services in the North of Scotland*, can be quoted as a valid criticism of McColvin's proposals:

[17] SLA, *Annual report* 1943 (1944), p. 15.
[18] Advisory Council report (1951), p. 47.

184

In suggesting that this area is fitted to become one of his proposed new library "units" Mr McColvin has apparently been guided more by a desire to embrace a population in keeping with standards he set for units in England than by his own proviso that the unit "shall as far as possible embrace a natural congregation of people and be related to their ways of living and their normal comings and goings." That I take to mean that the unit's main library should be situated in a town habitually resorted to by the population concerned or at least easily accessible to that population. It is only necessary to point out that the Outer Isles are over two hundred miles and, more important, over two days by normal means of travel from Aberdeen, to show the impracticability of this vast area as a "unit." The physical features of "North Scotland" make for a natural segregation, not a natural congregation, of people. . . . In such circumstances theoretical limits of numbers to be served are of purely academic interest and development must be related as closely as possible to existing population grouping and interests, giving due consideration to possible future changes. The islesman of the Hebrides is out of a different mould from the fisherman of the east coast and —north of the Great Glen—possibly the only feature they have in common is that each lives in a static community of extremely narrow geographical limits. Social life in such communities springs from within rather than from without, and the villager can, at best and under any organisation, choose his books only from a small deposited or itinerating collection. His recreational reading needs can be reasonably met in this way. For more serious reading and research he has access to the whole book stock of the country through the Scottish Central Library. What virtue then, of sufficient magnitude to outweigh administrative complexities, lies in regionalisation? To strengthen the Scottish Central Library organisation and improve the present county services, rather than add to the financial burden of book supply a whole supervisory staff of big guns and little guns firing broadsides from a hundred or two miles away, would seem to offer more solid prospects of practical advance.

THE MINTO REPORT

The Minto survey was undertaken, indeed, as a direct result of the Scottish Library Association council's belief that the proposals of the McColvin report were "unworkable in Scotland."

It originated in a suggestion made by W. E. C. Cotton, librarian of the Scottish Central Library for Students, in his presidential address to the Scottish Library Association in 1945:

> If we are to advise local authorities effectively we must have at our disposal up-to-date information of what the libraries are doing, and this information must be of unimpeachable reliability. I believe that we can ensure its possession only by collecting the data for ourselves. The published results of surveys undertaken by other people, useful and stimulating though they have been, show how easily visitors with an inadequate background of knowledge may be misled. If we cannot at present undertake a survey of the library services of the whole of Scotland, can we not attempt a survey of a region covering the territories of several authorities, preferably including some of the sparsely populated parts of the country where the provision of adequate services is admittedly difficult? The results would enable us to make constructive proposals to set against those advanced in the McColvin Report and in the proposals published by the Library Association in 1943 which we believe to be unworkable in Scotland.[19]

A survey committee was appointed, and with the assistance of the Carnegie Trust the survey was made and the report published.

The report describes in detail, county by county, the library services Minto surveyed, in a region "more difficult to serve than any other in this Kingdom."[20] He went everywhere, it seems, and saw everything. His comments are shrewd, forthright and illuminating, and display an attractive sense of humour.

In general, despite the north's "long experience of insufficient budgets for library services," the surveyor found evidence of "real efforts to improve matters."

> New headquarters, though perforce in adapted buildings, have recently been occupied by Aberdeen, Banff, Ross and Cromarty and Shetland while replanning is in progress in both Caithness and Orkney. The counties which have little prospect of early improvement are Moray, Nairn, Inverness and Sutherland. The independent burgh services are faced with the prospect of steady retrogression until such time as the rate limit is removed. . . .

[19] SLA, *Annual report* 1946 (1947), p. 28-9.
[20] L. R. McColvin, "The North Scotland Survey," *Library Association Record*, vol. 51 (1949), p. 109.

There is wide variation in the degree of cleanliness tolerated in the books themselves, some systems being good in this respect but far too many are shockingly bad. . . .

Book selection standards show similar wide divergence, many systems buying poor quality fiction much too freely. This last criticism applies equally to burgh and county systems. The main failing of the latter, taking a wide view, lies in the smallness of deposited collections which are commonly of fifty volumes or less and much too infrequently changed. It is only fair to say, however, that the majority of the county librarians are alive to these shortcomings and will rectify them as soon as possible.

The statistical tables that follow summarize the general position. They are accompanied by a note urging that they should be used with "much more than average caution." For example, the "curious item" of £46 for *Salaries and Wages* for the burgh authorities in Sutherland

consists of £7 salary and £39 wages in Dornoch. The £7 is an allocated amount from the Town Clerk for supervision. The librarian's emolument of £39 is certainly for part-time services only and is supplemented by the provision of a free house, but it is interesting to note that, regarded as per head expenditure, even this pittance represents a sum greater than the whole library expendiure per capita of many burghs and counties.

The figures for *Book Stocks and Issues*

show an overall provision of roughly 140 books per 100 of the population—not bad on paper but quite illusory in fact.

Recommendations, first put forward in some detail, are summarized in the following terms:

1. The development of existing county library services and of co-operation between them.
2. The complete co-ordination of burgh and county services throughout the area.
3. The merging of the present separate services in Moray and Nairn.
4. The creation of a joint service for the shires of Ross and Cromarty and Sutherland.
5. The reorganisation of the present joint scheme of Inverness burgh and county under one chief official.

6. The creation of a Central Scottish Library Advisory Authority with power to make grants to local authorities.

7. A sliding scale of grants designed to create satisfactory and uniform standards of service throughout the area.

8. The recruitment of trained and qualified personnel.

9. The employment of mobile lending libraries in suitable areas.

10. The expansion of the Scottish Central Library's services, and of postal services generally.

In the detailed recommendations a further suggestion is made when the amalgamation of Moray and Nairn is under discussion:

Quite possibly the most satisfactory solution of this problem and one advantageous to all three counties would result from the amalgamation or close co-operation of Moray-Nairn with Banff. A network of good roads covers the whole of this area which seems one that would lend itself well to the use of a mobile lending library or libraries.

Another important suggestion that does not appear among the summarized recommendations concerns Lewis and Harris. The authorities for Inverness-shire and for Ross and Cromarty should consider the advisability of Ross and Cromarty's taking over the library service in Harris and of Stornoway's supplying all centres in both parts of the island. A Stornoway experiment of 1929 and 1930 is recalled with approbation:

Catalogues and request slips were issued to twenty-seven sub-postmasters in all districts [of Lewis and Harris] and the request slips, which provided for three alternative choices, were returned by readers to the postmasters for forwarding to Stornoway. Regular dates were organised and books were forwarded, individually addressed in special envelopes, in batches by bus or carrier to the sub-postmasters. In the first year of working over 8000 books were issued, and though the second year was not completed before finances "dried up" this figure had been exceeded. A steady demand for reading was being adequately met for the first time, and it is extremely regrettable that the experiment could not be continued. The counties of Ross and Inverness should jointly consider its revival.

The recommendation concerning the use of mobile libraries is important:

In Caithness, Ross, Moray, Nairn and Banff service could be greatly improved by the use of mobile lending libraries as there is a sufficiency of suitable roads in these areas. . . . The success of the Stornoway request scheme, while it lasted, lay in comparative wideness of choice even though that choice was from a catalogue. There is no reason to doubt that a similarly sized collection of *books* would prove still more attractive. A carefully selected stock in a mobile library, even if the size of the vehicle were restricted by the necessity to accommodate it to narrow and winding roads, could comprise about 1000 volumes and would provide a stimulus to reading that has so far been lacking.

The last recommendation, in its summary form, reads perhaps a little strangely. It follows, however, from a reference to the Library Association's proposal for the development of "regional reference libraries."[21] The surveyor, having pointed out that in Scotland "reference needs in so far as they can be met by travel are already well catered for," goes on to say:

Behind every library in the country stands the excellent service of the Scottish Central Library for Students most of the work of which lies in the supply of books for research. . . . The Scottish Central Library . . . is now one of the cornerstones of the whole Scottish Public Library service and the keystone of research in the remoter parts of the country. Its expansion and development . . . are of the utmost importance.

Perhaps the most important of Minto's recommendations are numbers 6 and 7, which urge "the creation of a Central Scottish Library Advisory Authority with power to make grants to local authorities," and "a sliding scale of grants designed to create satisfactory and uniform standards of service throughout the area." If the standard rate of grant is 100 per cent, by the "sliding scale of grants" he proposes "Orkney, Caithness and Shetland might receive a 120 per cent grant, Ross and Inverness 140 per cent and Sutherland 150 per cent."

The question, he points out,

is not one of how many people are included in a given local authority's area or of how much per head a given authority

[21] Library Association, *The public library service: its post-war reorganization and development* (1943), p. 10.

can spend, but of whether the authority can afford, from its own resources, a sum sufficient to meet certain basic costs.

The Minto report was generously reviewed by McColvin:[22]

This is an excellent document, highly creditable to both the Surveyor and the S.L.A. It is realistic, courageous, clearly presented and well produced.

The reviewer underlines the central problem of these sparsely populated and impoverished counties:

For a proper appreciation of the problem it is not enough to note that the average expenditure per head in every one of the counties is much below the average for Great Britain and Northern Ireland, or that in poor counties it is less than one shilling, or that in only two counties is the average expenditure per head on books, periodicals and binding together higher than the Great Britain and Northern Ireland average for books alone. What matters is that a threepenny rate levied over the whole area would not produce as much per head as *half* the average per capita expenditure for Great Britain and Northern Ireland.

He examines the effect of Minto's proposed grants-in-aid, "not in criticism of Mr Minto's recommendations but, instead, to support them—and, especially to urge that they must be considered *as a whole.*"

McColvin points out in conclusion that the Minto report is "essentially 'moderate' and based upon the appreciation of things as they are."

The report provoked much interest and immediate improvements in many services in the area were "directly attributable to the effects of the survey."[23] At Banff the burgh library became "an important branch of the very active County service"; in Caithness replanning and stock revision were undertaken at Wick; and the Ross and Cromarty county library planned to provide a mobile library for Lewis. In Sutherland the county library was reorganized and branches were opened in autumn 1952 in several towns that had had little or no service of books for many years. Improvements such as these, it was felt, showed "a tangible return

[22] *Library Association Record,* vol. 51 (1949), p. 108-9.
[23] SLA, *Annual report* 1950 (1951), p. 7.

on the Association's interest and on the Carnegie Trust's generous financial backing of the *Report*."[24]

It was the Minto report, the least pretentious—but most specific—of these various surveys, that had the most noticeable and immediate effect. The McColvin report was a major contribution to the developing "public library idea." In both cases the report was the result of an individual librarian's field-work. The Library Association's team of surveyors did not attempt to elaborate recommendations: their work has its historical interest. The Kenyon report, inspiring as it is, and the Mitchell report have at times the somewhat unreal quality that any report must have that relies largely upon statistics and memoranda instead of first-hand information.

(2) DEVELOPMENT OF SERVICES

Over the years library practice in general has tended to become less formal and more flexible: the invariable trend has been "from the static to the mobile, from the inconvenience of the fixed to the convenience of the elastic."[25]

Index cards have replaced ledgers for accessioning and cataloguing; in arrangement the fixed place in bookcase and shelf has given way to a relative position to other books; methods of recording issues have been evolved from a ledger page to the mobility of the book card; our ancestors chained their books, we permit the readers to select freely and carry them away.

OPEN ACCESS

In this move to greater freedom and flexibility no step has been more important than the introduction of free or open access.

What is known as the free or open access system in libraries means simply the absence of barriers between readers and books. The term is used to distinguish between two methods: the old, under which readers selected books from catalogues,

[24] In 1964 Mr Minto made a second tour of public libraries in the north of Scotland and recorded his impressions in an article "Sixteen years on," published in *SLA News* (no. 66, September/October 1964, p. 3-16) with "related comments from the librarians of the authorities concerned" (p. 17-20).
[25] G. W. Shirley, "Presidential Address": SLA, *Report . . . May-December, 1934* (1935), p. 28.

191

lists, etc., and made application for them; and the new, that of admitting readers direct to the shelves.[26]

In December 1892 James Duff Brown, the Edinburgh-born and Glasgow-trained librarian of Clerkenwell Public Library, writing anonymously, contributed to *The Library* an article, " 'A Plea for Liberty' to Readers to help themselves," in which he formulated his ideas on the "safeguarded open-access system."

> The outstanding fact and universal cry in all popular lending libraries, is not only that borrowers cannot get the books they want, but also that they cannot chance upon any book likely to suit them, owing to catalogues being mere inventories, and the existence of all sorts of barriers, which make the selection of books a heart-break and a labour tinctured with disgust. . . . What lending libraries want, in addition to a less suspicious method of dealing with the public, is a better means of making their book-wealth known. . . . The proposal simply amounts to this: *Let the public inside, and place the staff outside, the counter.* . . . The book shelves are ordinary standards about seven feet six inches high, raised nine to twelve inches from the floor by a narrow step, and spaced about six feet apart. In these the books are closely classified according to subjects and authors (in the case of fiction), and properly numbered and marked. . . . The whole to be so plainly labelled and marked, that only the blind would be unable to find a given subject— author or number. . . . The educational value to the readers would be enormous, and the popularity and standard of reading of every library would be largely increased.

Brown introduced his system at Clerkenwell in 1894. Thirteen years later Aberdeen Public Library issued a *Special Report on Indicators, Open-Access, and other Methods of Lending Library Work* in which it was stated:

> Few libraries that have once adopted Open Access have gone back to the former arrangement.

Nevertheless, the report pointed out that Bishopsgate Foundation Library in London had abandoned the system, because of losses, excessive wear and tear, and misplacement; that Hyde had followed the same course for the same reason after three years' trial; and Chester also, after six months' trial with "disastrous results."[27]

[26] Kenyon report (1927), p. 68.
[27] Aberdeen Public Library, *Special report on indicators* . . . (1907).

In Scotland by 1900 "partial" open access had been introduced in the lending department of Aberdeen Public Library, where in the reference department there had been open access "to 700 reference books and all new additions" three years earlier. Several Scottish libraries, Edinburgh, Perth and Arbroath among them, had granted this unrestricted access to selections of suitable reference books, and a few small libraries had thrown open the whole of their reference collections.[28]

Montrose Public Library, officially opened by Andrew Carnegie in October 1905, was the first in Scotland to adopt the open-access system from the start. At a meeting of the public library committee in January of that year, Mr John Strong, rector of the Academy, initiated a discussion on the indicator and the open-access systems in lending libraries, and asked for a report "as to the merits and demerits of the two systems." A month later the committee heard the rector's report "of his recent visit to London where he inspected several Libraries, and saw the various systems of issuing Books in operation." His inquiries had led him to favour the system known as "Safeguarded Open Access," and the committee agreed unanimously to urge upon the town council the desirability of adopting this system.[29] Councillor John G. Milne, who supported the rector throughout, was to tell the Scottish Library Association at its annual meeting in Montrose in 1914 that at this time, when they had been "swithering between whether to make it an open-access Library or an indicator Library, . . . their Chairman, Rector Strong, . . . had the good fortune to fall in with the late Mr Duff Brown, who was really the final cause of their Library being an open-access one."[30] Councillor Milne regarded that "happy step" as being the means of making the library.

Nevertheless, despite this example and the claim made by another speaker at the Montrose conference, that "in these days open access needed no champion; it had proved its worth," the closed library was the rule rather than the exception until the early 1920s.[31] Many readers who use the open lending libraries of today can vouch for the vivid accuracy of the picture presented in the Advisory Council's report:

[28] Greenwoood's *Library Year Book* (1897), p. 117; *British Library Year Book* 1900-1 (1900), p. 267-8.
[29] Montrose Public Library Committee Minutes, 17 January; 27 February 1905.
[30] Councillor J. G. Milne: SLA, *Annual report* 1914-15 (1915), p. 19.
[31] F. Kent: ibid. p. 16.

Tall cliffs of indicators with columns of orderly numerals on a variegated background of blue and red; intervening counters across which the business of the library was transacted; a wooden gate, ostentatiously private, through which none might pass but the library staff and a few highly privileged persons; a tantalising and receding vista of bookshelves; well-thumbed, printed catalogues as firmly attached to the building as the chained bibles in former days.

The Kenyon report, observing that the merits of free access had been very widely recognized, had urged "that the system should be universally adopted"; but Scottish caution is shown in Stirling Public Library committee's decision ten years later to try "experimental open-access." Wherever free access was introduced it was welcomed as an improvement; and no Scottish library reversed its decision in this matter. However, at least four indicators survived the Second World War. At Stirling the indicators were removed only in February 1947; at Lossiemouth in 1948 Minto found a "Cotgreave Indicator . . . still used for charging purposes although readers are admitted to the shelves" and at Stornoway "the only fully working indicator system" of his tour; and as late as 1951 the Scottish Library Association reported :

Dumbarton's conversion to open-access saw the disappearance of the last "Cotgreave" indicator in the country.

In face of this steady move towards greater freedom and flexibility it is surprising to know that some libraries continued to make a charge for the issue, and sometimes for the renewal, of borrowers' tickets, all the more so in that such a charge is illegal. Its legality was challenged as long ago as 1894, when a Hawick stationer objected to a by-law, proposed for the public library there, that sought to levy a 2d charge for a reader's ticket. The sheriff was quite emphatic that the charge was illegal. The plea advanced in its defence, that other libraries made a charge of this kind, he dismissed in his decision : if other libraries chose to act illegally, that was no reason why Hawick should do so.[32]

[32] *Hawick Advertiser*, 5 October 1894. The case is cited in an interesting pamphlet, *The plundering of the public by public libraries*: *the case against the Aberdeen Public Library*, by J. Cyril M. Weale (Aberdeen, 1904). Weale shows that something like £800 had been taken illegally from the public of Aberdeen in charging for the issue and renewal of tickets (at 1d each) against the clear intention of sections 32 and 7 of the Act of 1887 and against the Hawick decision of 1894. His protest had an immediate effect: the charges for readers' tickets were abolished in Aberdeen on 21 October 1904.

Public libraries traditionally include a reading room, a lending department and a reference department, although the value of the tradition has been questioned.[33] The division of the main book stock into the two categories, "lending" and "reference," is often artificial. While there are certain books of reference that the library should never be without, books that are usually consulted for some particular purpose, even for one specific detail, and that are rarely if ever read through, there is perhaps too much of a tendency to immobilize in the reference department books that would be better used in the lending department. The artificial and arbitrary distinction between the two departments reaches a height of absurdity when the two collections of books are separately catalogued, and the reader is confronted with virtually two separate libraries under one roof.

The development of county library services has had a marked effect on the burgh libraries' policy of lending "reference library" books, for it is the essence of the county library service to bring the books to the readers. What a burgh library might consider "reference library" books, "standard histories . . . editions of the classic works of literature . . . expensive scientific and technical books," the county library lends to its readers without hesitation. In the county library branches the reference collection will be of "quick-reference" books only, and even these are frequently available on short-term loan. When the county reader wants the type of service only a reference library can provide, although he may find it in part at the county library headquarters, he is best advised to make the journey, if he can afford it, to one of the larger towns. A postal request service can provide almost all the specifiic books any reader wants: it cannot attempt to bring him the advantages of a comprehensive reference library, well arranged and efficiently staffed.

Mobile branch libraries were introduced into Scotland in 1949 by Edinburgh Public Libraries: "a new feature in Scottish municipal library practice made necessary by the prevailing conditions in regard to the erection of new buildings, the need for immediate service to newly-established communities, and general considerations of economic administration."[34] Its service was supplemented by a second mobile library some two years later,

[33] See, for example, J. W. Forsyth, "The future development of public libraries in Scotland": SLA, *Annual report* 1948 (1949), p. 35-6.

[34] *Edinburgh Public Libraries: a handbook and history of sixty years' progress* (1951), p. 30.

while Aberdeen had put a similar vehicle on the road in the interval.

By 1955 these three remained the only mobile branch libraries in the urban services, but there were then no fewer than seven mobile libraries in the counties, one each in Dunbartonshire, Fife, Kirkcudbright, Ross and Cromarty, and Sutherland, and two in Midlothian. The mobile branch libraries, as their name indicates, served a different function from the earlier library vans of which there were several in Scotland: in this development Perthshire led the way.[35]

LOCAL COLLECTIONS

Public libraries are inevitably general rather than special in their scope, but special collections, of varying size and importance, are to be found in a great number of public libraries. From the first beginnings of the movement a "local collection" has been considered a desirable, even an essential part of a public library.

The Select Committee thought so:

> In all our chief provincial towns it is requisite that there should be Topographical Libraries . . . where history may find a faithful portraiture of local events, local literature, and local manners;

and one of the witnesses the committee examined urged the "great moral advantage in collecting everything that is connected with the town or province, its history, its biography, books relative to its manufacturing and agricultural interest:"

> The population is more attached to its own town, to its historical souvenirs, and . . . there is a stronger local patriotism when there is a library, where the past can be studied and where the future can be prepared.[36]

[35] There is a photograph of the original Perth van in the proceedings of the Carnegie Rural Library Conference, 1920 (1921), p. 47. Minto gives a clear description of the routine working of a van of this type in his report (1948), p. 8-9.

[36] Select Committee Report (1849), p. x-xi; 706, 710 (M. Van de Weyer). George Blake, the Scottish novelist, was to express the same point of view: "I am quite certain that the average librarian can do more than he does at present to foster that sense of belonging, that awareness of the *genius loci* from which, I suggest, the full understanding of life begins. I would have every librarian beginning his charity at home. I would have him see to it that his library contained, as a first condition of its existence, every book and every paper that could be held to bear on the history of his district" ("Libraries and life," SLA, *Annual report* 1933-34 (1934), p. 42).

The Kenyon report urged that the library should supply "books dealing with subjects of local importance":

Even the smallest [urban library] should aim at possessing a full stock of books dealing with local history and local trades and industries;

and in the view of the Advisory Council:

All local librarians can and should [collect "everything"] in one particular field—the local collection.[37]

The members of the council had "noted with pleasure" the large number of local collections in Scottish burgh libraries. County libraries, initially handicapped by their late arrival on the scene, are none the less aware of their responsibilities in this connexion.

In a local collection the aim should be "to furnish with abundant material not only the bibliographer of the future but the historian too."

Our task then is to amass all the material possible relating to our own district, however trivial some of it may appear to us to be. Its evaluation can safely be left to posterity. . . .

The local collection should not approximate to a local bibliography, but must exceed it.[38]

Among "local collections" of particular interest and importance in Scottish libraries may be mentioned the Edinburgh Room in the Central Public Library in Edinburgh, opened in 1932 after a bequest in 1929 from Mr Cowan of 1370 books, pamphlets, engravings and plans (in 1951 it contained 19,708 books and pamphlets, 7214 prints and illustrations, 1833 lantern slides and 1078 photographic negatives); the Glasgow collection in the Mitchell Library, Glasgow, containing 20,000 volumes, "the main purpose of the collection being the preservation of copies of all books, pamphlets, plans, periodicals, illustrations and other papers which illustrate the growth and life of the city;" the Dundee collection in the Dundee Public Library of some 5000 books dealing with Dundee or by Dundee authors, which is supplemented

[37] Kenyon report (1927), p. 60; Advisory Council report (1951), p. 29.
[38] J. Egarr, "The establishment, maintenance and administration of a local collection: extracts from the essay awarded the SLA Annual Scholarship, 1934," *Library Association Record,* vol. 2 (4th series) (1935), p. 190-1.

by the Lamb collection of material other than books (such as pamphlets, manuscripts, cuttings, and so on); and the 300 volumes, either printed in Stirlingshire or written by natives or by authors who resided there, bequeathed by William Harvey to Stirling Public Library, to be kept there as "The William Harvey Collection."[39] In the Dumfries and Galloway collection in the Ewart Library at Dumfries, the task of preparing an analytical catalogue, which had been proceeding intermittently for some years, reached completion within the year 1954-5:

> 8461 items, comprising books, pamphlets, news cuttings, family papers, etc., have now been sifted, arranged and recorded with meticulous care by the chief cataloguer.[40]

A collection of local literature was being formed in Perth almost twenty years before the public library was established. In March 1879 the directors of the Mechanics' Library, as a result of the first annual conference of the Library Association held in Oxford in October 1878, issued an appeal for "Local Publications of all kinds."

> What might seem of little or no value at the present time, or at the date of issue, may ultimately come to be regarded with considerable interest. There will, therefore, be included all Works by Resident or Native Authors—works having any relation to the Town or Neighbourhood or County—Squibs, Pamphlets, Broadsheets, of whatever size or date—all will be included.

[39] *Edinburgh Public Libraries: a handbook and history of sixty years' progress* (1951); Glasgow Corporation, *Public libraries* 1874-1954 (1955); Dundee Public Libraries, *Report* 1949-50 (1950); *Stirling Journal*, 21 January 1937. See also the interesting paper by Norman Crawford, burgh librarian of Arbroath, "The local collection," SLA, *Proceedings . . . Arbroath* (1963), p. 17-26.

[40] Dumfriesshire Libraries, *Annual report for the year ending 15 May 1955* (1955), p. 2. It is to be hoped that the catalogue card service provided by the Council of the British National Bibliography receives the full support it deserves. Co-operative cataloguing of this kind was recommended in the Kenyon report and by McColvin. In 1955 the BNB offered it "as an opportunity to save cataloguing costs;" it might also release the time and staff necessary to undertake such specialized work as the detailed cataloguing and indexing of a local or other special collection. These are not only interesting and rewarding tasks, they can be a significant contribution to the bibliographical resources of the country. Further, more time might profitably be spent on improving the speed and extending the coverage of periodical indexing.

The directors hoped for "the assistance of the Literary Public" to carry their task "to a successful issue:"

They look for help to the generosity of Authors for Presentation Copies of each Work or new Edition as it may be issued; to Publishers and Book-buyers for gifts; and to the Public of both Town and County generally—many of whom have doubtless in their possession old, embrowned Pamphlets, lying undisturbed, but which, by being transferred to this Public Collection, would acquire a new value and increased usefulness.

By 1889 the "Special Department of Local Literature . . . consisting of works by authors belonging to Perthshire, or published within the City or County" was well established. An index of the collection had been "partly written out" and might be consulted "by arrangement with the Librarian."[41]

OTHER SPECIAL COLLECTIONS AND DEPARTMENTS

Special collections have sometimes developed through the particular interest of the library committee or the librarian, or a collection on a special subject may have been presented to the library as a gift. Among special collections of the second kind in Scottish libraries are the Atholl collection of Scottish music which the Sandeman Public Library in Perth accepted in 1938, or the Murison Burns Collection that was presented to Dunfermline Public Library in 1921 by Sir Alexander Gibb, the famous engineer.

Among special collections that have been formed as a result of the direct policy of the library committee the most comprehensive is the Burns and Scottish Poetry Collection in the Mitchell Library. Shortly after the first librarian, F. T. Barrett, commenced his duties in March 1877 it was resolved that the Mitchell Library should form "special collections . . . of editions of Robert Burns and books relating to his history and personality, and of Scottish poetry . . . to constitute a treasury of national poetical literature."

The principal objective . . . has been the acquirement of copies of all editions of the works of Robert Burns and all Scottish poets, selections and collections of Scottish poetry, historical

[41] Perth Mechanics' Library, *Appeal*, 31 March 1879; *Supplement to the catalogue* (1889), p. 2.

199

and critical dissertations on the poetry of Scotland and biographies of Scottish poets. The Burns Collection is believed to be the largest collection of books (3500 volumes) on the National Bard in any library in the world.[42]

The smaller libraries are not without their special collections. The Scottish collection in Falkirk Public Library, for example, is claimed to be "with the exception of the four city libraries, . . . one of the largest and most representative public collections of Scottish books in Scotland."[43]

It is only in the largest libraries that it is practicable to adopt the division of the library into special subject departments that Dr Savage carried through so successfully in Edinburgh. There at the Central Public Library there were in 1955 the Economics and Commercial Library, the Fine Art Library, and the Music Library. In Glasgow there are the Commercial Library, opened in 1916, the first municipal commercial library in the United Kingdom, and now accommodated in the Royal Exchange Building; the Music Room at the Mitchell Library; and the special collection of books in foreign languages at the Gorbals District Library. In the Central Public Library in Dundee an Art Room was opened in 1950 to provide "a quiet room for study and reading in close proximity to the books needed" and to make available to the student in "open access" many more volumes than it was possible to display in the "limited shelving space" of the Reference Department.[44]

MATERIAL OTHER THAN BOOKS

Etymologically a library is a place for books, and the provision of books must be the main purpose of a public library, yet even the first Public Libraries Act permitting the purchase of books, the Public Libraries (Scotland) Act, 1854, allowed the purchase also of "Maps and Specimens of Art and Science." The principal Act for Scotland, the Act of 1887, defined the powers of a library committee in this direction to cover the purchase of

books, newspapers, reviews, magazines, and other periodicals, statuary, pictures, engravings, maps, specimens of Art and

[42] Glasgow Corporation, *Public libraries* 1874-1954 (1955), p. 14, 21-3. The catalogues of the Murison Burns collection in Dunfermline Public Library and of the Robert Burns collection in the Mitchell Library, Glasgow, were published in 1953 and 1959 respectively.

[43] *Falkirk Herald,* 30 September 1939.

[44] Dundee Public Libraries, *Report* 1949-50 (1950), p. 14.

Science, and such other articles and things as may be necessary for the establishment, increase, and use of the Libraries and Museums under their control.

Among the "other articles and things" that have been found "necessary for the . . . increase and use" of libraries are films, film strips, and gramophone records.

Motherwell and Wishaw Public Library committee agreed in March 1953 to introduce a scheme, claimed to be the first of its kind in Scotland, for the issue of gramophone records on loan to the public in the area.[45] There was to be a selection of a thousand records, including both classical and popular music. The scheme was a success from the start.

Clackmannan County Library about the same time had a collection of almost 200 gramophone records, not available to the general public, however, although Linguaphone language courses in French, German and Spanish, had been followed by sixteen readers, ten readers and five readers respectively.[46]

The Scottish public libraries' interest in films is indicated by the formation in 1940 of a joint committee of the Scottish Library Association and the Scottish Film Council (the agency through which the British Film Institute operates in Scotland), one of its purposes being "the stimulation of the use of educational films in public library extension work." In the same year six libraries had accepted from the Ministry of Information the loan of a talking-film projector, and were organizing regular public displays of propaganda and educational films.

While several library authorities continue to give film shows with considerable success, it is doubtful if any library would be justified in acquiring a collection of films for loan, a service that is adequately provided by the Scottish Central Film Library of the Scottish Film Council. Film strip collections are a different matter, however: by 1955 Clackmannan County Library already possessed a collection of 400, much used by schools in the area, "although on occasion requests have been made . . . by some local organization."

Collections of illustrations, mounted and classified, have been built up in several libraries, Dundee among them; and the Dumfriesshire Libraries, working on behalf of the Dumfries Educational Trust, administer a scheme for circulating some 330 prints, reproductions of famous paintings, to schools in the county.

[45] *The Scotsman,* 12 March 1953.
[46] Clackmannan County Library, *Annual report* 1954-5 (1955), p. 8.

Activities of this kind, however, must be kept in proper perspective. The fundamental objective of librarianship, as the members of the Scottish Library Association were reminded by their president in 1947, remains constant:

> the acquiring of books, the preservation of books and the placing of books at the disposal of those who require them. . . .

> An institution which gave film shows, organised lectures and other oral means of conveying information, which had large collections of gramophone records, micro-films and lantern slides would, no doubt, be highly popular—it might justify the description of the cultural centre of the community, but if it did not give pre-eminence to its book-stock, it would not be a library and we should have to think of another name to supersede Librarian.[47]

A year later the point was driven home in another paper:

> I am not in favour of regarding the library as the cultural centre of the community. There is a grave danger here that a multiplicity of tails will wag the dog. You know that wishful argument that every venture into extension work brings ignorant citizens into the lending library and sends them away as registered readers. . . . Only two things, in my opinion, will convert non-readers into readers—books; and the urgent need for books, whether this be created by the library or by outside agency. Converts will not be won, I maintain, by frittering away our time and energies on schemes of social service which clutter up the building and interfere with our legitimate work.[48]

LECTURES

Nevertheless, lectures have for long been considered an appropriate library activity, although when they began in Manchester Public Library in 1852, Edward Edwards noted: "Lectures will involve a very serious interference with ordinary business of the library."[49]

The lectures sponsored each year by the Glasgow Corporation Public Libraries Committee are well known, not only for the high

---

[47] A. G. Mackay, "Presidential Address": SLA, *Annual report* 1947 (1948), p. 30, 31.

[48] J. W. Forsyth, "The future development of public libraries in Scotland": SLA, *Annual report* 1948 (1949), p. 38.

[49] Quoted in Munford, *Penny rate* (1951), p. 112.

standard the lectures reach and maintain, but for the excellent reading lists, carefully edited and annotated, that are issued shortly before each lecture. Galashiels Public Library runs "Celebrity Lectures" with speakers like Peter Churchill and Lady Violet Bonham Carter, and Clydebank sponsors both a series of lectures and a Literary and Philosophical Society.

These lectures are on general topics and are encyclopedic in their range, as the quotation of a few titles will show: "The Companionship of the Countryside," "Conflicting Influences in the Scottish Theatre," "Atoms," "Twentieth-century Music," an ambitious series of seven lectures on "The Literary Heritage," "Then and Now: Changes in Scottish Life," "The Most Intelligent Animal—the Elephant," "Mountaineering and Travel in the Garhwal Himalayas," and "Spies in Fact and Fiction."

More specific in content are the lectures given in a library on the best use of the library's resources. Lectures of this kind were given in Edinburgh in 1891 and 1892, when it was decided to have a series of meetings for men engaged in certain trades, to encourage a greater use of the books in the reference library. In 1891 two such meetings were held, one for masons, carpenters and plasterers, the other for gasfitters, plumbers, brassfounders and tinplate workers; and the following year there were lectures for cabinet-makers, wood-carvers, painters, decorators and glass-workers, and for printers, lithographers, engravers, type founders and bookbinders.[50]

In this connexion one may recall that one of the witnesses before the Select Committee drew attention to the "remarkable circumstances that in manufacturing districts works upon the steam-engine, and similar works which would be useful to those constantly attending the library are comparatively little read," and explained the indifference in this way:

> Many of them have an impression that they know more about the steam-engine than anybody else can tell them; and the same with regard to the power-loom; and the same with lectures.[51]

Library lectures of this kind are still given: in the annual report from Clackmannan County Library for 1954-5, for example, it is reported that the Alloa Business and Professional Women's Club visited the library headquarters one evening "when, after an introductory talk by the Librarian, the members were

[50] Edinburgh Public Libraries, *Report* 1887-94.
[51] Select Committee Report (1849), 2495, 2496.

conducted to all departments of the Library and were rather amazed at the large amount of work necessary in the administration of a modern County and Public Library system."

No modern library authority considers its service other than in terms of its relation to the whole local community: yet there are many people who never use the public library.[52]

A regular feature of early public library reports was a table showing the occupations of the readers using the library.[53] Such records are not normally kept now, and it is not easy to ascertain who uses or does not use the library, and why.

If there was a change in the 1950s it was that more and more the public library was attracting the type of reader who used to use the commercial subscription library. It is interesting to remember that in 1927 the Kenyon committee was pointing out that "the needs of those who require the newest books while they are new are sufficiently catered for by the subscription libraries. The patron of the public library can afford to wait." This view was rightly challenged at the time by G. W. Shirley of Dumfries:

> The Committee here fails to see that the very existence of the subscription libraries constitutes a criticism and demonstrates the limitations of the public service.[54]

There are in the community, however, certain groups of people who are debarred, temporarily or permanently, from using the general services provided by the public library, but the library authority is frequently prepared to recognize an obligation to provide additional services for these members of its public.

PROVISION FOR THE BLIND

Blind readers form one of these groups. According to the Kenyon report: "It is clearly the duty of the community, either

[52] See E. R. Luke, "The 'lost seventy-five'—or the case of the missing borrowers," *Librarian,* vol. 39 (1950), p. 215-19; F. S. Green, "The missing three-quarter," *Library Association Record,* vol. 57 (1955), p. 392-8.

[53] See the Parliamentary Return (439), 14 August 1876, for a classification of borrowers from Dundee and Paisley libraries; Library Association, *Monthly notes* (1881), p. 44, for Glasgow; and various library reports, such as that of the Sandeman Public Library, Perth, for 1900, Table X.

[54] G. W. Shirley, "The Scottish public book service: a reconnaissance": SLA, *Report* 1929-30 (1930), p. 44.

through the public library, or by other means, to take steps to secure that the blind reader shall have as much attention paid to his needs as the sighted."

In the Scottish public libraries books for the blind were first provided in Aberdeen in 1900. A small section for blind readers was established in the lending department with a stock of 132 volumes, 112 in Braille and 20 in Moon. In the first year 19 borrowers' tickets were issued: and one reader, a blind boy of about 13, had read through every Moon book in the collection.[55]

The collections of books for the blind in Scottish public libraries are both few and small. At the time of his survey Professor Adams found only seventeen libraries in Scotland that made any provision for the blind; and some of these do so no longer. By 1955 most of the libraries that offered a service to blind readers borrowed books for them from the National Library for the Blind, and many of the libraries that had small stocks of their own supplemented their resources with loan collections from the National Library. Dundee, for example, supplemented its stock of 257 Braille volumes and its monthly magazines in Braille with 150 volumes from the National Library, exchanged every three months; and in Glasgow, also, the special provision that was made for blind readers was augmented as required by special loans from the National Library.[56]

HOSPITAL LIBRARIES

The provision of hospital libraries in Scotland was raised at the Scottish Library Association's annual meeting in 1932 when the question was remitted to the council for consideration and report. In the following year the council examined the Library Association's 1931 Memorandum on Hospital Libraries, which had been circulated to every public library in Scotland. The council unanimously approved the Memorandum's principles and recommendations and urged library authorities

to give their sympathetic consideration to the desirability of establishing where possible a library service to hospitals in their area.

It was not until 1947, however, that the subject was discussed at a Scottish library conference. In that year Robert Butchart, the

---

[55] Aberdeen Public Library, *Annual report for the year ended 30 September 1900.*

[56] Dundee Public Libraries, *Report 1952-54* (1955), p. 15-16; Glasgow Corporation, *Public libraries 1874-1954* (1955), p. 35.

principal librarian of Edinburgh Public Libraries, read a paper, "Hospital Libraries," in which he described "the recently established scheme in the Edinburgh City Hospitals." In Edinburgh the hospital library service was financed by the Public Health Department and administered by the Libraries Committee. Later it was arranged that the Libraries Committee should pass the appropriate accounts to the Regional Hospital Board.

In Glasgow prior to the establishment of the National Health Service in 1948, fourteen hospitals administered by the Public Health Department were supplied with books by the Libraries Department, a service that was continued into the fifties, although on a smaller scale, while its future was being considered by a joint-committee of the Libraries Committee and the Western Regional Hospital Board.[57]

Towards the end of 1950, at the request of the British Red Cross, a joint meeting of representatives of the Society and the Scottish Library Association discussed the provision of hospital library services. Thereafter the council of the Association set up a Hospital Libraries Committee with D. C. Stark, the county librarian of Stirlingshire, as chairman. It was agreed that under the National Health Service, accommodation, staff and books should be financed by the hospital authority.

A service of this kind was established by Stirlingshire County Library and the Stirlingshire Branch of the British Red Cross Society at Killearn Hospital in 1949.[58] The Stirlingshire Branch built the library, which accommodated between two and three thousand books, and they paid to the county council the amount of a full-time librarian's salary. The hospital librarian was appointed by the county council as a member of the county library staff; the books in the hospital library belonged to the county library: the hospital library was in effect a branch of the county library service. Stirlingshire later opened a similar branch library for the patients in Bellsdyke Mental Hospital, Larbert. Here again the books were part of the county library service, and the librarian a member of its staff, but in this case the accommodation was provided and the salary of the hospital librarian was paid by the Hospital Board.

The Advisory Council in their report "specially commend the hospital library service operated by certain Authorities, which should be extended to cover all hospitals;" and the Scottish Library Association almost twenty years earlier had urged public

[57] Glasgow Corporation, *Public libraries* 1874-1954 (1955), p. 36-38.
[58] *Scottish Red Cross News*, no. 148, January and February 1950, p. 7-9.

206

library authorities to give their sympathetic consideration to the desirability of establishing where possible a library service to hospitals in their areas. Nevertheless, the Scottish libraries, city, burgh and county, in 1955 claimed to be providing only 45 hospital libraries (and one library's return includes "other institutions" in its figure), while there were over 400 hospitals in Scotland.[59]

Library services are also provided by various library authorities to children's homes, eventide homes and social welfare institutions, and to eleven prisons and borstal institutions.[60]

CHILDREN'S DEPARTMENTS AND SCHOOL LIBRARIES

The Kenyon committee advocated "the universal formation of juvenile departments (lending as well as reading) in public libraries, with personal access to the shelves," and most public libraries make some provision on these lines for young readers, yet in 1955 the "juvenile department" might still be, perhaps, a corner of the adult lending library. The inhibiting rate limit had prevented some libraries from providing the "separate accommodation" that the Kenyon report described as "highly desirable," "if young people of school age are to use the public library."

Among juvenile departments that are notable in one way or another it is right to mention the children's department of Dunfermline Public Library, opened in 1935, and the new junior library opened at Coatbridge in January 1949, uniquely equipped with a wash-hand basin.[61]

The Advisory Council report paid its tribute "to what the public libraries have done specially for children of school age" and mentioned with approval the arrangements made by several libraries for "story-hours" and the organized visits of classes of school children to the library "to enable pupils to become familiar with the contents and resources of the library and the way in which books may be consulted or borrowed." Elsewhere it is reported:

The county librarian encourages a class visit near the end of the pupils' school career, and describes all the facilities and benefits available.[62]

[59] Department of Health for Scotland, *Scottish Hospitals Directory* (1955).
[60] Library Association, *Replies to questionnaire* (1955).
[61] *Dunfermline Press*, 28 September 1935; *Bulletin*, 27 January 1949.
[62] Scottish Education Department, *Young citizens at school* (1950), p. 29.

Whether or not the public library service is to be responsible for the provision of school libraries, it is highly important that good school libraries should be provided. We have Edward Edwards's word for it:

> I do not believe a more prudent or a more wise subsidiary measure could be taken with reference to education, than to connect with schools lending libraries of a good kind.[63]

And over a century later the Advisory Council was pointing out:

> The emphasis in schools should not be nearly so much on putting over a systematic scheme of factual information, as on the discovering and creating of lively interests, and the training of children from their earliest school years in the method of getting information from books when and where it is required for any purpose in hand. . . .
>
> A school library is not a luxury that one can decide to do without. A school without a library and without the desire to have one gives itself away as being completely out of touch with modern needs and conditions. . . .
>
> Rapidly as the library system has developed in this country, it has not taken such a hold nor played such a part in national life as its sponsors hoped and foretold. On the contrary, very many children leave school without any urge to continue their education or broaden their interests by the greatest single instrument open and available to every individual in the community, namely, the public library service. . . .
>
> Libraries have reached or are approching a temporary limit to their usefulness, because the schools have not yet given adequate training in the use and power of books. . . .
>
> The public library stands to gain by the systematic training in school of a future generation of readers and borrowers who have already acquired the library habit and will be able to make fuller and more systematic use of library resources after they leave school.[64]

Opinions on the provision of school libraries range between two extremes. One is stated in the Kenyon report:

> In respect of schools there is no doubt that the main responsibility for the supply and use of books lies with local education

[63] S.C. Report (1849), 326.
[64] Advisory Council report (1951), p. 13, 33, 39, 43.

authorities. . . . It is not, of course, the function of the public library to supply school libraries.

The other is expressed in these terms by the Advisory Council on Education in Scotland:

School libraries should be regarded as a highly important constituent part of the national library service. From the point of view of the professional librarian each secondary school may be regarded as a special kind of branch library.

In Scotland the basic contradiction is confused by the fact that apart from the four counties of cities, only county councils are education authorities and that every county council providing a library service under the Education (Scotland) Act, 1946, is also by definition a statutory library authority, and is so for the whole of its administrative area, without the exclusion, as in England and Wales, of independent burgh library authorities. A Scottish burgh library committee, then, agreeing with the Kenyon report that the provision of libraries in the burgh's schools is not the function of the public library but is the responsibility of the local education authority, might well find that the education committee of the county council refers the question to its library committee who may decide that the school library should be provided as part of the county library service. The libraries in Scottish schools, when they exist at all, even in the schools in burghs that are independent library authorities, are very likely to be "branches" of the county library.

In the counties of cities the detailed arrangements for providing school libraries vary slightly, but all conform to the pattern that the service is controlled by the library committee. In Edinburgh, under a scheme of co-operation with the education committee that was approved in 1925, the Libraries Committee of the corporation is wholly responsible for the administration of all libraries in the rate-supported schools in the city: the library rooms, shelving, tables and chairs are provided by the education committee, books and staff by the Public Libraries Committee.[65] In Dundee thirteen school libraries are administered by the Public Libraries Committee on behalf of the education committee, an arrangement that has been in operation since 1933.[66]

In Glasgow the corporation education committee announced in 1954 "some very definite steps which should have an effect in

[65] R. Butchart, "School library or public library? A city librarian's viewpoint," *Scottish Educational Journal*, 16 October 1953.
[66] Dundee Public Libraries, *Report* 1952-54 (1955), p. 16.

the near future." A basic grant and annual grant was being given to each school, primary and secondary, junior or senior, and a junior assistant from the corporation public libraries would be employed half-time in each new secondary school library, if the libraries committee approved the suggestion.[67]

Of the other burghs of Scotland only five claimed to provide or control the school libraries in their area: four of these, Falkirk (for three junior schools), Grangemouth, Inverness and Kilmarnock, made this provision from their own funds; Clydebank administered libraries in the schools in its area out of funds provided by the education authority as part of the return for "double rating." The county library services provided or were prepared to provide school libraries in the other burghs with independent libraries.[68]

Nevertheless, the library provision in Scottish schools is not satisfactory. In 1952, of 741 secondary schools (718 grant-aided secondary schools out of a total of 869, and 23 independent schools) 495 claimed to have libraries of their own books, but 75 of these, including three senior secondary schools, had 100 or fewer books. In 54 schools (again including three senior secondary schools) the library contained fiction only; and in 370 fewer than fifty books were added to the library each year.

One headmaster of a senior secondary school in central Scotland stated that, before 1952, no book had been added since 1906.

Of the 741 schools 270 received no loans from burgh or county libraries: of the 471 schools receiving loans, 208 received more than 200 books exchanged twice a year or oftener.[69]

In March 1951 it was decided to establish a Scottish branch of the School Library Association, which had been founded in 1937 "to promote the use of the school library as an instrument of education." A School Libraries Section of the Library Association had been formed in that same year (1937), but its existence was terminated in 1946 "in order to make possible a single association of school librarians."

The aims of the School Library Association and the [School Libraries] Section being virtually identical, it had been found

[67] School Library Association in Scotland, Annual general meeting 1955, *Report.*

[68] SLA, *Replies to questionnaire on school libraries,* May 1953.

[69] School Library Association in Scotland, *Report on secondary school libraries* (1953).

from the outset that grave disadvantages resulted from the duplication of effort, and conversely that the best work was achieved by collaboration.[70]

The School Library Association in Scotland has focussed attention on the question of library provision in Scottish schools, a matter that was given detailed consideration in the Advisory Council's report. The Association and the Council disagreed, however, on one important point. The Association was emphatic: the librarian should be a full-time teacher. The Council took the view that the school librarian should be a member of the library staff:

In some cases this librarian may be an independent school librarian, but there are considerable advantages in the system whereby the head librarian for the area would make available the services of a junior librarian during the hours considered necessary for the purpose.

This difference of opinion was a new manifestation of the contradiction already mentioned. The honorary secretary of the School Library Association in Scotland stated "the real problem" thus:

Should school libraries be autonomous, managed by the school staffs and pupils; or should they be branch libraries of the public library, managed by public library assistants, with books supplied by the public library organization?[71]

To the present writer it appeared that in the Scotland of 1955 there were three possible lines of development:

(1) Where there were independent burgh libraries the county education committee might authorize—and pay—the burgh library committee to provide libraries in the schools in the burgh. By an arrangement of this kind, with the library service for the town and the schools in it under one control, it might be easier to achieve a greater "amount of carry-over . . . to future use of the public library."

(2) The county education committee might provide school libraries as part of its county library service.

(3) The county education committee might give grants to the schools under its control to enable them to establish school

[70] School Library Association, *School libraries today* (1950), p. iii.
[71] George More, "School library or public library?" *Scottish Educational Journal,* 9 October 1953.

211

libraries, either partially or entirely independent, leaving it to the headmaster and staff to decide how they should co-operate with the public library service, burgh or county.

That there should be close co-operation between school and public library was generally agreed.[72] That school libraries in Scotland should be much better than they were was clearer than ever. The propaganda of the School Library Association in Scotland, and its parent body, had driven this point home to education authorities and teachers.

Librarians had been more conscious of the true state of affairs. In 1905 the Library Association resolved:

> In order that children from an early age may become accustomed to the use of a collection of books, it is desirable (a) that special libraries for children should be established in all public libraries, and (b) that collections of books should be formed in all elementary and secondary schools.[73]

A year earlier, speaking to the American Library Association, John Ballinger, then librarian of the Cardiff Public Libraries, had said:

> The most satisfactory way of reaching children is through libraries deposited in the schools, the books being distributed by the teachers to the children for home reading. The teacher, knowing the capabilities and tasks of the individual child, can get closer contact with them than a librarian can. But there is need of the librarian's special qualifications in the selection, purchase, organization, and supervision of the school libraries.[74]

When the Scottish Library Association met in Perth in 1926 the president, Ryrie Orr, chairman of Greenock library committee and editor and proprietor of the *Greenock Telegraph,* discussed "the provision of well-stocked libraries in all elementary schools" and agreed that "a library policy for schools should be consciously evolved as a training ground for adolescent and adult reading." In 1943 the council of the Scottish Library Association

---

[72] For ways in which the two services might co-operate see article by the present writer, "Co-operation between the school library and the public library," *School Librarian,* vol. 7 (1954), p. 167-72.

[73] *Library Association Record,* vol. 7 (1905), p. 611-17.

[74] American Library Association, *Papers and proceedings,* 1904 (1904), p. 46-9.

adopted a memorandum that included the following recommendations :

1. The provision of libraries in all schools should be part of the policy of education authorities.

2. Co-operation between education authority and public library authority might be developed to a much greater degree, particularly by the establishment in school buildings of branch libraries to serve both children and adults. At the same time the view was expressed that in some districts the public library branch might with advantage form part of a community centre. . . .

4. Bibliography and the use of books should also be a recognised feature of school work. In this connection it was suggested that talks by librarians, visits to libraries, where exhibitions, film shows and other attractions could be arranged, would be of value. . . .

7. School libraries, whether for children only or for children and adults should be administered by trained librarians.

Again, in 1947 the county librarian of Midlothian pointed out that libraries in schools had been "grossly neglected:"

The remedy lies in *our* hands—if we are allowed to supply it. Let the education authority provide the accommodation in the school—accommodation planned and equipped in consultation with the library authority—and thereafter let the library authority administer the service. . . . This is work of the greatest importance and there should be complete correlation of library work within the school and in the public library itself to provide a balanced whole.[75]

Nevertheless, the demand for a school library must originate with the school. No library committee or librarian, however enthusiastic, can force a library with any success on an uninterested headmaster or a staff reluctant to recognize its value. But the public librarian can play an important part in the movement for better school libraries:

Good school libraries are essential for the encouragement of reading among young people. Their establishment and development should be welcomed and encouraged and assisted by

[75] A. G. Mackay, "Presidential address": SLA, *Annual report* 1947 (1948), p. 31-2.

public librarians, and they will be most effectively administered as part of, or in collaboration with, the public library service in city, county, and where possible, burgh. Plans for new schools and for the modernisation of existing schools now include reasonable accommodation for a library, and we should use all our persuasion and influence to ensure that adequate facilities are provided, that book-stocks and furnishings are on as generous a scale as possible, that financial provision is adequate, and that full use is made of the service for the encouragement of reading among children.[76]

The Ministry of Education and the Scottish Education Department had at this time both declared their interest in the establishment of more and better school libraries.[77] With this official encouragement, with local authorities increasingly aware of the importance of school libraries, and with teachers more appreciative of their value, school libraries developed rapidly and extensively throughout Scotland. Their development is bound to have a significant and far-reaching effect on the public library movement as a whole.

[76] W. B. Paton, "Forward to freedom": SLA, *Proceedings . . . Alloa* (1955), p. 10.
[77] See, for example, the Ministry's pamphlet, *The school library* (1952), the recent annual reports of the Secretary of State, *Education in Scotland*, the memoranda relating to the school curriculum issued by the Scottish Education Department, and the report of the Advisory Council on Education, *Secondary education* (1947), p. 145-7.

CHAPTER 8

PUBLIC LIBRARIANS:
THEIR QUALIFICATIONS, EDUCATION
AND ASSOCIATIONS

FROM THE BEGINNING of the library service under the Acts the capacities and qualifications of public librarians varied considerably. It was a new profession with no standards of training and in consequence it attracted recruits of a very heterogeneous character. Scotland must have had its share of librarians who had been "soldiers, sailors, pensioners, clerks, teachers, and booksellers."[1] One of the speakers at the Scottish Library Association's annual meeting at Montrose in 1914, for example, recalled that

> the first librarian he knew in Montrose was a worthy, an ex-soldier, and one of the survivors of the Light Brigade. He had charge of 20,000 volumes but he knew nothing about books, although he could keep order and command silence.

James Craigie, again, successively librarian at Brechin, Arbroath and Perth, and later first secretary of the Scottish Library Association, was we know originally trained as a bookseller, although this would seem to be a reasonably relevant qualification.

Yet the new profession attracted from the first some men of real quality and distinction, among them several trained or experienced librarians. John Maclauchlan, who was appointed librarian, secretary and curator at Dundee in 1874 in succession to the first librarian, James Cargill Guthrie, who "resigned when the books had been fully put in order," had been librarian and secretary of the Mechanics' Institute in Perth from 1865. The first librarian of Aberdeen Public Library, Alexander Webster Robertson, M.A., had been for four years on the staff of Aberdeen University Library. John Minto, M.A., who became Perth's city librarian in 1896, was also trained in Aberdeen University Library, and had had four years' experience as sub-librarian in Aberdeen Public Library.

[1] T. Greenwood, *Public libraries* (1890), p. 482.

215

Thomas Mason, later librarian of St Martin-in-the-Fields, the famous James Duff Brown, and H. Y. Simpson, who was the first librarian of Kilmarnock Public Library, all served in the Mitchell Library. George McNairn, Hawick's second librarian, and later librarian at Motherwell, had been for five years an assistant in a private library before his appointment to Hawick, where he trained an assistant, Archibald Macdonald, who was later to be librarian at Dumbarton.

Greenwood "unhesitatingly and emphatically" affirmed that "the best librarians are the men who have been trained in public libraries, and who have grown up in the work," and he urged library committees to assist "in raising the status and standard of librarians by refusing to recognise as candidates the large number of broken-down schoolmasters, clergymen, soldiers, journalists and others who apply for such positions."

Only too many of these applicants would, as a rule, be dear at half the salary offered.[2]

Nevertheless in 1916 the Carnegie Trustees were making this comment:

The importance of the librarian as the vitalising link between the books and the readers seems apt to be overlooked, or— at all events—not placed in its proper perspective. . . . At present the attitude of Local Authorities is too frequently to regard the librarian as a person whose sole duty is to hand books over a counter, and to consider that an employee with the slightest qualifications and training is sufficient for the purpose. The term "librarian" is lightly used, and often is applied to an official who is placed in charge of a collection of books, with very meagre knowledge of their contents and still less knowledge of the profession to which he purports to belong.

For the county library schemes they were assisting the Trustees wanted "competent librarians." In 1920 they announced their decision

that where more than 100 centres are to be served, the post must be a whole-time appointment carrying a salary of not less than £300 a year,

[2] J. Irving, *The book of Scotsmen* (1882), p. 188 (for Guthrie); other particulars from Greenwood, *Public libraries* (1890), p. 482-3; *British Library Year Book* 1900-1 (1900).

and Col. Mitchell maintained

> the rural librarian is conceived not as an old-time janitor keeping his books safe in the dusty security of locked bookcases, but as a type of adult education officer travelling through the country, and stimulating intellectual interest throughout the area which he serves.

Even in the 1930s it was still necessary to emphasize:

> The appointment of an ex-this, or ex-that, is an imposition on the public and detrimental to efficient local government service.[3]

* * *

"To promote whatever may tend to the improvement of the position and the qualifications of Librarians" is one of the objects of the Library Association as defined in its Royal Charter of Incorporation (1898).

The Association had been founded in 1877 at the end of the first international conference of librarians in London: a resolution, "That a Library Association of the United Kingdom be founded," was unanimously adopted at an evening meeting on the last day of the conference, 5 October 1877, when as it happens the chairman was J. T. Clark, the keeper of the Advocates' Library in Edinburgh. John Winter Jones, principal librarian of the British Museum, was elected president of the new Association; J. T. Clark was one of the three vice-presidents; and the first council included among its twelve members, F. T. Barrett, of the Mitchell Library, and the librarian of Edinburgh University, John Small.

The Association's main object was "to unite all persons engaged or interested in library work, for the purpose of promoting the best possible administration of existing libraries and the formation of new ones where desirable." To this end the Association in its early years arranged ordinary meetings, usually in London, and an annual conference has been held each year, apart from the war years. By 1955 eight of these annual conferences had been held in Scotland.

The Association's first Scottish conference, and its third annual meeting, was held in Edinburgh in October 1880. It has been pointed out already how this meeting helped to arouse there an interest in the library movement that eventually led (with,

---

[3] Library Association, *Small municipal libraries* (1930), p. 60.

217

admittedly, notable assistance from Andrew Carnegie) to the adoption of the Public Libraries Acts. On that occasion the speakers included J. T. Clark, the keeper of the Advocates' Library, John Small of the University Library, Thomas Mason, assistant librarian at the Mitchell Library, and John Maclauchlan, librarian and curator at Dundee.

The Association's second visit to Scotland took place in 1888 when the Rev. Professor W. P. Dickson, curator of Glasgow University Library, was president. At the time of the third Scottish conference, at Aberdeen in 1893, the Association's president was Dr Richard Garnett of the British Museum. The Library Association's later conferences in Scotland have included two in Glasgow (1907 and 1924), one in Perth (1911), and two in Edinburgh (1927 and 1951).

The Edinburgh conference of 1927 merits special mention: it was the Association's jubilee conference, it was a "thoroughly international gathering," and it followed shortly after the publication of the Kenyon report—it "may be said to have inaugurated a new era in the history of the public library movement in this country."[4]

It was at the Edinburgh meeting of the Library Association in 1880 that it was resolved that "the Council . . . should consider how library assistants may best be aided in their training in the general principles of their profession." More than ten years earlier Edwards had noted the need for it:

> The day will come when in Britain we shall have courses of bibliography and of bibliothecal-economy for the training of librarians, as well as courses of chemistry or of physiology for the training of physicians. But, as yet, there is no such training, even in London, or in Edinburgh—though it is provided at Naples. When that day comes, the election of Librarians for a Free Library will be much simplified, and the requirement of a diploma from the candidate for a librarianship will be as much in the common order of things as the requirement of a degree from the applicant for a curacy. In the interval, the proof of adequate qualification will sometimes be difficult.[5]

After a committee had been appointed and had reported that the training of library assistants might best be served by the

[4] The conference proceedings were printed in the *Library Association Record*, vol. 6 (new series), March 1928.
[5] E. Edwards, *Free town libraries* (1869), p. 30.

Association's "providing for the examination of candidates and the granting of certificates of proficiency," examinations were held in July 1885, in London and Nottingham, and "at irregular intervals at a number of centres throughout the country until 1891."

In 1891 and again in 1894 the Association's syllabus of examinations was revised; and in 1898 the Royal Charter affirmed that it was one of the Association's objects "to hold examinations in librarianship and to issue certificates of efficiency."

Some seven years later an allied question came under discussion. In a paper to the monthly meeting of the Association in London in November 1905 W. R. B. Prideaux suggested "the establishment of a professional register of librarians."[6] While the subject was under debate in the ensuing years it was apparent that although most librarians were agreed that some form of professional registration was desirable, there was disagreement over the best method of initially establishing a register, and considerable doubt whether the Library Association, which had never been an Association exclusively for librarians, was competent to constitute such a register.

Early in 1908 a joint meeting of the Library Association and the Library Assistants' Association heard a paper written jointly by the two Associations' honorary secretaries, L. Stanley Jast and W. C. Berwick Sayers.[7] Its central theme was that the registration of librarians was desirable and timely, and that the Library Association was the correct body to undertake the task—by virtue of its prestige, its charter, its representative character, its educational work, and its standing as a recognized examining body. In the subsequent discussion the chairman of the Library Assistants' Association, W. Benson Thorne, argued that librarians wanted something to consolidate their profession. To point his argument he quoted the case of the "recent appointment at Dundee:"

> Here was a man, not only not a librarian, but a journalist of twenty-seven years' experience on the staff of a local paper. He had had information too (he believed authentic) that Mr Millar was a man sixty-one years of age, and further, a few months back, the Committee of the Dundee Library passed a resolution, ordering that no servant under the Library Authority should be allowed to serve after he had reached the age of sixty-five, so they had deliberately put a man in office who

[6] W. R. B. Prideaux, "Professional education and registration: some suggestions," *Library Association Record*, vol. 8 (1906), p. 1-6.
[7] "The registration of librarians: a criticism and a suggestion," *Library Association Record*, vol. 10 (1908), p. 325-35.

was only to serve four years. He did not think he could use a more forcible argument in favour of registration.[8]

A special committee's report on the subject was discussed at the Association's annual meeting in 1908, and it was resolved that a scheme of registration was desirable, that any such scheme should take the form of a classification of the membership to distinguish between professional and non-professional members, and that the council should prepare a scheme in accordance with the report under discussion.

The scheme asked for was submitted to the Association's annual meeting in 1909 in the form of remodelled by-laws and was adopted by 65 votes to 7. The new by-laws proposed that the Association should consist of Fellows, Honorary Fellows, Members, Associates Members, and Student Members. Four categories were to be accepted as Fellows:

(*a*) Any Member of the "Library Association of the United Kingdom" elected within the first year of its foundation; (*b*) Chief Librarians responsible for the administration of a Library or Library system, and holding or having held office on or before 31st December, 1914; (*c*) Librarians of approved status, not holding chief positions and holding or having held office on or before 31st December, 1914; (*d*) Holders of the Diploma of the Library Association and of the complete certificate issued prior to 1901;

and two categories as Members:

(*a*) Librarians, not qualified for election as Fellows, twenty-five years of age or over, and having not less than six years' approved experience, and holding or having held office on or before 31st December, 1914; (*b*) Librarians holding four Certificates of the Library Association, and with three years' approved experience.

Fellows and Members were to have the right of using the initials F.L.A. and M.L.A. respectively after their names.

The Association's *Year Book* for 1914 (the first it had been possible to issue since 1909) contained a list of Fellows and Members, "entirely revised consequent upon the adoption of the new classification" created by the by-laws, and showed 280 Fellows, 14 Honorary Fellows, 36 Members, 87 Associate Members and 3 Student Members.

[8] *Library Association Record,* vol. 10 (1908), p. 357-8.

A complete revision of the by-laws was allowed in 1928, under which it was provided that the Association should consist of Honorary Fellows, Members, Institutions and Corresponding Members, and that the council of the Association should maintain a register of librarians who should be classified as Fellows or Associates of the Association, according to certain principles that are then stated. From 1949, when the by-laws were again revised, until the introduction of a new examination syllabus in 1964, classification as Fellow or Associate was granted only to members who had passed the final or the registration examinations of the Association, respectively. Fellows and Associates have the right to use the letters F.L.A. and A.L.A. and may describe themselves as "Chartered Librarians."

* * *

The standard of the Library Association's examinations initially "had to be adapted to the educational level of the ordinary library assistant:"[9] the preliminary test in general knowledge that had been discontinued in the revision of the syllabus in 1904 was restored in 1916, in view of "the evident deficiency in the elementary education of many candidates." Since 1924, however, candidates for the professional examinations have required to hold a certificate of university matriculation standard.

Over the years the syllabus has been altered, modified, revised and enlarged, and by 1955 the registration examination—the general professional examination—consisted of seven three-hour papers, arranged in four groups, designed to "assess the candidates' possession of the knowledge necessary to competent practising librarians," while the four-part final examination leading to Fellowship of the Association approximated to ordinary degree standard.[10]

[9] W. A. Munford, *Penny rate* (1951), p. 80.
[10] The Library Association's professional examinations were substantially restructured in 1964. Admission to the register of Chartered Librarians as an Associate is gained by passing the Association's Part II examinations (for non-graduates), or its post-graduate professional examination (for graduates), and after the requisite service in an approved library. Many of the schools and departments of librarianship offer their own degrees (some through the Council for National Academic Awards) and diplomas, which are recognized by the Library Association. Fellowship of the Association is awarded to Associates of at least five years' standing who successfully submit a thesis upon some aspect of librarianship.

Of the Library Association's 10,814 personal members at 31 December 1954, 1400 (or 13.0 per cent) were Fellows, and 2632 (24.3 per cent) were Associates.

As the standard of the examinations has been raised and as the number of chartered librarians has increased—in fact, as the profession has become both better qualified and better organized —a firmer stand has been taken on the question of the appointment of unqualified persons as chief librarians.

In 1923 the council of the Scottish Library Association had occasion to deplore

the principle of inviting candidates to state the amount of remuneration they desire. . . . They foresee the danger of the appointment of a candidate whose qualifications are proportionate to the salary he asks rather than to the importance of the office he seeks,

and the president, John Minto, in his address expressed the hope that:

Gone . . . were the days when library authorities, even in some of the larger centres of population, could reconcile it with their duty to the public to appoint to chief librarianships persons with no previous training, who had, of necessity, to buy their experience at the expense of the community.

The Kenyon committee realized the need "to educate public opinion to demand that trained librarians should be the rule and not the exception" and the council of the Scottish Library Association in 1930 "approved a standard letter, to be sent by the Honorary Secretary to any authority about to make an appointment, urging that only candidates with experience and qualifications should be considered eligible for the principal positions in the library service," and requested the council of the Library Association, in a resolution unanimously adopted by the Library Association at its annual conference, "to bring to the notice of all library authorities the standard of qualifications and experience which is essential in the officer responsible for the administration of a library system." Nevertheless, there had been far too many unqualified chief librarians in the public library service in Scotland, and fresh appointments of this kind were still being made.

If there was a lack of qualified chief librarians, there were even more cases where a qualified or experienced chief librarian had no adequately trained assistants. It has been pointed out that "in some large and important areas, the gap between the salary of chief librarian and that of the assistant immediately below in seniority is disgracefully large" and the gap in salary all too frequently indicated a similar gap in qualifications and training.[11]

> Outside the cities and largest counties, the post of Deputy Librarian in Scotland is too often non-existent. . . . Every full-time Branch library, however small, should be under the charge of a qualified librarian.

In the county library service considerable reliance was still laid on the voluntary local librarian, the lineal descendants of Samuel Brown's "gratuitous librarians." While it was scarcely practicable to give these local librarians any instruction that could be called training, it was early recognized that "Annual Conferences of Local Librarians are well worth the money they cost," and the Advisory Council strongly commended the practice of those authorities who brought together "once a year these part-time librarians for an instructional conference which is happily combined with a social function."[12] The Stewartry of Kirkcudbright was one of these authorities: the first of the post-war series of conferences was held in 1947, after a gap of eight years, when the speakers included the late William Power and R. D. Macleod, who had been the librarian in charge of the Carnegie Trust's pioneer North of Scotland scheme.[13]

*   *   *

Munford has pointed out that the public library movement "failed from the outset to recruit its fair proportion" of university graduates:

> The rate limitation made it impossible, in nearly all areas, to pay salaries which were sufficiently attractive.[14]

The intake of graduates only began after the First World War, when post-graduate students from the first school of librarianship —in London—found openings in the new county libraries.

In Scotland, where the rate limitation persisted for a further generation, the graduate who would enter the library profession

[11] W. B. Paton, "Forward to freedom": SLA, *Proceedings . . . Alloa* (1955), p. 9.

[12] CUKT, *County Libraries . . . Report,* 1927-28 (1928), p. 46; Advisory Council report (1951), p. 59.

[13] "Library service: Conference in the Stewartry," *Dumfries Standard,* 28 May 1947.

[14] Munford, *Penny rate* (1951), p. 72.

found it difficult to get an appointment, even if he were prepared to accept the "unattractive" salary. Apart from the school of librarianship in London the only way to achieve registration as a qualified librarian was to take the Library Association examinations; but the graduate could not be registered as a qualified librarian, even if he had been allowed to join the Association and had sat and passed its examinations, until he had completed three years' service in a library; and as a graduate, four or five years older than a schoolboy with his Higher Leaving Certificate, he would find few authorities prepared to pay an assistant who was after all only a beginner in the profession the salary appropriate to his age and general qualifications, and fewer still to accept his services, even if he were ready to work for the wage of a school-leaver. The vicious circle was almost unbreakable. If a graduate did break through, however, and qualified as a chartered librarian, his university degree later became a considerable asset.

As in England and Wales, graduates have more frequently found their senior appointments in the county library service, perhaps because education committees are more familiar and at home with academic qualifications. On at least one occasion a county library committee, proceeding to the appointment of a chief librarian, interviewed only chartered librarians with a university degree in addition to their library qualification.

PROFESSIONAL EDUCATION

The Library Association's work as an educating body included also tuition and training. A summer school was first held in London in 1893; and correspondence courses were begun in 1904.

By 1955 there were throughout Great Britain nine full-time schools of librarianship, administered by various bodies, all preparing candidates for the Library Association examinations, in addition to the school of librarianship at University College London, established in 1919 with the assistance of the Carnegie Trustees, which awarded its own diploma. The correspondence courses continued under the care of the Association of Assistant Librarians; there were part-time courses in twelve centres in the London area, and in thirty-three places in the provinces; and there were usually at least two summer schools each year.

In Scotland, as we shall see, the functions of the Library Association are fulfilled by the Scottish Library Association, and the two associations, originally separate but affiliated in 1931, have usually worked amicably together. Occasionally, however, the feeling has been expressed that the Scottish Library Association should be more than a regional branch of the Library Association. In his presidential address to the Scottish Association in 1945, W. E. C. Cotton, an Englishman and librarian of the Scottish Central Library, had this to say:

> The first question for us to decide is whether we are content to leave everything to the Library Association, whether we should spur the Library Association to greater efforts or whether we should act independently.

He continued, and one wonders if there is a touch of wistful regret in his "perhaps: "

> Completely independent action is perhaps impossible, as it would involve the establishment of a separate scheme of professional education. We have neither the numbers to justify this course nor the funds to put it into operation, and the scheme would hamper the free exchange of librarians between Scotland and England, which is to the advantage of the library systems of both countries.

The Scottish Library Association, while it has always claimed to be "a representative body with a National character and interested in Acts of Parliament which affect our country only,"[15] has never set out to rival the Library Association by holding examinations in librarianship or issuing certificates of efficiency. It has, however, played its part in providing professional training.

The desirability of a library training school in Scotland is first recorded in the Scottish Library Association report for the years 1915-19. Glasgow, the council agreed, was the "natural location" for such a school, while summer schools should be held at Edinburgh, Dundee and Aberdeen. Nevertheless it was felt that adoption of the scheme must await the extension or abolition of the rate limit.

In the winter of 1919-20, however, the Glasgow and West of Scotland Branch of the Scottish Library Association organized a class in library routine under Mr A. Strain that attracted 35 students. The following winter there were 50 students for another evening class in library routine, conducted again by Mr Strain. In the following year, 1921-2, the Branch's educational activities were extended: two classes were organized, one in library routine, under Mr Strain once more, and one in cataloguing under C. A. Bradley. The enrolments were 34 and 29 respectively.

---

[15] G. W. Shirley, "Presidential address": SLA, *Annual report* 1935 (1936), p. 28.

In the autumn of 1922 a week's course of lectures in library practice was held in Glasgow. Nevertheless, the local branch of the Association continued throughout the winter its evening classes in library routine and cataloguing, but this was their last session. Ten years later, in 1932-3, a course of weekly lectures was held in the High School, Elmbank Street, Glasgow, on Wednesday evenings during the winter months, from mid-September to March. Two classes were arranged, one in preparation for the elementary examination, under Mr Strain, and the other on classification, under A. B. Paterson—with a total enrolment of sixty students. Courses of this kind were held each winter until 1938-9. Mr Strain continued his connexion with the classes until 1937. In the last two sessions, 1937-8 and 1938-9, the teacher was W. B. Paton, then of Airdrie, who was later to become the first Head of Scotland's first full-time school of librarianship. These later classes were held under the auspices of the Glasgow Corporation Education Department.

In June 1921 at its tenth annual meeting, in Edinburgh, the Scottish Library Association adopted a resolution instructing the council to institute in 1922 a spring or summer school in librarianship. The council discussed the matter and agreed to hold such a school, contingent on adequate enrolments, in one of the larger towns, Edinburgh, Glasgow, Aberdeen or Dundee, "but Ayr, Montrose and similar resorts are to be considered." The school to be held in Glasgow in September 1922 would be preparatory to the Library Association examinations. It was hoped it would be self-supporting: lecturers, it was thought, might be available without fee beyond expenses. Library authorities were to be asked to give staff time off and to assist with fees and expenses.

The first school was finally arranged for the first week of October. The 80 students came from 17 library systems from Dundee to Dumfries, 55 of them from Glasgow. There was a reception and musical evening on the Monday, and a charabanc trip to Aberfoyle and the Trossachs on the Saturday. In between, five lectures were given in the Jeffrey Room of the Mitchell Library, with visits to paper makers, printers and bookbinders, and to the Mitchell Library, the Commercial Library and representative district libraries. The expenditure of £16 12s 6d was adequately covered by the fee of 5s each, as Councillor D. McOwan, Convener, Glasgow Libraries Committee, gave a donation towards the expenses of the reception.

A year later, in October 1923, there were 81 enrolments for the second autumn course in librarianship. It was again held in

Glasgow with the same five lecturers—Kent, Savage, Macleod, Minto and Pitt. On this occasion the council decided to invite essays on the subjects dealt with by the lecturers and to make an award for the best essay in each section, but the entries were disappointingly few.

The third autumn school of library practice followed two years later, in October 1925, and was the first to be held in Edinburgh. There were 45 students and the syllabus offered nine lectures from six lecturers: Minto, Savage and Kent continued their connexion with these schools, and the other lecturers were A. Strain, J. Campbell and Dr W. K. Dickson. This year the president (Mr Ryrie Orr, chairman of the Greenock Library Committee) offered two prizes (£3 and £2) for the best essays on the week's proceedings. Nine were submitted and the prizes were awarded to Mr J. A. Burnett and Miss Jean M. Allan, both of Edinburgh.

The fourth school was held in Glasgow the following year, and until 1934 schools were held every second year alternately in Edinburgh and Glasgow, and always in October.

In 1936 the school was held in Edinburgh again, but the council had decided to attempt something new: the school was arranged for the summer (6-11 July), it was residential, and its syllabus was based on "the Elementary and Intermediate Sections of the Diploma Course of The Library Association." The first residential summer school at Buchanan Hostel, Edinburgh, was attended by forty-one students from Scotland, England and Ireland, and "although a financial loss [of £8 1s] was incurred, the school from a practical point of view was a success and an advance upon the Autumn School formerly held."

The following year the summer school was held at Newbattle Abbey College and was attended by 53 students (45 resident at the College) including two from Sweden and one from Iceland. The schools of 1938 and 1939, both at Newbattle Abbey, followed the same pattern, offering a syllabus directly preparatory to the elementary and intermediate examinations of the Library Association.

No summer schools were held during the war years or immediately following the end of hostilities. Indeed nine years elapsed before the fifth residential summer school was arranged in St Andrews in July 1948. In the interval the pattern of professional education had changed: the Library Association's syllabus of examinations had been drastically revised, and with the end of the Second World War full-time schools of librarianship had been established throughout Great Britain.

It was in 1945 that the council of the Scottish Library

Association received and examined the Library Association's new regulations and syllabus of professional examinations which eventually came into force in January 1946. The council had already expressed its desire for the establishment of a library school in Scotland, so the Library Association's proposal to set up a number of schools throughout Great Britain, including one in Scotland, was warmly welcomed.

Towards the end of 1945 it became clear that the Library Association's scheme to establish the Scottish library school in Edinburgh was hanging fire. After prolonged negotiations a home for the school was found in Glasgow, and the Scottish School of Librarianship was opened in September 1946 at the Glasgow and West of Scotland Commercial College with W. B. Paton, formerly librarian of Greenock Public Library, as Head and twenty-five full-time students. The main activity of the school was to be a year's course in preparation for the registration examination of the Library Association, but even in the first year part-time courses were organized for candidates preparing for the entrance examination and parts of the final examination.

Since its establishment the school has never looked back. After four years as Head, Mr Paton relinquished this post, on his appointment as county librarian of Lanarkshire, when he was succeeded by W. E. Tyler.[16]

The existence of this full-time school, with its thorough-going instruction in preparation for the different stages of the Library Association's examinations had its effect on the scope and organization of the Scottish Library Association's summer school.

The first post-war school was held at St Andrews in July 1948. (It had been hoped to hold a summer school during 1947 but suitable accommodation could not be found and the plan was abandoned.) Under the general title, "New Ideas for Old," seventeen lecturers delivered a series of lectures on a wide variety of special aspects of librarianship, and there were the usual visits to interesting libraries in the neighbourhood. The school attracted 62 students, of whom 42 were present for the entire period, from

[16] The subsequent history of the Scottish School of Librarianship and how it evolved into the Department of Librarianship in the University of Strathclyde falls outside the scope of this study, but it is difficult to overestimate the part W. E. Tyler played in this development. At Strathclyde he established the pioneer first-degree courses in Britain with librarianship as a principal subject (the first of these degrees were awarded in June 1969) and a year later there was general satisfaction when it was announced that the University had approved the establishment of a chair in librarianship and that Mr Tyler had been appointed professor.

practically every type of library, half from Scotland and the other half including librarians from England and Ireland and one from Switzerland.

The following year 44 students (28 for the whole course) attended a similar course, again at St Andrews, with the title, "Beyond the Textbooks." The third summer school at St Andrews, in 1950, "The Voice of Experience," was the last of the series. There were only 38 enrolments and the financial loss was heavy.

Nevertheless, the Scottish Library Association council decided to hold another school in July 1951, but agreed that year to return to Newbattle Abbey College where three very successful schools had been held before the war. The attendance was small (27, the lowest on record) but apart from this the school was judged "eminently successful and worthwhile," and there was even a small credit balance. The achievement was repeated in 1952 and again in 1953 when 37 and 34 students attended further schools at Newbattle Abbey College. The summer school became a regular feature of the Association's work each year, and the connexion with Newbattle has been maintained.

THE SCOTTISH LIBRARY ASSOCIATION

The Library Association remains an organization for the United Kingdom although the phrase "of the United Kingdom" was officially dropped from its title in 1896. However, in view of the differences that have always existed in library legislation north and south of the Border, the Library Association, with its head-quarters in London and a preponderance of English members, has tended to be predominantly English in outlook and influence. It is certainly true that in its first seventy-eight years of existence, although several notable Scots had been elected president of the Association, only one Scottish-born librarian (J. Y. W. MacAlister) had held that office, and he was never a librarian in Scotland. The three librarians of Scottish libraries who became presidents of the Library Association in that period were all Englishmen.[17]

It was during the fourth Library Association conference in Scotland, in Glasgow in 1907, that a meeting of Scottish librarians discussed the question of forming a branch of the Association or

[17] The appointment of W. B. Paton, county librarian of Lanarkshire, as president of the Library Association in 1962, however, brought to that office for the first time a Scottish-born librarian, living and working in Scotland and closely involved with all that is forward-looking in Scottish library development. He was also the first county librarian to be president of the Library Association.

of establishing a separate Association for Scotland. "It was decided that as Scottish libraries are administered under separate Acts of Parliament and have problems of their own, the better plan would be to have a separate Association for Scotland, but affiliated to the Library Association."[18]

Several regional branches of the Association had been formed already, and almost twenty years before, Greenwood had been urging Scottish librarians to follow this course:

It would be a good thing for the Scotch Public Librarians to form a small association among themselves.

The Association was formally inaugurated at a meeting held in Edinburgh on 24 October 1908. F. T. Barrett presided and James Craigie, Sandeman Public Library, Perth, acted as secretary. A fortnight later a circular letter signed by Craigie announced the formation of the new Association "with sixty-five Librarians and Assistants—all of whom are employed in Scottish libraries— . . . as Members."[19]

At a general meeting of the Association in Glasgow in February 1909 rules and regulations were adopted, and the Association's first annual meeting was held in Edinburgh on 12 May 1909.

The first annual report of the association appears to be that for 1909-10. It records that two council meetings were held in the course of the year, both at Stirling. At the first "the compilation of a Bibliography of Scottish Periodical literature was mentioned:" nothing more is heard of this ambitious project.

By 1913-14 there were 138 members, of whom 104 worked in the four great cities (Glasgow 63, Edinburgh 21, Dundee 17, Aberdeen 3).

The report for 1912-13 records the first district meetings held in December, January, and March, at Edinburgh, Motherwell, and Dundee respectively. The holding of district meetings had been suggested and discussed in council the previous year: it was felt that one annual meeting was not sufficient. Another district meeting was held at Dunfermline in April 1914; and then, with the outbreak of war, apart from two meetings held at Glasgow and Lanark in 1916, there were no more district meetings for five years. During the war years it was found impossible to hold even the regular annual meeting.

[18] Minto, *History* (1932), p. 247.
[19] In the *Annual report* for 1912-13 the number of original members is given as 68; in the *Annual report* for 1913-14 it is stated to have been 63, and the Association is said to have been founded in 1907.

The seventh annual meeting of the Association was held at Dundee in 1915 and the eighth at Aberdeen in 1919, when a four-year report was given. At the council meetings then reported, two important topics had been discussed: the desirability of a Library Training School, located in Glasgow, was emphasized, with summer schools at Edinburgh, Dundee, and Aberdeen, but it was felt that "fruition of the scheme must await extension or abolition of the rate limit;" and it was decided that district meetings should be organized in three areas: Glasgow and the West; Edinburgh and the East; Dundee, Aberdeen and the North. Meetings were arranged in Glasgow and the West in 1919-20 with John Dunlop as local secretary.

The special conferences of 1919 and 1920 to discuss the library rate have been reported in chapter 3.

At the tenth annual meeting, at Edinburgh in June 1921, it was resolved that the council should inquire into conditions of service, and that the council should institute in 1922 "a spring or summer school in librarianship." As we have seen the first Scottish Library Association school of librarianship was held in the autumn, in Glasgow from 2 October to 7 October 1922. As to the inquiry into conditions of service: seventy-three copies of a questionnaire were sent out, but in the first instance only twenty-six replies were received. The attempt was made to obtain more information but even so there were insufficient replies for the purpose of a detailed report. A printed summary was circulated by the honorary secretary in July 1922.

In the year 1923-4 local meetings were organized in two of the suggested areas: two meetings were held in Glasgow and the West and four in Edinburgh and the East. From this date on these branches of the Association have had a continuous and active existence, providing professional talks and social meetings for their members.

In the same year the Association made some constitutional changes. At the 1923 annual meeting in Stirling D. E. Edward of Ayr had raised the question of the election and constitution of the council. The matter was remitted to the council for consideration, and at the annual meeting at Glasgow in the following year certain amendments were submitted and adopted. Hitherto councillors had been elected for a period of two years, at the annual meeting. Now the president and three vice-presidents (an increase of two vice-presidents) were to be elected annually by the council, and at the annual meeting the Association would elect the honorary secretary and the honorary treasurer and (by voting paper) four councillors to serve for three years. Two years later it was agreed that the secretary and treasurer, like the president and vice-presidents, should be elected annually by the council and not by the annual meeting. At the first election twelve councillors (an increase of two) would be elected, the first four in the election for three years, the second four for two years, and the third four for one year, and all were to be eligible for re-election at the end of their periods of office. Thereafter there would be an annual election for four councillors who would serve for three years and be ineligible for re-election for one year after their term of office.

The first election under the new constitution took place at the fourteenth annual meeting at Greenock in June 1925 with the following result:

Miss Maud S. Best, Aberdeen	125	
John McDonald, Dunfermline	113	*To retire in 1928*
Frederic Kent, Glasgow	112	
Robert Bain, Glasgow	111	
Lt. Col. J. M. Mitchell, C.U.K.T.	100	
G. M. Fraser, Aberdeen	99	*To retire in 1927*
W. Graham Waugh, Stirling	91	
R. Butchart	88	
A. H. Millar, LL.D., Dundee	83	
James Craigie, Perth	81	*To retire in 1926*
Miss J. M. Cuthbertson, Glasgow	71	
James Christison, Montrose	70	

At this time too the Association agreed to the election of an honorary president and honorary vice-presidents and the council proceeded to fill these offices. The Earl of Elgin was elected honorary president and six honorary vice-presidents were chosen.[20]

At a council meeting in 1925-6 it was proposed that an annual scholarship should be established. It was suggested the annual award should be £15 and the council allocated £50 towards the necessary £300. Five hundred appeals were issued to members "and to persons interested in literature and its dissemination." The president, Ryrie Orr, offered to defray the cost of the first scholarship. This was won by Miss Jean M. Allan, M.A., Edin-

[20] The Earl of Elgin, for many years chairman of the Carnegie United Kingdom Trust, and president of the Library Association in 1927, was to remain honorary president of the Scottish Library Association until his death on 27 November 1968 in his 88th year.

burgh Public Libraries, with an essay "A plea for co-operative catalogues in printed form." Miss Allan used the award towards the cost of a tour of the principal libraries of England. She later submitted to the council a report of her tour, and she spoke of her experiences at meetings of both the Glasgow and Edinburgh branches of the Association. No award was made in 1927, and in the year 1928-9 the council prudently agreed to suspend the competition until the capital had reached £300. The scholarship was next offered in 1931.

It was in 1928-9, after the annual meeting of 30 May 1928 at Aberdeen when Guy W. Keeling, the secretary of the Library Association, had been welcomed for the first time to a meeting of librarians in Scotland, that the Scottish Library Association was invited to become a branch of the Library Association. The jubilee conference of the Library Association in Edinburgh in 1927 had strongly recommended the strengthening of the Association by a unification of the different local and special associations of librarians. With this end in view it had been decided to appoint a full-time secretary and to obtain suitable premises for the Association's headquarters. The executive committee of the Library Association council had approached the Carnegie Trust for a grant towards this policy, and a generous offer was made, subject to certain conditions, of which one was "that the Association undertake to make an effort to induce the other library groups and associations to come within a single unit." At Aberdeen the secretary had underlined the importance of unity in purpose and organization, but the special committee of the council appointed to consider the matter concluded that "having regard to the national character of the Scottish Library Association, the interests of Scottish libraries and librarians would be best served by the retention of its separate identity," a recommendation the council adopted.

However, at the annual meeting of 1929, at St Andrews, when for the first time it had been found necessary to extend the meeting to two days, Mr Keeling made a second appearance. He was introduced by the president (E. A. Savage, principal librarian of the Edinburgh Public Libraries) and "briefly addressed the meeting on the urgent necessity for the closest co-operation between the organisations representing areas or aspects of the library service throughout the Kingdom." In the succeeding winter the council "considered very carefully the invitation to this Association to become a branch of the Library Association, and, having regard to the obvious value of a co-ordinated body representative of the entire library service of the Kingdom, and to the fact that under the proposed agreement of union the Scottish Library Association would retain its national entity," they came to the conclusion "that the interests of both the Scottish library service and the Association would be best served by the closest possible affiliation with the Library Association."

A draft agreement between the two Associations, which the council of the Scottish Association had approved and recommended its members to accept, was printed in the council's report for 1929-30, and it was agreed to hold a postal ballot, for or against union on these conditions, after the annual meeting in 1930. The Scottish Library Association was to retain its constitution and whatever title its members might select ("provided always that the title chosen shall indicate the connection and/or union with the Library Association"), and it would become also the branch of the Library Association in Scotland.

Members of the Scottish Library Association who were already members of the Library Association were to pay in future only the appropriate subscription of the Library Association, and any new members enrolled "after the date of union" were to join the Library Association in accordance with its by-laws; "members of the Scottish Library Association not being members of the Library Association" were to be recognized as Transitional Members and would continue to pay to the officers of the Scottish Library Association the subscription payable at the date of the agreement, but "it shall be part of the policy of the Scottish Library Association to persuade Transitional Members to become members of the Library Association." Transitional Members were to enjoy all the privileges of membership of the Library Association, except that they would not receive the *Library Association Record* nor would they be entitled to registration. The Scottish Library Association was to receive towards its expenses "the equivalent of a rebate of not less than Three Shillings per Guinea of the subscription of members of the Library Association who are members of the Scottish Library Association, or who elect to become members of the Scottish Library Association."

In the postal ballot 182 voting papers were returned (there were over 300 members of the Association at the time), 174 being in favour of the union and 8 against.

With this authority the Council authorised the President and Honorary Secretary to sign the agreement on behalf of the Scottish Library Association at the Conference of the Library Association at Cambridge.

This was done on 26 September 1930 and the agreement came into force on the first day of January 1931.

The credit for the successful outcome of the negotiations is very largely due to the untiring efforts of the Hon. Secretary, Mr Ernest A. Savage, whose advocacy of the amalgamation was whole-hearted, and who spared neither time nor trouble to bring about this happy result.[21]

At the time, Dr Savage was both honorary secretary of the Library Association and president of the Scottish Library Association.

In its twenty-two years as an independent Association the Scottish Library Association had increased its membership from 65 to 350; it had arranged a series of six short-term schools in librarianship; it had organized branch meetings in the Glasgow and the Edinburgh areas; and it had established a fund to provide an annual scholarship. The Association's annual meetings had given both local authority representatives and librarians the opportunity of discussing problems, arguing differences, and formulating policies. The Association's council had become an important deliberative body.

The new "branch" of the Library Association retained the constitution of the Association it superseded, and the fact that Scottish libraries operate under their own Acts of Parliament gave the new branch a status in the Library Association different from that of the regional branches in England and Wales. As we have seen, problems peculiar to Scottish library legislation were already occupying the attention of the Scottish Library Association council at the time of the affiliation, and they were to be its main concern for the next twenty-five years.

It will be recalled that when local or district meetings of the Association were suggested in the report for 1915-19, it was hoped there would be meetings in three areas; but while meetings were early organized in Glasgow and the West and in Edinburgh and the East, it was found difficult to establish a branch of the Association in the third district, Dundee, Aberdeen and the North of Scotland. At length, in April 1933, an inaugural meeting was held at Inverness, when Col. Mitchell spoke, and a local committee was appointed with Daniel Hay, Caithness County Library, and A. B. Peters, Inverness Public Library, as joint honorary secretaries. A second meeting, held six months later, was the branch's last. A branch for Dundee and Central Scotland,

---

[21] Minto, *History* (1932), p. 206.

however, was formed in 1949, and continues to function successfully.[22]

In 1933 the Library Association, at a meeting of branch and section chairmen and secretaries, suggested "that all Branch and Section Councils and Committees be elected to hold office as from 1st January." It had been the practice in the Scottish Library Association from its formation to elect office-bearers and council members to hold office from one annual meeting until the next, but the annual meeting at Perth in May 1934 approved the council's recommendation to amend the Association's rules and regulations affecting the date of election of office-bearers and councillors, the amendments to become operative on 1 January 1936. As a natural consequence of the change of the Association's year to synchronize with that of the Library Association and its branches, a short-term report, covering the period from May to December 1934, was issued. Thereafter, the reports have covered twelve months, as they did previously.

There were further negotiations in 1935 and the council's sub-committee on the proposed re-organization and closer union of the Library Association and the Scottish Library Association had two meetings during the year with the joint-committee of the Library Association and the Association of Assistant Librarians. A draft scheme for closer union, approved by the Scottish Council, was after all suspended, in view of the Assistant Librarians' rejection of the proposals for amalgamation with the Library Association.

Relations with the Library Association were again under discussion ten years later. During 1945 a memorandum setting out the position as it appeared to the council of the Scottish Library Association was issued to the Library Association council, which received a Scottish deputation at its December meeting. The Scottish Library Association proposed:

(1) Direct representation of the Scottish Library Association on the Council of the Library Association.

(2) Formal notification to the Scottish Library Association of any decisions affecting Scotland reached by the Library Association.

(3) Prior notification to the Scottish Library Association of any approach which the Library Association intended to make to Scottish bodies.

[22] The North of Scotland branch was successfully revived in 1963.

236

(4) That copies of official letters from the Library Association office to Scottish members should be sent to the Honorary Secretary of the Scottish Library Association.

(5) An increase in the rebate from three shillings to six shillings in the guinea.

(6) That steps should be taken to ensure that newly joined Scottish members of the Library Association were immediately made aware that membership of the Scottish Library Association was open to them without payment of additional subscription.

The Scottish representatives were given a sympathetic hearing and all but the first of these six proposals were adopted. The first proposal, as the Scottish representatives realized, conflicted with the Library Association's by-laws. However, it was referred to the Library Association's executive committee for examination.

The annual report of the Scottish Library Association for 1945 continues:

The Council are confident that the new agreement, besides ensuring a welcome increase in the annual income of the Scottish Library Association, will facilitate joint action between the two associations in matters of common interest, and will prevent a recurrence of misunderstandings which have existed in the past. Before this interview took place the Library Association had made a special grant to the Scottish Library Association towards the extraordinary expenditure incurred in connection with the promotion of new legislation. The Council are most grateful to the Library Association for their generous and sympathetic attitude.

Later the Library Association council invited the council of the Scottish Library Association to send an observer to its meetings. The invitation was eagerly accepted, and it was moreover agreed that the Scottish Library Association could be represented by a substitute if the duly appointed observer found it inconvenient to attend a meeting to which he had been called. The observer, of course, had no power to vote in the Library Association council. Then with the revision of the Library Association's by-laws in 1949 it was agreed to include in the council from 1 January 1950 a representative from each of the branches of the Association, and under these new by-laws the Scottish Library Association observer became a full member of the council.

That there remained a particular reason for including a representative of the Scottish Library Association in the Library Association council was made clear at the Library Association's annual meeting in 1953, when the by-laws were again under discussion, for an amendment to abolish branch representation (it was not, however, adopted by the Association) excepted the Scottish Library Association and the Northern Ireland and the Wales and Monmouthshire Branches.[23]

Hitherto, in the matter of finance also the Scottish Library Association, in receiving under the 1930 and 1945 agreements an agreed proportion of the Library Association subscriptions raised in Scotland, had been treated differently from the other regional branches of the Association, which had to prepare each year for approval and possible modification by the council of the Library Association, an estimate of the expenditure likely to be incurred in the ensuing year. Under the new by-laws which became effective in January 1950 all members of the Library Association residing or working in a branch district were deemed to be members of that branch and the council agreed to pay to the branch "such proportion of the annual subscriptions received from the Members of that Branch as may from time to time be determined."

At the same time the deletion of the proviso permitting branches to admit "persons residing in the district, who are not professional librarians and not Members of the Association, . . . to Branch Membership" on the payment of an annual subscription made it necessary for the Scottish Library Association to abolish Transitional Membership and Transitional Associate Membership, and this step was taken at the annual meeting in Perth in 1949 to be effective from January 1951.

From January 1951 the Scottish Library Association was allowed a sum equal to 10s per member of the Library Association resident or working in Scotland instead of the grant at the rate of 6s for every guinea paid by those members of the Association in Scotland who had notified their desire to become members of the Scottish Library Association. The change was slightly to the advantage of the Scots. In 1950 the Library Association payment (at 6s per guinea for the subscriptions from 530 members) amounted to £272 13s 1d and transitional members' subscriptions (at December 1950 there were 9 Transitional Members and 27 Transitional Associate Members) were £7 3s 6d, a total of £279 16s 7d. In 1951 the Library Association payment at 10s

[23] *Library Association Record,* vol. 55 (1953), p. 92, 189.

per head for 582 members was £291. A year later membership stood at 640 and the Association received £320. In December 1954 the membership was: Personal 603, Institutional 86; a total of 689.

Apart from the Scottish Library Association there were in Scotland in 1955 several other associations of librarians, both official and unofficial.

There were, for example, Scottish branches of two of the sections of the Library Association. The branch of the Youth Libraries Section had been formed in 1948 and had held regular meetings since that time. Then 1953 saw the formation of a Scottish branch of the University and Research Section: its membership at 31 October 1955 stood at 122 and was by no means limited to librarians working in "university and research" libraries.

A Scottish branch of Aslib—the Association of Special Libraries and Information Bureaux, founded in 1924—has been in existence since 1949 and operates both on its own account and in joint meetings with the regional branches of the Scottish Library Association.[24]

Scottish county librarians have an association of their own in the County Library Circle which was founded in 1927. Following a preliminary meeting in December 1926 circulars suggesting the formation of the Circle had been sent to all county librarians in Scotland. Replies from "practically every one" approved the decision, and a subsequent meeting on 12 January "proceeded to consolidate the Circle."

This lively body has held regular quarterly meetings (apart from the years of the Second World War) and provides an excellent forum for the discussion of county library problems. It fulfils this function so adequately that there was no support among Scottish librarians for the suggestion, brought forward in 1951, that a Scottish branch of the County Libraries Section of the Library Association should be formed. It was felt that the County Library Circle already did all that the proposed branch could do.

The Strathclyde Librarians' Club is a social meeting, and its professional membership is confined to male chief librarians, mainly in the west of Scotland, but although it is "unofficial" it is not uninfluential. Later the female chief librarians in Scotland founded, in emulation or retaliation, the Scotia Club.

[24] SLA, *Calendar of library activities in Scotland,* 1954-5, 1955-6.

239

While the committee that governs a public library is finally responsible for the policy to be pursued and for financial control and the librarian is nominally only the executive officer, it is generally in fact the librarian who initiates developments by advising the authority and bringing before it recommendations for its consideration. Nevertheless, the responsibility of accepting or rejecting these recommendations lies with the committee.

The Scottish burgh library committee is an executive with its constitution and powers laid down by statute. It appeared in its present form—not more than twenty members, half of whom are to be members of the council, and half chosen by the council from householders—in the Public Libraries (Scotland) Act 1867. In Edinburgh, however, the town council, by the Edinburgh Public Libraries Act 1887, reserved to itself the control of capital for land and buildings and the annual audit of all expenditure, both capital and current. In Glasgow, where the libraries are administered under a local Act by a committee of the town council, there are no co-opted householder-members. In Edinburgh, again, in 1953 and 1954, there was a move to eliminate the co-opted members, but in the end their representation was only reduced to a number not exceeding one-half and not less than one-third of the membership of the committee. Similar steps have been taken in Aberdeen and Dundee.

Co-option is not favoured in present-day municipal politics, but there is no doubt that the library service as a whole has benefited greatly from the advice of co-opted committee members.

> Clearly when co-option was permitted the intention of Parliament was to encourage local authorities to choose men who were fit to administer libraries. . . . Men of this type either can't or won't stand for a town council, but they are glad to put their knowledge at the disposal of a committee doing work of interest to them. Co-option is one way of checking the apotheosis of the amateur, democracy's great weakness.[25]

The Kenyon committee did not doubt "the value of co-option in securing a more expert committee," but thought "the majority of the committee, and the chairman, should as a general rule be

---

[25] E. A. Savage, *The librarian and his committee* (1942), p. 11. Dr Savage, in a memorandum he prepared for the Departmental Committee on Public Libraries in 1927, advocated "governing bodies elected and selected especially to manage public libraries; the Scottish constitution of such bodies being taken as a model" (Minto, *History* (1932), p. 159).

elected members." Miss Carnell on the other hand was not in favour of the principle:

Co-opted members either add to the size of a committee or dilute its voting strength on the main body. . . . Very few individuals are worth obtaining at either price.[26]

The power of co-option, it is clear, must be wisely exercised; the co-opted members should be obviously suitable for the committee on which they are asked to serve:

Co-option quickly falls into disrepute when members are chosen to represent parties or factions or sects, or to console them for bad fortune at the last election, or when local politicians elbow their way into the committee room and use it as an arena for boosting their candidature to the council.[27]

County libraries in Scotland are administered by the county education committees, generally through a sub-committee. By statute education committees must include certain co-opted members, although "at least a majority of the committee" must be members of the council. A sub-committee may consist "to an extent not exceeding one half" of persons who are not members of the council and may include persons who are not members of the committee: in other words, the county library sub-committee may have members co-opted to it for their knowledge and experience of libraries who are neither members of the education committee nor of the county council. Provision of this kind was made in Clackmannanshire, for example, at the time of the amalgamation of the burgh library service in Alloa with the county library service. A county library sub-committee was appointed with fourteen members: seven were county councillors, members of the education committee, three were members of the education committee but were not county councillors, and four were specially co-opted to the library sub-committee. As a gesture to the superseded Alloa burgh library committee four of its members were the first to be co-opted to the new sub-committee. Co-option to the county library sub-committee only is, however, rare.

As the county library committee is itself a sub-committee, it does not often establish further sub-committees to carry out its work. Burgh library committees, however, frequently appoint such sub-committees. There is usually a Books Committee, and

[26] E. J. Carnell, *County libraries* (1938), p. 45.
[27] Savage, *The librarian and his committee* (1942), p. 12.

other sub-committees are sometimes appointed for Accounts, Staff and Buildings. The Books Committee may well be a survival from the days of the subscription library when the guiding power was the committee of directors and the librarian was little more than a caretaker.

In the burghs the librarian is sometimes clerk to the library committee, but it is more and more common for the duties of clerk to the committee to be undertaken by the town clerk or a member of his department. In only two burghs is the librarian treasurer to his committee as well as clerk.

The burgh librarian holds a status slightly different from the county librarian. The burgh librarian, although he may not rank among the chief officials of the authority he serves, is the chief officer of an *ad hoc* committee with considerable powers. The county librarian administers a service on behalf of a sub-committee of the education committee, whose chief executive officer is the director of education. The county librarian, then, is an assistant to the director of education, with particular responsibility for a specialized service within the general educational service, in much the same way as the sanitary inspector is a specialized assistant to the medical officer of health. There have been those, burgh librarians among them, who have not been slow to point out the county librarian's subordination to the director of education, and there have been unfortunate cases where librarian and director have signally failed to work well together. The Advisory Council has a wise footnote on this very point:

> We do not believe that it is either important or desirable that senior officers or others holding responsible posts should be placed in a self-conscious hierarchy. Such officers are carrying out functions on behalf of the County Council, where each one is an expert in his own line and where any definition of relative importance is always difficult and seldom necessary.

The public librarian's conditions of service have been governed for some years by the National Joint Industrial Council's scheme, which was generally adopted on its introduction in 1946. Under this scheme it is normal to work 38 hours per week; yet in 1922 two Scottish libraries had a working week of 84 hours while three worked 70 hours. In one case where the hours worked weekly was given as 70 there was only one member of staff.[28]

[28] SLA, *Statistics of public libraries in Scotland* (1922).

242

At that time salaries for chief librarians ranged from £700 to £70 (with house, etc.); thirty years later they ranged from £1725 to £300.

Earlier in this chapter the qualifications that a librarian should possess have been referred to in terms of the professional examinations he should pass. His more general qualifications are briefly stated by Edwards:

> The two main things to be looked for in a librarian,—then as now,—will be these:—(1) A genuine love of books; (2) An indomitable passion for order. Neither quality will, of itself, suffice. There must be an union of the two.[29]

A librarian must have administrative ability, technical competence, a good business head, sound judgement, the capacity to "get on" with people, an alert intelligence and a wide range of general knowledge, but none of these important qualities in itself distinguishes the librarian from the men and women of other professions. It is his knowledge of books that is or should be the librarian's hall-mark:[30]

> A library is dead unless it is under the direction of an enthusiastic librarian who is able to make the great books of the past still live.[31]

Many tributes have been paid to the librarian. None perhaps is more emphatic than the statement in the Kenyon report:

> The success of a library . . . depends to an extent which is seldom realised on the librarian. The qualities, both of character and knowledge, required of a good librarian are very

[29] E. Edwards, *Free town libraries* (1869), p. 30.
[30] The librarian is not infrequently an author, although his pen is usually turned to deal with professional topics and technicalities. Among Scottish public librarians with a literary gift may be mentioned: Thomas Mason of Glasgow, whose novel, *Adam Dickson,* was published in 1888; John Gardiner of Airdrie, author of a novel, *Harry Rutherford;* W. F. Cuthbertson of Hawick (son of a sub-librarian of Edinburgh University Library, who was also a writer), a poet and the author of several children's books and western "thrillers"; James Christison, burgh librarian of Montrose, to whom Violet Jacob "used to submit her drafts for revisal" (*see* Douglas Young, *"Plastic Scots" and the Scottish literary tradition* (1947), p. 24); and R. D. Macleod, founder and editor for 37 years (1927-64) of *Library Review,* "a quarterly magazine on libraries and literature," who has written authoritatively on John Davidson and William Morris, and on *The Scottish publishing houses* (1953).
[31] J. Arnold Fleming, *The medieval Scots scholar in France* (1952), p. 110.

243

high. . . . For the large majority of the population the librarian and his staff are the guides who introduce them into the kingdom of knowledge. For such a service no qualifications can be too high, while it is a disaster to the community if they are too low.

None more inspiring than the words of the Advisory Council on the "trained professional librarian":

a man who lives among books, is never tired of savouring them, and has acquired by long experience the sense of quality that will enable him, particularly if he also knows something of the tastes and standards of the reader, to put before him, however tentatively, a selection of books from which he may himself choose those that will give him the greatest pleasure and satisfaction.

A librarian can derive much encouragement from the knowledge that it was a statesman and historian of the standing of the late Viscount Bryce, O.M., who declared:

One of the best justifications for the existence of libraries is, that they provide a librarian.[32]

---

[32] Library Association, *Public libraries: their development and future organization* (1917), p. 42.

CHAPTER 9

SCOTTISH LIBRARY LEGISLATION

THE HISTORY of Scottish public library legislation in the twentieth century has been singularly unhappy.

As we have seen, although the Public Libraries Act of 1919 had abolished the penny rate in England and Wales, the Public Libraries (Scotland) Act of the following year had merely raised the limit from 1d to 3d. Certainly the increase gave some immediate relief to the more sorely pressed authorities, but later the three-penny rate was to prove as crippling a limitation as the penny rate had been.

Again, when the Education (Scotland) Act of 1918 created in Scotland an entirely new type of library authority, there was no general protest, although the Scottish Library Association expressed some concern and submitted its views on the matter to the Secretary for Scotland; for the proviso to section 5 of that Act kept the two types of authority financially apart. It was some ten years later before library legislation in Scotland became the "real live issue" that the president of the Library Association called it at the Dunblane conference of 1931.[1] It was to remain a live issue for twenty-five years.

The Scottish Library Association's efforts to obtain new library legislation may be said to have begun at a special general meeting of the Association on 21 December 1928, which had been called to consider the Local Government (Scotland) Bill. The council had previously considered this measure, benefiting from the guidance and advice of A. B. Hyslop, treasurer of the Carnegie United Kingdom Trust, and recommended its approval. At the special general meeting the discussion centred mainly around sub-section 5 of section 18, which proposed the repeal of the proviso to section 5 of the Education (Scotland) Act, 1918. A resolution, moved by Mr Shirley of Dumfries Public Library and seconded by Mr Reekie of Paisley, was adopted, to the effect that the meeting approved clause 18 (5) "with the proviso that where a burgh is operating a library under the Public Libraries Acts, it

[1] L. S. Jast, *Proceedings of the Scottish Library Conference, Dunblane* (1931), p. 37.

245

shall be given, for the portion of the county assessment for libraries raised from it, an equivalent service."

A second motion, by Mr Reekie of Paisley and the Rev. P. R. Landreth of Perth, was defeated. It sought to express the meeting's disapproval of the council's recommendation of the Bill, and urged "that the whole question of library legislation be reconsidered with a view to creating a single Authority in burghs and counties."

A further motion, by Mr Shirley and Mr Paterson, was, however, adopted. It remitted to the council "to consider the provisions requisite to a new Libraries Act for Scotland, and to report to the Annual Meeting."

The council of the Scottish Library Association implemented this remit by appointing a committee which held several meetings in the ensuing year and reached conclusions which were, in the main, accepted by the council. The committee was of the opinion that new legislation was urgently necessary, and that "it should take the form of a Consolidating Act, with such amendments and additions as the efficient operation of the Scottish library service demands." The council agreed to engage, at the Association's expense, a competent legal authority to draft a Bill embodying their proposals.

Meantime, the double library rate was under discussion again at a meeting of the Scottish Library Association. At the annual meeting in St Andrews in June 1929, a month after the Local Government (Scotland) Act reached the Statute Book, Mr Shirley read a paper on "The Scottish Public Book Service: a Reconnaissance" in which he referred to the motion adopted at the special general meeting six months before, and then described the double library rate on burghs as "this curious anomaly."

Exactly what services the Burghs will secure from the Counties for their contributions had not yet emerged and solutions, doubtless, will be studied with much attention by librarians.

The following year, when the Association met in Dumfries in May, Colonel Mitchell read a paper on "Public libraries under the new regime," afterwards issued by the Scottish Library Association along with Mr Savage's presidential address as a pamphlet under the title, *Scottish Public Libraries under the new Regime.* Colonel Mitchell dealt in some detail with the situation arising from the Act of 1929. On the question of double rating he said:

There has been a certain amount of discussion as to what service might be rendered by the counties to these burghs in

246

return for the financial contribution which hitherto the counties have not received from them. It is unadvisable in the interests of the library movement that an exact *quid pro quo* should be demanded. As has been pointed out, the whole tendency of educational policy has been to provide service where it is required, and it seems desirable that the same spirit should enter into the library service. At the same time County Authorities should bear in mind that there may at first be some feeling of resentment in the burghs at having to contribute to the County Library service. They are naturally jealous of their powers, and they may, quite unjustifiably, suspect that the new arrangement is the thin edge of the wedge of county control. The new Act, however, puts an additional power into the hands of the county, which can therefore well afford to be generous in its attitude towards the burghs.

It is difficult to make any general suggestions as to the form which service by the county to the burgh should take. The character of the need will vary in different localities, and arrangements will have to be made according to the particular requirements of the burgh. The following suggestions have, however, been put forward : —

(i) Loans of sets of books for continuation and other classes.

(ii) School libraries.

(iii) An annual contribution towards running expenses.

(iv) Purchase of more expensive non-fiction.

(v) Structural alterations required for the modernisation of a library building.

Here again an intelligent grasp of the possibilities and a spirit of mutual confidence will spread even more widely the harmonious and efficient co-operation which is working so admirably in such counties as Angus and West Lothian. The very small towns would be well advised to consider complete amalgamation, but this can only occur of their own absolutely free will, and most of them will be content for the present to explore the advantages of co-operation. These advantages are so great and so well authenticated by experience that it will be discreditable to all concerned if *a priori* suspicion, based on ignorance and ill-will, shuts the door which the new system has thrown open. . . .

Where, however, the burgh is a very small one, the withdrawal of the proviso to Section 5 may be an inducement to it to rescind its powers in favour of the county and allow the County Council to take over complete control of the library. From the burgh's point of view this would be an economy if the cost in future were to be met from county funds. From the county's point of view it might be advantageous if development on a regional basis, as outlined above, were in contemplation.

Despite Colonel Mitchell's reassurances the difficulties arising from double rating persisted.

In March of the following year (1931) the Dunblane conference, jointly convened by the Carnegie United Kingdom Trust and the Scottish Library Association, adopted four resolutions, of which two referred explicitly to the burgh-county controversy, one of these including the hopeful phrase: "pending future legislation."

The findings of the conference are well worth noting:

(1) That Public Library Committees should be empowered to enter into arrangements with other Library Authorities for the interloan of books and other library material.

(2) That there should be established in Scotland a National Central Lending Library on a similar scheme to that approved for England and Wales.

(3) That, pending future legislation, with the object of regulating co-operation between Burgh and County Library Authorities, where money is raised as part of the Education rate by the County Authority for Library purposes, some reasonable return should be given to the Burgh Authority, such return to be determined after consultation with the Burgh Authority.

(4) That in order to facilitate and encourage co-operation between County and Burgh Authorities the principle embodied in the proviso in Section 5 of the Education Act of 1918 be restored.

Those resolutions are to recur in slightly varying form for more than twenty years.

Throughout the year 1930-1 the Scottish Library Association council had continued to consider the problem of Scottish library legislation, and its conclusions were embodied in "a rough draft Bill for a Consolidated Public Libraries Act for Scotland," the main provisions of which were submitted for the consideration of members at the annual meeting of 1931 in Kirkcaldy. The

248

Association's consideration of the council's recommendations was preceded by the presidential address in which Mr Pitt reviewed "existing legislative provision for Public Libraries in Scotland, and the special need at this time for its revision and extension." Towards the end of his talk he quoted the two complementary resolutions adopted by the Dunblane conference (numbered 3 and 4 above) and made this comment:

> The first resolution may, I think, be said to reflect the view that the cancellation of the proviso had brought about a state of affairs which was not of a permanent nature, and which, as experience had already shown, was much more conducive to constant discord than to the complete harmony desirable in a developing service. The second resolution was obviously intended to expedite legislation which would give effect to that view.

The council's recommendations for new library legislation for Scotland were eight in number:

1. The Scottish Public Libraries Acts, 1887 to 1920, to be consolidated.
2. Public Library Committees to be given powers to enter into arrangements with other library authorities for the interloan of books and other library material.
3. Public Library Committees to be empowered to provide public lectures and to defray the cost from the library rate.
4. County Councils to be empowered to levy a separate rate for library purposes.
5. The repeal of the clause in the Local Government (Scotland) Act, 1929, the effect of which is the double rating for library purposes of burghs which already maintain a public library under the Public Libraries Acts.
6. Power to adopt the Act to be restricted, so far as burghs are concerned, to burghs with populations of 20,000 and upwards, without affecting those burghs which have a library service in being at the time of the passing of the new Act.
7. The abolition of the rate limit of 3d in the £.
8. The establishment of a National Lending Library for Scotland.

The annual report records that "after considerable discussion paragraphs 1, 2, 3, 6, 7, and 8 were approved unanimously, and paragraphs 4 and 5 were adopted by majority votes." The council was instructed "not to proceed in the first instance with a parliamentary Bill, but to draft a memorandum embodying the approved, and any contingent, proposals," and to submit it to a later meeting of the Association.

The existence of divergent points of view in burgh and county, however, was apparent. A further motion, proposed by two burgh librarians, to the effect that the council should obtain from each burgh library authority an estimate of the assessment for library purposes in the education rate imposed on the burgh, with a statement of any return made by the county council to the burgh, was opposed when the direct negative was moved by a county librarian and a director of education. On a vote the motion was adopted.

Following the annual meeting the council considered the preparation of a memorandum on the requirements of new Scottish library legislation. A drafting committee was appointed, but in view of the financial situation of the country it was decided, while proceeding with the preparation of the necessary data, to defer public discussion of the memorandum.

This decision was discussed at length at the next annual meeting of the Association (at Motherwell in June 1932), and it was agreed to leave the matter in the hands of the council with an additional remit—

> to consider and to make recommendations on suitable forms of return which might be made by the counties to the burghs, for the amount raised for library purposes by the counties in urban areas, where libraries are already maintained under the Public Libraries (Scotland) Acts.

This additional remit was discharged in the annual report of the council for 1932-3 when the council submitted the following recommendations:

1. Apart from the *form* of return, a reasonable return would be the repayment of the amount raised by the county in the burgh for library purposes, less an agreed percentage for administrative expenses.

2. The Council would deprecate the return from the county being applied to the reduction of the public library rate.

3. Forms in which the returns might be made: —

    (*a*) Cash payment.

    (*b*) Equivalent expenditure on books and book-binding.

    (*c*) Loans of books from the county library, at an agreed rate per hundred.

(d) Service. This form of return should be carefully considered in the case of the smallest burghs whose
interests would be best served by entering into the
closest co-operation with the county service.

Meanwhile the draft memorandum had been submitted to a
special general meeting of the Association held in the St Andrew's
Halls, Glasgow, on 11 January 1933, when there was an attendance
of about 150 members and delegates. The president, G. W.
Shirley of Dumfries, occupied the chair, and in his introductory
remarks made a strong appeal for uniformity of conditions of
administration and employment, and urged upon members the
desirability of unanimity in their decisions. The memorandum
then submitted, paragraph by paragraph, embodied the eight
clauses previously laid before the Association at its annual
meeting in 1931, and already quoted on page 249.

At the special general meeting in January 1933, clauses 1, 2,
7 and 8 were adopted unanimously. Clause 3 was adopted after
the defeat of two amendments—one moving its deletion, the other
seeking to limit the public lectures to be provided "to literary and
scientific subjects." Clause 6 was also adopted after the defeat of
an amendment which sought to introduce, as an exception to the
limit of 20,000 as the minimum population of counties or burghs
given power to adopt the Act, "the case of a County or Burgh
which can show that it can provide an efficient library service."
Both clauses 4 and 5 were remitted back to the council for further
consideration, clause 5 with the added instruction "that this
meeting is in favour of the abolition of 'double rating'." A
suggestion, that in reconsidering clause 4 the council should
"appoint another sub-committee, with powers to co-opt four
County representatives," was initially adopted but was overruled
by a further amendment moving a simple remit back to the
council for further consideration.

The council's second thoughts on clauses 4 and 5 were submitted to the annual meeting at Coatbridge in June 1933. The
council recommended that clause 4 should be amended to read:

County Councils shall administer their libraries by a statutory
committee, the expenditure to be met from the County Fund
(Education Account), with a proviso excluding Burghs operating
the Public Libraries (Scotland) Acts from contributing to it,

and that clause 5 should stand as printed in the memorandum.
The meeting approved the council's recommendations and it was
agreed that in the final print of the memorandum, clause 5 should

precede clause 4. The memorandum, as now amended and approved, was again remitted to the council "with powers to take the requisite action towards placing the necessary legislation on the Statute Book, at the earliest opportune time." At the same meeting the Association appointed as its first honorary legal adviser Andrew Shearer, town clerk of Dunfermline.

The memorandum was then presented to the council of the Library Association, receiving its approval and promise of support. The memorandum was also submitted to the Association of County Councils and the Convention of Royal Burghs. The Association of County Councils opposed the establishment of a statutory library committee as suggested in clause 5 of the memorandum. The Convention of Royal Burghs approved the memorandum with two exceptions: (1) they considered the limit on the public library rate of 3d per £ to be sufficient, and (2) they suggested that one of the Association's supplementary recommendations, for exemption from liability to assessment for Rates, Income and Property Taxes, should be omitted.[2]

Further, the memorandum was submitted to the Secretary of State for Scotland, who later convened a conference in the Scottish Education Department offices in Edinburgh, on 26 October 1934, to which were invited representatives of the Scottish Library Association, the Association of County Councils, the Convention of Royal Burghs, and the Association of Counties of Cities, together with officers of the Scottish Office and the Scottish Education Department.[3]

At this conference, while there was general agreement on the need for an improvement in public library legislation, and while there was among the representatives a degree of unanimity on the proposals of the memorandum, it was made clear that some of the representatives could not accept certain of the proposals. It was unanimously resolved to appoint a committee of twelve, composed of three representatives from each of the three local authority organizations along with three representatives from the Scottish Library Association "to endeavour to formulate agreed Proposals for the amendment of Scottish Public Libraries legislation" and that all questions of policy relating to legislation should be referred to this committee. The Scottish Office agreed to take the initiative in bringing such a committee together.

[2] Convention of Royal Burghs, Minutes 1933-4 (1934), p. 66-9, 73; Convention 1934, Minutes, p. 11-12.

[3] Joint Committee on Scottish Public Libraries Legislation, Scottish Public Libraries Legislation: Report, 23 July 1936 (1937), p. 1. The proposed Bill is printed at the end of this report.

This committee first met early in 1935. In June the president of the Scottish Library Association was able to report:

A considerable measure of agreement among the representatives has been revealed. Agreement, by the terms of the remit, is the essential feature of the Proposals which the Committee can formulate, and such progress has been accomplished that a remit has been made to a Sub-Committee to draft a Bill. I have hope that this draft Bill will be ready in the early autumn, and I anticipate that it will be the duty of your Council to convene a Special General Meeting and place it before you. Such reference as that must be made by their representatives to the other Associations concerned as well as ourselves, and if their and our sanction is obtained the Bill will go to the Government with a by no means negligible body of opinion in support of it and good prospect of little opposition.

By the end of the year the draft Bill had been forwarded to the four Associations represented on the joint committee, and early in 1936 the committee was able to report that it had been accepted in principle.

On 24 October 1936 the joint committee had a meeting with the Permanent Under Secretary of State when the draft Bill was fully discussed. The Secretary of State, however, was unable to support the Bill as drafted "as he was not satisfied that it would be generally acceptable throughout Scotland."[4]

At the annual meeting of the Scottish Library Association in Kilmarnock almost a year later two of the Association's representatives on the joint committee, the Rev. R. P. Fairlie and G. W. Shirley, submitted a report which, however, could not be discussed, the president ruled, "in view of the fact that negotiations were still in progress between the joint committee and the Secretary of State for Scotland." A year later in Aberdeen the Rev. R. P. Fairlie again "reported on the stage of progress reached in the endeavour to obtain the proposed legislation."

He stated that the Joint Committee had reached agreement on certain principal points and had submitted their recommendations in the form of a Draft Bill to the Scottish Office. The Secretary of State for Scotland had intimated, however, that he was not prepared to propose legislation covering all the

[4] Convention of Royal Burghs, Memorandum on Report of the Advisory Council . . . (1951), par. 9.

points dealt with in the Draft Bill, but that he was prepared to give further consideration to the question of legislation to facilitate the establishment of a Regional Library Bureau in Scotland, provided such legislation would not give rise to controversy.

After this report it was "unanimously decided to protest against the attitude of the Secretary of State, and to re-state the Association's support of the Joint Committee in their effort to obtain acceptance by the Scottish Office of all their recommendations." It was also decided to suggest to the joint committee that they should send to every Scottish Member of Parliament a copy of the draft Bill along with a letter informing them of the Secretary of State's attitude.

With this encouragement the joint committee made further representation to the Scottish Office and obtained another interview with the Secretary of State on 20 January 1939, when the necessity of the proposals contained in the draft Bill was carefully explained. The Secretary of State "promised to give consideration to the matter and to the desire and need for dealing with the whole situation." Whatever may have been done in the interval, the outbreak of war in September put an end to the hopes of any immediate legislation for Scottish libraries.

Two years later, at the second war-time annual meeting, there were two addresses on "The Place of the Public Library in Post-War Planning," the first by Hector McNeil, M.P. for Greenock, and the second by the president, Alfred Ogilvie of Lanarkshire. Mr McNeil referred to the abolition of the rate limit on library expenditure in Scotland "as the first urgent and essential step towards future development."

The Scottish public must be wakened to the need to cancel the existing law restricting Scottish local authorities to spending more than threepence in the pound on libraries, and thus hoist themselves into a position of parity in this respect with the English public.

Mr Ogilvie spoke as a professional librarian, drawing attention to present needs and problems and indicating some future developments. There was a lively discussion at the end of which it was moved that "the Council be instructed to consider and report on the whole question of the future of public libraries in Scotland."

A memorandum prepared by the council, following this resolution, was considered by a special general meeting of the Association held at Glasgow early in 1942. In contrast to the

1933 memorandum which had been "a mean between conflicting opinions," this new memorandum "visualised the library service as a whole." After several speakers had contributed to the discussion, the clauses in the third part of the memorandum were submitted to the meeting. All were approved unanimously, with the exception of clauses 6 and 7 (referring to government supervision and grants), which were approved by a large majority. Thereafter a resolution, adopted without division, instructed the council "to take such steps as they consider expedient to place [the memorandum] before the appropriate committee appointed by the Government to deal with matters affecting post-War reconstruction."[5]

The memorandum was first submitted to the council of the Library Association, by which it was remitted to its Post-War Policy Committee. In face of this further delay the Scottish council decided to submit the memorandum to the Secretary of State for Scotland forthwith, informing him that the Library Association had yet to declare their policy regarding the substance of clauses 6 and 7 (the only clauses affecting interests outside Scotland and likely to be contentious), and to inform the council of the Library Association of the action taken.

In 1943, in response to the invitation of the Library Association's Post-War Policy Committee, the council studied the proposals of the McColvin report in relation to the memorandum. In June five members of the Scottish council met the Post-War Policy Committee to place before them the council's views on the McColvin report and the question of post-war policy in general. Later in the year, when the proposals of the Post-War Policy Committee were approved and published by the Library Association council, it was found that most of the recommendations of the memorandum were included.[6] It was agreed, however, that so far as the Scottish Library Association council was concerned the memorandum remained the overriding document.

Throughout the year the matter was kept alive "by personal contacts with the appropriate Government departments," and the council had the assurance that "no action will be taken by the Government in connection with the library service of the country without an opportunity being given to the Association to express its views."

[5] The 1942 *Memorandum* is printed, with amplifications added in 1947, as an appendix to the Minto report of 1948 (p. 36-40).
[6] Library Association, *The public library service: its post-war reorganization and development. Proposals by the Council of the Library Association* (1943).

The next year the council decided to seek a personal inter-view with the Secretary of State for Scotland, and on 1 December 1944 the Rt. Hon. Thomas Johnston gave a sympathetic hearing to a deputation appointed by the council. The deputation of eight, including the president and honorary secretary of the Association and the chief librarians of Edinburgh and Glasgow, was introduced by Lord Elgin, honorary president of the Association and a former president of the Library Association. The president, W. E. C. Cotton, submitted a statement in amplification of the eleven points set out in the 1942 memorandum and other members of the deputation spoke in support of it.

Mr Johnston did not counter the arguments in favour of new legislation advanced by the deputation. He agreed that some changes appeared to be necessary, but he pointed out that one of the Scottish local authority associations had already expressed disapproval of part of the Association's programme and that the time was inopportune for the introduction of con-troversial legislation. He suggested that, in order to secure an amendment to the current Acts within a reasonable time, the Association should confine their efforts in the meantime to those of the proposals on which it seemed possible to secure general agreement. He instanced the abolition of the rate limit, the discontinuance of double rating and freedom for co-operation between authorities. He suggested that a renewed approach should be made to the Association of Councils of Counties of Cities, the Association of County Councils and the Convention of Royal Burghs, with the object of securing their support for this three-point programme, and he undertook to do what he could to facilitate the passage of amending legis-lation on these lines if it had the support of the organizations mentioned.

Later in the month, at a specially convened meeting, the council decided to act on the Secretary of State's advice. Although there was some disappointment that, even as a temporary compromise, any part of the memorandum should be dropped, there was a general feeling that "a substantial advance would have been made if the three principles of single rating, no rate limit and freedom to co-operate were established." The council, in a further effort to ensure that Scottish library legisla-tion should receive early consideration, invited Kenneth Lindsay, Independent M.P. for the Kilmarnock burghs, who accepted the invitation, to watch the Association's interests in the House of Commons.

During 1945 the council followed the advice given by the Secretary of State in December 1944. The support of the Scottish local authority associations was sought for a measure embodying the three chief points of the legislative programme—single rating, no rate limitation, and freedom to co-operate—that were already embodied in the Bill drafted by the joint committee of the three local authority associations and the Scottish Library Association, which had been accepted in principle nine years before. It was now found, however, that the abolition of double rating was opposed by the Association of County Councils, although the Association's decision was not unanimous. The Convention of Royal Burghs, on the other hand, regarded this reform ("or rather restoration to the position which existed, to everyone's satisfaction, before 1929") as a necessary preliminary, a view the Scottish Library Association endorsed.

The General Election of 1945 and the consequent change of Government "prevented the fulfilment of any hopes which the Council may have had of securing new legislation" that year, but the council was active in drawing the attention of Scottish peers and all M.P.s representing Scottish constituencies to the three-point programme and to the arguments in support of it: Scottish libraries, after all, were asking "only for opportunities which have been possessed by English libraries for twenty-five years or more." Towards the cost of this campaign the Library Association made a special grant of £100.

In 1946 the Association extended its campaign by issuing a pamphlet, *Scottish Public Library Law: the present position and the need for reform*. This is an eloquent and lucid statement of the case. It compares the powers given to library authorities in Scotland with those enjoyed by authorities in England and Wales, while pointing out that "legislation is not perfect South of the Border."

> The Scotish Library Association is contenting itself, as an immediate objective, with the attainment of that degree of freedom which authorities in the South have enjoyed for so long that it is now regarded as a prescriptive right.

Five points are considered in detail: The two types of authority, The rate limit, Double rating, Inter-library co-operation, and Amalgamation of Authorities. The last paragraph is headed "Immediate rectification of two of the anomalies is essential" and continues:

> If the rate limit is not quickly removed (a) book stocks will deteriorate and it will be impossible to make up for the lean

257

years of war when supplies were inadequate even for normal replenishment, (b) staffs will be underpaid and the service will not attract recruits of the right type, (c) buildings will fall into disrepair and become out-of-date, and (d) much needed branches will not be built. If double rating is continued friction between authorities will continue to be engendered and the way to free co-operation will be barred. As these two reforms are so vitally important the Council of the Scottish Library Association is ready to devote all its energies to their attainment and for the time being to relegate the remainder of its programme to the background. If Parliamentary time really cannot be spared for the introduction of a Public Libraries Bill for Scotland the solution to the two rating questions can and should be incorporated in the next Scottish Local Government Bill.

It will be seen that the three points of 1945 were now reduced to two.

Later, in 1946, it was agreed to press for one only—the removal of the rate limit. The Under-Secretary of State for Scotland had advised the council "that . . . he could only hope that library legislation might be secured within two years." In the council's view burgh libraries could not wait for two years for the removal of rate limitation and it was suggested "that some consideration be given to the possibilities of aiding Scottish libraries in the contemplated Local Government (Scotland) Bill." As this was impossible, the council again approached the Secretary of State, suggesting a one-clause Bill to remove the rate limit, but "received the same reply as previously."

The annual meeting in Hawick in September, however, unanimously adopted a strongly worded resolution :

That this Conference of the Scottish Library Association, representative of the library authorities and the library profession throughout Scotland, is of the opinion that the immediate removal of the rate limit of 3d in the £ imposed on the expenditure of Scottish burghs for library purposes is urgently necessary and calls upon the Secretary of State for Scotland to introduce legislation into Parliament for this purpose without delay.

It may have been this resolution, it may have been Dundee's action in securing powers, under section 16 (1) of the Local Government (Scotland) Act, 1929, to exceed the statutory rate limit of 3d in the £ for library purposes, it may have been the publication of a second pamphlet, *Scottish Public Libraries: why the rate limit must be removed*, that provoked the Secretary of State's letter of 21 January 1947:

> The Secretary of State has decided that if a town council should apply for his approval, in terms of section 16(1) of the Local Government (Scotland) Act, 1929, to expenditure on public library purposes in excess of the amount obtainable from the maximum library rate laid down in the Statute, he will be prepared to give the application his sympathetic consideration.[7]

But by this time, however, consideration of Scottish library legislation had been remitted by the Secretary of State for Scotland to the Advisory Council on Education in Scotland. The remit, dated 9 January 1947, was in the following terms:

(1) To review
  (*a*) the libraries and museums conducted under the Public Libraries (Scotland) Acts, 1887 to 1920, and other libraries and museums providing similar services;
  (*b*) school libraries; and
  (*c*) the arrangements for the provision of books by the education authorities of counties under section 12 of the Education (Scotland) Act, 1946;

(2) To consider the arrangements for co-operation between the bodies providing the services described in Head (1) (*a*) *inter se* and (*b*) with the managers of central libraries and museums;

(3) To consider the administration and finance of the services described in Head (1); and

(4) To make recommendations.

Although problems of legislation continued to occupy the Scottish Library Association council's attention during the ensuing years, the Secretary of State could only reply, when his opinion was sought, that the matter was *sub judice;* and more than four years were to pass before the Advisory Council's report, *Libraries, Museums & Art Galleries*, was published as Cmd. 8229.

The report begins by stating the three main problems affecting public library provision in Scotland which at once confronted the

---

[7] Before the Act of 1955 removed the rate limitation no fewer than thirteen Scottish burghs had promoted Provisional Orders to increase or abolish the limit.

Advisory Council—(i) "double-rating," (ii) abolition or raising of rate limitation and (iii) inter-library co-operation—and it is agreed that, of these, numbers (ii) and (iii) seemed to be necessary and generally demanded. The report accordingly records the Council's belief that "the imposition of rate-limitation for libraries, if it was ever justified, is now an anachronism," and their recommendation that it be abolished. The report further recommends that in an officially recognized national lending library service there should be an "extension and standardisation of the practice . . . that books wanted by readers at a distance should be sent to them at their homes." In facing the problem of double rating the Advisory Council made their central recommendations: (1) That the burgh and county library systems should be amalgamated and double rating thus "brought to an end, not by any new form of financial manipulation but by unification" and (2) "That the Education Authority be the Library Authority."[8]

> The recognition of the Education Authority as the library authority for the area will involve (a) the transfer of the functions of the burghs which have adopted the Public Libraries Acts and (b) the formal transference of the library functions of the four cities to themselves as Education Authorities.

> The library assets of the burghs which are library authorities should be transferred to the County Council. This involves the transfer of all buildings, book-stocks and equipment. . . . Library staffs would require to be taken over and their rights properly safeguarded.

Indeed, this identification of the library authority and the education authority is the simple solution the report propounds for all its problems:

> If it is accepted that local library provision should be included in the duties of Education Authorities under the Education Acts, such anomalies as rate limitation, "double-rating," unfair discrimination as regards grants, and lack of power to co-operate with other libraries will automatically disappear; and we think it is infinitely better that they should disappear in this way than that any of them should be the subject of

[8] There are thirty-five education authorities in Scotland—the four counties of cities and all of the administrative counties, with the exception of Kinross and Nairn, which are combined with Perth and Moray respectively for certain local government purposes, including education.

a small amending Act dealing with relatively minor difficulties and leaving the major problems unsolved.

The solution is what one might have expected from an Advisory Council on Education—

> After careful deliberation we have come to the conclusion that the library service cannot be regarded as other than an educational service

but the arguments advanced in support of the recommendations are reasonable and by no means narrowly "educational":

> There is no question of one type of library being more efficient or more necessary than the other; the plain fact is, as has already been shown, that they have grown up separately, and the time is ripe for unification. Each type of library has much to contribute in experience and resources for the common benefit. We think it would be very wrong to perpetuate what is, generally speaking, a division between town and country at a time when close understanding and relationship between them are more essential than ever to our national future. . . .

> So far as the borrowing of books is concerned, a burgh boundary is an artificial and irritating barrier. Many who dwell beyond it make their living within the burgh; and others within a considerable radius—much extended by bus travel—visit the town regularly for shopping or recreation. To equate library privileges with the fact of ratepaying in a particular area is a parochial attitude that few will now attempt to justify.

The point of view of the burgh library authorities is represented with considerable sympathy:

> Burghs already operating the Public Libraries Acts . . . would in particular resent being deprived of their libraries, one of the few remaining services free from the control or supervision of a Government Department. The local "free" library, probably gifted or subscribed for expressly to benefit the people of the burgh, is usually a noticeable building in which the inhabitants take some pride. They have struggled on for years with inadequate resources, and may feel that all they need is complete liberty of rating.

Then the "possible future arrangements" are considered, in the first instance as they affect the case of the small burgh:

Take first the actual building. . . . Now these buildings cannot be spirited away; continuing in use for the same purpose, they must remain the same familiar local landmarks as before, perhaps improved and extended by resources drawn from the wider area. Morally and practically speaking, a public building belongs to the people in the neighbourhood who familiarly enter and make use of it from day to day; it does not appear to be a matter of moment who actually holds the title deeds.

Again,

it is generally true that most towns operating the Libraries Acts have round them a sphere of influence which is more sharply defined and more significant than it was even a generation ago. In many cases it corresponds to the catchment area of the local senior secondary school; in others to the radius of the bus service and the attractiveness of the town as a recreation and shopping centre. . . . We are convinced that nothing could be more helpful to that end than a library service including both the burgh and its natural hinterland.

Finally,

the books in the burgh library. Regarded as possessions, books belong far less to the legal owner who holds them as property than to the person who can use or profit by them. The reader most truly "possesses" the book who has mastered what the author has sought to convey. Therefore the legal ownership of the book-stock is of as little consequence as the title deeds of the library building. There are however some other things that do matter enormously to the reader. The book-stock should be fresh: not only in appearance, but as a result of regular additions and the withdrawal from the shelves of volumes which for one reason or another no longer arouse interest. The reader would like someone available to give him friendly, expert advice. He would like to be able to get within reasonable time any book he may want, on any subject, for reading, study, or consultation. Now, all these needs are best met by a library organisation of sufficient size and resources, controlled by a professional librarian.

262

"The large burghs" it is noted "are in a special position."

Superficially the case for isolating the libraries in these burghs and allowing them to carry on as before would seem to be stronger than in the case of the small burghs. But we doubt whether it is. Just because they are larger, they have usually a considerable peripheral population in the adjoining county area who regard the town as their natural centre for a large variety of purposes, and many of whom have their place of work or business in the town. Even with a county area for administrative convenience, the prestige, responsibilities and usefulness of the libraries in the large burghs will be greater than ever before.

The Advisory Council's recommendation "that the Education Authority be the Library Authority" is elaborated in two supplementary recommendations—that the library functions of the education authority should be delegated to the education committee and that each education authority prepare and submit for the approval of the Secretary of State a scheme for the exercise of its functions relating to libraries. The recommended delegation of library functions to the education committee is subject to certain provisos of which the most important are that the counties of cities shall have the power to set up a library committee as an *ad hoc* committee of the council if they wish to do so, and that counties containing large burghs shall have a similar power which, if it is not used, the Secretary of State may instruct them to exercise, on the representation of any of the large burghs within the county. The scheme for the discharge of library functions should provide, among other things, for the appointment of a chief librarian for the whole of the education authority area, and adequate staff to secure an efficient library service, including the recruitment of part-time librarians on a paid basis, for a reference and information service throughout the area, for the continuance, extension and setting up of local collections, and for the encouragement of research based on such collections, and for the establishment of a complete system of co-ordination between the library service for the area and all library services of a wider or national character.

The Advisory Council, in pursuit of their ideal that "so far as it is geographically possible an equal and full provision of library service [should] be made throughout Scotland, . . . suited to all ages, capacities and interests," make certain recommendations about the provision, development and administration of school libraries, and discuss the position in the national library service

263

of the Scottish Central Library, of the National Library of Scotland, and of the semi-private general and specialist libraries of the country. The Council further recommend that library expenditure incurred by all local authorities be aided by adequate annual grants, that such grants be at the same rate for all library authorities, making no distinction between services formerly administered under the Education Acts and services formerly administered under the Libraries Acts, and that a condition of grant should be the securing and maintenance of standards. The Central Lending Library, in addition to its annual grant from Treasury sources, should receive aid from the education authorities (in their new role as local library authorities) in proportion to their population.

Finally, a Library Council for Scotland should be appointed with the following functions:

(a) To ensure that the grant-aided local services reach and maintain a national standard of efficiency;

(b) To administer the Central Lending Library;

(c) To advise on general library policy and schemes of library development in Scotland.

The Library Council for Scotland would have certain executive functions, to be exercised through a full-time Development Officer for Libraries.

The duty of this officer, who would be chosen from persons of high qualifications in the library service, would be to visit all libraries in receipt of grants, give the local librarians and committees all possible help in the maintenance and raising of standards, advise about projects for extension of facilities, and report to the Library Council on the efficiency of the service in each area.

The report contains in addition (apart from its recommendations regarding museums and galleries) two chapters of general interest: "The Library and its Functions," a stimulating philosophy of librarianship that says a great deal that had never been said so well before, and "The Present Position," a rapid survey of the history of Scottish libraries and their status that is vividly written and within its limits comprehensive.

The report was presented to Parliament as a Command Paper on 22 May 1951. The next day *The Scotsman,* noting that the report favoured "the unification of burgh and county libraries in a national library system," commented:

Naturally the burghs would be reluctant to lose control of their libraries, which are one of the few services remaining to them. This argument commands a good deal of sympathy at a time when small communities are being deprived of their functions; but the advantages of larger areas for library administration are obvious.

At the conference of the Library Association which opened in Edinburgh a fortnight later a discussion on the report was introduced by J. W. Forsyth, burgh librarian of Ayr, and president of the Scottish Library Association.

Mr Forsyth summarized the report, after a brief introduction that explained its background, and was frankly critical.

How do they [the Council] propose to meet the three insistent demands of the Scottish Library Association—demands which have been crying for attention for the past twenty years? The answer is a master stroke.

> (Para. 159.)
> While making every allowance for the difference in origin, administration, and methods of procedure between the burgh and the county library systems, we can find no sufficient justification for continuing the division between them, and we recommend that they be amalgamated.

Or in other words, abolish the burgh libraries altogether! There you have the simplicity of genius, and, I venture to add, its impracticability. . . .

Amalgamation is not used in its generally accepted meaning of a uniting or coming together of common interests, but of a complete relinquishment and handing over by one party to the other.

Mr Forsyth emphasized, and the president of the Library Association in introducing him had also pointed out, that he spoke as an individual. His paper was not an expression of the policy of the Scottish Library Association, but it is interesting to note how closely, in the event, the line adopted by the Association followed Mr Forsyth's criticisms. In view of his attitude to the report in general, it was scarcely to be expected that Mr Forsyth could be fair to the report in all its recommendations. While he pointed out, for example, that 11 out of the 33 counties in Scotland had populations of less than the report's basic figure of 30,000, he omitted to mention what was pointed out in the discussion following the paper—that 32 of the 53 burgh library systems in Scotland served burghs of under 20,000, the Scottish Library Association's recommended minimum figure.

Again he deplored the proposed abolition of the burgh library committee:

In place of the present autonomous committee appointed by the Town Council, the burgh library would be administered by a local committee responsible to the county library committee which in turn would be responsible to the education committee which itself is responsible to the county council—and is usually, in addition, within the grip of the county council finance committee. In short, local control is abolished.

It was left to speakers in the discussion to point out that in counties containing large burghs the report suggested there might be an *ad hoc* library committee on which the burghs would be proportionately represented, and that the regionalization recommended in the report would rather enhance the status of existing burgh libraries.

Towards the end of the month the report was discussed by the Convention of Royal Burghs, when it was agreed that the Convention could not support the conclusions of the report, and that their Libraries Committee should take all adequate steps, in conjunction with other bodies interested, to oppose the recommendations' being put into effect, in so far as they affected the libraries of large burghs. Later the Convention's Libraries Committee agreed to indicate "its desire to discuss with the Secretary of State the methods by which Library Services could be developed without removing such an important public service from Burghs which had done valuable work in the field for many years and were well able to render further great service in the future."[9]

In September the report was again under discussion at the annual conference of the Scottish Library Association at Aberdeen, when for the first time for many years the Library Association was represented by a high-powered delegation, consisting of the president (James Wilkie), the honorary secretary (L. R. McColvin), the chairman of he County Libraries Section (Miss Cook), and the secretary (P. S. J. Welsford). The Scottish president, J. W. Forsyth of Ayr, explained that the council of the Association had decided to offer this opportunity of absolutely free and open discussion, that a verbatim report of the proceedings would be taken, and that thereafter the council would prepare a

[9] Convention of Royal Burghs, Minutes 1951-2 (1952), p. 40; Ordinary Convention, 29 June 1951, p. 54; Libraries Committee, 1 August 1951.

statement to be submitted to a special general meeting of the Association which would be called as soon as possible.

The speakers who opposed the main recommendations of the report did so on the grounds that the public library could not be regarded as a part of the formal educational service, and that in many cases education committees were already overloaded and overworked to such an extent that they could not easily assume other responsibilities.

The speakers in favour of the report pointed out that almost half the population of Scotland was already enjoying a public library service controlled by education committees, that the proposals for a library service on a county basis were a substantial step forward, that for the small burgh library nothing but good would come from amalgamation with the county library system, that the burghs were an essential part of the counties in Scotland, and that no burgh need fear loss of status in taking its appropriate place in the county administration.

Of the Library Association representatives only Miss Cook and Mr McColvin spoke. Miss Cook had come to Aberdeen at the request of her committee because there were matters in the report which "were likely to have repercussions throughout the British Isles." She deplored the library's being part of the education department. Mr McColvin, although he was convinced that the small independent library could not give its public the service that was necessary, and that that objective might be achieved by the creation of the larger units which were his dream in 1941-2—or they might be built up on a voluntary basis of co-operation and co-ordination—thought the report would not benefit the library users of Scotland to any great extent. "Legislation had never made people good, and it would not make libraries good." So the advice of the Library Association representatives was heavily weighted against the report. (It is ironical that a decade later the Library Association was to welcome for England and Wales new library legislation not very different from that proposed for Scotland in the Advisory Council report.)

Yet even the opponents of the report's central proposals felt "there were some good things in the report" or agreed that in the Report "many things were well said that needed saying."

With this expression of opinion to guide it the council of the Scottish Library Association tackled the problem of preparing a statement on the report for submission to a special meeting of the Association. The drafting of the statement was remitted to a committee, their draft was in due course considered by the council, and the statement, dated 4 December 1951, was eventually issued for consideration at a meeting of the Association called for 16 January 1952.

The statement records agreement with many of the report's particular recommendations, but is opposed to the two major recommendations, (1) that the county should form the basis of the library unit, and (2) that the education authority should be the library authority. The main points of agreement are as follows:

(a) The removal of rate limitation in burghs.

(b) The abolition of double rating of burghs for library purposes.

(c) Legal approval of co-operation between authorities for library purposes.

(d) The extension and development of a national library service both for reference and lending with financial assistance from the Exchequer.

(e) The extension to all public libraries of the principle of national Exchequer grants.

(f) The formation of a Library Council for Scotland.

(g) The development of school libraries.

The statement welcomes two interdependent suggestions of the report—grant aid to all public library authorities and the creation of the new advisory body to be called the Library Council for Scotland, and enlarges on the proposed functions of the Library Council:

Before setting out what we consider these functions should be we have first to determine what exactly the Advisory Council's recommendation is in regard to grant aid (paras. 163 and 164 of the Report). The wording "such grants be at the same rate for all library authorities" has been variously interpreted but if it is the contention of the Advisory Council that, for instance, the County of the City of Edinburgh and the County of Sutherland should each receive from national funds the same percentage of local expenditure, then we would most strongly challenge this recommendation. There is here no relationship to need and consequently no substantial advance to be achieved towards that national standard of service that is so desirable. At the same time we are not unaware of the importance of a basic grant but we would suggest that besides the basic grant common to all public library services there should be created a Central Grant Fund from which special grants could be

268

made for approved library developments that could not be financed from ordinary income (including the basic grant) and to meet the exceptional needs of the marginal library areas. Experience would show what proportion should go direct to local authorities and what proportion it would be necessary to divert to the central fund but we consider it essential that some such Central Grant Fund should be created and that it should be in the administrative care of the Library Council for Scotland. Only in this or some similar way will it become possible for that body "to ensure that the grant-aided local services reach and maintain a national standard of efficiency."

We therefore suggest that there be added to the functions of the Library Council for Scotland, as given in paragraphs 203-206 of the Report, the administration of the proposed Central Grant Fund.

The composition of the Library Council for Scotland is discussed and a definite recommendation is made.

The statement, naturally enough, elaborates the two points on which the Scottish Library Association council found itself in disagreement with the report. On the question of the library unit the statement's final word is:

Briefly, we recommend that the creation of a national standard of service should spring from co-operation between existing authorities fostered by a Library Council or similar body and not from the statutory elimination of smaller authorities, many of which are now efficient units and would certainly increase their efficiency and their influence given freedom from rate limitation.

In discussing the library authority the statement quotes approvingly the opposition of the Kenyon report to "any transfer of the libraries to the domain of the Education Committee" and adheres to the view already expressed by the Library Association and incorporated in an earlier statement by the council of the Scottish Library Association:

No libraries should be controlled by committees charged also with the responsibility for other functions, such as education, nor by sub-committees of such committees.

The eleven proposals of the Scottish Library Association's memorandum on the post-war development of public libraries in Scotland are re-affirmed as the council's policy, and the statement concludes:

It should be possible within a reasonable time to pass a new and comprehensive Libraries Act embodying the points on which there is general agreement with the Advisory Council; the removal of the rate limitation and of double rating, legal powers of co-operation, and the establishment of a Library Council, and this is the action which we strongly recommend to the Secretary of State for Scotland.

The special general meeting, under Mr Forsyth's chairmanship, was asked to consider this statement under the following motion:

That this meeting of the Scottish Library Association approves the Statement as an expression of the Association's opinion on the Advisory Council's Report.

After some lively discussion this motion was carried by 115 votes to 52 and the statement went forward to the Secretary of State for his consideration.[10]

At the same time the council of the Scottish Library Association were considering what further action might be taken. As a first step a letter was sent to the Secretary of State pointing out "the increasingly serious plight of certain burgh libraries" and suggesting that legislative action might follow on the non-controversial recommendations of the Advisory Council: (1) removal of rate limitation, (2) powers to co-operate, and (3) powers to organize and finance extension activities. It is interesting to note that these are not the same three points that the Association was pressing for in 1945. The principle of "single rating" (still a controversial issue) had been dropped: powers to organize and finance extension activities were now sought.

The Secretary of State, however, felt it incumbent upon him to consider the Advisory Council's recommendations as a whole: it was desirable that any legislation arising from the report should be as comprehensive as possible, and as certain of the recommendations had proved controversial, further discussions with interested bodies would have to take place before any legislation was initiated.

In 1953 the Association's council made a further approach to the Secretary of State. On this occasion the council agreed to ask again for legislation to cover the three non-controversial recommendations of the Advisory Council, but added a fourth, and entirely new point. With the needs of the Scottish Central Library

[10] *The Scotsman,* 17 January 1952.

in mind, in view of the announced withdrawal of Carnegie United Kingdom Trust support at the end of 1955, the council's deputation to meet the Secretary of State was instructed to press for legislation:

To authorise Library Authorities to contribute to the Scottish Central Library on such basis as may be fixed from time to time by the Secretary of State for Scotland.

This request from the Scottish Library Association council is similar to a recommendation of the Advisory Council's report, although the question does not appear as one of the "main points of agreement" with the report in the Scottish Library Association's statement. For the first time the principle of compulsory contributions to the Scottish Central Library is announced as an essential part of the Association's programme for new legislation.

In 1954 it became known that the Scottish Education Department had the question of library legislation under review in the light of the Advisory Council's recommendations and with a full appreciation of the local authority associations' comments on them. Early in the year the president and the honorary secretary of the Scottish Library Association (A. B. Paterson, city librarian of Glasgow, and Alex Dow of Coatbridge) were invited to St Andrew's House where they learned that talks on legislation were imminent and that the local authority associations, the Scottish Library Association, and the representatives of the Scottish Central Library would be consulted before legislation was introduced.

Later the council of the Scottish Library Association was asked to express an opinion on several points that had arisen in connexion with the legislation under consideration, and a last deputation had a meeting with Scottish Education Department officials in May 1954 when there was general agreement on the scope of possible legislation.

The bill that was eventually prepared was introduced to the Commons on Wednesday, 16 March 1955, as a private member's Bill by Sir William Y. Darling, supported by Sir Ian Clark Hutchison, Major McCallum, Mr Rankin, Mr M. K. MacMillan, Sir David Robertson and Mr Oswald.

The five clauses of the Bill covered three of the four points that the Scottish Library Association had agreed to press for. Clause 1 removed the limitation on expenditure and borrowing; clause 2 made provision for co-operation among statutory and non-statutory library authorities, and authorized a statutory library authority to contribute, with the consent of the Secretary of State, towards the expenses of any non-statuory library

271

authority, the payment of such contributions to be compulsory, if their amount was agreed to by the Associations representing the local authorities, if each Association resolved that the statutory library authorities among its members contribute, and if the Secretary of State endorsed the Association's resolution.

Clause 3 permitted the revocation of the decision to adopt the principal Act, and thereby offered legal sanction for what had been done, for example, in Alloa when in 1936 the burgh ceased to operate the Public Libraries Acts on the amalgamation of the burgh library service with the service for Clackmannanshire.

Clause 4 extended the lending powers of burgh libraries as defined in the principal Act of 1887, under which a library committee could lend out books only, although it could purchase "books, newspapers, magazines and other periodicals, stationery, pictures, engravings, maps, specimens of Art and Science, and such articles and things as may be necessary."

The last clause, a formal clause covering "Interpretation, citation, and extent," was notable in one respect. The phrase "statutory library authority" is defined to include the education authority of a county within the meaning of the Education (Scotland) Act, 1946.

On 1 April the Bill was read a second time and committed to the Scottish Standing Committee, but before the Committee met on Thursday, 21 April, to debate the bill, the Prime Minister had announced that Parliament would be dissolved on 6 May. In the circumstances it is scarcely surprising to find that before they settled to debate the Bill the members of the Scottish Standing Committee tried to satisfy themselves that they were not wasting their time, that there was in fact any hope at all of the Bill's reaching the Statute Book. The debate on clause 1, however, began and continued with some vigour for almost an hour and a half, when unfortunately it was found that the committee did not have its quorum of fifteen members and the meeting was adjourned to the following Tuesday.

The Scotsman, on 22 April, regretted "that a chance of carrying out an overdue reform in Scottish library legislation has apparently been lost by the failure of the Scottish Grand Committee to muster a quorum yesterday." It welcomed Sir William Darling's Bill as a simple solution of the problem: "Its provisions have seemingly been deliberately limited to the points on which there is general agreement"; but its news-columns carried Sir William's own comment that the Bill, he thought, was "virtually dead."

The next day both *The Scotsman* and the *Glasgow Herald* printed letters from Sir Alexander Gray, as chairman of the executive committee of the Scottish Central Library, and W. B. Paton, as president of the Scottish Library Association. *The Scotsman* gave these letters pride of place and a two-column heading: "Public Libraries Bill. Appeal to M.P.s to secure its passage." In the following Monday's issue a letter from Sir William Darling that headed the correspondence column renewed the appeal.

I hope that my fellow Scots Members (most of whom, I observe, read "The Scotsman" in the House of Commons) will join me at 10.30 a.m. on Tuesday in the Scottish Grand Committee. There are four clauses in the Bill. They can be passed in one hour. If they do so, they will do a service to all library users in Scotland.

It will be the responsibility of the Government to give—or refuse—Parliamentary time for this useful measure.

The proceedings in the Standing Committee began with an eloquent speech from the Member for Dunfermline Burghs, James Clunie, in the course of which he referred to Dunfermline as "the home of libraries," and in half an hour clause 1 was agreed to.

In the debate on clause 2 Henderson Stewart, Joint Under-Secretary of State for Scotland, disclosed that the local authority associations had already made "a provisional agreement for contributions on a prescribed formula to be made to the Scottish Central Library by each library authority for the next five years." The Bill, he pointed out, made "an informal agreement into a formal agreement."

Clause 3 provoked no discussion, and the debate on clause 4 (Extension of lending power of public libraries) is notable in particular for the surprising question of a Member who wanted to know if the new Act would make it easier in the future for a reader to obtain "Palgrave's *Golden Treasury* or a work of that kind."[11]

In an hour and five minutes the Scottish Standing Committee had agreed that the Bill should be reported, without amendment. The next day, *The Scotsman* rejoiced that the Scottish M.P.s had redeemed themselves:

Although the Bill is concerned with a minor reform, it is one for which library authorities have been pressing for many

[11] House of Commons, Scottish Standing Committee, Official Report, 26 April 1955, col. 37, 43, 47, 50.

years. The 3d limit on the rates for library services is an archaic restriction which takes no account of currency depreciation and the rise in the price of books. It has long ceased to apply in England, and the liberation of Scottish authorities is greatly overdue. The measure will also stabilise the position of the Scottish Central Library, although it was reassuring to learn from Mr Henderson Stewart, Joint Under Secretary of State, that arrangements had been made for its continuation, even if the Bill failed to be enacted,[12]

and Dr Savage, "as an ex-librarian of Edinburgh and a past-president of the Library Association," was quick to thank *The Scotsman* for its "powerful support" of the Libraries Bill.

On the same day, 27 April, the Public Libraries (Scotland) Bill passed the Report stage and was read a third time formally.

On the 28th the Bill was brought from the Commons to the Lords, and on the Tuesday following (3 May) it received "a speedy and cheerful Second Reading."

On 5 May there were no amendments during the Committee stage and the Bill formally passed through the Report stage before being read a third time and passed.

The Bill received the Royal Assent on 6 May, the day on which Parliament was dissolved, and became the Public Libraries (Scotland) Act, 1955 (3 & 4 Eliz. 2, c. 27).

The Scottish Library Association met in Alloa less than three weeks later in an atmosphere of "buoyancy and expectancy," not only that "the continuous struggle . . . to obtain legislation" had been successful, but that success had been won when all seemed hopeless. The president in his presidential address was "inexorably driven to acceptance of one inevitable theme," and its title, "Forward to Freedom," clearly indicates his attitude to the situation. Clause by clause Mr Paton examined the full implications of the new Act, and outlined the opportunities it afforded. His address is an inspiring exhortation at the beginning of a new day.

In looking back over the thirty-five years that separate the Public Libraries Acts of 1920 and 1955 one must deplore that for so long the energies and activities of Scottish librarians were so largely preoccupied with attempts to remove or to mitigate the effect of restrictive and irritant legislation. One wonders why the Act of 1920 only raised the rate limit from 1d to 3d when the English Act of 1919 had abolished the rate limitation for library authorities in England and Wales; one wonders why the Local

[12] *The Scotsman,* 27 April 1955.

274

Government Act of 1929 repealed the proviso to section 5 of the Education Act of 1918 and thereby introduced the double rating of independent burgh library authorities. Were there any cogent reasons for these enactments?

For an explanation of the retention in 1920 of a rate limit on Scottish burgh library expenditure, when rate limitation on library expenditure in England and Wales had been removed, one can point to the unique status of the burgh library committee in Scotland. Under the principal Act of 1887 the duly appointed library committee of a Scottish burgh, on which the town council representatives are joined by an equal number of non-councillors, had the power to demand from the town council, who must raise the rate, whatever sum within the statutory limit they required for their library service. The town council had no control over the estimates of the committee provided they did not exceed the statutory limit. The powers of a Scottish burgh library committee and its composition, as defined in the Act of 1887, so placed it outwith the control (or the interference) of the town council that it has been said that the public libraries committee is, in effect, a little local authority on its own.[13] It is not surprising then that when rising costs made the removal or the increase of the rate limit urgently necessary, the town councils of Scotland, through their association, the Convention of Royal Burghs, sought to retain the only control the 1887 Act imposed on the burgh library committee. When the Secretary for Scotland was asked in Parliament why a limit should be retained in Scotland when it had been abolished in England and Wales, he took refuge behind the Convention's decision that only an increase was necessary, despite his earlier expressed contention that any difference in the matter of rate limit between the two countries was "unthinkable."

While the Convention's attitude was understandable, its influence unfortunately resulted in the retention of a restriction that before long became crippling and that continued to cripple burgh library services, unless the town council went to the expense of removing or alleviating it, long after its value as a control on burgh expenditure had been lost in the direct control the town council obtained by section 41 (2) of the Local Government (Scotland) Act of 1929, which stipulated that "every estimate of sums required by a committee under the Public Libraries Acts shall be subject to the approval of the town council."[14]

[13] Library Association, *A survey of libraries* (1938), p. 19.
[14] The Convention of Royal Burghs agreed in 1937 that with the enactment of this section "the reason for the limitation has very largely, if

For the following twenty-five years, then, the rate limitation was a useless anomaly.

While there was some show of reason for the retention of the rate limit in the Act of 1920, it is difficult to find any explanation of the "curt and somewhat bleak" subsection 5 of section 18 of the Act of 1929, which repealed the proviso relating to burghs or parishes in which a library rate was levied.[15]

At the Scottish library conference at Dunblane in 1931 Principal Rait defended the section because it achieved "what has been adopted as a cardinal principle in educational administration in Scotland, a flat rate for the County," but the Lord Provost of Perth even suggested that the clause had reached the Statute book by accident.[16]

It is generally agreed that the clause was aimed at securing a greater degree of co-operation—if not complete amalgamation—between the two kinds of library.

The depute county clerk of Fife expressed this view at the 1931 conference:

> The purpose of the Local Government Act of 1929 was to amalgamate services, to centralise with a view to making the most out of the common pool or common stock. Suppose no legislative provision had been made, what steps could have been taken to compel the Burghs to co-operate with the Counties, and vice versa, and so to take advantage of the common pool or common stock? I think, therefore, the legislature did attempt this, and the position is as it is today in order to compel a measure of co-operation.

It is obvious that after the repeal of the proviso both types of library had to take cognizance of the other. They were certainly thrown together, though often at loggerheads. If the clause was to encourage co-operation, it signally failed to do so, with the certain

not altogether, disappeared" (C.R.B. Minutes 1936-37 (1937), p. 82). See also the evidence led in March 1954 during the inquiry in connexion with the Edinburgh Corporation Provisional Order to abolish the rate limit and transfer control of the libraries to a committee of the Town Council.

[15] The descriptive phrase was used by W. A. F. Hepburn, *Proceedings of the Scottish Library Conference, Dunblane* (1931), p. 13.

[16] In the debate on the Bill in the House of Lords an amendment, which stood in Lord Arnold's name, that an "equitable contribution" should be made by county to burgh in respect of double rating, was not in fact moved (H.L. Papers, 1925-9 (53), p. 9; 73 H.L. Deb. 5s., 25 March 1929, col. 913).

exceptions we have already examined. "Co-operation" the town clerk of Stirling pointed out:

Co-operation means two bodies free to contract entering into a voluntary arrangement for their mutual good.

Following the repeal of the proviso there was nothing of this freedom to enter into voluntary arrangements in the relationship between the county council on the one hand and the town council and burgh library committee on the other. Co-operation was under compulsion.

More than ten years later McColvin underlined this point:

If we are right in assuming that this was to induce the burghs to throw in their lot with the counties we can only say that this is an example of legislation trying to do by indirect implication what it should have had the courage to achieve by direct injunction. . . .

The system is indefensible. It creates a sense—and indeed a reality—of injustice which might well militate against co-operation and good relations between authorities, though one must admit that there was a spirit of friendship and professional fellowship among the librarians themselves which it would clearly take more than "dual rating" to destroy.

It is good to be able to report that although there have been exceptions where the relationship has been sometimes strained, the returns in respect of double rating have been mainly "reasonable," and that while the Act of 1955 leaves the problem of double rating untouched, the anger seems to have gone out of the former irritant. In his presidential address to the conference at Alloa Mr Paton could refer lightly to the "erstwhile burning issue of double-rating . . . which hindered agreement on other more important questions, and thus delayed for twenty years the passing of urgent library legislation."

Double rating is no longer a problem, and now that its anomalous nature can be contemplated with equal equanimity by Burgh and County alike, the more clear-sighted among us might be prepared to confess that the nature of the problem in the past was largely of our own making. In retrospect, all fairminded persons will admit that double rating has been of great value to the burgh libraries during the lean years of rate restriction, and indeed that through the financial or other return made by County Authorities to Burghs, the most serious effects of rate limitation were mitigated. Such a return continues to be made, I hope, on an equitable and improving basis, by County authorities all over the country, so that double rating still brings benefits to Burghs, and does no harm to others. The framers of the Bill were wise in this matter to leave well alone, and except for urging that all County Councils should make generous return to Burghs in compensation for any double rate levied, the library profession should contentedly follow suit.[17]

[17] The Convention of Royal Burghs, incidentally, "reserved its position" in the matter of double rating, "and if in fact fair financial treatment was not given by the Counties to the Burghs . . . the question of principle might be taken further." (C.R.B., Minutes, 1954-55 (1955), p. 43).

CHAPTER 10

THE SCOTTISH PUBLIC LIBRARY
SERVICE IN 1955 — AND AFTER?

THE PUBLIC LIBRARIES that now cover the whole of Scotland vary greatly in size, as one would expect. At one end of the scale is the service in Glasgow; it was, indeed, in 1955 the largest single public library service in the United Kingdom and includes the largest rate-supported reference library in Scotland.[1] At the other extreme is the small burgh library serving a population of less than 2500 that spent in 1952-3 only £1 on the purchase of new books.

Nevertheless, however unequally, library services are provided throughout Scotland and it should be possible for any reader anywhere to get the serious books he requires.

A picture of Scottish libraries in 1952-3, in so far as it can be given in statistics, is contained in the pamphlet, *Statistics of public (rate-supported) libraries in Great Britain and Northern Ireland 1952-3*, published by the Library Association. Returns are printed for 65 Scottish libraries, 40 urban (city or burgh) and 25 county. There are no returns for 12 libraries (7 burgh and 5 county). The librarians (or clerks) of six of these libraries, three county and three burgh, have been good enough to supply for this survey the data missing from the Library Association's official publication. The remaining six libraries (4 burgh and 2 county), which are not taken into consideration in the following calculations, together serve about 2.0 per cent of the population of Scotland.

In the Library Association pamphlet the libraries for which statistics are given are arranged in alphabetical order. The returns for the 65 Scottish libraries, along with the six additional returns already mentioned, will be found in the statistical appendix, where, however, a more systematic arrangement by population groups has been adopted. The libraries are re-arranged according to the populations of their areas in descending order in the population groups 1 to 14 of the Library Association's summary of statistics. A few obvious errors in the Library Association's

---

[1] Glasgow Corporation, *Public libraries* 1874-1954: *an historical summary* (1955), p. 36.

population figures have been corrected by the Registrar-General's estimates: the alterations are indicated.

The population served by the 71 libraries is estimated at approximately five millions; of this total 57.0 per cent are served by the 43 urban libraries and 43.0 per cent by the 28 county libraries. Among the urban libraries are the services in the four counties of cities, with a population of 1,917,284, or 38.1 per cent of the total. The large-burgh libraries and the small-burgh libraries serve populations of 755,588 and 197,633 respectively, or 15.0 per cent and 3.9 per cent of the total.

The library service throughout Scotland functions through well over 3000 branches and other service points. The full-time branches reported in the returns total 121, and to this total must be added the central libraries, in at least all the burgh library systems. Several counties, it is known, consider their administrative headquarters a full-time branch, for a return such as this, if provision is made there for direct borrowing. In these statistics a full-time branch is a branch open not less than 30 hours per week. Other points include part-time branches, centres, mobile libraries giving a service similar to that provided by a part-time branch library, and school, hospital and prison libraries supplied by the local library authority.

The total stock of books, lending and reference, is given as 6,063,747. The book stocks vary in size from the total of 1,290,126 volumes provided for Glasgow, to the 4500 volumes reported by Inverurie.

The number of reference books is about one-fifth of the total; but the Library Association points out:

In most cases where no figure is given under the heading Reference, it may be assumed that the number of reference books is included in the figure given under Lending. This particularly applies to county libraries.

The scale of book provision per hundred of population throughout the country is, on the average, 120; 132 in the cities and burghs and 105 in the counties. This is what experience leads one to expect. A system of branch libraries and centres, co-ordinated from a central headquarters, can share a relatively smaller yet a more comprehensive reserve stock of the older standard works and past popular successes than a multiplicity of independent units, even when the population of the county area is considerably larger.

For example, a county serving a population of 100,000 may

buy six or ten sets of Churchill's War Memoirs. When the time comes that these books are as little read by the general public as Lloyd George's War Memoirs are now, one or two sets in reserve will adequately cover the likely demand for the book: but five or six independent libraries serving the same total population would be preserving at least one set each.

All statistics at all times have to be used with caution, but perhaps figures for books in stock should be treated with particular care: the total is very easily swollen by an accumulation of obsolete lumber. Minto in 1948 had this to say about Dornoch:

> The stock of 345 books per 100 . . . is four-fifths moribund . . . and includes almost all the books originally bought for or gifted to the library.

A total of 29,463,370 issues from lending libraries is reported. The issues per head range from a very doubtful 18.7 to 1.6: the average is 5.9. Seven libraries record over 10 issues per head of population, and no fewer than 15 libraries had under 5 issues per head. Four of the libraries recording over 10 issues per head of population serve populations of less than 11,000; but it is often in the smaller towns that the library, if it is used at all, is used most frequently. In Perthshire, for example, one of the most lively branch libraries serves Doune, with a population (mid-1952) of 852, where the issues for 1952-3 were as high as 18.8 per head of the population; in the seven Perthshire burghs with populations between 852 and 2430 the issues per head were 18.8, 9.3, 10.9, 6.9, 10.9, 6.5 and 7.3, giving an average of 9.2 per head, while in Perth itself, with a population of over 40,000 the issues recorded represent 8.6 per head (a figure which is, however, well above the national average).[2] But in the larger towns there are not only a greater variety of attractions; there are also other libraries of different kinds—private, professional and commercial.

The total expenditure of these 71 Scottish libraries in 1952-3 was £992,929, of which the city and burgh libraries spent £659,778 and the counties £333,151. This represents an average expenditure over the country as a whole of 3s 11.3d per head, the burgh average being 4s 7.2d per head and the county 3s 0.9d. The counties should have been spending considerably more:

> It is a universal axiom that it must cost more to give adequate library services the more sparse the population.[3]

[2] Perth & Kinross Joint County Council, Education Committee, *County librarian's report* 1952-3 (1953), p. 6

[3] L. R. McColvin, "The North Scotland Survey," *Library Association Record*, vol. 51 (1949), p. 109.

The total expenditure on books was £251,410 (burghs £126,280; counties £125,130) an average of 1s per head (burghs 10.6d; counties 1s 1.9d). In their expenditure on books the counties were on the average more generous than the burghs; and rightly so, in view of the unavoidable initial duplication of stock that a multiplicity of distribution points necessitates.

The total of full-time staff (excluding manual workers) is shown as 1070 (745 in burgh libraries and 325 in the counties), giving a ratio of staff to population of one to 4700 approximately (in the burghs 1:3850, in the counties 1:6660).

In the summary of statistics the figures for issues, expenditure and book expenditure per head, and the number of staff in relation to population are shown group by group in the form of the highest figure, the lowest and the median for each group. It is in this table that the inequalities of the standards of service are most clearly demonstrated.

The expenditure per head ranges from 5s 9.7d in Coatbridge to 6d in Peeblesshire; the expenditure per head on books from over 2s in Roxburghshire, Coatbridge and Dumfriesshire (an exceptionally high figure of 3s 10.9d per head in Sutherland includes in addition expenditure on binding and some other items) to a minute fraction of a penny in Innerleithen; the number of staff in relation to the population served ranges from a ratio of 1 to less than 2000 to a ratio of 1 to more than 20,000.[4]

While the average expenditure per head on the library service is 4s, 20 authorities (serving 21.25 per cent of the population) spent less than 3s per head; 9 of these (serving 11.15 per cent of the population) spent less than 2s per head. While the average expenditure per head on books is 1s, 23 authorities (serving 22.2 per cent of the population) spent less than 9d per head.

It is clear that the poorer libraries must be improved if there is ever to be "an equal and full provision of library service . . . throughout Scotland."[5] The backward authorities must be encouraged to do more, and it would appear that the stimulus of healthy rivalry alone between authorities is not invariably effective. One hesitates to suggest the laying down of agreed minimum standards by some central authority—too often a minimum standard becomes the maximum beyond which few attempt to go—but a set of standards and a system of inspection

[4] In Orkney the county librarian worked alone until the spring of 1955; he then obtained 4 assistants, 3 full-time and 1 part-time.
[5] Advisory Council report (1951), p. 37.

282

might help immeasurably.[6] Inspection does not necessarily imply a bleak uniformity or destructive criticism. One president of the Scottish Library Association underlined this very point:

> My experience in administering a library service which is already grant-aided has convinced me that the appropriate connotation for the attitude of the government officials concerned is the positive one of interest and encouragement, and not a negative one of interference and obstruction which the pessimists so readily accept and fear.[7]

Through the influence of the Kenyon report primarily, the library service, although it has remained the direct responsibility of local authorities, has become a truly national service. "No other Local Government service, however grant-aided, supervised and inspected, is so closely integrated nationally."[8] Without waiting for the explicit legal sanction now embodied in the Public Libraries (Scotland) Act of 1955, the library authorities of the country gathered round the Scottish Central Library to form a network of inter-library co-operation.

One manifestation of this readiness to pool resources for the benefit of all is to be found in the Scottish Fiction Reserve scheme initiated by the Scottish Library Association and launched in March 1955.

The Scottish Fiction Reserve originated in a request from the Edinburgh and East of Scotland branch of the Scottish Library Association that the council of the Association should "consider a scheme whereby older novels could be preserved and made available for loan." The request came before the council in May 1951 and a sub-committee was appointed to investigate the question and report. After careful consideration it was decided, in the first instance and in view of the existence of a general fiction reserve in the Glasgow libraries, to limit the Scottish Fiction Reserve to the "systematic collection and preservation of the works of Scottish novelists, major and minor." The sub-committee further decided, in the light of the replies to a questionnaire which had been sent to all Scottish libraries to ascertain which novelists' works they were already collecting, that the allocation of an author to a specific library under the scheme

---

[6] Standards for the public library service in Scotland have now been recommended in the report, published in 1969, of the Working Party appointed in October 1967 by the Secretary of State.

[7] W. B. Paton, "Forward to freedom": SLA, *Proceedings* . . . *Alloa* (1955), p. 14.

[8] W. A. Munford, *Penny rate* (1951), p. 51.

should not be alphabetically (and arbitrarily) by the author's surname but on "a basis of regional association, each library making itself responsible for the authors born in its area or closely connected with it." It was suggested that the next step was the preparation of "a complete list of Scottish novelists, contemporary and classical, whose works should be preserved" and the council of the Association was asked to name a "suitable compiler" and to appoint a small standing committee to administer the scheme.

The then chairman of the council's General Purposes committee, the late Angus Mackay of Midlothian County, was appointed chairman of the Scottish Fiction Reserve committee, the librarian of the Scottish Central Library was to be correspondent, and the present writer was asked to undertake the compilation of the list. With the publication in 1955 of the *List of Authors included in the Scheme* the Reserve could begin to operate.

The scheme is intended to facilitate both the borrowing of Scottish novels and the disposal of surplus copies. The list contains in alphabetical order the names of approximately 650 authors covered by the scheme and shows the library or libraries —62 in all—responsible for collecting their works. Librarians, whether borrowing or giving, communicate directly with each other and not through the Scottish Central Library.

The Scottish Central Library has asked that certain records should be kept, which the library will collect periodically, to show "how the scheme operates in practice." In Perth and Kinross County Library in the first six months three Scottish novels were supplied to other libraries in response to requests through the scheme, and three of five novels required were located and borrowed. Further, the library acquired fifteen novels by Perthshire authors previously not represented in its collection, and no fewer than 44 duplicate copies of novels of which, in several cases, the library had possessed only one very tattered copy.

The Scottish Fiction Reserve scheme can be developed in various ways. At present the handbook to the scheme is merely a list of the authors to be included in it: it might well be expanded to contain a bibliography of each author's novels, and this could be done co-operatively, if each collecting library reported its holdings of works by novelists allocated to it. Once the list becomes a list of novels, instead of a list of novelists, it will be possible to include in it the "Scottish" novels that have been written by non-Scottish novelists: the Scottish novels of Jules Verne, for example.[9] It has been suggested also that the list of

[9] *Les Indes-Noires* (*The child of the cavern*) (1877) and *Le rayon vert* (*The green ray*) (1882).

284

Scottish novels might be annotated and that a subject index to the annotations would provide a key to historical and topographical information that is often overlooked.

A further suggestion is that the idea "might well be extended to other types of literature than the novel:" a similar list might be prepared to show the local connexions of Scotland's many minor poets, for example.

Another co-operative project of considerable importance is the *Union List of Current Periodicals in Edinburgh Libraries,* compiled and edited by H. Phillips of Edinburgh University Library for the Edinburgh Committee for Library Co-operation. The first edition, published in 1953, listed 5000 periodicals in 18 Edinburgh libraries: the second edition (1955) listed 6250 titles and the holdings of 36 libraries. A similar catalogue of periodicals in Glasgow and the West of Scotland, then reported as under compilation, has yet to appear.

Co-operative schemes of this kind, however, whether among public libraries themselves or between public libraries and special libraries of various kinds, imply beyond the will to co-operate a degree of dependable efficiency in the co-operating libraries. The partners to an agreement, whatever their size and relative import-ance, must be equally reliable.

In discussions of library organization and development one frequently finds an attempt to estimate the minimum, or in some cases the ideal, size of the "library unit," usually in terms of the population to be served. This preoccupation with the minimum or the ideal size of the library unit is fundamental. A library service cannot be efficient if it is run on too small a scale, and a prolifera-tion of small units is bound to be ineffective and uneconomic, par-ticularly when the small units are proudly independent and quite uncoordinated. Too often the small library cannot justify, even if it could afford, the purchase of the expensive and authoritative book on the subject and has to remain content with a popular exposition—that will be duplicated in every library of a similar size throughout the country. The book stock of these small inde-pendent libraries, if considered in mass, is inevitably ill balanced.

Again, in the matter of staff, where small libraries are operating independently, there is a considerable wastage in the repetition of comparatively unimportant routine duties and there is no real opportunity for the training and the employment of specialists. Indeed, the very small unit often cannot afford to pay the salary of even one trained librarian.

One can look at this question from the other side. To provide a good reference service large and often specialized resources are required and staff with particular interests and qualifications to use them effectively.

With arguments of this kind in mind the Public Libraries Committee of 1927 found that with a population under 20,000 "economic factors become so strong as to defeat the efforts of any community to provide itself with an efficient library," while on the other hand they considered that "any town of over 20,000 inhabitants must be regarded as able to maintain a library in a reasonable state of efficiency." The Scottish Library Association accepted the same minimum figure for burghs:

> A burgh with a population of less than 20,000 cannot, as a general rule, provide economically a full range of library services of a satisfactory standard. The figure for counties must be higher, 50,000 being suggested as a minimum,[10]

and the Advisory Council on Education increased it: they felt certain that a "lively and healthy" library service could not be economically provided for a population of less than 30,000.[11]

In 1955 the Library Association adopted a memorandum on the public library service and local government reorganization which recommended that as a first step to the creation of suitable library authorities "the library powers of all local authorities where the 1953-4 Rateable Value is less than £300,000 should be surrendered to their county councils or arrangements should be made for joint services."[12] This memorandum refers primarily to England and Wales, but if the recommendation is applied to Scotland it would exclude as independent library authorities all those authorities excluded by acceptance of the Scottish Library Association's minimum figures, excepting the counties of Clackmannan and Roxburgh, and would exclude in addition the three large burghs with populations between 20,000 and 30,000 (Rutherglen, Dumbarton and Stirling) that fall below the Advisory Council's recommended minimum, the burgh of Airdrie with a population (mid-1954) of 31,769 but a rateable valuation of only £223,300, and the counties of Banff and Ross and Cromarty.

At the other end of the scale we find the McColvin report's

---

[10] Kenyon report (1927), p. 32, 33; *Statement on essential requirements of new library legislation* (1947), clause 3. The *Statement* is reprinted as an appendix to the Minto report (1948), p. 36-40.

[11] In the memorandum the council of the Scottish Library Association submitted in October 1966 to the Royal Commission on Local Government in Scotland a population figure of at least 100,000 was recommended as desirable.

[12] *Library Association Record,* vol. 57 (1955), p. 315.

proposals for library units of which the smallest was to serve a population in the neighbourhood of a quarter of a million, and the largest well over one and a half millions, and the suggestion of the council of the Library Association that in general the population of the library area should lie between one-quarter and three-quarters of a million.[13]

Admittedly McColvin's schedule of library units is the most contentious section of his report, and the paragraphs relating to the library authority, paragraphs 12-16 of the *Proposals,* including the population estimate just quoted, came under heavy fire at the Blackpool conference of the Association in 1946, when it was agreed by 314 votes to 218 that they should be withdrawn for further consideration.[14] Yet though these optimum figures provoked this stormy opposition, the minimum figures quoted above reveal a remarkable unanimity.

But population is not the only factor in determining the most suitable size for the library unit. McColvin had to admit the "special difficulties" that arise from sparsity of population: it is no solution of the library problem to suggest the amalgamation of sparsely populated counties until a hypothetical "ideal" population figure is reached, if the resultant unit covers too wide an area.

The Minto report on the north of Scotland drives this point forcibly home, and similar conditions are found in the Border counties. McColvin admits that four of the units he proposes for Scotland, "two in the North and two in the South, cover exceptionally wide areas," and adds: "This cannot be avoided owing to the absence of large towns suitable as main libraries."

The third factor to be considered in the delimitation of library areas is hinted at in the phrase of McColvin's just quoted: the distribution of the population within the area, in particular the way the small towns and villages are grouped in relation to the larger towns, on which, probably, the roads converge and to which the inhabitants of the surrounding district travel for business and pleasure and for the amenities of town life.[15]

When this point of view is given the consideration it merits, it is frequently found that the existing local government boundaries, burgh and county, cut across areas that might form coherent

[13] McColvin report (1942), p. 150-6; Library Association, *The public library service: . . . proposals* (1943), p. 7.

[14] *Library Association Record,* vol. 48 (1946), p. 140.

[15] This information was usefully presented in the Ordnance Survey map, "Local Accessibility: the hinterland of towns and other centres as determined by an analysis of bus services" (1955).

library units. Only a service nationally administered, such as the Post Office, can afford to ignore these local authority boundaries, linking, for example, Kincardine in Fife to Alloa in Clackmannanshire, or Aberfoyle in Perthshire to Stirling.

It is not easy to resolve the contradiction between the library unit as determined by existing local government boundaries and what one might call the "natural" library unit dictated by the normal comings and goings of the people in a given area.[16] If, however, library service is to retain its local character, with at least part of its revenue derived from local rates, then library administration must continue to be linked with the already-existing administrative and rating areas, although steps should be taken to ensure that the artificial barriers of burgh and county boundaries interfere as little as possible with a reader's use of whichever library is most convenient to him. There should be, for example, complete interavailability of readers' tickets and as much uniformity and standardization as can be reasonably achieved in the details of method and routine.

If the Scottish Library Association's figures are strictly applied, no small burgh, except the burgh of Buckhaven and Methil, would remain an independent library authority, while the burgh of Arbroath, the counties of Berwick, Bute, Caithness, Clackmannan, Kirkcudbright, Orkney, Peebles, Roxburgh, Selkirk, Sutherland, Wigtown and Zetland, and the combined counties of Moray and Nairn (less the burgh of Elgin), fall below the stated minima. In all, something like 37 of the present library authorities would be excluded. These "under-size" authorities together serve a population of approximately 485,800, or about 9.5 per cent of the population of Scotland.

On the other hand there are cases—Dumfries county is one—where both burgh and county supply the minimum figures of the Scottish Library Association's memorandum, where each might be able separately to "provide economically a full range of library services of a satisfactory standard." Yet how much more satisfactory and economical, in the truest sense, is the library service provided by burgh and county since their amalgamation in 1932.

In other words, it must be emphasized that while "the Scottish

[16] The writer developed his thoughts on the library unit in his presidential address to the Scottish Library Association meeting at Oban in 1965, when he suggested "that the multiplicity of Scottish library authorities should be replaced by a Scottish library authority, under the Secretary of State, administered in appropriate regions by boards similar in composition and function to the Regional Hospital Boards" (SLA, *Proceedings . . . Oban* (1965), p. 9-18, particularly p. 15-16).

Library Association are of the opinion that a burgh with a population of less than 20,000 cannot, as a general rule, provide economically a full range of library services of a satisfactory standard" and that "the figure for counties must be higher, 50,000 being suggested as a minimum," it cannot be said that every burgh with a population over 20,000 and every county over 50,000 is capable of providing "economically" a satisfactory standard of library service.

The question of suitable library areas is fundamental, because although the library service is and ought to be essentially a local service administered to meet the needs of each particular community, it is also, and ought to be, a national service that covers the country as a whole and places at the disposal of every reader resources organized at the national level, and this national organization will function to greatest advantage only when the separate units are individually capable of reaching, and in fact reach, at least a uniformly satisfactory minimum standard. As long as there are local services that fall below this adequate minimum standard, the national services will be hindered in the performance of their proper functions. If, for example, local book stocks are impoverished, or if bibliographical tools and the trained staff to use them are lacking, then the Scottish Central Library's routine is liable to be clogged with requests that should have been dealt with in the local library. The achievement of appropriate library areas, then, seems to be a necessary prelude to the "equal and full provision of library service . . . throughout Scotland, suited to all ages, capacities and interests" that is our ideal.

There are, we have said, twelve Scottish counties whose population figures fall below the minimum of 50,000 mentioned in the Scottish Library Association's memorandum—six southern counties, Berwick, Kirkcudbright, Peebles, Roxburgh, Selkirk and Wigtown; one central county, Clackmannan; two northern counties, Caithness and Sutherland; and the three island counties of Bute, Orkney and Zetland—but by a judicious policy of combining certain of them for library purposes with larger neighbours, or in some instances by amalgamating two or more of these counties with small populations, it is possible to reach the minimum figure without creating areas too large for effective library administration. The combination of authorities for purposes in which they are jointly interested was permitted by the Local Government Act of 1947, and the combination of two county authorities for library purposes (even although county libraries in Scotland operate under an Education Act and are normally administered by a sub-committee of the education committee of the county council) has a precedent in the joint library service for the counties of Angus and Kincardine.[17]

It is suggested that a similar joint county library service might be established by voluntary agreement, in the best interests of all concerned, for Wigtown and Kirkcudbright. In the south-east Border counties it is not so easy to suggest the amalgamation of neighbouring authorities. There are long-established burgh libraries of some importance in Galashiels, which at present operates a service for Selkirkshire, and in Hawick, where there is a particularly good collection of Border literature, and there are also libraries at Innerleithen and Peebles in Peeblesshire, Selkirk in Selkirkshire, and Jedburgh and Kelso in Roxburghshire. Berwickshire might most readily join forces with East Lothian, and Peebles with Midlothian; and Selkirkshire and Roxburghshire and the burghs therein might combine their resources and use Hawick and Galashiels as the main centres of a joint library service.

Clackmannanshire, the smallest Scottish county, is a unique case. Although its population falls below the Scottish Library Association's recommended minimum for a county, its area is compact and its population density is relatively high. Under any scheme combining library authorities this small county would retain its present character of a convenient unit or sub-unit: and it might well retain its independence. If it is to be combined with a neighbour, however, the obvious partner is Stirlingshire.

In the far north it might seem reasonable to suggest the combination for library purposes of Caithness and Sutherland—they are already combined as a Parliamentary constituency—but communications are difficult and there is more to recommend Minto's solution that Sutherland and Ross and Cromarty should establish a joint service, despite the vast area these counties cover.

In view of their isolation the island counties of Orkney and Zetland cannot readily combine either with each other or with a mainland county, although the creation of a joint service for Orkney and Caithness is worth considering. On the other hand, Bute, in an echo of the 1946-50 association with Kilmarnock, might combine with Ayrshire.

Agreements of this kind—accepted voluntarily and implemented wholeheartedly—could quickly raise the standard of library provision in those less populous counties.

The game of suggesting possible amalgamations has been played for more than thirty years. In the Mitchell report of 1924, for example, it is suggested that Clackmannan and Kinross might

[17] See also chapter 5.

join with Fife, and that Nairn, Moray and Banff might join forces. This was, of course, prior to the combination of Kinross with Perthshire and Nairn with Moray by the Act of 1929. Minto, it may be noted, in 1948 also recommended the combination of Moray and Nairn with Banff.

In the small burghs, by and large, the wisest course to recommend is complete amalgamation with the county service. In Scotland this has already occurred in Caithness (Thurso and Wick), Clackmannanshire (Alloa), Dumfriesshire (Annan and Lockerbie, and also the large burgh of Dumfries), Kirkcudbright (Castle Douglas), Midlothian (Bonnyrigg), and Orkney (Kirkwall and Stromness). Of the remaining small burgh libraries, the best struggle, some with a show of success, to provide a library service. For the majority their independence is illusory, or bought at the expense of the service. With a population of less than 10,000 no burgh can provide a library service worthy of the name, though some are providing a service that compares not very unfavourably with the service offered by the counties in which they lie.

The position of the seventeen large burghs with independent libraries is different. With the exception of Arbroath all in 1955 exceeded the Scottish Library Association's minimum figure of 20,000, and Arbroath was only 250 short of it, although three others (Dumbarton, Rutherglen and Stirling) fell below the Advisory Council's minimum of 30,000. In addition the largest of the small burghs, Buckhaven and Methil, had a population greater than Arbroath's by approximately a thousand.

Most of these burghs were capable of providing, and most of them provide, library services "of a satisfactory standard," but the influence of their libraries extends far beyond the burgh boundaries into the surrounding landward areas, and the better the library service the wider its sphere of influence.

If Scottish library legislation had followed a different pattern these burgh libraries might have become legally responsible for the surrounding county districts, and could have drawn some revenue from them by levying a library rate; but in Scotland the legal responsibility for burgh library provision and the library's income from rates ends at the burgh boundary, and readers from the county beyond, if they wish to use the burgh library, are frequently charged an annual subscription. The two kinds of library service, in burgh and in county, are now well established, and in view of their origins and their histories and in the face of local pride and jealousy, any suggestion to impose amalgamation or unification by statute is bound to meet with strong opposition.

The Kenyon report emphasized this very point:

Compulsion can only lead to resistance, to grudging compliance, to resentment, which will ensure unpopularity for the very idea of a library. Persuasion and example are the stimuli on which we should rely. . . .

Tempting as it may be to use compulsion in order to turn a bad service into a good service, the Committee are not convinced that compulsion would have that result. It is contrary to the whole spirit of the library movement, which has derived its main value from the fact that it is a spontaneous growth.[18]

Amalgamation or unification is best achieved by voluntary agreement. Nevertheless, a greater degree of co-operation—indeed, in certain cases, some form of co-ordination—would be mutually advantageous.

The seventeen large burghs that administer independent libraries are to be found in the eight counties of Angus, Ayr, Dunbarton, Fife, Lanark, Perth, Renfrew and Stirling; and in seven of these eight counties the headquarters of the county library services is in a large burgh. The seven towns in Scotland with two public libraries—the urban municipal library and the county library headquarters—are Ayr, Dumbarton, Hamilton, Kirkcaldy, Paisley, Perth and Stirling. In addition the county library headquarters of Aberdeenshire is in Aberdeen. McColvin mentions that in Great Britain there are altogether 54 cases of the kind. With 9 out of 54 Scotland has in this instance exceeded its share by the Goschen formula.

McColvin summarizes the evils of this duplication thus:

Most of the counties have some collections, large or small, available either for those who call or for postal service; most have some reference and bibliographical material—though seldom enough; all maintain reserve stocks and the like. The urban library—possibly within a stone's throw—does much the same. Those who do not live in the town may use the county library; those who do may not. The better the two services the greater the duplication of effort; when, as is usual, one is much better than the other, the more ironical the situation. If the two were to be amalgamated the people served by both authorities would benefit not only by increased facilities but by greater economy.[19]

[18] Kenyon report (1927), p. 38, 108.
[19] McColvin report (1942), p. 109.

292

If it is found impossible to agree voluntarily either to the combination of burgh and county services under a joint committee (as at Inverness) or to complete unification under the education committee of the county council (as in Dumfriesshire), something may still be done to mitigate the evils of duplication. The two authorities can encourage an official co-operation that remains just short of amalgamation; they can instruct their librarians, who probably co-operate closely, if informally, already, to consult together on book purchase, particularly of the more expensive multi-volume standard works, and the direct interchange of stock, and in defining the limits of each library's local collection to avoid unnecessary competition in acquiring rare items; they can consider the practicability of compiling a union catalogue of, at least, their local collections; they can ensure that as far as possible the two services are equally available to readers in burgh and in county—that the tickets of either library are accepted by the other and that no additional subscription is levied. Agreement on a co-ordination of the services should not be difficult to achieve, for although the two kinds of authority administer library service under quite distinct Acts of Parliament and although their library committees differ in status, it frequently happens that some members sit on both committees.

In at least one instance in Scotland the duplication McColvin deplores might have been avoided, even if it had been impossible to establish any degree of co-operation beyond the formal connexion at a distance through the Scottish Central Library. The new headquarters of Fife County Library could have been built in Cupar, the county town, where there is no burgh library, instead of in Kirkcaldy; but Kirkcaldy was the administrative centre of the Fife Education Authority when the county library was established.

If the Scottish Library Association's figures are adopted as minimum standards (with the possible exceptions of Arbroath and Clackmannanshire), and if the present statutory library authorities realize the advantages of the amalgamations we have discussed or of similar arrangements of the kind, the number of library authorities in Scotland might well be reduced substantially. At present there are, in addition to the libraries in the four counties of cities, twenty-nine county libraries, seventeen large burgh libraries, and about forty small burgh libraries of which all but ten are only nominally indepedendent: a total of about 90, of which perhaps 60 are "effective." After amalgamation of the kind discussed this total might be reduced to something like 45— four city libraries, twenty-three county libraries and eighteen burgh libraries.

Amalgamations such as we have suggested are implied in the Scottish Library Association's memorandum, and they have been recommended both by the surveyors in the Library Association survey in 1938 and by Minto in his report on the north of Scotland. McColvin's recommendations are much more sweeping, but the amalgamations we have suggested would not prejudice a later scheme of regionalization, if it was agreed to proceed on the lines of McColvin's proposals, yet they can be realized under existing legislation and without the creation of special rating areas.

Scotland, as we have seen in chapter 5, has provided examples of four types of library amalgamation:

(1) In Angus and Kincardine a county library service for two counties is administered by a joint committee appointed from the two county education committees.

(2) In Invernessshire a library service for the entire county was administered for 28 years, from 1933 to 1961, by a joint committee of the town council of the burgh of Inverness and of the county council.[20]

(3) In Dumfriesshire a library service for the entire county is administered by the education committee of the county council in whose favour all the burghs in the county that had adopted the Public Libraries Acts, including the large burgh of Dumfries, have resigned their powers under the Acts.

(4) In Selkirkshire the committee of Galashiels Public Library, in addition to their service for the burgh of Galashiels, provide a library service for the county (apart from the burgh of Selkirk) for which the education committee of the county council make an agreed annual payment.

Other cases of amalgamation conform to one or other of these types. With the exception of Inverness-shire (where the friction that intermittently arose between the combining authorities eventually led to the dissolution of the partnership), all are admittedly successful and likely to continue, although each formal minute of agreement provides for the possibility that one side or the other might wish to abandon the joint scheme.

The voluntary amalgamation of library authorities should be planned towards "creating, as the area for each independent local

[20] The Minute of Agreement is printed as an appendix to the Minto report of 1948 (p. 32-4). The two library services resumed their independent status in May 1961 (see *SLA News*, 96 (1970), p. 36-42).

service, a suitable local unit sufficiently large to facilitate co-ordination and to ensure efficiency and economy."[21]

The advantage of combining small authorities to make larger units and of eliminating unnecessary duplication are obvious. Most important of all is the creation of library units that can afford "to employ and make full use of the services of those qualified people whom we know to be necessary in any efficient service."[22] It is worth pointing out that there were in 1955 only seven librarians with professional qualifications in the forty-odd libraries, burgh and county, serving populations below the Scottish Library Association's minimum figures of 20,000 and 50,000 respectively. It is even more distressing to realize that (in 1955) 26.6 per cent of the population of Scotland lived in areas where the chief librarian was unqualified, including 17.9 per cent in areas where there were no professionally qualified librarians at all in the public library service.

This is a serious matter, and the only hope of improvement lies in the creation of library units that can afford to offer the salary appropriate to a qualified librarian and in their realization that it is as wrong to appoint an unqualified person as librarian as it is impossible to appoint any but a qualified doctor as medical officer of health. The employment of properly qualified staff throughout the public libraries of Scotland, in libraries of suitable size administered by committees that are ready to finance their services adequately, would improve not only the individual libraries; it would facilitate their co-ordination and their co-operation through the Scottish Central Library and in other joint projects.

The distribution of the population in Scotland makes it difficult to achieve the "equal and full provision of library service" that the Advisory Council on Education in Scotland recommend, "so far as it is geographically possible." There are important functions that only libraries of a certain magnitude can discharge efficiently and economically: there are some functions that only the largest libraries can discharge at all. No scheme of regional reference libraries, for example, however it is financed, could justify the establishment of a Mitchell Library in Inverness. But it is vitally important that throughout the country there is a realization of the extent of the total resources of the library service as a whole, and that as far as possible the resources that are naturally concentrated in the libraries in the large centres of

[21] McColvin report (1942), p. 116.
[22] ibid. p. 118.

295

population should be made available on request, to the smallest and most remote library.

As time goes on the public library, particularly the smaller public library, must increase in importance as a place of research, or at least as the link between the research-worker and the appropriate special library or research association. This implies that even the smallest library needs more than a rudimentary knowledge of the main research organizations and the subjects they cover, and of the technical periodicals that are published and where copies can be found. To the research student, in the humanities and in the sciences, the public librarian should be an unfaltering guide through the bibliographical maze.

In the '50s the responsibilities of the public library to industry were to receive considerable attention. Lord Elgin dealt with the subject in general terms at the conference of the Library Association in Edinburgh in 1951.[23] Two years later Dr D. J. Urquhart of the Department of Scientific and Industrial Research read a paper to a joint meeting of the East and West of Scotland branches of the Scottish Library Association, in which he pointed out that there were few firms sufficiently alive to the value of books and periodicals to maintain libraries or to use the public library services.[24] The larger industrial concerns may have good collections, and sometimes employ their own librarians or information officers; but the great majority of firms are small, and could profitably make use of the public library service—if they were aware of its existence. Following on this talk the D.S.I.R. provided a leaflet which could be issued from public libraries to industrial firms in their area, drawing attention to four ways in which the public library could help—by providing literature through inter-library co-operation, by providing special lending services for firms, by providing information about libraries, and by helping industrial firms to obtain the answers to technical inquiries.[25]

That the public library should contain a collection of books dealing with local industries has long been a principle of the service. The principle was enunciated in the 1849 Report of the Select Committee:

It would seem that in our large commercial and manufacturing towns, as well as in our agricultural districts, . . . libraries would naturally spring up, illustrative of the peculiar trade,

[23] Library Association, *Proceedings . . . Edinburgh* (1951), p. 84-6.
[24] D. J. Urquhart, *Public libraries and industry* (1953), p. 11.
[25] D.S.I.R., *Public libraries and industry* (1954).

manufactures, and agriculture of the place, and greatly favourable to the practical development of the science of political economy;

and the Mitchell report noted:

It may fairly be said nowadays that every library does its utmost to provide adequately for persons interested in the development of local industries and manufactures, where such exist and are sufficiently concentrated.[26]

The whole problem in its widest aspects was considered at the Royal Society's Scientific Information Conference in 1948, when this recommendation, among others, was recorded:

Library Committees are urged to give more attention to co-operation between libraries with the object of reducing undesirable duplication and of extending access to a greater proportion of the world's literature. It is suggested that co-operation should commence in local areas and that regional centres should be linked with national and international systems of interchange.[27]

The Library Association thereupon set up, at the request of its University and Research Section, a working party whose interim report was published in December 1949.[28] This report outlined a long-term plan "for the complete coverage of useful English and foreign published material," so that the libraries of this country can play "their full part in scientific and humanistic research."

The basic plan envisaged five categories of library:

Category A. The National Libraries. The British Museum, the National Library of Scotland and the National Library of Wales . . . "Every effort must be made to secure that they are genuinely comprehensive."

Category B. First Line Special Libraries. "So far as possible they should be all-embracing (in their fields) . . . A First Line Special Library should be the recognized bibliographical and research centre in the field."

Category C. Second Line Special Libraries "free to develop their resources as may seem best to their providers. . . . They shall co-operate with their appropriate First Line Libraries and with one another."

---

[26] Select Committee report (1849), p. xi; Mitchell report (1924), p. 53.
[27] Royal Society Scientific Information Conference, *Recommendations,* sect. 10.3.
[28] *Library Association Record,* vol. 51 (1949), p. 383-7.

"Category B and Category C Libraries will include special libraries and special departments of *all* kinds, government, research institution, society, firm, public, etc., etc."

Category D. Major Regional Reference Libraries which will provide "(*a*) general, pervasive reference materials and (*b*) materials of a specialized character needed in a region but not adequately provided by Category B or C Libraries operating in the region."

Category E. Lending Libraries "willing to lend freely to the general public, and in the majority of cases . . . therefore . . . public libraries. The field of specialization will need to be divided between them (*a*) so far as possible on the basis of natural local interest or existing and appropriate special holdings, and (*b*) on a purely arbitrary basis."

An essential first stage of this ambitious project is "a survey of specialist resources of all libraries" and "the continuation of the survey on a permanent basis." The interim report discusses some further details, and the council in approving the report in principle asked the working party to continue its work with a pilot survey covering the Dewey Classes 620 (Engineering) and 700 (Fine Arts).

The importance of this plan and the service that may emerge from it can scarcely be overestimated. The public libraries enter into the scheme as Category D and E libraries. The Regional Reference Libraries are to be "existing public libraries in the major centres, strengthened and, if necessary, re-organized to bear their additional responsibilities."

In the lending libraries "the allocation of subject fields must be determined after a survey of holdings and local interest," so that each selected library may be given "fields which will be of the maximum local and regional use."

It has been known for many years that in the public libraries of Scotland there has been a certain amount of subject specialization, quite apart from the usual provision of a local collection, but there has been so far no overall plan to systematize or to co-ordinate this specialization, beyond an abortive attempt initiated in April 1936 by the County Library Circle.[29] After appointing a committee who gave the scheme careful consideration it was decided in November that "the time was not yet ripe for the

---

[29] Letters from W. E. C. Cotton, librarian, Scottish Central Library, as honorary secretary of the County Library Circle, 23 April, 10 August and 27 November 1936.

inauguration of any formal scheme." The question was deferred until such time as a Regional Library Bureau had been established, when it would be "much easier to ascertain the existing resources of Scottish libraries, both county and burgh:" the Circle's scheme had concerned county libraries only.

In 1955 the question of a subject-specialization scheme for Scotland was considered by the executive committee of the Scottish Central Library. In March of that year the librarian issued a questionnaire designed to ascertain the degree of subject specialization at present existing. From the replies received, it was obvious that there was considerable ambiguity in the definition of a special collection. One library claims to have a special collection of 400 volumes on a subject; another has a collection of 750 volumes, while a third has approximately 26,000 volumes on the same subject. These divergent figures indicate that some librarians in claiming a "special collection" scarcely realize the full extent of the subject they claim to cover and the potential size of their special collection. Stanley Jast's definition is worth remembering:

> A special collection is such by virtue of its aim, to gather together a complete collection of books on the particular subject, and the extent to which it realizes that aim. There must be a reasonable proportion between what it has and what it *might* have, between the actual and the possible contents. Alternatively, if the books are few, they must be rare or remarkable in some other respects. To apply the term indiscriminately to collections which are "large" only in comparison with the representation of other subjects in a particular library is to rob it of any real meaning. The comparison must be with the literature. The library of Slocum-cum-Podgham, which has fifty volumes on Napoleon, may call it a special collection, but the literature on Napoleon runs into thousands of volumes, a veritable library in itself, and Slocum-cum-Podgham's use of the term is a foolish and misleading use. A special collection must be worth while to the specialist.[30]

The part that the executive committee of the Scottish Central Library and its librarian are playing in forwarding this question of a subject-specialization scheme for Scotland suggests that this body may be able to perform some of the functions of the Library Council for Scotland recommended in the Advisory Council report and agreed to in the Scottish Library Association's statement on that report. It will be recalled that the three functions to be referred to the Library Council for Scotland were:

[30] L. S. Jast, *The library and the community* (1939), p. 93.

(*a*) To ensure that the grant-aided local services reach and maintain a national standard of efficiency;

(*b*) To administer the Central Lending Library;

(*c*) To advise on general library policy and schemes of library development in Scotland.

The Scottish Central Library executive committee is specially charged with the second of these functions; could it possibly—and properly—assume the others? The report pointed out:

> The three functions mentioned above are on a national level; they all require the participation of library experts and others specially interested; and they all involve some measure of control in the interests of the general public whether as taxpayers, ratepayers or consumers.

The executive committee is fully representative: the local authority associations, different kinds of library, and other related and interested organizations are all represented. It is more influential in many ways than the council of the Scottish Library Association, for although the Scottish Library Association includes both librarians and local authority representatives, it has more of the character of a professional association, and the local authority representation in it, frequently from the co-opted and not the elected members of the library committee, is not strong. The executive committee of the Scottish Central Library, particularly since the representation of local authority associations was increased, is in a strong position to formulate policy and get it carried into effect. As a nationally representative body it is well able to advise on general library policy and schemes of development, and to ensure that local services reach and maintain desirable standards of efficiency.

Throughout this study the National Library of Scotland has been referred to only incidentally. The library of the Faculty of Advocates was handed over to the nation in 1925 and its new building was opened in July 1956. The National Library is a public library of a very special kind: it is Scotland's British Museum.

The 1849 *Abstract return relating to public libraries in Scotland* mentions only the Advocates' Library and the libraries of the four Scottish Universities.[31] If such a return of Scottish public libraries

---

[31] Parliamentary Return, Public Libraries, 9 March 1849 (18-II).

were made today it is doubtful if these five libraries would be included. The term "public library" has come to mean almost exclusively the "rate-supported" library. But it is not the least interesting point that emerges from a survey of the history of the public library movement in Scotland that over the years the university libraries through their ready assistance by inter-lending are probably more public today than they have ever been: especially is this true of Edinburgh University Library. The library that contains Clement Little's bequest has indeed become "ane commoun Librarie," and two of the University's librarians have served with distinction as presidents of the Scottish Library Association.[32]

Over the years, too, the public library idea has evolved from the mere provision of a supply of reading matter, usually limited in numbers and frequently in appeal, to the ideal of "a public library which concentrates on making recorded fact, opinion and experience generally available . . . through a really high standard of service."[33]

But, as a national service locally administered, a public library can be no better than its community wants it to be. At its best the public library will be "the centre of the intellectual life of the area which it serves," a university of the people which "all may attend and none need ever leave."[34]

---

[32] F. C. Nicholson (1928-9); L. W. Sharp (1949, 1950). Later, in 1960, the librarian of the National Library of Scotland, Professor William Beattie, also served as president.

[33] W. A. Munford, "The public library idea," *Library Association Record,* vol. 57 (1955), p. 350.

[34] Kenyon report (1927), p. 39; George V at the opening of the new building of the National Central Library, 7 November 1933.

THE PERTH MECHANICS' LIBRARY was instituted in November 1823 in a small room in the High Street.[1] The first catalogue still extant is dated 1832. It lists 130 volumes, including Chambers' *Dictionary of Arts and Sciences* in 2 volumes with the 2-volume supplement, Brewster's edition of Ferguson's *Mechanics*, and Brewster's Ferguson's *Astronomy*, both in 2 volumes, Gregory's *Mechanics* in 3 volumes, 12 volumes of the *London Mechanics' Magazine* and 4 volumes of the *Glasgow Mechanics' Magazine*, Johnson's *Dictionary* in a 2-volume edition, books on arithmetic, algebra, geometry, trigonometry, natural philosophy, chemistry and mineralogy, Adam Smith's *Wealth of Nations* in 4 volumes, 15 volumes of the *Library of Entertaining Knowledge*, Birkbeck's *Mathematics*, McCulloch's *Commercial Dictionary*, Ware's *Body of Architecture*, and Chippendale's *Cabinet Makers' Director*.

A supplement of Addenda lists books numbered from 131 to 173, among them 14 marked as donations. The Addenda include, in addition to works of science such as Sir David Brewster's *Optics* and Ritchie's *Illustrations of the Differential and Integral Calculus*, six volumes of Rollin's *Ancient History*, *The Sketch Book* by Washington Irving (in two volumes), a history of New York, and two volumes called *Working Man's Companion*, the one with the sub-title *Rights of Industry*, the other, *Cottage Evenings*.

The next catalogue that has been found is actually an "Additional Supplement," dating from about 1850, to a catalogue now lost. In the interval the library had obviously changed in character. Four of the eight pages of the "Additional Supplement" list novels, many of them in 3 volumes, and there is a note that says:

Members are entitled at a time to a Novel of 1, 2, or 3 volumes, and any other Miscellaneous work of the same

[1] The material on which this account of the Perth Mechanics' Library is based is to be found in the Sandeman Public Library in Perth. Unfortunately no Minute Books of the Mechanics' Library have survived; the Minute Book of the Perth Anderson Institution came into the writer's hands when he was invited to examine a private library that was being dispersed on the owner's decease.

number of volumes, or one volume of any of the Periodical Works.

The "Additional Supplement" lists about 300 works (the earlier practice of giving a separate number to each volume of a work in several volumes had been abandoned, the one number was now given to all the volumes of a work) and one of the highest numbers used is 1318, for a copy of *The Adventures of Oliver Twist,* but some early numbers have been used again. The numerical order of the previous catalogues is abandoned for an approximate alphabetical arrangement, mostly by title but occasionally by the author's surname. Thus *The Adventures of Oliver Twist,* just mentioned, follows *The Commissioner* by Charles Lever, and *The Life and Adventures of Martin Chuzzlewit,* and precedes *The Chevalier, a Romance of the Rebellion, 1745* (in 3 volumes) and *The Moneyed Man, or the Lesson of a Life* (also in 3 volumes), while Ainsworth's *Tower of London,* Bulwer's *Last of the Barons,* and James' *Arabella Stewart* are so catalogued. Seven novels by Mrs Trollope and nine by Mrs Gore are listed under M, between *Marmaduke Herbert, or the Fatal Error* and *Mary Barton, a Tale of Manchester Life.*

The list of 130 Miscellaneous works begins with about thirty works with "Adventures" as the first word of the title. While such books as Humboldt's *Cosmos,* and the *Panorama of Science, or Guide to Knowlelge, The Mechanic's Own Book,* and *The History of Useful Invention,* still find their place in the catalogue, they are now in the minority. Biography, travel, history and belles lettres all make an appearance: among them *Confessions of a Young Sailor Boy,* Lewis' and Clark's *Travels to the Source of the Missouri, The War in Affghanistan and Scinde,* and *Memoirs of the Literary Ladies of England.*

Perhaps it was this radical change in the character of the Mechanics' Library that prompted the "meeting of the inhabitants of Perth" that was held in the City Hall "on Wednesday the seventeenth day of February 1847 for the purpose of forming a Philosophical and Scientific Institution, the Lord Provost in the Chair."

The following Resolutions were moved and unanimously agreed to:

First. Moved by the Rev. Mr Gilfillan of Dundee and seconded by the Rev. Mr Jacque of Auchterarder, namely "That the diffusion among all classes of a sound knowledge of the truth of Science, Literature, and the Arts, is essential to the happiness and greatness of the people."

Second. Moved by the Rev. Dr Young, and seconded by Mr Nairne, Milnhaugh, "That a Philosophical and Scientific Institution be organised in Perth."

Third. Moved by Mr David Lowe, Wright, Perth, and seconded by Bailie Barlas, "That the existence of a popular Institution for the dissemination of useful knowledge is of manifold and varied advantage to the working classes, and the hearty support and warm co-operation of those classes in Perth and its vicinity are earnestly invited and anxiously expected in behalf of this Institution."

Fourth. Moved by the Rev. J. Anderson, East Church, and seconded by Mr Sheriff Barclay, "That the name of the association shall be the 'Perth Anderson Institution' in memory of Adam Anderson, LL.D., Professor of Natural Philosophy in the University of St Andrews and formerly Rector of Perth Academy."

The fifth resolution detailed the aims and objects of the Institution:

. . . by Lectures and otherwise, to disseminate amongst the population of Perth a knowledge of Philosophy, Science, General Literature, and the Arts.

Persons subscribing "£5 at once or 5s annually" were to be members of the Institution, entitled "to attend the Lectures, and to have the benefit of the Observatory, Library, or other means of instruction connected with the Institution."

. . . The Institution, if sufficient funds be obtained, shall have an Observatory and philosophical apparatus, a Library of Books on Science, General Literature, and the Arts, with a Museum of Exhibition of Models and Works of Art.

Six patrons are listed, Mr Sheriff Barclay was to be president, and two secretaries, a treasurer, and twelve directors were nominated. The Institution's motto was later agreed upon: "It is a Godlike attribute to know."

When the directors held their first meeting two days later the secretaries were instructed:

To write Mr Andrew Davidson requesting him to call a meeting of the Committee of the Perth Mechanics' Institution for the purpose of having the Library and apparatus belonging to them transferred to the Anderson Institution.

and a committee of three was appointed "to enquire into the

305

condition of the books and also to look out for a suitable library-room." A week later when this committee confessed that "there had existed a difference of opinion amongst them regarding the size, rent and intended uses of this room," it received further instructions "to look for a good room capable of containing the Library alone." The yearly rent was not to exceed £5.

At the first meeting of directors it was agreed to write "Mr Chambers of Edinburgh making enquiry about a course of lectures on History now delivering before the Philosophical Institution there, and . . . Mr Kettle of Glasgow about a course of lectures on Rhetoric."

At a later meeting the directors decided to write to the secretary of the Dundee Watt Institution to ascertain whether its directors would be disposed to enter into an arrangement with the Perth Institution "to have the same course of lectures delivered alternately in the two towns."

The directors regretted they could not accept the offer of a Revd. Mr Paterson of Glasgow to give two lectures to the Institution "as the only nights convenient for him unfortunately happen on the Sacrament week in Perth."

The Institution's introductory lecture, by Rev. Dr Anderson of Newburgh, was delivered in the City Hall on 19 March, "with no charge for admission: a collection however to be made at the door."

A Mr Cuthbertson delivered the first course of lectures. As for his remuneration, it was agreed that his travelling expenses should be paid forthwith: "the Directors were desirous to make him some consideration for his services—which would be done at some other time." At the same time it was agreed to write to the lecturer with whom the directors had been in communication over a second course of lectures, to say that in the present condition of their funds they could not "venture on his course in the meantime."

A handsome present of books for the library was gratefully acknowledged by the directors in May 1847, with unanimous thanks to the donor "for the very timely aid he had so readily afforded them."

In October 1847 it was agreed that the first session should finish at Candlemas, and that the second should be "from 1 February to 1 October next." The directors "had a conversation about Mr Emerson and Dr Samuel Brown" and a "course of lectures on phrenology" was suggested. Again arrangements were made to join forces with the Watt Institution in Dundee and through this co-operation the directors engaged "the services of Mr George Dawson for a course of six lectures."[2]

The library was open to mechanics for 1s for one quarter and to apprentices for 6d. Indeed apprentices and all persons under 15 years of age were admitted "to the full benefits of the Instituttion at half price on producing a certificate from their masters." For admission to single lectures the prices ranged from 1d to 1s. The directors allowed "admission to centre seats at half price to those below 12 years of age; Sabbath scholars and others under 12 admitted to side seats, 1d."

When the Rev. George Gilfillan of Dundee lectured on "Old Testament Poetry" the admission charges were to be 6d, 3d and 1d. A lecture by Mr J. H. Pepper of London on "the Electric Light" was arranged at a cost of £7 10s, and on that occasion the charges for admission were 1s, 6d and 3d, with special reserved seats at 2s. When a Dr Hudson of Glasgow offered "the services of Mrs Hudson and himself, each to deliver a lecture," it was agreed "to write and ask their charges. If accepted, to charge for admission to Mrs Hudson's lecture 3d, 6d and 1s and to Dr Hudson's 3d and 6d. Agreed that if gratuitous to accept Mrs Hudson."[3]

The final entry in this Institution's first Minute Book refers to the library once more:

Perth, 25 January 1849 . . . It was stated to the Directors that the Perth Reading Society in the Kirk Close was about to be broken up and the books dispersed. Dr Frew, Mr Hepburn, and Mr Fleming were appointed a Committee to visit the members of the Society and ascertain if the books could be got for the Anderson Institution.

The Institution is mentioned twenty-four years later in the preface, dated March 1873, to the supplement to the 1870 cata-

[2] Emerson did lecture in Dundee, but the suspicion of scepticism that surrounded him made a timid committee wary of engaging him; Dr Samuel Brown is almost certainly the chemist son of the founder of the East Lothian Itinerating Libraries; and George Dawson later gave evidence before the Select Committee on Public Libraries. Phrenology, to the founders of the Mechanics' Institutes, was an important science: let the working man by this science ascertain his true bent, and then let him educate himself by reading.

[3] Probably Dr J. W. Hudson, author of a *History of Adult Education* (1851), on the title-page of which he is described as "Secretary of the Manchester Athenaeum, Founder of the Scottish and Northern Unions of Literary and Mechanics' Institutions."

logue of the Mechanics' Library. The librarian, John Maclauchlan, points out that:

A considerable number of the Scientific Books in this Supplement are not of the most recent date; but the explanation is, that these (276 vols.) were kindly presented to the Library by the surviving Trustees of the Perth Andersonian Institution.

It is most interesting to find, then, that although in 1847 the members of the Anderson Institution obviously thought that the existence of their association would mean the end of the Mechanics' Institution and the transfer to them of its "library and apparatus," in the event it was the reverse that happened.

In 1856 the Mechanics' Library had found most commodious accommodation in the hall of the Hammermen Incorporation, where it steadily increased for thirteen years—there were 400 members and the books eventually numbered 7000—until early in the morning of 8 April 1869 a fire broke out in the premises under the library, when nearly all its books were destroyed.

By September the library had found a new home. The £500 for which the books had been insured (less than half their original cost) and sums contributed by members had enabled the directors to purchase more than 2500 new volumes and rebind about 1500 which had been only partially damaged in the fire. These, with the volumes in borrowers' hands at the time of the fire, formed the library's new stock, and a fresh catalogue was issued in March 1870, compiled by the librarian and secretary, John Maclauchlan, who was to become librarian of the public library in Dundee in 1874, after seventeen years' service in the Perth Mechanics' Library.

It was his successor as secretary, Charles Tulloch, who issued in 1879 the appeal for material to form a "local collection" that we have noted in chapter 7. He was responsible also for the new catalogue published in July 1882: this was an "Alphabetical Index-Catalogue," "generally admitted" to be "best suited for a popular Library such as the Mechanics' . . . where the Readers are not allowed to examine the shelves for themselves." Maclauchlan's catalogue, which it superseded, had been arranged in subject groups within which the arrangement was by author, title or subject, treating "each class by the rule that seemed best fitted for it."

At this time the library was open ten hours a week, every Tuesday and Friday from 1 p.m. to 3 p.m., and on Monday, Wednesday and Saturday evenings from 7.30 to 9.30. The subscription, which had to be paid in advance, was $1\frac{1}{2}$d per week, or 1s 6d for a quarter of thirteen weeks; but any member whose circumstances rendered him unable to continue in the Society might have reading gratis, if recommended by two members and if the directors approved. At the death of a member his nearest heir was entitled to his share in the library.

Members were entitled to have "two Works of not more than three Volumes each," and to exchange their books twice a week. Current issues of certain magazines and reviews were issued on special payments of "Twopence for three Nights during the first Month, One Penny for three Nights during the second Month, thereafter . . . free of charge for one Week."

A "Suggestions Book" was maintained in the library wherein members could insert "the name of any Work or Works which they may think would be for the advantage of the Library to purchase," and if a member wanted to read a book on loan to another borrower, it would be kept for him on its return "till Nine o'clock on the next evening the Library is open, after which it shall be given to the next Member on the List who may be present."

Each Member will be furnished with a copy of these Rules, so that none can plead ignorance of them.

In 1896, the Public Libraries Acts were adopted in Perth, and in November of that year the secretary of the Perth Mechanics' Library wrote to inform the city clerk that the following motion was to be discussed at the library's annual general meeting in April of the following year:

That the Perth Mechanics' Library be thereafter discontinued and that the Books be handed over to the Committee of the Sandeman Public Library, on such terms as may be agreed upon by the meeting.

The clerk was instructed "to thank the Directors of the Mechanics' Library for their handsome and considerate indication of intention."

In March 1897, the Public Library Committee was told by its librarian, John Minto, "that the amount proposed to be spent on the Lending Department was conditioned by the prospect of the Mechanics' Library being handed over to the Committee. If the negotiations to that end should fail more than £1000 would have to be spent on the Lending Department."

The next month, however, the Public Library Committee's Books Sub-Committee learned from the secretary of the Mechanics' Library that it had been agreed that the Mechanics'

Library should be discontinued and its books handed over to the Sandeman Public Library on certain conditions:

(1) That the Committee of the Sandeman Library relieve the Mechanics' Library of rents and taxes from the date of possession; (2) that the local collection should be kept distinct from the Lending Library as a nucleus to the Perth collection; (3) that county readers be granted the privilege of reading on the same terms as at present. . . .

It was agreed that it should be a hard and fast stipulation in handing over the Library that Mr Gullen (the Librarian) should get a pension of not less than £15 per annum.

The Books Sub-Committee agreed to recommend acceptance of the collection on these terms, "as far as it may be in the power of the Committee to fulfil the same," and the directors and members of the Mechanics' Library were thanked for their "valuable gift."

By June, Minto had examined the stock of the Mechanics' Library and submitted his report:

Of about 11,000 volumes, 6,300 will be available for placing on the shelves. Of these about 5,300 are suitable for the Lending Department and 1000 for the Reference. To this has been added 153 volumes of the *Times* newspaper. The remainder of the stock is either worn out or consists of three- and two-volume novels which are unsuitable for the purposes of a lending library.

The 1000 volumes for the Reference Department included the local collection.

The Sandeman Public Library Committee were at this time using the Mechanics' Library as storage accommodation for the books that were being accumulated for their library. In November they brought in a local book-binder to undertake "the mending and repairing of the Mechanics' Library stock of books" and also to number "the whole of the books." In April this work was "well advanced" and likely to be completed "before the books are removed to the new building."

The Sandeman Public Library was officially opened in October 1898. The Mechanics' Library is last heard of in August 1900. On the 7th of that month the directors met in the Sandeman Library. It was found that after meeting all liabilities they had at their disposal a sum of over £20.

It was unanimously agreed to wind up the affairs of the Mechanics' Library, and to hand over the free surplus to the managers of the Home for Consumptives at present in course of erection at Barnhill, to be devoted to the purchase of books and magazines for the use of the patients.

With this generous gesture the Perth Mechanics' Library came to an end almost exactly 77 years after its foundation. It is perhaps worth noting that several of its members in its later years were active in the establishment of Perth's Public Library under the Acts, and that twenty years later in 1917 some of the same people were involved in the Carnegie Trust's pioneer scheme for the Perthshire Rural Library that preceded the rate-supported county library.

(b) THE INSHEWAN READING SOCIETY

THE INSHEWAN READING SOCIETY was proposed in 1796 by some persons in the three Inshewans—Easter, Middle and Wester—that are now included in the village of Birnam, near Dunkeld, Perthshire.[1] The "new Rules and Regulations" adopted on 9 January 1810 make a bold start. Rule 1 reads:

1. That the Society shall be permanent and shall be called the Inshewan Reading Society.

The Society was to be under the direction of a Preses, and if he did not attend at the hour fixed "the meeting shall fine him threepence or a satisfactory excuse given." There are the usual Rules governing membership, but sometimes with a unique turn:

If any member shall reside twenty miles from the seat of the Society he shall no more be considered a member, but that he shall not lose his right he shall have it in his power to transfer his share of the library to his son or his brother or his son-in-law, providing he is of a good moral character, until his return.

If any member was convicted of lending the Society's books he had in his custody to any person not connected with the Society, he was to pay a fine of threepence for each day the book

---

[1] This account is based on a typescript of the Society's Minute Book in the Perth and Kinross County Library. The original is referred to in Elizabeth Stewart's *Dunkeld, an ancient city: local lore, persons and places* (Perth, 1926)—"The title page is beautifully transcribed by hand and would adorn any age"—but its present owner is unknown.

was lent, and if he refused to pay, he was to be "expelled from the Society and forfeit all he may have contributed."

Rule 14 decreed:

That if any member use improper language such as swearing, or assumes the character of a director at any of their meetings, he shall pay for the first offence one penny, and double for the second, and lose his vote for that meeting;

and Rule 19 added:

That if any member be convicted of raising factions or tumults or disturb the Society with idle discourse till such time as business be over, he shall pay twopence for the first, and double for the second offence.

Fines for overdue books were to be charged—"twopence for each week"—and the librarian had authority to charge "a halfpenny for every turned down corner and the same for a spot or soiled margin."

The early minutes are brief and formal. In April 1811 there is, however, a reference to a book for the Society: it was unanimously agreed to purchase Dean Prideaux's *Connections* at "the first opportunity."[2] In August the librarian reported that the four volumes had been bought for one guinea, and the "considerable number" of the members present "balloted for the volumes for reading."

In January 1812 it was proposed that the Society should get "a good history of Great Britain" and the members agreed "to deliberate upon what author or history at some future meeting." A year later they were still deliberating: three members of the Society were "impowered" severally to consult with the minister and two other gentlemen in the neighbourhood, "as to their opinions what history would be best for the Society to purchase." One gathers the Society received conflicting advice: a year later again in 1814—

The meeting was still of their former opinion of having a good history of Great Britain and Dr Henrie's *History* was thought as the best adapted for the Society and to be got as soon as possible on the easiest terms.[3]

[2] *The Old and New Testament connected in the history of the Jews and neighbouring nations,* by Humphrey Prideaux, Dean of Norwich (2v. 1716-18). The sixteenth edition, in four volumes, "to which is now first added the Life of the Author," was published in 1808.

[3] *The history of Great Britain,* by Robert Henry, was first published in six volumes in 1771-93. A fourth edition, in twelve volumes, was published in 1805.

In 1815 it was agreed, "as there was cash in hand," to purchase Hume's *History* with Smollett's *Continuation,* and during the year this was done, for in 1816 the meeting directed "Smollet's volumes to be bound in a substantial manner." At the 1816 annual meeting, incidentally, the president, "having failed to appear or send a reasonable excuse," was fined "threepence, stg." in accordance with the Rule we have already referred to

Gifford's *History of the Wars*[4] was being purchased in parts by one of the Society's members in 1816, and at an extraordinary meeting of the Society in December it was agreed that the Society should take over this reader's subscription "provided he would bind the half of the numbers already taken out by him;" the Society was prepared to purchase and bind the other parts.

In 1817, "taking into consideration the pressure of the times," the Society agreed to defer the collecting of the "quarterages . . . as they have money enough to meet the present demand."

A catalogue was planned in 1819: all the members, when called upon, were "to send in the books in their custody or a list of them." At this time it was resolved to reduce the quarterage from sixpence to threepence per quarter.

The annual meeting in January 1822 "empowered the librarian to buy Waverley and Rob Roy's novels" and it was agreed that the Society should get "a type for marking all the books belonging to the Society with the following inscription 'Inshewan Reading Society.' . . . After partaking of the fruits, ham and salmon the meeting adjourned." In April the librarian reported that "Mr Thomas Stewart of Dunkeld had purchased all Sir Walter Scott's novels in sixteen volumes new and that he offered them at £4 10/-," and it was unanimously agreed to take them.

Throughout the twelve years covered by the minutes we have been quoting the librarian and clerk had been invariably a Harris from Middle Inshewan—in the first instance, and again at the end of the period, a certain William Harris, and at other times, James Harris, or Thomas Harris his brother, or Thomas Harris, jun. In 1824, however, William Harris was elected Preses, and William Stewart, Wester Inshewan, was appointed librarian, "but as the present library is not sufficient to hold the books, it is hereby agreed that the books shall remain with Wm. Harris till the half yearly meeting in July, when members will meet and carry the books to Wm. Stewart's in Wester Inshewan."

Mr Wm. McAra was appointed chaplin to walk in front of the procession carrying Dr Dodridge Family expositor and to

---

[4] C. H. Gifford, *History of the wars occasioned by the French Revolution, from* 1792 *to* 1814 (1816).

consecrate the books after being placed in the new library with a prayer.

The same meeting agreed "to get a new library made 6 ft. long and 4 ft. wide of larch wood."

In January 1825 the story is recapitulated, and we are told that the new bookcase that had been ordered in 1824 had not been ready "at the time appointed, and the removal of the books was postponed till this date."

After collecting the quarterages from the members present the meeting adjourned to Birnam Inn and removed the books to the Librarian's house and placed them in the new bookcase and after partaking of a plentiful dinner resumed the business of the Society.

The members then resolved to half-bind the novels by the author of *Waverley* and dealt with other matters demanding their attention.

This ended the business of the Society, then the country beverage, whisky toddy, was ordered and the members continued together till a late hour. Many appropriate toasts were drunk in course of the evening and the members, inspired by the enlivening spirit of genuine Glenlivet, sang many national airs with real Scotch glee.

The Society was again seeking advice on book selection in 1827.

The meeting proceeded to consider what books they would purchase for the funds in hand amounting to £1 18/-. The meeting fixed upon the lives of remarkable characters since the Reformation and as none of the members knew where such a work could be had, they ordered the Librarian to write the Rev. W. Aird Thomson, Perth, for information on the subject, and to lay his answer before the following Committee, Viz. James Hettles, Middle Inshewan, Thos. Harris, there, and Thos. Harris, elder, Easter Inshewan, Wm. Macfarlane, Middle Inshewan, and Donald Bory, Inver, any three of them to be a Quoram.

Unfortunately it is not recorded what Mr Thomson recommended.

Towards the end of the year an emergency meeting was called to consider the appointment of a librarian as William Stewart was "leaving the place." William Harris was again "fixed upon," and the meeting ordered "the Library to be removed to his house on Monday first." There is no record of any ceremonial at this removal.

In 1828 "the stock in the Librarian's hand being £1.19/- stg.," the members fixed upon the purchase of certain books: Cook's *History of the Church of Scotland* and Knox's *Memoirs*, but three years later the books are still "to be bought" and funds are dwindling: the members present "empowered the Librarian to purchase any of these two books the funds would cover, as there is only £1 stg. in the Librarian's hands."

There follows a long gap of twenty-three years in the minutes, and the next entry is the last. On 19 June 1854 "a general meeting of the Inshewan Reading Society assembled in terms of a requisition from the Librarian for the purpose of dissolving the Society."

The Librarian, Wm. Harris, produced all the books in his custody.

They were divided among the members equally, according to the value of the books.

There was also £1 stg. in the Librarian's hands which divided amongst the poor of the district. The book-holder was then disposed of and Inshewan Society was then declared dissolved mutually.

So, one year after it became legally possible to set up rate-supported public libraries in Scotland, this little Society that had so ambitiously set out to be "permanent" came to the end fated for so many voluntary schemes of the kind.

PERTHSHIRE RURAL LIBRARY

T HE PRESENT Perth and Kinross County Library traces its origin to an informal meeting in Perth on 23 March 1917 of the General Committee of the Sandeman Public Library Committee, with in addition the chairman and three members of Perth School Board. The meeting had been called to hear A. L. Hetherington, secretary to the Carnegie United Kingdom Trust, on a possible scheme of rural libraries for Perthshire.

The Carnegie Trustees were prepared to finance in its experimental stage a scheme "under which all the parishes in Perthshire, if they wished, could have the services of a Circulating Library for a year or two free of any expenses, or at least at a nominal cost," in the hope that after the experimental period these parishes would adopt the Public Libraries Acts and combine with the Sandeman Public Library in carrying out the provisions of these Acts.[1]

A month later the Public Library Committee accepted the Carnegie Trust's suggestion, and a sub-committee of six was appointed "to enquire and report . . . as to the preliminaries of the Scheme." James Craigie, city librarian of Perth and clerk to the Public Library Committee, was appointed clerk. This sub-committee had a meeting with Mr Hetherington in May and received "much useful information . . . as to what the Carnegie United Kingdom Trust was prepared to do and as to ways in which the Trust suggested the Scheme might be carried out."

On 19 May a circular letter was sent to the head teachers of the schools in the twenty-six parishes "in the vicinity of Perth . . . chosen for the initiation of the Scheme," inviting them to attend a meeting on 26 May.[2]

A large number of teachers attended the meeting, and nearly all who were not present sent apologies for absence and expressed interest in the movement and their willingness to

[1] The secretary was, in fact, outlining and promising the Trust's financial backing for a plan that had already been considered by the Sandeman Public Library Committee some seventeen and a half years before (Minutes, 21 November 1899).

[2] By the census of 1911 these 26 parishes had a population of 32,501 (or about 37 per cent of the population of the county apart from the city of Perth).

help. Mr A. D. Miller, H.M. Inspector of Schools, was also invited to the meeting and was present. . . .

It was unanimously agreed by those present to do all they could to assist in the work.

With this indication of the teachers' interest and support the sub-committee in July sent a circular to the School Boards of the selected parishes, "requesting that the Boards grant the use of the schoolrooms as far as might be necessary for the Libraries, and give the teachers permission to volunteer their services as local librarians during the experimental period of the Libraries."

By the end of August the sub-committee had heard from all the School Boards they had approached, and "all were in favour of the Scheme." A shop in Kinnoull Street, no. 23, directly opposite the Sandeman Library, was mentioned "as a very convenient repository for the Rural Library books." The committee agreed to report progress to the General Committee of the Public Library, and asked for powers to complete negotiations with the Carnegie Trust and to appoint a librarian or other assistants.

At a further meeting with Mr Hetherington in September provisional estimates for "the institution and annual operations of the Scheme" were agreed. The capital expenditure amounted to £1305, including 8000 volumes at an average of 2s 6d per volume, shelving to cost £130, a typewriter, catalogue cabinets and cards, and an honorarium of £25 to the "Sandeman Library Librarian for preliminaries." The annual expenditure was estimated at £325 —salaries £150; allowances to schoolmasters at £2 2s each, £65; rents, taxes, heating, lighting and cleaning, £80; carriage of boxes, postages and stationery £30.[3]

A bank account was opened in the name of "The Perthshire Rural Library Committee," and in November the Carnegie Trust placed a first instalment of £500 to its credit. The shop at 23 Kinnoul Street was rented for a period of five years, and it was agreed "to advertise for a Librarian lady or gentleman, to take charge of the Scheme at a salary of £130 per annum."

Booksellers were rivalling each other in the discounts they were offering to the committee on the purchase of new books— 30 per cent, 47½ per cent, 65 per cent and even 80 per cent. In making their initial selection of books for the Scheme, the com-

[3] For comparison, the expenditure of the Sandeman Public Library Committee for the year ended 15 May 1917 was £1320. The population of Perth at the time (1911 census) was 35,854.

mittee had before them a list of the books in the eighteen Coats libraries in the schools they were intending to supply.

In December the committee were considering the applications received for the post of librarian, and four candidates were interviewed on the 19th of the month: Miss Mary B. Smith, Royal Technical College, Glasgow; Miss Jean Watterston, University College, Dundee; Alexander Jack, c/o Mrs Gowans, Comely Bank House, Bridgend, Perth; and Alexander Porteous, Ancaster House, St Fillans. At the interview each candidate was invited

to make up a specimen list of books for consignment to a rural district. . . . After careful consideration had been given to their qualifications and experience the Rev. P. R. Landreth proposed that the situation be offered to Miss Jean Watterston, L.L.A., assistant in the University College Library, Dundee.

The salary was to be £130 a year paid monthly and the appointment subject to a month's notice on either side. Hours were 9 a.m. to 5 p.m. on weekdays, with an interval of an hour for lunch, and 10 a.m. to 1 p.m. on Saturdays. The librarian was to have a fortnight's holiday in July or August and "all days declared by the Perth Town Council to be Public Holidays."

Her duties:

Everything necessary for organising, instituting, conducting and developing the Carnegie United Kingdom Trust Scheme of Rural Libraries for Perthshire.

Miss Watterston assumed her new responsibilities on 22 January 1918.

Efficient as Miss Watterston was, she did not maintain a Minute Book as Mr Craigie had done. The story of the development of the Rural Library Scheme is rather sketchy until the education authority took it over on 1 August 1919.

The newly established education authorities had obtained powers under section 5 of the Education (Scotland) Act, 1918, to provide "books for general reading," and at the second meeting of the Perthshire Education Authority, on 19 May 1919, Miss Haldane of Cloan had moved "the appointment of a Special Committee—to be known as 'The Library Committee'— . . . which would deal with matters connected with rural Libraries."[4]

[4] Miss Haldane was appointed chairman of this committee and took a great interest in its work. In her autobiography she tells how she "thoroughly enjoyed going round a Highland district in the Librarian's van and seeing how all classes of a scattered community came out to get the books required" (E. S. Haldane, *From one century to another* (1937), p. 220).

In June Mr Hetherington of the Carnegie Trust and Miss Watterston met this Committee.

After full discussion, it was unanimously resolved to recommend the Authority to adopt the provisions of Section 5 of the Education Act, 1918, and institute Libraries in the Schools of the County (exclusive of the City of Perth) or to carry on those already existing in connection with the Sandeman Library, provided arrangements could be made with the existing Committee. These recommendations, however, were subject to the condition that the Carnegie United Kingdom Trust would subsidise the scheme to the extent of:

1. Handing over the existing stock of books which is supplying about 30 Parishes, and also shelving, etc., sufficient for a larger number of volumes.

2. Supplying a sum which would approximate to £2,000 for the purpose of providing a Building, extra boxes necessary, and new Books sufficient to carry on the Scheme for some years.

The cost of upkeep was estimated as follows:—Salaries, £200; Rates, £10; Heating and Lighting, £30; Carriage of Boxes, £30; Travelling Expenses, £10; Printing, Stationery, and Postages, £30; Miscellaneous, £25—in all, £335. This figure did not include any payment to Head Teachers, but it was thought that if they were supplied with a sufficient number of books, they would be willing to carry on the distribution free of charge. At present they are each paid £2 yearly.

These recommendations were accepted by the local committee and by the Carnegie Trust, and the education authority agreed to them on 22 July. The transfer at 1 August 1919 was reported to and authorized by the authority on 11 August. Miss Watterston resigned in October, "in view of her approaching marriage," and was followed by Mr James Caithness, whom the present writer succeeded in 1949.

The subsequent history of the Scheme is best shown as a statistical summary. Here it is clearly seen how the service grew —in the number of centres supplied, the number of books available to maintain them, and the number of issues recorded. It is interesting to note, too, that apart from the early experimental period and the grant to cover the purchase of the library's first book van, the Carnegie grants were entirely spent on books, and that it was not indeed until 1923-24 that the authority made any payment for books from its own funds.

	INCOME		EXPENDITURE		CENTRES		STOCK	ISSUES
Year	Carnegie Trust	Education Fund	Books	Admin.	Adult only	School and School & Adult		
To 1919	£929	£	£929			27	2,500	
1919-20	576		£	£		50	12,469	
1920-21	1,080	966	663	966	25	94	14,687	20,567
			Van 417					
1921-22	296	871	296	871	30	104	15,569	38,072
1922-23	90	1,010	90	1,010	34	127	16,848	60,411
1923-24	664	899	743	810	41	131	19,253	63,917
1924-25	276	902	381	797	48	148	20,495	88,412
1925-26	37	1,259	429	867	48	156	22,914	96,561
1926-27	—	1,348	402	946	49	158	26,790	108,080
1927-28	431	1,346	863	914	49	159	29,888	131,024
1928-29	—	1,809	800	1,009	51	164	34,285	161,948
1954-55	—	12,372	5,234	7,265	58	156	141,654	592,718

REPORT BY JOINT COMMITTEE OF THE COUNTY COUNCIL OF
THE COUNTY OF DUMFRIES AND THE TOWN COUNCIL OF
THE BURGH OF DUMFRIES IN REGARD TO LIBRARY PRO-
VISION IN THE EDUCATION AREA OF DUMFRIESSHIRE

The Joint Committee was appointed at a conference of representatives of the county council of the county and of the town
council of the burgh of Dumfries in regard to questions and proposals, including library provision, pending between these two
bodies. The remit to the Joint Committee was to consider and
report whether the library services in the county and burgh should
be unified and, if so, under what arrangements. The Joint Committee consisted of the Rev. R. P. Fairlie (Chairman), Provost D.
Brodie, and Councillor R. Dinwiddie from the town council, and
Colonel F. J. Carruthers, Mr John Henderson, and the Rev. C.
Rolland Ramsay from the county council. The Joint Committee
have had several meetings, and, having considered their remit
fully, now report and recommend as follows: —

1. In Scotland there are two methods of providing library
facilities at the cost of the rates. The first of these is under the
Public Libraries (Scotland) Acts, 1887 to 1920. The other is under
the Education (Scotland) Acts, 1872 to 1918. As after-mentioned,
certain of the provisions of these two series of statutes were
amended by the Local Government (Scotland) Act, 1929.

2. The Public Libraries Acts can only be operated in a burgh,
or in a landward parish, or in the landward part of a partly landward and partly burghal parish, in which these Acts have been
adopted by the "householders" in accordance with the elaborate
and antiquated procedure prescribed in the original Act. But in
burghs in which these Acts have been adopted their administration is really vested in an *ad hoc* committee consisting to the
extent of one-half only of members of the town council. That
committee are empowered to requisition the town council annually
for such sums as they (the committee) may consider necessary for
library purposes subject only to the limit imposed by the maximum rate of assessment. In any landward parish, and in any
landward part of a partly landward and partly burghal parish, in
which the Acts had been adopted, it was formerly obligatory on
the parish council to constitute a similar *ad hoc* administrative

committee, but such appointment is no longer necessary. The Public Libraries Acts cannot be adopted now in any landward parish, or in the landward part of any partly landward and partly burghal parish, without the consent of the county council.

3. In Dumfriesshire the Public Libraries Acts have been adopted in the three burghs of Dumfries, Annan, and Lockerbie. In Dumfries reasonably efficient provision has been made for that burgh at the Ewart Library. In the other two burghs the town councils (or more correctly, the *ad hoc* administrative committees which the town councils are bound to set up) have made such library provision as is possible with the limited funds raised in these burghs under these Acts.

4. Since 1924 the education authority of the county (now, of course, the county council) have, as empowered by Section 5 of the Education (Scotland) Act, 1918, provided library facilities throughout practically the whole of the council's education area, with the exception of the three burghs above-mentioned in which, it is understood, the library provision available from the education authority was not desired. In addition to the headquarters library at Dumfries, with an increasing stock of more than 18,000 books, there are eighty-five distributing centres throughout the county. The books placed at these centres for circulation are changed from the library headquarters three times a year. The cost of all library provision by the county council is borne by the Council's education fund. Prior to 15th May, 1930, the balance of the annual expenditure chargeable to that fund (i.e. after deduction of the government education grant and other receipts) was raised by means of the education rates levied over the whole education area. Since 15th May, 1930, the balance of the annual expenditure just mentioned is allocated (1) to the landward part of the education area, and (2) to the several burghs which constitute part of that area, in proportion to their rateable annual values. The proportion applicable to the landward part of the area is included in the cumulo county rate levied directly by the county council on the ratepayers therein, and the proportions applicable to the burghs are requisitioned by the county council from the several town councils who include the amounts so requisitioned in the cumulo burgh rates levied by them on the ratepayers in their burghs.

5. Section 5 of the Education (Scotland) Act, 1918, above-mentioned provided that, where the Public Libraries (Scotland) Acts had been adopted and a rate under these Acts was levied, in any burgh, or in any landward parish, or in any landward part of a partly landward and partly burghal parish, the amount raised

322

in such burgh, or landward parish, or landward part of a parish, for library purposes by means of the education rate should be reduced by an amount equal to the estimated produce of the rate levied in the same area under the Public Libraries Acts. That requirement was repealed by Sub-section (5) of Section 18 of the Local Government (Scotland) Act, 1929.

6. The county council are accordingly now bound to raise the money required from the rates for education, including library, purposes by means of what is in effect a uniform rate over their whole education area irrespective of whether the Public Libraries Acts have been adopted, and a rate under these Acts is levied, in any part or parts of that area. In consequence of the legislation just recited the position now appears to be that, if the town council of any burgh in that area elects to continue to levy, and to make library provision in their burgh by means of, rates under the Public Libraries Acts, the inevitable result must be the double assessment of the ratepayers in that burgh and also the duplication of the library services if the burgh public library committee and the county council as education authority both make library provision in the burgh.

7. Suggestions were put forward by the representatives of the burgh of Dumfries that there might be a combination of (1) the county council as education authority and (2) the town councils (as local authorities under the Public Libraries Acts) of the three burghs of Dumfries, Annan and Lockerbie, in which these Acts have been adopted, and that a joint committee of these four councils might be constituted for the purpose of making library provision throughout the county council's education area; but the representatives of the county council stated the following objections to these suggestions: —

(1) The county council (and every other local authority) should be responsible for administration within their area and for the spending of the rates which they levy or of which they requisition the levy;

(2) The town councils of the three burghs in the county who have adopted the Public Libraries Acts are already fully represented on the county council, and these town councils would be doubly represented on the suggested joint committee;

(3) The suggested joint committee could hardly supersede the statutory *ad hoc* administrative committees in the three burghs nor extinguish these committees' power of requisition; *and*

(4) None of the three town councils could bring any funds into

the combination without continuing the anomalous double assessment of the ratepayers in their burgh.

8. After careful consideration of the whole circumstances the Joint Committee have come unanimously to the conclusion that, pending further legislation, library provision should be made under the Education Acts and at the cost of the education fund throughout the whole education area. While it will be desirable that some understanding as to the intended standard of library provision should be reached precedent to the necessary changes being introduced, there does not seem any material difficulty in the way of all reasonable library facilities being provided efficiently under the Education Acts for all parts of the education area.

9. Assuming acceptance of the view that library provision should now be made under the Education Acts, the Joint Committee, speaking generally, are of opinion and suggest that the scheme for the whole education area of Dumfriesshire should embrace provisions and arrangements of the following effect: —

(1) The Ewart Library buildings in Dumfries to be leased to the county council for the purpose of being used by them as part of their library accommodation for the whole county, a portion of these buildings to continue to be used as a newspaper reading room;

(2) The county council (*a*) to maintain the buildings and to defray all expenditure incidental to their maintenance and use, including rates and taxes, and (*b*) to continue the services now provided by the town council of Dumfries under the Public Libraries (Scotland) Acts, 1887 to 1920;

(3) The county council to erect, as near to the Ewart Library as practicable, such additional library accommodation as they may consider necessary for the purposes of library provision by them;

(4) The books in all the libraries in the county to be pooled;

(5) Branch or district sub-libraries of moderate dimensions to be established at Annan and Lockerbie if satisfactory arrangements are reached with the town councils of these burghs in regard to existing buildings;

(6) Similar branch or district sub-libraries might be established at other centres if such are considered necessary;

(7) The circulation of books from the remainder of the existing distribution centres in the county to be continued;

(8) One library staff, under one librarian, to be employed;

(9) All library provision throughout the education area of Dumfriesshire to be made under the Education (Scotland) Acts by a committee of the county council (to be known as the "Library Committee") consisting of (1) seven county councillors who represent electoral divisions in the landward area of the county, (2) four county councillors who represent the burgh of Dumfries, and (3) two county councillors who represent small burghs in the county;

(10) The library committee to prepare an annual estimate of their expenditure and to transmit such estimate to the education committee with a view to that committee (*a*) including it in the education estimates for the then current or ensuing year, (*b*) making such observations on the details or amount of such library estimate as they may consider called for, and (*c*) transmitting the library estimates and any such observations to the finance committee of the county council in accordance with the council's administrative scheme; and

(11) Subject to satisfactory grants being received from the Carnegie Trustees the expenditure of the library committee not to exceed £4000 in the first year nor £4500 in any of the remainder of the first five years.

10. The draft of this report was submitted to and considered fully at a conference of (1) the sub-committee of the convener's committee by whom the county representatives on the joint committee were appointed, and (2) the county councillors who represent the small burghs in the county and the town clerks of these burghs. At that conference the burgh representatives, except of one burgh, approved the proposals in the report. In the excepted case the representatives desired to give further consideration to the report and to consult their town council.

11. It is recommended that, immediately this report has been approved by the county council, and by the town council of Dumfries, the proposed Library Committee be appointed and be authorised to proceed with the contemplated arrangements with a view to these becoming operative as from and after 15th May 1932.

In name and by direction of the joint committee

ROBERT P. FAIRLIE, *Chairman.*

Dumfries, April, 1932.

FORFARSHIRE AND KINCARDINESHIRE JOINT COUNTY LIBRARY

THIS MINUTE of AGREEMENT by and between the EDUCATION AUTHORITY of the COUNTY of FORFAR, constituted under the Education (Scotland) Act, 1918, and having their office at Forfar, (hereinafter referred to as the First Party) *of the first part,* and The EDUCATION AUTHORITY of the COUNTY OF KINCARDINE, constituted under the said Act, and having their office at Stonehaven, (hereinafter referred to as the Second Party) *of the second part,* WITNESSETH THAT WHEREAS in the year Nineteen hundred and sixteen the Carnegie United Kingdom Trust set up in Montrose a special library for the supply of books to borrowers in certain rural parishes in the Counties of Forfar and Kincardine: AND WHEREAS by section five of the Education (Scotland) Act, 1918, Education Authorities were empowered to provide books for general reading and to do in the premises as is therein mentioned; AND WHEREAS the parties hereto, after sundry proceedings and by arrangement with the said Trust and the Town Council of Montrose and their Public Library Committee agreed, in exercise of their powers under the said section of the said Act, to take over as from the fifteenth day of November Nineteen hundred and twenty the existing Montrose Rural Library Scheme and to carry on the same jointly for behoof of the school and adult population resident in their respective areas: AND WHEREAS the parties hereto have continued to carry out the scheme then formulated and have administered and conducted, in terms of the said section five of the said Education (Scotland) Act, 1918, a joint library: AND WHEREAS it was agreed that the terms and conditions of the joint arrangement should be reduced to writing, NOW THEREFORE the parties hereto have agreed and do hereby agree as follows, THAT IS TO SAY,

FIRST. The parties hereto shall continue to administer the library scheme before mentioned while this agreement subsists under the style "The Forfarshire and Kincardineshire Joint County Library" (hereinafter referred to as the Library) subject to the conditions and regulations after-written.

SECONDLY. The general management of the Library shall be entrusted to an executive committee (hereinafter referred to as the

Committee) consisting of such number of members to be appointed by the First Party and the Second Party equally, as the parties may from time to time decide, but the Committee shall at no time consist of less than six members at which figure it stood at the date of these presents. Such committee shall be reconstituted as soon as may be after each fresh election of education authorities and shall remain in office, subject to the terms of Paragraph Eleven of the Second Schedule to the Education (Scotland) Act, 1918, until dissolved or reconstituted. Members of the Committee shall hold office during the pleasure of their respective constituents, who shall fill casual vacancies in their representation as they occur. So long as the Repository of the Library shall be housed in property belonging to the Town Council of Montrose or their Burgh Library Committee, the said Council or their Burgh Library Committee shall be entitled, for their interest, to elect three representatives to the Committee, but such representatives shall have no vote in the proceedings of the Committee.

THIRDLY. The Committee shall appoint their own convener, who shall have a casting as well as a deliberative vote on all matters delegated to the Committee. The Committee shall conduct their business at meetings specially called for the purpose, and shall meet as they may find necessary for the transaction of business. The Committee may appoint sub-committees and may delegate to such sub-committees any of their minor functions. Minutes of the proceedings of the Committee and of its sub-committees shall be suitably kept and the Committee shall have full power to regulate their proceedings in such manner as they may decide. The Clerk to the Committee shall be such permanent official of either of the parties hereto as the Committee may, with the consent of the pary concerned, appoint.

FOURTHLY. The parties hereto delegate to the Committee all their functions in connection with the administration of the said library except those relating to the general control of expenditure and the acquisition, leasing, and holding of land and heritable subjects generally, and in particular, but without prejudice to the said generality (i) the fixing of the amount to be made available for the Committeee's purposes during each financial year, (ii) staffing arrangements and the remuneration of the staff employed or to be employed, and (iii) the provision of a repository for the library and the financial arrangements thereanent. But subject to the terms of the next succeeding article all matters relating to the exercise by the parties of the said excepted functions shall stand referred to the Committee, and the parties hereto before exercising any such functions shall receive and consider the report of the Committee with respect to the matter in question. Notwithstanding the foregoing delegation of the functions of their constituents, the Committee shall, for information, submit to the parties hereto minutes of all their proceedings. No decision on such matters as stand referred to the Committee for report only shall become operative until the parties hereto have individually approved the Committee's proposed findings.

FIFTHLY. Notwithstanding the terms of the immediately preceding Article either of the parties hereto may at any time, and in their absolute discretion, take into consideration at their own hand any matter relating to any library function, but any decision reached shall not become operative or in any wise affect the proceedings of the Committee until, and in so far as, it has been approved by the other party. Any instruction given by the parties jointly in terms of any resolution adopted and approved as aforesaid shall, however, be accepted and acted upon by the Committee. If any resolution so adopted and approved is general in effect and does not relate to any particular event, matter or business, the procedure formulated by the latter part of Article Eighthly hereof shall be followed.

SIXTHLY. An account to be kept by the Clerk to the Committee for the time being shall be opened for recording the financial transactions of the Committee. To this account shall be credited all receipts applicable to the scheme while all payments passed by or chargeable against the Committee shall be debited against it. A bank account in name of the Committee shall be opened, and through it shall be passed all receipts and payments of the Committee. Such bank account shall be operated on by the properly accredited member or members and official of the party whose officer is acting for the time being as Clerk to the Committee. The accounts of the Committee shall be subject annually to a cash audit by the auditor appointed by the party whose officer is for the time being acting as Clerk to the Committee. A certified copy of the accounts signed by the responsible official and the auditor shall annually, as soon as may be after the audit, be transmitted to the Treasurer of the other party.

SEVENTHLY. The Committee shall annually take into consideration an account of their estimated receipts and expenditure during the financial year commencing the sixteenth day of May next ensuing, and shall determine the deficiency thereon. Before the thirty first day of May in each year the Committee shall apportion such deficiency between the parties hereto in the ratio of two parts to the first party, and one part to the second party, and shall certify to the parties the amount of the deficiency as apportioned. If the individual parties approve they shall take account of the sum so certified in their budget for the said financial year. If either of the parties disapprove, such party shall forthwith notify the other of their decision, and the parties shall thereupon make such arrangements as they may think fit to determine the total sum to be made available for the Committee's purposes during the said financial year. Instalments to account of the deficiency apportioned against either party shall be payable on the certificate of the Treasurer for the time being of the party operating the bank account of the Library but proportional payments shall be made concurrently by both parties.

EIGHTHLY. This agreement may be terminated as at the fifteenth day of May in any year by either party giving notice in writing to the other party at least six months beforehand, and may be otherwise varied, altered or amended by consent of the parties at any time, but any such variation, alteration or amendment shall forthwith be incorporated in a new agreement or by way of an addendum to this Minute.

NINTHLY. If at any time the parties hereto should determine to discontinue the scheme whether for the purpose of (a) the parties disjoining, (b) one party abandoning the scheme, or (c) both parties abandoning the scheme, the parties, failing agreement, shall refer to arbitration by a sole arbiter to be mutually chosen all matters, questions and disputes which may arise between them, whether during the subsistence of the Library or at or after its dissolution, and that subject to the terms of the article next after written, universally and without limitation; and failing agreement in the choice of an arbiter as before mentioned a sole arbiter shall be appointed by the Sheriff of Forfarshire, on the application of either party.

LASTLY. It is expressly agreed and declared that in any arbitration proceedings which may arise in terms of the foregoing reference (*Primo*), the interests of the First and Second parties respectively shall be deemed to be in the ratio of two to one, and (*Secundo*), in the event of the scheme being discontinued on account of abandonment by both parties, neither party having resolved to established a new scheme under section five of the Education (Scotland) Act, 1918, or under any Act varying, modifying or amending the same, or to make provision otherwise for a similar service, and if, during the period of five years immediately preceding the discontinuance of the scheme, the Carnegie United Kingdom Trustees have made any contribution in cash or kind towards the cost of the scheme, then the arbiter shall award to the said Trustees such proportion of the assets of the scheme or of the capital value of such assets by whatever means of reckoning or distribution he may adopt, as shall equal the proportion of the contribution last made by the Trustees which the unexpired term of the said period of five years, reckoning from the date of payment of the said contribution, shall bear to the full term: And the parties consent to the registration hereof for preservation: IN WITNESS WHEREOF these presents typewritten on this and the five preceding pages are executed in duplicate as follows *videlicet*: — they were sealed with the Common Seal of the First Party and signed by George Hitchcock, their Chairman, and John Eadie, their Clerk, on behalf of, and as specially authorised by, the First Party at a Meeting of them duly convened and held at Forfar on the fifth day of June Nineteen hundred and twenty nine before these witnesses, William Cameron, Cashier, and Margaret Fell Nairn, Typist, both to the Education Authority of the County of Forfar; and they were executed by the Second Party, on whose behalf they were signed by Thomas Laurie, their Chairman, Alexander Thomson, their Vice-Chairman, Ernest Lees, Convener of their Finance Committee, and John Miller, their Executive Officer, all as specially authorised by the Second Party at a Meeting of them duly convened and held at Stonehaven on the twenty sixth day of the month and year last mentioned before these witnesses, Henry Smart Taylor, Cashier, and Annie Bain, Typist, both to the Education Authority of the County of Kincardine.

(Sgd.)

WM. CAMERON *Witness*	GEORGE HITCHCOCK
MARGARET F. NAIRN *Witness*	J. EADIE
H. S. TAYLOR *Witness*	THOMAS LAURIE *Chairman*
ANNIE BAIN *Witness*	ALEX. THOMSON *Vice-Chairman*
	ERNEST LEES *Convener of Finance Committee*
	J. MILLER *Executive Officer, Kincardineshire Education Authority*

THE SCOTTISH LIBRARY ASSOCIATION SURVEY OF NEW PREMISES

IN RESPONSE TO A REQUEST made at the first meeting of the Working Party on the Standards of the Public Library Service in Scotland, on 28 November 1967, a questionnaire on new, extended or renovated premises, during the period 1960-69, was compiled for circulation to Scottish public libraries. The questionnaire was circulated to 72 authorities during April 1968. For projects in 1968 and 1969, for which final figures were not available, librarians were asked to provide estimated figures if possible.

42 authorities submitted positive returns to the questionnaire and nil returns were received from 3—Peebles, Kelso and Maybole. The following 27 authorities did not submit returns: Paisley, Perth & Kinross, Inverness-shire, Kirkcaldy, Perth, Clackmannanshire, Falkirk, Airdrie, Inverness, Wigtownshire, Stirling, Kirkcudbrightshire, Caithness, East Lothian, Kirkintilloch, Orkney, Sutherland, Bo'ness, Montrose, Fraserburgh, Helensburgh, Dunoon, Campbeltown, Selkirk, Peeblesshire, Carnoustie and Inverurie. With one or two notable exceptions, it is probable however that the returns received cover the bulk of work during the decade.

The information received has been abstracted and is presented in three tables. Firstly, a *Summary of Returns,* which gives under each authority the number and type of projects, the number executed each year, the total cost, floor area and stock capacity of all projects and, to assist comparison, the cost per head of population and the cost per square foot of all projects. Secondly, an *Analysis of Branch Projects,* which notes under each authority the number of branch projects, the number serving populations of 10,000 or over, the number meeting IFLA standards of accommodation (see *Standards of Public Library Service in England and Wales,* Appendix III), and the number which fail to meet the minimum stocks prescribed by the Library Association and the Scottish Library Association. Thirdly, an *Abstract of Returns,* which lists under each authority details of each project reported.

From the various returns it may be noted that of the 178 projects reported 137, or 76 per cent, were branch libraries. Only two new central libraries were reported, though major extensions

331

were completed in a number of others. Of the branch libraries, only 8 met the IFLA standards of accommodation, a fact also commented on by the Working Party in England & Wales. 27 per cent of the branches had stocks below the minimum of 6000 volumes prescribed by the Library Association and 42 per cent stocks below the minimum 10,000 volumes suggested by the Scottish Library Association. 49 per cent of the 178 projects were new buildings, 14 per cent extensions of existing buildings and 37 per cent renovations of existing buildings. 1966-68 were the most productive years, the peak year being 1968 with 34 projects completed or nearing completion.

The total cost of all projects amounted to some £2½ million, giving an average cost per head of population of 13/11 for the ten year period. The total floor area involved amounted to 431,300 square feet, at an average cost of £5 10s per square foot. The total stock capacity of all projects amounted to some 2½ million volumes.

R. S. WALKER, *Hon. Secretary,*
Scottish Library Association.

SUMMARY OF RETURNS

Authority	Pop. in 1000s	Projects Tot	Bran	Oth	60	61	62	63	64	65	66	67	68	69	(a)	(b)	(c)	Costs Excluding Furniture	Furniture & Fittings (in £1000s)	Total	Per Head in shillings	Total in 100 sq. ft.	Cost per sq. ft. in £	Stock Capacity in 1000 vols.
Glasgow	1,001	13	9	4	1	1	1	1	–	–	2	–	4	1	6	1	6	–	–	469	9	603	7:14	156
Edinburgh	472	12	5	7	–	4	1	1	–	1	2	1	2	–	3	4	5*	–	–	208	9	457	4:10	228
Lanarkshire	357	8	8	–	1	1	1	–	–	2	1	1	1	–	7	–	1	122	12	134	8	273	4:18	125
Ayrshire	245	9	9	–	4	2	2	–	–	1	–	–	1	2	4	–	5	21	5	26	2	83	3:2	58
Fife	199	13	13	–	1	2	2	1	–	2	2	–	1	2	5	–	8	–	–	111	11	369	3	118
Aberdeen	186	4	4	–	–	–	–	–	1	–	–	1	–	–	2	–	1	64	6	70	8	80	8:15	62
Dundee	185	5	5	–	–	–	1	–	–	–	1	–	–	2	3	–	2	33	8	41	4	116	3:10	66
Renfrewshire	184	17	16	1	3	1	2	3	–	2	–	2	3	–	9	1	7	136	33	169	18	255	6:12	171
Dunbartonshire	126	6	6	–	–	–	–	–	1	–	–	5	–	–	5	†	–*	43	10	53	8	152	3:10	89
Midlothian	119	8	6	–	1	–	–	1	2	–	2	–	–	3	6	–	–	69	9	78	13	176	4:8	61
Stirlingshire	112	8	8	–	–	–	–	–	–	–	1	2	–	–	6	–	2	50	14	64	11	117	5:9	55
Aberdeenshire	107	7	7	–	–	–	–	1	1	1	–	–	2	1	4	1	2*	50	8	58	10	96	6	60
West Lothian	99	8	8	–	2	–	–	2	2	1	1	–	2	–	8	–	–	–	–	156	32	260	6	96
Dumfriesshire	88	4	3	1	–	–	–	–	–	–	–	–	–	1	–	–	4	–	–	17	4	46	3:14	47
Motherwell	76	1	–	1	–	–	–	–	–	–	–	1	–	–	–	–	–*	50	5	55	14	70	7:17	–
Greenock	75	2	1	1	1	1	–	–	–	1	–	–	–	1	2	–	–	237	16	253	67	252	10	120
Angus & Kincardineshire	68	7	6	1	–	–	–	–	1	1	2	–	2	–	1	–	5*	–	–	7	2	32	2:3	20
Moray & Nairn	59	3	3	–	–	–	–	–	1	1	1	–	2	–	1	–	1	7	4	11	4	103	1:1	43
Ross & Cromarty[1]	58	4	3	1	1	–	–	–	–	–	–	2	2	–	–	–	4	16	8	24	8	–	–	28
Coatbridge	54	1	1	–	–	–	–	–	–	–	–	–	–	–	1	–	–	–	.7	.7	.25	9	0:15	4
Clydebank	51	3	2	1	–	1	1	–	–	–	–	–	1	–	2	1	–*	44	9	53	21	181	2:18	85
Dunfermline	50	1	1	–	–	–	–	–	–	1	–	–	–	–	1	–	–	3	3	6	2	6	10	6
Kilmarnock	48	8	3	5	–	–	–	–	–	–	2	1	2	2	4	1	3	5.5	11.6	17	7	86	1:19	69
Ayr	46	1	1	–	–	–	–	–	–	–	–	1	–	–	–	1	–*	7.5	1.5	9	4	15	6	6

SUMMARY OF RETURNS (Continued)

Column groups: **Projects** = Tot / Bran / Oth; **Openings per Year** = 60–69; **Nature of Work** = (a)(b)(c); **Costs** = Excluding Furniture / Furniture & Fittings (in £1000s) / Total / Per Head in shillings; **Area** = Total in 100 sq. ft. / Cost per sq. ft. in £; **Stock** = Capacity in 1000 vols.

Authority	Pop in 1000s	Tot	Bran	Oth	60	61	62	63	64	65	66	67	68	69	(a)	(b)	(c)	Excl. Furniture	Furn. & Fittings	Total	Per Head	Total 100 sq.ft.	Cost per sq.ft. £	Capacity 1000 vols.
Hamilton[2]	46	3	2	1	–	–	–	–	1	–	–	–	–	1	1	2	–	42	10	52	21	30	14	32
Banffshire[3]	46	1	–	1	–	–	–	–	–	–	–	1	–	–	–	–	1	–	–	–	–	45	–	120
Argyll	44	4	2	2	–	1	–	1	1	–	–	–	1	–	3	–	1	1	1·5	3	1	26	1:13	20
Roxburghshire	43	3	2	1	–	–	1	–	–	–	–	1	1	–	–	1	2*	4·8	·9	6	3	13	4:12	3
Dumbarton	26	1	–	1	–	–	–	–	–	–	–	–	–	1	–	1	1*	31	4	35	27	45	7:7	50
Rutherglen	26	2	1	1	–	–	–	–	1	–	–	–	1	–	1	1	–*	–	–	30	23	59	5:2	60
Berwickshire[4]	22	1	–	1	–	–	–	–	–	–	–	–	–	–	1	–	–*	25	8	33	30	–	–	–
Arbroath	21	1	–	1	–	–	–	–	–	1	–	–	–	–	1	–	–*	2	2	4	4	5	8	23
Grangemouth	21	1	–	1	–	–	–	–	–	1	–	–	–	–	1	–	–	11	9	20	19	34	5:17	56
Buckhaven & Methil	20	1	–	1	–	–	–	–	–	–	1	–	–	–	–	–	1*	14	3	17	17	16	10:12	50
Zetland	18	1	–	1	–	–	–	–	–	–	1	–	–	–	1	–	–	30	6	36	40	46	7:18	75
Hawick[5]	16	1	–	1	–	–	–	1	–	–	–	–	–	–	–	–	1	–	4	4	5	–	–	–
Galashiels	15	1	–	1	–	–	–	–	–	–	–	1	–	–	1	1	1	12·5	3·5	16	21	46	3:9	0
Bute[6]	14	2	1	1	–	–	1	–	–	–	–	1	–	–	–	–	–	·3	·2	1	1	67	0:3	48
Peterhead[7]	13	1	–	1	–	–	–	–	–	–	–	–	–	–	–	1	1	·3	·2	1	1	6	1:13	–
Forfar	10	1	–	1	–	–	–	–	–	–	–	–	1	–	–	–	–*	24	3	27	54	16	16:17	30
Leven	9	1	–	1	–	–	–	–	–	–	1	–	–	–	1	–	–	5·2	·2	6	13	13	4:12	24
Brechin	7	1	–	1	1	–	–	–	–	–	1	–	–	–	–	–	1*	8	1	9	26	9	10	35
Totals		178	136	42	13	17	10	12	11	15	21	23	34	20	87	26	65	1169·1	220·3	2389·7	582·25	4313	215:10	2439

* Shows combination of types of work, i.e. new building and extension or extension combined with renovation

Nature of work:
a New building
b Extension of existing building
c Renovation of existing building

1 No floor area given
2 No opening date given for Burnbank Branch
3 No costs given
4 No floor area or date for project given. Also applies to Motherwell, Berwickshire and Hawick
5 No floor area given
6 No costs given for H.Q. project
7 No floor area or date for project given

ANALYSIS OF BRANCH PROJECTS

Authority	No. of Branch Projects	No. serving pop. of 10,000+	No. meeting IFLA standards of accommodation	No. with stocks below L.A. min. of 6,000 vols.	No. with stocks below S.L.A min. of 10,000 vols.
Glasgow	9	9	0	0	0
Edinburgh	5	4	1	1	1
Lanarkshire	8	3	3	0	1
Ayrshire	9	1	0	5	7
Fife	13	4	3	5	7
Aberdeen	4	3	0	0	1
Dundee	5	4	0	1	2
Renfrewshire	16	5	0	3	12
Dunbartonshire	6	3	0	1	3
Midlothian	6	1	0	0	1
Stirlingshire	8	1	1	4	7
Aberdeenshire	7	0	–	3	4
West Lothian	8	4	0	0	1
Dumfriesshire	3	0	–	1	2
Motherwell	0	–	–	–	–
Greenock	1	1	0	0	0
Angus & Kincardineshire	6	0	–	6	6
Moray & Nairn	3	1	0	0	0
Ross & Cromarty	3	0	–	1	2
Coatbridge	1	0	–	1	1
Clydebank	2	1	0	0	0
Dunfermline	1	1	0	0	1
Kilmarnock	3	0	–	2	3
Ayr	1	0	–	0	1
Hamilton*	2	1	0	0	0
Banffshire	0	–	–	–	–
Argyll	2	0	–	1	1
Roxburghshire	2	0	–	2	2
Dumbarton	0	–	–	–	–
Rutherglen	1	0	–	0	0
Berwickshire	0	–	–	–	–
Arbroath	0	–	–	–	–
Grangemouth	0	–	–	–	–
Buckhaven & Methil	0	–	–	–	–
Zetland	0	–	–	–	–
Hawick	0	–	–	–	–
Galashiels	0	–	–	–	–
Bute	1	0	–	0	1
Peterhead	0	–	–	–	–
Forfar	0	–	–	–	–
Leven	0	–	–	–	–
Brechin	0	–	–	–	–
	136	47	8	37	67

* Information not given for second project

335

ABSTRACT OF RETURNS

Symbols used

Col. 1:
- B Branch library
- C Central library
- D Subject department
- E Educational/School library
- J Juvenile library
- L Lending library
- N Newspaper room
- P Periodicals room
- R Reference library
- S Study/Reading rooms
- W Work room
- X Extension work premises

Col. 4:
- a New building
- b Extension of existing building
- c Renovation of existing building

Authority & Premises	1 Function	2 Pop. served (in 1000s)	3 Year of Opening	4 Nature of Work	5 Cost in £1000s (excld. furniture, etc.) £	6 Cost of furniture and fittings £	5+6 Total cost in £1000s £	7 Total floor area (in 100 sq. ft.)	8 Number of separate departments	9 Stock at opening (in 1000 vols.)	10 Ultimate stock capacity (in 1000 vols.)
GLASGOW											
Elder Park	R	30	60	c			4	15	1	4	6
Castlemilk	B	40	61	a			28	30	3	20	13
Elder Park	B	30	62	c			15	43	2	22	13
Mitchell Library											*
(Periodicals room)	P		63	b			10	25	1	10	10†
(Science library)	D		65	c			10	32	1	26	18
Partick	B	35	66	c			20	70	3	4	4
Elder Park	J	30	66	c			4	8	1	26	16
Pollok	B	40	67	a			75	70	3	26	16
Drumchapel	B	40	68	a			79	70	3	22	16
Dennistoun	B	30	68	a			35	54	3	21	12
Easterhouse[1]	B	30	68	c			19	36	2	21	16
Pollokshaws	B	40	68	a			79	80	2	20	16
Cardonald	B	30	69	a			91	70	3	24	16
12 projects							460	602		220	155

EDINBURGH

Library	Code	Year	Type							
Central library (Edinburgh room)	D	61	bc			47	11	1	24	24*
(Lecture hall)	X	61	b				9	1		†
(Periodicals room)	P	61	c				11	1	37	37‡
(Scottish library)	D	61	b	6			81	1	2	2
Corstorphine	B	62	b			7	9	1	25	35
Portobello	B	63	a			33	72	2		§
Trinity College Apse	N	65	c			10	17	1	10	11**
Central Children's library	J	66	c			2	45	3	27	45
Blackhall[1]	B	66	a			58	133	3	6	6
Portobello	J	67	c				8	1	38	38
McDonald Road	B	68	c	3	2	5	7	1	17	30
Sighthill	B	68	a			48	54			
12 projects						210	457		186	228

* Plus 22,759 non-book items. 3 carrels
† 500 periodicals
‡ Plus 4,917 non-book items
§ 80 current newspapers

** Plus 5,139 non-book items
[1] Including car park, exhibition area, central courtyard, ramp for prams

LANARKSHIRE

Library	Code		Year	Type						
Springboig[1]	B	5	60	a	4	5	12	1	8	8
New Stevenston[2]	B	4	61	a	8	9	14	1	11	11
Newmains[3]	B	6	62	a	9	10	20	2	12	12
Halfway[4]	B	7	65	a		1	16	2	10	10
Carluke[5]	B	8	65	a	25	27	38	2	16	16
Baillieston	B	15	66	a	25	27	49	3	16	18
Cathkin[6]	B	10	67	a	26	28	56	4	20	20
Bishopbriggs[7]	B	18	68	c	25	27	68	5	25	30
8 projects						134	273		118	125

[1] In school playground
[2] Part of community centre
[3] With 'Coventry Cathedral' inclined walls, inset windows
[4] In rented premises
[5] Hyperbolic paraboloid roof, glass walls
[6] In shopping centre. On first floor. Display cases a feature
[7] Reconstructed from former school

Page 338

Authority & Premises	1 Function	2 Pop. served (in 1000s)	3 Year of Opening	4 Nature of Work	5 Cost in £1000s (excld. furniture, etc.)	6 Cost of furniture and fittings £	5+6 Total cost in £1000s £	7 Total floor area (in 100 sq. ft.)	8 Number of separate departments	9 Stock at opening (in 1000 vols.)	10 Ultimate stock capacity (in 1000 vols.)
AYRSHIRE											
Catrine	B	3	60	c	·6	·4	1	8	2	4	5
Drongan	B	4	60	a		·4	·4	8	2	4	4
Patna	B	3	60	a		·3	·3	4	2	3	4
Stewarton	B	4	60	c	1	·6	1·6	13	2	6	8
Crosshouse	B	2	61	c	3	·3	3·3	6	2	3	3
West Kilbride	B	4	61	c	·5	·3	·8	5	2	3	5
Irvine	B	20	65	c	·6	1	1·6	14	2	10	12
West Kilbride[1]	B	4	69	a	12	1	13	15	2	6	10
Tarbolton	B	2	69	a	3		4	10		5	7
9 projects							26	83		44	58
1 With car park											
FIFE											
Lochore[1]	B	10	60	a			12	35	3	12	12
North Queensferry[2]	B	·8	61	c			·6	6	1	2	2
St Monance[2]	B	1	61	c			·6	6	1	2	2
Newport[3]	B	3	62	c			2	9	1	7	6
St Andrews	B	12	63	c			14	60	3	30	30
Markinch[3]	B	3	65	c			2	12	1	7	6
Burntisland[4]	B	6	65	c			6	80	3	14	12
Lochgelly[5]	B	9	66	a			15	40	3	13	12
Falkland[3]	B	1	66	a			2	7	1	6	3
Kinglassie[1]	B	2	66	c			4	12	1	4	5
East Wemyss[6]	B	3	68	c			5	12	1	12	4
Cowdenbeath[5]	B	12	69	a	20	2	22	45	3	12	12
Glenrothes West[7]	B	16	69	a	23	3	26	45	3	15	12
13 projects							111	369		126	118

1 Let. disc ... per rack   With clinic
2 Part of community centre   3 Part of school

ABERDEEN (continued)

Kaimhill[2]	B	5	64	c		.7	.7	4	1	6	6
Kincorth	B	10	67	a	19	2	21	25	3	12	20
Airyhall[3]	B	10	68	a	34	2	36	28	2	12	20
4 projects							70	80		42	62

2 Rented premises   3 With lecture/exhibition room

1 Converted shop

DUNDEE

Camperdown[1]	B	8	62	c		1.5	1.5	12	1	5	6
Fintry[2]	B	10	67	c		1.5	1.5	8	1	5	5
Douglas[2]	B	10	68	a	11	2	13	24	2	10	15
Menzieshill[2]	B	10	69	a	22	3	25	27	2	12	20
Kirkton[3]	B	15	69	a				45	3	12	20
5 projects							41	116		44	66

2 In community centre   3 In community centre. May open 1970

1 Shop library

RENFREWSHIRE

Neilston[1]	B	5	60	c	2	1	3	10	1	6	7
Barrhead[2]	B	16	60	c	3	1	4	8	1	8	9
Clarkston[3]	B	12	60	a	5	2	7	16	1	12	14
Crum Memorial	B	5	61	c	4	1	5	14	1	6	7
Bishopton[4]	B	3	62	a	2	1	3	5	1	4	5
Johnstone[2]	B	14	62	c	2	3	5	20	2	13	15
Howwood[5]	B	3	63	a	1	1	2	5	1	4	5
Inverkip[5]	B	3	63	a	1	1	2	6	1	4	5
Eaglesham[3]	B	4	63	a	3	2	5	9	1	5	6
Lochwinnoch	B	4	65	c	4	1	5	13	2	6	7
Ralston[6]	B	6	65	a	16	1	17	16	1	7	8
Gourock[7]	B	11	66	c	16	2	18	13	1	10	12
Johnstone Castle[8]	B	8	67	a	16	2	18	14	1	6	9
Headquarters[1]	C		67	b	20	6	26	45	4	20	22
Kilbarchan	B	4	68	c	3	2	5	10	1	7	8
Bridge of Weir[9]	B	6	68	a	12	2	14	14		7	8
Renfrew[10]	B	20	68	a	26	4	30	37	3	17	24
17 projects*							169	255		142	171

* In addition, 18 school libraries have been opened during the period. Average area, 2,000/2,500 sq. ft., stocks 4,000/8,000 vols. Separate reading rooms available in several instances.

1 With car park   2 Larger branch planned   3 With car park. Separate wing of public hall

4 Separate wing of primary school. Reading accommodation in garden   5 Separate department of primary school

6 With car park. Separate wing of public hall   7 Separate wing of Gamble Institute   8 Separate wing of community centre   9 Including layout of grounds

10 With car park. In group of public buildings. Many decorative features

	1	2	3	4	5	6	5+6	7	8	9	10
Authority & Premises	Function	Pop. served (in 1000s)	Year of Opening	Nature of Work	Cost in £1000s (excld. furniture, etc.)	Cost of furniture and fittings	Total cost in £1000s	Total floor area (in 100 sq. ft.)	Number of separate departments	Stock at opening (in 1000 vols.)	Ultimate stock capacity (in 1000 vols.)
DUNBARTONSHIRE					£	£	£				
Bearsden[1]	B	22	64	a	7	1	8	35	3	10	18
Cumbernauld[2]	B	20	67	a	17	6	23	67	3	19	35
Duntocher	B	5	67	a	11	1	12	15	1	5	6
Rhu	B	1	67	a	3·5	·1	3·6	6	1	6	7
Alexandria[3]	B	19	67	bc	1	1	2	22	2	17	18
Rosneath	B	1	67	a	3·5	·4	3·9	7	1	4	5
6 projects							53	152		61	89

1 With story room, car park
2 Regional library. Access by stairs, ramps and lifts. Car park. Library in 'first phase' only
3 With story area

	1	2	3	4	5	6	5+6	7	8	9	10
MIDLOTHIAN											
Penicuik[1]	B	8	60	a	9	1	10	23	2	8	11
Mayfield[2]	B	7	63	a	11	1	12	24	1	5	7
Newtongrange[3]	B	5	64	a	12	2	14	26	3	6	10
Musselburgh[4]	B	17	64	a	15	2	17	34	3	8	12
Currie[5]	B	9	66	a				34	2	8	11
Loanhead[3]	B	6	68	a	22	3	25	35	3	7	10
6 projects							78	176		42	61

1 With car park   2 With car park   Part of school, clinic and community centre   5 With car park.   In school
3 With car park   Exhibition area   4 With exhibition area

STIRLINGSHIRE

Place	Type		Year	Code							
Plean	B	2	62	c	10		1	3	1	3	3
Bonnybridge	B	7	63	a		2	12	20	1	8	8
Fallin	B	3	66	a		1	9	11	1	7	7
Slamannan	B	3	67	a	3	1	4	5	1	3	3
Balfron	B	2	67	a	9	.3	9.3	12		6	6
Cowie	B	3	69	a				13		5	5
Burngreen	B	10	69	a	28	10	38	46	2	20	20
Milton of Campsie	B	1	69	c		.7	.7	7	1	3	3
8 projects							74	117		55	55

[1] Shop library   [2] Converted house   [3] Including car park

ABERDEENSHIRE

Place	Type		Year	Code							
Culter[1]	B	4	61	bc	3	.5	3.5	4	1	5	5
Dyce	B	1	63	c		.6	.6	3	1	3	3
Turriff[2]	B	3	64	c	4	.4	4.4	9	1	5	6
Cults[3]	B	5	66	a	11	1.5	12.5	18	1	11	13
Bucksburn[3]	B	7	68	a	15	2	17	27	1	14	15
Bridge of Don[3]	B	4	68	a	12	2	14	27	1	14	15
Kemnay[3]	B	1	69	a	5	1	6	8	1	3	3
7 projects					50	8	58	96		55	60

WEST LOTHIAN

Place	Type		Year	Code					
Armadale	B	6	63	a	13	22	2	8	10
Bathgate[1]	B	14	63	a	18	32	3	15	
Broxburn[2]	B	15	64	a	26	54	2	17	22
Fauldhouse	B	5	64	a	12	22	2	8	10
Whitburn	B	10	65	a	21	39	2	11	20
Blackburn[3]	B	10	66	a	28	41	2	10	17
Linlithgow[4]	B	4	68	a	22	30	2	6	10
South Queensferry	B	4	68	a	16	20		5	7
8 projects					156	260		80	96

[1] Will take second floor   [2] With car park   [3] In new commercial centre   [4] In new town centre

Authority & Premises

	1 Function	2 Pop. served (in 1000s)	3 Year of Opening	4 Nature of Work	5 Cost in £1000s (excld. furniture, etc.) £	6 Cost of furniture and fittings £	5+6 Total cost in £1000s £	7 Total floor area (in 100 sq. ft.)	8 Number of separate departments	9 Stock at opening (in 1000 vols.)	10 Ultimate stock capacity (in 1000 vols.)
DUMFRIESSHIRE											
Ewart library[1]	C	27	60	c			2	12	2	20	
Sanquhar	B	2	60	c			3	8	1	4	
Langholm	B	2	65	c			3	9	1	6	
Annan	B	6	69	c			9	17	3	17	
4 projects							17	46		47	
1 Reference department											
MOTHERWELL											
Central library[1]	C	45	67	bc	50	5	55	70	4		
1 With exhibition room and public lounges											
GREENOCK											
John Reid library	B	20	61	a	10	2	12	70	2	12	20
Central library[1]	C	75	69	a	227	14	241	182	9	60	100
2 projects							253	252		72	120
1 Probably 1970											
ANGUS & KINCARDINESHIRE											
Stonehaven	B	5	61	c			·1	3	1	3	5
Banchory	B	2	64	c			·2	2	1	3	4
Inverbervie	B	1	65	c			·6	3	1	3	3
Headquarters	C		66	bc			2·5	10	4		
Portlethan	B	1	66	c			·5	6	1	1	1
Laurencekirk	B	2	68	c			·5	4	1	3	3
Newtonhill[1]	B	1	68	a			2·4	4	1		4
7 projects							7	32		13	20

MORAY & NAIRN

Elgin	B	19	61	c	1	1	2	60	4		20
Forres[1]	B	9	64	a	5	2	7	25	3	13	13
Lossiemouth	B	9	66	b	1	1	2	18	3	10	10
3 projects							11	103		23	43

1 With car park

ROSS & CROMARTY

Headquarters	C	10	67	c	7	3	10			10	10
Stornoway	B	6	67	c	2	2	4			10	10
Kyle of Lochalsh	B	·5	68	c			·5	1		2	2
Invergordon	B	2	68	c	7	3	10		1	6	6
4 projects							24	1		28	28

COATBRIDGE

Whiffiet[1]	B	8	69	a		·7	·7	9	1	4	4
1 project											

1 Rented premises.   Part of community centre

CLYDEBANK

Parkhall	B	9	62	a	11	2	13	20	2	7	12
Faifley[1]	B	12	66	a	18	2	20	35	2	11	13
Central library[2]	C	50	68	bc	15	5	20	126	4	52	60
3 projects							53	181		70	85

1 With exhibition area   2 New reference and news rooms, Lending extension, exhibition corridor

DUNFERMLINE

Abbey view (Shop branch)	B	15	61	a	3	3	6	6	1	5	6
1 project											

Authority & Premises	1 Function	2 Pop. served (in 1000s)	3 Year of Opening	4 Nature of Work	5 Cost in £1000s (excld. furniture, etc.) £	6 Cost of furniture and fittings £	5+6 Total cost in £1000s £	7 Total floor area (in 100 sq. ft.)	8 Number of separate departments	9 Stock at opening (in 1000 vols.)	10 Ultimate stock capacity (in 1000 vols.)
KILMARNOCK											
Dick Institute (Junior library)[1]	J		65	c	1	1	2	7	1	4	4
(Reserve accommodation)[1]	W	6	66	b	2	1	3	6	1	4	4
Bellfield[2]	B		66	a		·6	·6	6	1		
Dick Institute (Reference library)	R		67	c	1·5	2	3·5	25	1	4	6
Onthank[2]	B	6	68	a		·7	·7	6	1	3	3
Dean[2]	B	6	68	a		·8	·8	7	2		
Dick Institute (Lending library)	L		69	c		4	4	23	1	40	40
(Reserve accommodation)[3]	W		69	a	1	1·5	2·5	6	1	12	12
8 projects							17	86		67	69

[1] Stage 1   [2] Building not charged to library   [3] Stage 2

	1	2	3	4	5	6	5+6	7	8	9	10
AYR											
Forehill[1]	B	5	67	bc	7·5	1·5	9	15	1	4	6
1 project											

[1] With car park

	1	2	3	4	5	6	5+6	7	8	9	10
HAMILTON											
Burnbank	B	12	64	b	3	1	4	30	3	12	32
Hillhouse	B		69	a	14	5	19				
Central library	C	46		bc	25	4	29	30		12	32
3 projects							52				

Keith (Old) Grammar School	C	46	68	c			45		6		120
1 project											
ARGYLL											
Inveraray	E	·5	63	a	·3	·3	3	1		2	3
Bowmore (Islay)	E	1	64	a	·7	·7	8	1		3	4
MacCaig Institute (Oban)[1]	B	8	65	a			10			6	10
Kinlochleven	B	2	68	c	·5		5	2		3	3
4 projects					1·5	3	26			14	20
[1] Costs met from bequests. Including car park											
ROXBURGHSHIRE											
Denholm[1]	B	1	67	c	·5	·1	·6	3	1	2	2
Newcastleton[1]	B	1	68	c	·3	·1	·4	2	1	1	1
Headquarters[1]	C	43	69	bc	4	·7	4·7	8			
3 projects							6	13		3	3
[1] With car park											
DUMBARTON											
Central library[1]	C	26	69	bc	31	4	35	5	4	38	50
1 project											
[1] Mezzanine balcony for exhibitions											
RUTHERGLEN											
Blairbeth	B	5	67	bc			10	9	1	7	10
Central library	C	26	68	c			20	50	3	34	50
2 projects							30	59		41	60

Authority & Premises	1 Function	2 Pop. served (in 1000s)	3 Year of Opening	4 Nature of Work	5 Cost in £1000s (excld. furniture, etc.) £	6 Cost of furniture and fittings £	5+6 Total cost in £1000s £	7 Total floor area (in 100 sq. ft.)	8 Number of separate departments	9 Stock at opening (in 1000 vols.)	10 Ultimate stock capacity (in 1000 vols.)
BERWICKSHIRE Headquarters[1] 1 project	C	22	68	ab	25	8	33		4		
[1] New Local History room and Museum. Also new reference section											
ARBROATH Central library 1 project	C	21	68	b	2	2	4	5	1	5	23
GRANGEMOUTH Central library[1] 1 project	C	22	65	bc	11	9	20	34	3	45	56
[1] Extension of Lending and new Reference library											
BUCKHAVEN & METHIL Central library[1] 1 project	C	21	68	bc	14	3	17	16	4	43	50
[1] With car park											
ZETLAND Headquarters[1] 1 project	C	17	66	a	30	6	36	5	5	45	75
[1] With Museum in same building											

HAWICK Central library[1]	C	16	67	c	12·5	3·5	4	46	3	24	40
1 project											
[1] Renovation of Reference and Junior rooms											
GALASHIELS Central library	C	15		c			16				
1 project											
BUTE Kildonan (Old School)[1]	B	3	68	b	·3	·2	·5	9	1	4	8
Headquarters	C	9	69	a			1	58	2	25	40
2 projects								67		29	48
[1] Headquarters of travelling library											
PETERHEAD Central library	C	16	67	c	·3	·2	·5	6			
1 project											
FORFAR Meffan Institute	C	10	68	bc	24	3	27	16		30	30
1 project											
LEVEN Central library	C	9	68	c	5·2	·2	6	13	1	15	24
1 project											
BRECHIN Central library	C	7	66	bc	8	1	9	9	1	35	
1 project											

347

Fig. 1

GROWTH OF THE PUBLIC LIBRARY MOVEMENT IN SCOTLAND

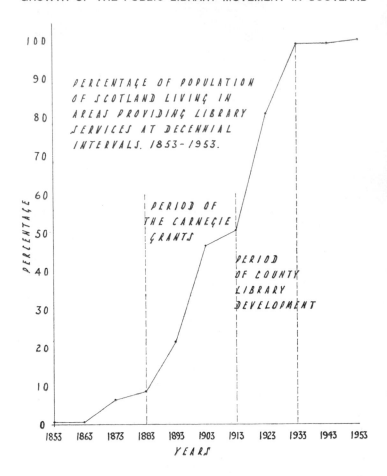

This graph shows how the movement was slow in getting under way: after ten years Airdrie was still the only library service in Scotland. A marked increase from 1863 to 1873 slackened off in the succeeding decade. From 1883 to 1913, and particularly from 1893 to 1903, Carnegie's grants produced a revolution, but their effect was less noticeable between 1903 and 1913, and even then little more than half of the population of Scotland was living in areas providing library services. Between 1913 and 1933, with the encouragement of the Carnegie Trustees, the various county library services developed to cover the rest of the country, except Argyll. With the establishment of a library there in 1946-7, the public library service, in the last decade of its first century, covered the whole of Scotland.

TABLE 1

GROWTH OF THE PUBLIC LIBRARY MOVEMENT IN SCOTLAND

(a) Burgh and Parish Libraries: Dates of adoption of Public Libraries Acts (or other Acts authorizing the provision of public libraries).

Year	Authority	Year	Authority
1853	*Airdrie	1900	*Lockerbie (burgh & parish)
1866	*Dundee		*Tain (burgh & parish)
1867	Paisley	1901	Newmilns
1870	Forfar		Clackmannan (parish)
1872	Galashiels		*Bo'ness
	*Thurso		*Corstorphine (parish)
1877	*Inverness		*Larbert (parish)
1878	*Hawick		*Lossiemouth
1880	*Dunfermline		*Coatbridge
1881	*Dumbarton		*Kelso
1883	*Tarves (parish)		*Hamilton
1884	*Aberdeen		*Rutherglen
1885	Alloa	1902	*Castle Douglas
1886	*Edinburgh		*Innerleithen
1887	*Grangemouth		*Montrose
	*Wick (burgh & parish)		*Prestonpans
1888	Selkirk		*West Calder (parish)
1890	Brechin		*Motherwell
	*Ayr		*Dingwall
	*Kirkwall	1903	*Cromarty (burgh & parish)
	*Peterhead		*Fraserburgh
1891	*Elgin		*Inverurie
1892	*Jedburgh		*Annan
1893	*Drumoak (parish)		*Maybole
	Kilmarnock	1904	*Bellie (parish)
1895	Newburgh		*Burntisland (burgh & parish)
1896	*Falkirk	1905	*Kinross (burgh & parish)
	Perth		*Dornoch
	*Arbroath	1906	*Dyce (parish)
	Campbeltown		Maxton (parish)
1897	*Stirling	1907	*Bonnyrigg
	*Stornoway	1909	Alloa (parish)
1898	Tarbat (parish)	1911	*Clydebank
1899	*Glasgow		Peebles
	Kirkcaldy		*Torryburn (parish)
	*Dumfries	1914	Dunoon
	Creich (parish)	1919	Buckhaven
	*Banff	1937	Blairgowrie
	Stromness(burgh & parish)	1938	Leven
1900	Edderton (parish)	1945	Crieff
	Meldrum (burgh & parish)	1947	Carnoustie
	*Greenock	1949	Helensburgh

* Libraries so marked were assisted, either initially or at a later date, by Andrew Carnegie.

349

(*b*) County libraries: Dates when education authorities began to provide library services under the Education (Scotland) Act, 1918.

Year	Authority	Year	Authority
1919	Perthshire	1924	Zetland
1920	Caithness		Moray
	Angus & Kincardine		Kinross-shire
	Renfrewshire		West Lothian
	Berwickshire		Dumfriesshire
	Kirkcudbright	1925	Roxburghshire
	Midlothian		Ross & Cromarty
	Sutherland		Ayrshire
1921	Peeblesshire		Stirlingshire
	Clackmannanshire		Bute
	Fife	1926	East Lothian
1922	Lanarkshire		Aberdeenshire
	Wigtownshire		Banffshire
	Nairnshire		Inverness-shire
1923	Dunbartonshire	1946	Argyll
	Orkney		
	Selkirkshire		

TABLE 2

PROGRESS IN PUBLIC LIBRARY PROVISION IN SCOTLAND

	No. of Libraries	Volumes	Issues	Expenditure £	Book Expenditure £	Staff
1884*	9	104,304	224,046†	6,467	—	—
1913-14‡	77	1,551,068	5,339,884	74,404	14,724	591
1952-3§	71	6,063,747	29,463,370	992,929	251,410	1,070

* Parliamentary Return (106), 1885.
† For two libraries only.
‡ Adams Report (1915).
§ Library Association Statistics (1954).

TABLE 3

STATISTICS OF PUBLIC (RATE-SUPPORTED) LIBRARIES
IN SCOTLAND, 1952-3

"We have no statistical evidence, and I am sure that we shall need this evidence if we are to persuade backward authorities of the need for a new outlook."

—W. E. C. COTTON,
President of the Scottish Library Association,
11 April 1945.

These tables are based on the information contained in the Library Association's pamphlet, *Statistics of public (rate-supported) libraries in Great Britain and Northern Ireland* 1952-3 (1954), supplemented by returns from a further six libraries. The remaining six libraries not taken into consideration together served about 2 per cent of the population of Scotland.

Table 3(*a*) shows the distribution of the population in library areas, burgh and county, grouped according to the population served.

Table 3(*b*) summarizes the information given in detail in Table 3(*e*). Here are shown the issues, expenditure and book-expenditure per head, and the staff in relation to population, group by group in the fourteen population-groups of Table 3(*a*). For each group three figures are shown— the highest, the lowest and the median. It is in this table that inequalities in the standards of service are most clearly demonstrated.

Table 3(*c*) shows the distribution of the population in library areas, burgh and county, grouped according to the expenditure per head. This makes it clear, for example, that no county authority was spending more than 5s per head on its library service, while 6 burghs, serving 25.4 per cent of the population of Scotland, were.

Table 3(*d*) shows the distribution of the population in library areas, burgh and county, grouped according to the book-expenditure per head. Here it is shown that 4 counties, together serving 3.6 per cent of the total population, were spending more than 1s 9d per head on books, and that only one burgh was doing so.

Table 3(*e*) gives the detailed statistics for each library. The libraries are arranged in descending order of population in the fourteen population groups of Table 3(*a*).

(a) Distribution of population in library areas, grouped according to population

Group Ref. No.	Population group	Burgh libraries			County libraries			All libraries		
		No.	Population	%	No.	Population	%	No.	Population	%
1	500,000 and over	1	1,089,500	21·6				1	1,089,500	21·6
2	300,000–499,999	1	466,770	9·3	1	314,955	6·3	2	781,725	15·6
3	200,000–299,999				1	227,924	4·5	1	227,924	4·5
4	150,000–199,999	2	361,014	7·2	2	363,829	7·2	4	724,843	14·4
5	100,000–149,999				3	318,263	6·3	3	318,263	6·3
6	75,000– 99,999	2	170,885	3·4	5	440,368	8·8	7	611,253	12·2
7	60,000– 74,999	1	69,100	1·4	1	72,653	1·4	2	141,753	2·8
8	50,000– 59,999				3	155,239	3·1	3	155,239	3·1
9	40,000– 49,999	8	353,051	7·0				8	353,051	7·0
10	30,000– 39,999	2	68,032	1·4	3	107,410	2·1	5	175,442	3·5
11	20,000– 29,999	4	95,218	1·9	4	97,251	1·9	8	192,469	3·8
12	15,000– 19,999	4	67,505	1·3	2	38,628	0·8	6	106,133	2·1
13	10,000– 14,999	4	41,352	0·8	1	13,664	0·3	5	55,016	1·1
14	Under 10,000	14	88,078	1·7	2	15,674	0·3	16	103,752	2·0
	Totals	43	2,870,505	57·0	28	2,165,858	43·0	71	5,036,363	100·0

(b) Summary of Statistics. Group standard figures: issues, expenditure, book expenditure and staff

Group No.	No. of Libraries	Issues per head — Highest	Issues per head — Lowest	Issues per head — Median	Expenditure per head — Highest (s. d.)	Expenditure per head — Lowest (s. d.)	Expenditure per head — Median (s. d.)	Book expenditure per head — Highest (s. d.)	Book expenditure per head — Lowest (s. d.)	Book expenditure per head — Median (s. d.)	Staff in relation to population — Highest (1:)	Staff in relation to population — Lowest (1:)	Staff in relation to population — Median (1:)
1	1			3·7			5 0·9			10·3			3,681
2	2	9·1	5·0		4 8·2	3 10·0		1 4·8	9·1		3,922	5,624	
3	1			5·1			1 11·2			7·4			7,352
4	4	7·1	3·8	5·9	4 3·5	2 6·0	4 0·1	1 4·8	6·4	9·5	3,962	6,393	4,579
5	3	7·2	3·8	5·4	4 4·4	1 10·4	3 5·3	1 4·3	8·4	4·0	4,166	10,660	5,941
6	7	8·5	3·6	6·3	4 10·9	1 7·7	3 0·3	2 0·1	5·6	11·0	4,288	11,371	7,953
7	2	7·8	4·5		4 6·5	1 8·0		1 8·4	7·9		4,065	12,109	
8	3	8·3	3·6	5·1	4 7·2	2 4·7	4 1·4	1 11·6	1 4·7	1 7·3	6,126	10,000	7,158
9	8	14·3	5·9	7·8	5 9·7	3 11·0	4 9·4	2 0·2	8·1	1 11·1	3,090	4,520	3,594
10	5	10·3	3·4	7·0	5 4·0	4 11·7	4 1·8	1 6·7	5·6	1 4·1	3,100	12,752	4,404
11	8	11·3	4·6	6·9	4 8·7	2 2·0	3 7·2	2 1·8	8·2	1 1·0	3,010	21,229	4,818
12	6	9·6	6·2	8·0	5 2·5	3 1·9	3 9·6	1 6·8	4·6	11·7	3,120	5,573	4,371
13	5	14·9	1·9	8·4	4 1·5	2 0·1	3 6·9	3 10·9*	5·3	11·2	2,152	13,664	5,000
14	16	18·7	1·6	7·6	4 6·8	3 6·0	3 1·7	1 4·5	0·1	7·5	1,927	9,028	4,770
	71	18·7	1·6	5·1	5 9·7	6·0	4 3·1	3 10·9†	0·1	10·3	1,927	21,229	4,166

* Includes binding and some other items; next highest is 1s. 0·9d.
† Includes binding and some other items; next highest is 2s. 1·8d.

353

(c) Distribution of population in library areas, grouped according to expenditure per head

Expenditure per head	Burgh libraries			County libraries			All libraries		
	No.	Population	%	No.	Population	%	No.	Population	%
5/6 & over	1	47,538	0·95				1	47,538	0·95
5/- & under 5/6	5	1,231,703	24·45				5	1,231,703	24·45
4/6 & under 5/-	8	710,220	14·1	2	135,764	2·7	10	845,984	16·8
4/- & under 4/6	5	289,859	5·75	7	432,120	8·6	12	721,979	14·35
3/6 & under 4/-	10	375,166	7·5	1	314,955	6·3	11	691,121	13·7
3/- & under 3/6	7	166,780	3·3	5	263,709	5·2	12	430,489	8·5
2/6 & under 3/-				2	126,378	2·5	2	126,378	2·5
2/- & under 2/6	4	31,844	0·6	5	350,380	6·9	9	382,224	7·6
1/6 & under 2/-				4	497,435	9·9	4	497,435	9·9
1/- & under 1/6	2	14,002	0·3				2	14,002	0·3
6d & under 1/-	1	2,393	0·05	2	45,117	0·9	3	47,510	0·95
Totals	43	2,870,505	57·0	28	2,165,858	43·0	71	5,036,363	100·0

(d) Distribution of population in library areas, grouped according to book-expenditure per head

Book expenditure per head	Burgh libraries			County libraries			All libraries		
	No.	Population	%	No.	Population	%	No.	Population	%
2/3 and over				1	13,664	0·3	1	13,664	0·3
2/- & under 2/3	1	47,538	0·9	2	113,692	2·2	3	161,230	3·2
1/9 & under 2/-				1	55,131	1·1	1	55,131	1·1
1/6 & under 1/9	4	164,762	3·3	2	87,636	1·7	6	252,398	5·0
1/3 & under 1/6	3	52,039	1·0	8	820,401	16·3	11	872,440	17·3
1/- & under 1/3	6	124,455	2·5	3	211,420	4·2	9	335,875	6·6
9d & under 1/-	12	1,911,743	38·0	5	316,031	6·3	17	2,227,774	44·3
6d & under 9d	9	509,357	10·1	3	417,840	8·3	12	927,197	18·4
3d & under 6d	3	30,329	0·6	3	130,043	2·6	6	160,372	3·2
Under 3d	5	30,282	0·6				5	30,282	0·6
Totals	43	2,870,505	57·0	28	2,165,858	43·0	71	5,036,363	100·0

355

(e) Statistics for all libraries, grouped according to population

L.A. Ref. No.	Library	Population	Branches Full Time	Branches Other Points	Stock Lending	Stock Reference	Issues Lending Libraries	Issues per head	Total Exp. £	Exp. per head s. d.	Book Exp. £	Book Exp. per head s. d.	Staff	Staff Pop. 1:
Group 1: 500,000 and over														
184	Glasgow	1,089,500	32	12	640,544	649,582	3,986,819	3·7	276,254	5 0·9	46,578	10·3	296	3,681
Group 2: 300,000-499,999														
155	Edinburgh	466,770	13	115	526,000	210,000	4,240,635	9·1	109,241	4 8·2	17,786	9·1	119	3,922
259	Lanarkshire	314,955	11	223	300,000		1,584,646	5·0	60,350	3 10·0	22,094	1 4·8	56	5,624
Group 3: 200,000-299,999														
20	Ayrshire	227,924	9	117	180,432		1,153,000	5·1	22,000	1 11·2	7,050	7·4	31	7,352
Group 4: 150,000-199,999														
379	Renfrewshire	185,411	1	97	120,000	68,000	718,205	3·8	23,208	2 6·0	7,993	10·3	29	6,393
2	Aberdeen	182,714	5	12	138,000		869,850	4·7	34,218	3 9·0	4,893	6·4	45	4,060
169	Fife	178,418	4	172	191,125		1,265,933	7·1	38,273	4 3·5	12,498	1 4·8	35	5,098
147	Dundee	178,300	7	12	209,414	66,025	1,270,352	7·1	37,996	4 3·1	6,368	8·6	45	3,962
Group 5: 100,000-149,999														
5	Aberdeenshire	117,263[1]	3	230	93,800		449,497	3·8	10,927	1 10·4	4,109	8·4	11	10,660
303	Midlothian	101,000		79	112,561		542,081	5·4	17,391	3 5·3	6,747	1 4·0	17	5,941
430	Stirlingshire	100,000	6	84	145,000		717,640	7·2	21,848	4 4·4	6,782	1 4·3	24	4,166
Group 6: 75,000-99,999														
146	Dunbartonshire	95,438	1	104	100,688		606,379	6·4	14,431	3 0·3	4,870	1 0·2	12	7,953
358	Perth & Kinross	94,753	3	217	135,000		574,674	6·1	12,052	3 6·5	5,738	1 2·5	9	10,528
348	Paisley	93,704			66,098	20,666	430,366	4·6	15,913	3 4·8	3,976	10·2	15	6,247
145	Dumfriesshire	85,656	1	94	144,000		725,355	8·5	21,023	4 10·9	8,601	2 0·1	17	5,039
243	Inverness-shire	84,926		189	63,634	10,200	181,109[2]	6·5	8,668	2 0·5	1,964	5·6	8	10,616
485	West Lothian	79,595[1]		60	65,139		287,168	3·6	6,549	1 7·7	3,395	10·2	7	11,371
195	Greenock	77,181	2		49,000	1,500	489,787	6·3	14,545	3 9·2	3,528	11·0	18	4,283
Group 7: 60,000-74,999														

No.	Place															
24	Banffshire	30,108		93	70,000~		410,303	8·3	11,311	4	4·7	4,028	1	7·3	1	7,??
14	Argyll	50,000		284	61,778		177,802	3·6	5,988	2	4·7	3,471	1	4·7	5	10,000

Group 9: 40,000–49,999

No.	Place															
256	Kirkcaldy	49,230		2	64,393	4,586	417,971	8·5	13,039	5	3·6	4,026	1	7·6	14	3,516
111	Coatbridge	47,538		1	41,613	2,178	453,775	9·5	13,817	5	9·7	4,800	2	0·2	13	3,657
110	Clydebank	45,927		9	44,372	4,051	304,401	6·6	10,942	4	9·2	1,967		10·3	12	3,827
148	Dunfermline	45,200	1	5	81,000	4,000	326,129	7·2	9,796	4	4·0	2,245		11·9	10	4,520
19	Ayr	42,377		1	39,575	9,884	248,980	5·9	8,861	3	2·2	1,550		8·8	12	3,531
253	Kilmarnock	42,140	1		79,000	3,000	602,902	14·3	8,248	11	11·0	1,425		8·1	13	3,241
357	Perth	40,466		1	50,000	25,000	346,042	8·6	9,692	4	9·5	2,392	1	2·2	11	3,679
204	Hamilton	40,173	1	1	39,865	4,289	260,444	6·5	10,705	5	4·0	1,669		10·0	13	3,090

Group 10: 30,000–39,999

No.	Place															
310	Moray	38,257[1]		57	23,023		131,011	3·4	1,866		11·7	892		5·6	3	12,752
107	Clackmannanshire	37,528	1	28	44,466	702	313,029	8·3	7,782	4	1·8	2,969	1	6·7	9	4,170
166	Falkirk	37,200			53,133	5,175	383,308	10·3	9,925	5	4·0	2,491	1	4·1	12	3,100
498	Wigtownshire	31,625		60	36,000		204,302	6·5	4,540	2	10·5	2,122	1	4·1	5	6,325
6	Airdrie	30,832	1		39,000	8,000	224,319	7·0	7,673	4	11·7	2,387	1	6·6	7	4,404

Group 11: 20,000–29,999

No.	Place															
388	Roxburghshire	28,036		81	69,000		237,185	8·5	5,824	4	1·9	3,005	2	1·8	5	5,607
429	Stirling	27,089			31,162		176,601	6·5	6,400	4	8·7	1,595	1	2·1	9	3,010
43	Berwickshire	25,060	1	95	29,000	3,022	152,685	6·1	4,295	3	5·0	1,534	1	3·2	8	6,265
393	Rutherglen	24,225			20,700	700	177,266	7·3	5,690	3	8·4	1,139		11·3	8	3,028
144	Dumbarton	23,703			13,000		116,783	4·9	4,385	3	8·4	812		8·2	6	3,951
	Caithness	22,926	2	75	43,634		169,701	7·4	3,995	3	5·8	857		9·0	5	4,585
	Orkney	21,229	1	80	35,000		97,142	4·6	2,303	2	2·0	1,094[4]	1	0·4	1	21,229
72	Buckhaven & Methil	20,201		2	33,312	600	228,384	11·3	3,475	3	5·3	1,137	1	1·5	4	5,050

Group 12: 15,000–19,999

No.	Place															
13	Arbroath	19,503		91	19,201	4,760	160,524	8·2	3,381	3	5·6	715		8·8	5	3,901
519	Zetland	19,343	1	14	36,142		120,184	6·2	3,988	4	1·5	1,404	1	5·4	4	4,836
79	Bute	19,285			19,794	397	172,816	9·0	3,050	3	1·9	900		11·2	4	4,821
211	Hawick	16,718			25,466	4,759	130,767	7·8	3,559	4	3·1	850	1	0·2	3	5,573
180	Galashiels[5]	15,684		11	19,607	1,697	96,835	6·2	2,575	3	3·4	300		4·6	4	3,921
191	Grangemouth	15,600			23,250	750	150,473	9·6	4,062	5	2·5	1,219	1	6·8	5	3,120

L.A. Ref. No.	Library	Population	Branches Full Time	Branches Other Points	Stock Lending	Stock Reference	Issues Lending Libraries	Issues per head	Total Exp. £	Exp. per head s.	Exp. per head d.	Book Exp. £	Book Exp. per head s.	Book Exp. per head d.	Staff	Staff: Pop. 1:
Group 13: 10,000-14,999																
446	Sutherland	13,664		50	11,352		25,755	1.9	2,820	4	1.5	2,670	3	10.96	1	13,664
309	Montrose	10,760			17,548	2,215	131,362	12.1	2,023	3	9.1	502		11.2	5	2,152
157	Elgin	10,535			19,654	2,505	156,994	14.9	1,233	2	4.1	231		5.3	3	3,512
56	Bo'ness	10,057[1]			15,572	675	55,544	5.5	1,011	2	0.1	345		8.2	2	5,029
177	Fraserburgh	10,000			14,000	1,000	84,430	8.4	1,786	3	6.9	536	1	0.9	2	5,000
Group 14: under 10,000																
176	Forfar	9,981			15,000	2,500	80,071	8.0	1,828	3	8.0	542	1	1.0	2	4,990
	Leven	9,028			10,000	50	68,235	7.6	1,467	3	3.0	612	1	4.2	1	9,028
370	Prestonpans	8,902			6,214		13,872	1.6	580	2	3.6	75		2.0	1	8,902
313	Nairn	8,814		12	10,000	120	49,839	5.7	900	2	0.5	360		9.7	1	8,814
213	Helensburgh	8,760			6,927		69,154	7.9	1,697	3	10.5	32		0.9	1	8,760
61	Brechin	7,264			24,000	250	55,021	7.6	1,574	4	4.0	324		10.7	2	3,632
350	Peeblesshire	6,860		20	7,890		15,642	2.3	171		6.0	104		3.6		
349	Peebles	6,013			11,100	1,000	91,125	15.2	700	2	3.9	200		8.0	2	3,007
74	Burntisland	5,811[1]			17,000	250	108,467	18.7	1,326	4	6.8	400	1	4.5	3	1,927
403	Selkirk	5,800			10,000	1,000	43,326	7.5	1,060	3	7.9	233		9.6		
	Carnoustie	5,239			4,500	100	40,000	7.6	602	2	3.6	197		9.0		
435	Stornoway	5,127[1]		1	19,200		44,339	8.6	1,015	3	11.5	50		2.3	2	2,564
244	Inverurie	5,100			4,500		30,274	5.9	364	1	5.1	50		2.3	1	5,100
201	Haddington	4,550			4,340	968	22,640	5.0	732	3	2.6	132		7.0	1	4,550
	Kelso	4,110			12,000	800	30,000	7.3	630	3	0.8	100		5.8	1	4,110
242	Innerleithen	2,393[1]			5,000	1,000	6,198	2.6	66		6.6	1		0.1		
	TOTALS: All groups	5,036,363	111	3225	4,925,791	1,137,956	29,463,370		£992,929	3	11.3	£251,410	1	0.0	1,070	4,700
	Burghs (43)	2,870,505	64	174	2,671,260	1,126,057	17,765,429		£659,778	4	7.2	£126,280		10.6	745	3,850
	Counties (28)	2,165,858	47	3051	2,254,531	11,899	11,697,941		£333,151	3	0.9	£125,130	1	1.9	325	6,660

1 Figure adjusted by Registrar-General's estimate, mid-1952
2 Issues for Inverness burgh only
4 Includes binding
5 & Selkirkshire

SELECT BIBLIOGRAPHY

1 GOVERNMENT PUBLICATIONS

House of Commons.
  Parliamentary returns. *Libraries.* 1849, 1852, 1856, 1857, 1870, 1876, 1877, 1885, 1890, 1912, 1933.
  Select Committee on Public Libraries.
    Report . . . together with the proceedings of the Committee, minutes of evidence, and appendix. 1849.
    Report. 1850.
Ministry of Reconstruction. *Third interim report of the Adult Education Committee: Libraries and museums.* 1919.
Board of Education.
  Public Libraries Committee. *Report on public libraries in England and Wales.* 1927. Cmd. 2868.
  Books in public elementary schools. 1928.
Scottish Office. Committee on Scottish administration. *Report.* 1937. Cmd. 5563.
Scottish Education Department.
  Education in Scotland. [Annual reports]
  Young citizens at school: a report on experiments in Education for Living. Edinburgh, 1950.
  Advisory Council on Education in Scotland.
    Secondary education: a report. Edinburgh, 1947. Cmd. 7005.
    Libraries, museums and art galleries: a report. Edinburgh, 1951. Cmd. 8229.
Ministry of Education. *The school library.* 1952.

2 PUBLICATIONS OF CORPORATE BODIES

Airdrie Public Library. *A century of reading: Airdrie Public Library, 1853-1953.* Airdrie, [1954].
Carnegie United Kingdom Trust.
  Annual reports. Dunfermline, 1915-
  County libraries in Great Britain and Ireland. Reports, 1924 (1925)—1927-28 (1928).
  Proceedings of the Carnegie Rural Library Conference . . . 1920 (1921); *County Library Conferences,* 1924 (1925); 1926 (1927).
  Report of the proceedings of the County Library Conference . . . 1935. (1936).
  Libraries in secondary schools: a report . . . by the committee appointed to inquire into the provision of libraries in secondary schools in Great Britain and Northern Ireland. 1936.

Carnegie United Kingdom Trust (*continued*).

Scottish Central Library for Students: transactions of a conference held in Stirling, 7-8 June 1923. 1923.

Report . . . by the Advisory Committee on the Scottish Central Library for Students. 1947.

Carnegie United Kingdom Trust *and* Scottish Library Association. *Proceedings of the Scottish Library Conference . . . Dunblane, 6-8 March 1931.* 1931.

Church of Scotland.

The Acts of the General Assembly of the Church of Scotland. Committee on Education and Religious Instruction in Scotland. *Reports,* 1826-48.

Convention of Royal Burghs. *Minutes,* 1900-

Earlston Library and Reading Room. *Catalogue and rules.* Earlston, 1909.

Edinburgh Public Libraries. *Edinburgh Public Libraries,* 1890-1950: *a handbook and history of sixty years' progress.* Edinburgh, 1951.

Glasgow Corporation. *Public libraries* [1874-1954]: *an historical summary.* Glasgow, 1955.

Glasgow. Town Council. *Report on free town libraries and museums.* Glasgow, 1864.

Joint-Committee on Scottish Public Libraries Legislation. *Scottish public libraries legislation: report of the Joint-Committee appointed at the invitation of the Scottish Office, 23 July 1936.* Scottish Library Association, 1937.

Library Association.

Annual reports of Council.

Proceedings of the annual conference.

Public libraries: their development and future organization. 1917. [Proceedings of the 40th annual meeting of the Library Association held at London, 3 to 5 October 1917]

Public libraries of the United Kingdom. Statistical return, 1919.

Small municipal libraries: a manual of modern method. 2nd ed. 1934.

Statistics of urban public libraries in Great Britain and Northern Ireland, 1935. 1936.

A survey of libraries: reports on a survey made by the Library Association during 1936-1937. General editor: Lionel R. McColvin. 1938.

The public library scrvice: its post-war reorganization and development. Proposals by the Council of the Library Association. 1943.

Statistics of public (rate-supported) libraries in Great Britain and Northern Ireland, 1952-53. 1954.

Library Association. County Libraries Section.

County Libraries in Great Britain and Ireland. Reports, 1928-29 (1929)—1938-39 (1940).

Library Association. County Libraries Section (*continued*).
   Report on branch library buildings, with statistical tables, 1929-30.
      1930.
   *Statistical and policy survey of the county libraries of Great
      Britain and Northern Ireland,* 1951. 1952.
   County libraries manual. Edited by A. S. Cooke. 1935.
National Central Library. *Annual reports.* 1917-
National Central Library *and* National Committee on Regional
   Library Co-operation. *Recommendations on library co-operation.*
   1954.
Perth Library.
   *An abstract of the articles, for establishing, and regulations,
      respecting the use of, The Perth Library.* Perth, Morison, 1786.
   *Catalogue of the Books in the Perth Library . . . by D. Morison,
      junr., Librarian.* Perth, Morison, 1824.
   Perth Library and Museum Record. Vol. 1-2, 1899-1901.
Perth Mechanics' Library.
   Catalogue. Perth, Taylor, 1832. *Addenda.* n.d. *Additional supple-
      ment.* n.d.
   Catalogue. Perth, *Perthshire Journal,* 1870. *Supplements,* 1873,
      1876.
   Catalogue. Perth, Wood, 1882. *Supplement,* 1889.
Regional Library Bureau of Scotland. *Annual reports.* 1946-53.
School Library Association. *School libraries to-day: being the
   second edition of* School libraries in postwar reconstruction, *the
   joint report of a panel of the School Library Association and the
   School Libraries Section of the Library Association,* 1945. London,
   1950.
School Library Association in Scotland. *A report on secondary school
   libraries in Scotland in* 1952. Edinburgh, 1953.
Scottish Central Library. *Annual reports.* Edinburgh, 1953-
Scottish Library Association.
   Annual reports of the Council. 1909-
   Minutes of the Council. 1908-
   Proceedings of the annual conference. 1950-
   Conditions of service in Scottish public libraries, July 1922.
Scottish Union Catalogue Committee. *Reports,* 1939-45. 1943-5.

3 MANUSCRIPTS

Kirkwood, *Rev.* James. *The Kirkwood collection of* MSS, *prints and
   books,* 1687-1708. [In New College Library, Edinburgh]
Inshewan Reading Society. *Minutes,* 1810-54. [Typescript in Perth
   and Kinross County Library: the original has not been traced]
Perth Anderson Institution. *Minute Book,* 1847-9. [In the Sandeman
   Public Library, Perth]

Aberdeen. *Proposals for a publick library at Aberdeen*, 1764. [Reprinted 1893]

Aberdeen Mechanics' Institution. *Notes and suggestions on the library*. By the Manager [James Sinclair]. Aberdeen, Lindsay, 1880.

Adams, *Professor* W. G. S. *A report on library provision and policy . . . to the Carnegie United Kingdom Trustees*. Dunfermline, CUKT, 1915.

Anderson, Alexander. *The old libraries of Fife*. Kirkcaldy, Fife County Library, 1953.

Anderson, John. *Prize essay on the state of society and knowledge in the Highlands of Scotland*. Edinburgh, Tait, 1827.

Arbroath. *An account of Arbroath Public Library, opened 4 June 1898*. Arbroath, Buncle, 1898. [Reprinted from *Arbroath Guide*, 28 May and 11 June 1898]

Baker, Ernest A. *The public library*. London, Grafton, 1924.

Bannatyne Miscellany, vol. 3. Edinburgh, 1855.

Besterman, Theodore. *British sources of reference and information*: *a guide to societies, works of reference, and libraries*. London, Aslib, 1947.

Brougham, Henry, *Lord Brougham*. *Practical observations upon the education of the people*. London, Longman, 1825.

Brown, James Duff.
Les bibliothèques municipales en Angleterre. Brussels, 1908.
A handbook of library appliances. London, David Stott, 1892.
Manual of library economy. 1st ed. 1903 - 6th ed. 1949.
The village library problem. 1894.

Brown, Samuel.
Reports of the East Lothian Itinerating Libraries. 1817-31.
First report of the Itinerating Libraries in Edinburgh, Leith and Mid-Lothian. 1834.

[Brown, Samuel, jr.] *Some account of Itinerating Libraries and their founder*. Edinburgh, 1856.

Brown, *Rev.* William. *Memoir relative to Itinerating Libraries*. Edinburgh, Balfour, [1830]. [Reprinted in *East-Lothian Literary and Statistical Journal*, vol. 1, no. 10, April 1831, p. 298-308.]

Burgoyne, Frank J. *Library construction*: *architecture, fittings and furniture*. 2nd ed. London, Allen, 1905.

Burgoyne, Frank J., *and* Ballinger, John. *Books for village libraries*. With notes upon the organization and management of village libraries by James D. Brown. London, Simpkin, 1895.

Carlton, Grace. *Spade-work*: *the story of Thomas Greenwood*. London, Hutchinson, [1949].

[Carnegie, Andrew] *Centenary of the birth of Andrew Carnegie*: *the British trusts and their work*. Edinburgh, 1935.

Carnegie Endowment for International Peace. *A manual of the public benefactions of Andrew Carnegie*. Washington, 1919.

Carnell, E. J. *County libraries*: *retrospect and forecast*. London, Grafton, 1938.

Chambers, George F., *and* Fovargue, H. West. *The law relating to public libraries and museums.* 4th ed. London, Knight, 1899.

Clark, Robert S. *Books and reading for the blind.* London, Library Association, 1950.

Coats, G. S. *Rambling recollections.* Paisley, 1920.

Cotgreave, Alfred. *Views and memoranda of public libraries.* London, Library Aids, 1901.

Couper, W. J. *The Gray Library, Haddington.* Haddington, Croal, 1916.

Craven, J. ,B. *Descriptive catalogue of the Bibliotheck of Kirkwall* (1683) *with a notice of the founder, William Baikie, M.A., of Holland.* Kirkwall, 1897.

Dickson, William P. *The Glasgow University Library: notes on its history, arrangements, and aims.* Glasgow, Maclehose, 1888.

Dobbs, A. E. *Education and social movements* 1700-1850. London, Longmans, 1919.

Douglas, James, *of Cavers. The prospects of Britain.* Edinburgh, Black, 1831.

Dow, Alexander. *Library service in Scotland: dual rating.* Gravesend, Philip, 1938.

Edwards, Edward.
Free town libraries. London, Trübner, 1869.
Memoirs of libraries. 2 vols. London, Trübner, 1889.

Esdaile, Arundell. *The British Museum Library: a short history and survey.* London, Allen & Unwin, 1946.

Fraser, G. M. *Aberdeen Mechanics' Institute: a record of civic and educational progress.* Aberdeen, University Press, 1912.

Glasgow.
Brief notices of Glasgow and its libraries. 1897.
Notes of Glasgow libraries. 1907.

Godard, John George. *George Birkbeck, the pioneer of popular education: a memoir and a review.* London, Bemrose, 1884.

Gray, W. Forbes. *Catalogue of the library of John Gray, Haddington.* Haddington Town Council, 1929.

Greenwood, Thomas.
Free public libraries: their organisation, uses and management. London, Simpkin Marshall, 1886. 2nd ed. 1887.
Public libraries: a history of the movement and a manual for the organization and management of rate-supported libraries. 3rd ed. London, Simpkin Marshall, 1890. 4th ed. London, Cassell, 1891 ; 1894.
Greenwood's Library year book, 1897: *a record of general library progress and work.* London, Cassell, 1897.
British library year book, 1900-1901: *a record of library progress and work.* London, Scott, Greenwood, 1900.

Hammond, J. L., *and* Hammond, Barbara. *The age of the Chartists,* 1832-54. London, Longmans, 1930.

Hendrick, Burton J. *The life of Andrew Carnegie.* 2 vols. New York, 1932.

Hessel, Alfred. *A history of libraries*. Trans. with supplementary material by Reuben Peiss. Washington, Scarecrow Press, 1950.

Hewitt, A. R. *A summary of public library law*. 3rd ed. rev. London, Association of Assistant Librarians, 1955.

Hibbert, James, *ed*. *Notes on free public libraries and museums*. Preston, 1881.

Hole, James. *An essay on the history and management of Literary, Scientific and Mechanics' Institutions*. London, Longman, 1853.

Hudson, J. W. *The history of adult education*. London, Longman, 1851.

Hunt, K. G. *Subject specialisation and co-operative book purchase in the libraries of Great Britain*. London, Library Association, 1955.

Hyslop, A. B. *The public library service: a summary for the guidance of students and the general reader*. Dunfermline, CUKT, 1926.

Jast, L. Stanley. *The library and the community*. London, Nelson, 1939.

Johnston, George P. *Notices of a collection of* MSS *relating to the circulation of the Irish Bibles of 1685 and 1690 in the Highlands and the association of the Rev. James Kirkwood therewith*. Edinburgh, 1904.

[Kirkwood, Rev. James]

    An overture for founding and maintaining of Bibliothecks in every Paroch throughout this Kingdom, humbly offered to the consideration of this present Assembly. 1699.

    A copy of a letter anent a project for erecting a library in every Presbytery or at least County in the Highlands, from a Reverend Minister of the Scots nation, now in England, to a minister at Edinburgh, with reasons for it, and a scheme for erecting and preserving these libraries. 1702.

Libraries Museums and Art Galleries Year-Book. Ed. by A. J. Philip. 1910; 1914; 1923-4; 1932; 1933; 1935; 1948. Advisory Editor: Lionel R. McColvin. 1955.

Lipman, V. D. *Local government areas, 1834-1945*. Oxford, Blackwell, 1949.

Livingstone, P. K. *Kirkcaldy and its libraries*. Kirkcaldy, *Fifeshire Advertiser*, 1950.

McBain, J. M. *History of the Arbroath Public Library from 1797 to 1894*. Arbroath, Brodie & Salmond, [1894].

McColvin, Lionel R. *The public library system of Great Britain: a report on its present condition with proposals for post-war reorganization*. London, Library Association, 1942.

McColvin, Lionel R., *and* Revie, James. *British libraries*. 2nd ed. London, Longmans, 1948.

Maclean, *Rev. Prof.* Donald. Highland libraries in the eighteenth century. *Glasgow Bibliographical Society. Records*, vol. 7. 1923. p. 36-43.

McLean, M. D. *"Fifty years a-growing": the Ewart Library attains its jubilee*. Dumfries, 1954.

Macleod, Robert D.
Rural libraries and rural education. London, Grafton, 1921.
County rural libraries: their policy and organisation. London, Grafton, 1923.
Martin, Burns. *Allan Ramsay: a study of his life and works.* Cambridge, Harvard University Press, 1931.
[Mason, Thomas] *The free libraries of Scotland.* By an Assistant Librarian. Glasgow, Smith, 1880.
Mason, Thomas. *Public and private libraries of Glasgow.* Glasgow, Morison, 1885.
Milne, John Duguid. *The success of free public libraries in industrial towns, and the necessity for a free public library in Aberdeen.* Aberdeen Philosophical Society, 1883.
Minto, C. S. *Public library services in the north of Scotland: their present condition and future development. A report and recommendations on a survey carried out during April 1948 for the Council of the Scottish Library Association.* Scottish Library Association, 1948.
Minto, John. *A history of the public library movement in Great Britain and Ireland.* London, Allen & Unwin and Library Association, 1932.
Mitchell, Alexander, ed. *Inverness Kirk-Session Records, 1661-1800.* Inverness, Carruthers, 1902.
Mitchell, J. M.
The public library system of Great Britain and Ireland, 1921-1923: a report prepared for the Carnegie United Kingdom Trustees. A sequel, with current statistical tables, to the Report prepared in 1915 by Professor W. G. S. Adams. Dunfermline, CUKT, 1924.
The Scottish Central Library for Students: an address delivered on 7 June 1922, before the Scottish Library Association. Dunfermline, CUKT, 1922. 2nd ed. 1923.
Munford, W. A. *Penny rate: aspects of British public library history, 1850-1950.* London, Library Association, 1951.
Murison, W. J. *The public library: its origins, purpose and significance as a social institution.* London, Harrap, 1955.
Newcombe, Luxmore. *Library co-operation in the British Isles.* London, Allen & Unwin, 1937.
The new statistical account of Scotland. 15 vols. Edinburgh, Blackwood, 1845.
Ogle, John J. *The free library: its history and present condition.* London, Allen, 1897.
Pafford, J. H. P. *Library co-operation in Europe.* London, Library Association, 1935.
Penman, Richard. *Memoir of Mr William Brown, late minister of the Gospel, Inverury.* Aberdeen, King, 1830.
Peterhead Free Library demonstration, 8 August 1891. Peterhead, D. Scott, 1891. [Reprinted from *The Peterhead Sentinel*]

Pinnington, Edward. *Montrose Public Library*. Montrose, *Standard Office*, [1905].

Ridpath, George. *Diary* 1755-1761. Ed. by Sir James Balfour Paul. Edinburgh, Scottish History Society, 1922.

Sanderson, Charles Rupert. *Library law: a textbook for the professional examinations in library organisation*. London, Bumpus, 1925.

Saunders, Laurance J. *Scottish democracy, 1815-1840: the social and intellectual background*. Edinburgh, Oliver & Boyd, 1950.

Savage, Ernest A. *The librarian and his committee*. London, Grafton, 1942.

Savage, Ernest A., *and* Mitchell, J. M. *Scottish public libraries under the new regime: two papers read at the annual conference of the Scottish Library Association, Dumfries, 21 May 1930*. Scottish Library Association, 1930.

Sewell, P. H. *The regional library systems*. London, Library Association, 1950.

Shirley, G. W.
William Ewart: pioneer of public libraries, a former Dumfries M.P. Dumfries, [1930].
Dumfriesshire libraries. Dumfries, 1933.

[Sinclair, James] *The free public library question discussed, with special reference to Aberdeen*. By Sigma. Aberdeen, Cornwall, 1883.

Sinclair, *Sir* John, *Bart. The statistical account of Scotland*. 21 vols. Edinburgh, 1791-9.

Smith, Robert Murray. *A page of local history: being a record of the origin and progress of Greenock Mechanics' Library and Institution*. Greenock, Pollock, 1904.

Society for Promoting Christian Knowledge. *A chapter in English church history: being the minutes of the S.P.C.K. for the years 1698-1704*. Ed. by the Rev. Edmund McClure. London, S.P.C.K., 1888.

Stewart, William. *Innerpeffray Library and Chapel: a historical sketch, with some notes on the books of the Library*. Crieff, Philips, 1916.

Strong, John. *The Education (Scotland) Act, 1918, with annotations*. Edinburgh, Oliver & Boyd, 1919.

Thornton, John L.
The chronology of librarianship: an introduction to the history of libraries and book-collecting. London, Grafton, 1941.
A mirror for librarians: selected readings in the history of librarianship. London, Grafton, 1948.

Thornton, John L., *and* Tully, R. I. J. *Scientific books, libraries and collectors: a study of bibiography and the book trade in relation to science*. London Library Association, 1954.

Urquhart, D. J. *Public libraries and industry*. London, D.S.I.R., 1953.

Vollans, Robert F. *Library co-operation in Great Britain: report of a survey of the National Central Library and the Regional Library Bureaux.* London, National Central Library, 1952.

Weale, J. Cyril M. *The plundering of the public by public libraries: the case against the Aberdeen Pubic Library, to which is appended a report of the Hawick Pubic Library test case,* 1894. Aberdeen, William Smith, 1904.

Webb, R. K. *The British working class reader,* 1790-1848: *literary and social tension.* London, Allen & Unwin, 1955.

Wellard, James Howard. *Book selection: its principles and practice.* London, Grafton, 1937.

Whyte, W. E. *The Local Government (Scotland) Act,* 1929. Edinburgh, Hodge, 1929.

Wodrow, Robert. *Analecta, or materials for a history of remarkable providences.* 4 vols. Edinburgh, Maitland Club, 1842-3.

SUPPLEMENTARY BIBLIOGRAPHY, 1956-1971

Studies and papers published since the thesis, with its original bibliography, was completed in 1955.

Altick, Richard D. *The English common reader: a social history of the mass reading public,* 1800-1900. University of Chicago Press, 1957.

Bain, Andrew. *Education in Stirlingshire.* University of London Press, 1965.

Ballantyne, G. H. *Comparative studies in Scottish county library organization and administration.* FLA Thesis, 1965.

Bramley, Gerald. *A history of library education.* Clive Bingley, 1969.

Burkett, J., *ed. Special library and information services in the United Kingdom.* Library Association, 1961. 2nd rev. ed. 1965.

Durbidge, L. G. Pioneer itinerator. *Times Literary Supplement.* 6 March 1969, p. 246.

Durkan, John, *and* Ross, Anthony. *Early Scottish libraries.* Glasgow, Burns, 1961.

Education, Ministry of.
The structure of the public library service in England and Wales. HMSO, 1959. Cmnd. 660. [The Roberts report]
Inter-library co-operation in England and Wales. HMSO, 1962.
Standards of public library service in England and Wales. HMSO, 1962. [The Bourdillon report]

English libraries 1800-1850. Three lectures . . . by C. B. Oldman, W. A. Munford, Simon Nowell-Smith. H. K. Lewis, for University College London, 1958.

Fry, W. G., *and* Munford, W. A. *Louis Stanley Jast: a biographical sketch.* Library Association, 1966.

367

Hamilton, J. T. *Greenock libraries: a development and social history,* 1635-1937. [Greenock Corporation, 1969]

Hepburn, A. G. *Guide to Glasgow libraries.* Glasgow, R. D. Macleod Trust, 1965.

Irwin, Raymond.

> *The English library: sources and history.* Allen & Unwin, 1966. [A revised and enlarged edition of the same author's *The origins of the English library* (1958)]
>
> *The heritage of the English Library.* Allen & Unwin, 1964. Supplementary notes. University College London, 1969.

Kaufman, Paul.

> Library news from Kelso. *Library Review,* vol. 17 (1959-60), p. 486-9.
>
> *Libraries and their users: collected papers in library history.* Library Association, 1969.
>
>> This volume reprints a number of Dr Kaufman's papers, including "The rise of community libraries in Scotland" (*Papers of the Bibliographical Society of America,* vol. 59 (1963), p. 233-94), "The earliest free lending library in Britain" [Dundee] (*Library Association Record,* vol. 63 (1961), p. 160-2), "A unique record of a people's reading" [Innerpeffray] (*Libri,* vol. 14 (1964), p. 227-42) and "Leadhills: Library of diggers" (*Libri,* vol. 17 (1967), p. 13-20).

Kelly, Thomas.

> *George Birkbeck: pioneer of adult education.* Liverpool University Press, 1957.
>
> *A history of adult education in Great Britain.* Liverpool University Press, 1962. Rev. ed. 1970.
>
> *Early public libraries: a history of public libraries in Great Britain before* 1850. Library Association, 1966.
>
> *Public libraries in Great Britain before* 1850. Library Association, 1966.

Keyse, F. A. The birth of county libraries: CUKT experiments 1915-1919. *Journal of Librarianship,* vol. 1 (1969), p. 183-90

Libraries and librarianship in Scotland. *Library World,* vol. 69 (1967-8), p. 307-26.

McDonald, William R. Circulating libraries in the north-east of Scotland in the eighteenth century. *Bibliotheck,* vol. 5 (1967-9), p. 119-37.

Munford, W. A.

> *William Ewart, M.P.,* 1798-1869: *portrait of a Radical.* Grafton, 1960.
>
> *Edward Edwards,* 1812-1886: *portrait of a librarian.* Library Association, 1963.
>
> *Annals of the Library Association,* 1877 *to* 1960. Library Association, 1965.
>
> *James Duff Brown,* 1862-1914: *portrait of a library pioneer.* Library Association, 1968.

Murison, W. J. How we got here: past history and future possibilities in Scottish and Irish public libraries. *Proceedings of the Joint Conference, Portrush, 1968.* Glasgow, SLA, 1968, p. 11-21. [Reprinted in *An Leabharlann,* vol. 26 (1968) p. 51-60.]

Ollé, James G. *Library history: an examination guidebook.* Clive Bingley, 1967. 2nd ed. revised and enlarged, 1971.

Robertson, William. *Welfare in trust: a history of the Carnegie United Kingdom Trust,* 1913-1963. Dunfermline, CUKT, 1964.

Ross, Anthony. Libraries of the Scottish Blackfriars. *Innes Review,* vol. 20 (1969), p. 3-36.

Royal Commission on Local Government in Scotland, 1966-1969. *Written evidence, 12. 1968. Report and Appendices.* 1969. Cmnd. 4150.

Scottish Education Department. *Standards for the public library service in Scotland. Report of a Working Party.* Edinburgh, HMSO, 1969.

Scottish Home and Health Department. *Local authority records.* Edinburgh, HMSO, 1962.

Scottish Library Association.
Recommendations of the Council on new library legislation affecting Scotland and standards in book provision, staff and premises. 1960.
Scottish libraries. Triennial reviews. Edited by Moira Burgess. 1963-65 (1966) ; 1966-68 (1969).
Memorandum on public library standards. 1968.

Smith, Colin. *The development of libraries in technical colleges and other institutions of further education in Scotland.* MA Thesis, University of Strathclyde, 1970.

Smith, Colin, *and* Walker, R. S., eds. *Library resources in Scotland.* Glasgow, SLA, 1968.

Stockham, K. A., ed. *British county libraries:* 1919-1969. André Deutsch, 1969.

Thompson, A. R. The use of libraries by the working class in Scotland in the early nineteenth century. *Scottish Historical Review,* vol. 42 (1963), p. 21-9.

Tyler, William E. *The development of Scottish public libraries.* MA Thesis, University of Strathclyde, 1967.

Vollans, R. F., ed. *Libraries for the people: international studies in librarianship in honour of Lionel R. McColvin.* Library Association, 1968.

The Library History Group of the Library Association was founded in 1962, and in 1967 launched a new periodical, *Library History* (two issues a year), which regularly prints notes on recent publications.

SLA News, the official journal of the Scottish Library Association, reached its hundredth number with the issue for November-December 1970. An invaluable index to the first 82 numbers, covering the years 1950-67, was published by the Association in 1968.

INDEX

371

Cotgreave indicators, 194
Cotton, W. E. C., 140, 186, 256; on relations between SLA and LA, 225
County libraries, 90-114; costs, 109-11, 168; graduates in, 224; relations with burgh libraries, 115-32, 245-70; urban branches, 104-9; discussed in the Kenyon report, 172-3
County Library Circle, 239, 298-9
Craigie, James, 215, 230, 232, 316
Crawford, Norman, 67n, 198n
Crossgates, itinerating library, 38
Cumbernauld, subscription library, 25
Cupar, 23
Cuthbertson, Miss J. M., 232
Cuthbertson, W. F., 243n

Darling, Sir W. Y., and the PL (Scotland) Act (1955), 271-4
Davies, E. Salter, 169; on the SCL, 146
Departments in libraries, 194, 200
Dickson, Dr W. K., 227
Dickson, Rev. Professor W. P., 218
Double rating, 115, 117-22, 127, 245-70, 276-8
Douglas, James, and itinerating libraries in Roxburghshire, 35
Doune, 281
Dumbarton, 194
Dumfries, subscription library, 18; Mechanics' Institute, 19; PL, an example of overbuilding, 78
Dumfries and Galloway Farmers' Club and Library, 43
Dumfriesshire, amalgamation of library services, 123-5, 294, 321-5
Dumfriesshire libraries, Dumfries and Galloway collection, 198; illustrations scheme, 201
Dunbar, Mechanics' Institute, 41
Dunbartonshire CL, 25; mobile library, 196
Dunblane conference, 118-23, 142, 248-9
Dunblane, Leightonian library, 2
Dundee, subscription library, 23; Mechanics' Institute, 41, 54; PL, 54; as an example in the Mitchell report, 164; Dundee collection, 197; illustrations collection, 201;

provision for blind readers, 205; school libraries, 209; subject departments, 200.
Dunfermline, tradesmen's and mechanics' library, 42; PL, 60, 174, 180; children's library, 207; Murison Burns Collection, 199
Dunlop, John, 231
Duns Public Library, 20

Earlston Library and Reading Room, 24-5
East Lothian, itinerating libraries, 30-4
Edinburgh, Duke of, opens SCL in Edinburgh, 154
Edinburgh, Mechanics' Subscription Library, 43; School of Arts, 41; subscription libraries, 23, 62; PL Acts rejected, 55-6, 61-2; adopted, 64
Edinburgh PL, Edinburgh Room, 197; hospital libraries, 206; lectures, 203; mobile branch libraries, 195; school libraries, 209; subject departments, 200
Edinburgh, SCL, new accommodation, 149
Edinburgh, UL, 155, 301; and Clement Little's bequest, 1, 301
Edinburgh and Leith itinerating libraries, 38
Education, Board of, Departmental Committee on public libraries, 142, 169-74
Education, Ministry of, on school libraries, 214
Education (Scotland) Act (1908), 97; (1918), 66, 97-9, 245, 318; (1946), 130, 272
Education authorities and county library services, 99
Education for librarians, 218-21, 224-9
Edward, D. E., 149n, 231
Edwards, Edward, evidence to Select Committee, 14-15, 44, 90; on children's libraries, 208; on a librarian's qualifications, 243; on lectures, 202; on the principle of rate support, 49; on professional education, 218
Egarr, J., 125, 197
Elgin, Earl of, 232, 256

Elgin, PL Acts rejected, 62
Erskine, Dr John, 154
Evening classes in librarianship, 225
Ewart, William, 43-52
Extension activities, 201-3

Falkirk, PL Acts rejected, 67; PL, 175, 200, 210
Farmers' libraries, 43, 47
Ferguson, J. P. S., *Scottish newspapers in Scottish libraries,* 159n
Fife CL, 113; mobile library, 196
Films and film strips in libraries, 201
Forfar, 58
Forfarshire, *see* Angus
Forsyth, J. W., 202; on Advisory Council report, 265-6
Fowler, Dr, and Corstorphine library, 72
Fraser, G. M., 85, 114, 142, 232
Fraserburgh, 174
Free Church, itinerating libraries in Peeblesshire, 38
Fremantle, Rev. W. R., evidence to Select Committee, 29, 90

Galashiels PL, 58-9, 177; amalgamation with Selkirkshire, 128, 294; lectures, 203
Gardiner, J., 243n
Glasgow, Baillie's Institution, 73; Stirling's Library, 21-2, 89; subscription libraries, 23; PL Acts rejected, 57-8, 62-3; powers included in local Act, 68
Glasgow, interlibrary lending, 141
Glasgow, Mitchell Library, 58, 68, 216; Glasgow collection, 197; Robert Burns and Scottish poetry collection, 199-200
Glasgow PL, hospital libraries, 206; lectures, 202-3; provision for blind readers, 205; Royal Exchange building, 89; school libraries, 209-10; subject departments, 200
Graduates in the library profession, 223-4
Graham, William, and his amendment on the rate limit (1920), 86-7

Gramophone records in libraries, 201
Grangemouth, 66, 210
Grants to library authorities, discussed in the Select Committee report, 50; in the Minto report, 188-90; in the SLA statement on the Advisory Council report, 268-9
Gray, Sir Alexander, 147-8, 154; foreword to *Scottish newspapers in Scottish libraries,* 159n; letters to the press on future of SCL, 273
Gray, Duncan, on libraries in northern Scotland, 174-6
Gray, Rev. John, and his library at Haddington, 5
Greenock, mechanics' library, 41-2; subscription library, 21; PL, 181
Greenwood, Thomas, 64, 66, 71-2, 75, 230; on librarians, 216; on village and rural public libraries, 91-2
Guthrie, J. C., 215

Haddington, Gray Library, 5; itinerating libraries, 30-3; Mechanics' School of Arts, 41
Haldane, Miss E. S., of Cloan, 99, 137, 318
Hamilton, subscription library, 24
Harris, Isle of, 188
Hawick, 177, 290; charges for borrowers' tickets, 194; an example of overbuilding, 78
Hay, Daniel, 235
Hepburn, W. A. F., at Dunblane conference, 120-2, 276
Highland libraries: Kirkwood's scheme, 6-11; General Assembly's scheme, 11-13; the Minto report, 185-91
Hospital libraries, 205-7
Hyslop, A. B., 245

Illustrations in libraries, 201
Imray, John, evidence to Select Committee, 15, 28-9
Indicators, 192-4
Industry, library services to, 296-7
Innerpeffray Library, 5
Inshewan Reading Society, 311-15

378